Israel

the Bradt Travel Guide

Samantha Wilson

edition
2

www.bradtguides.com

Bradt Travel Guides Ltd, UK
The Globe Pequot Press Inc, USA

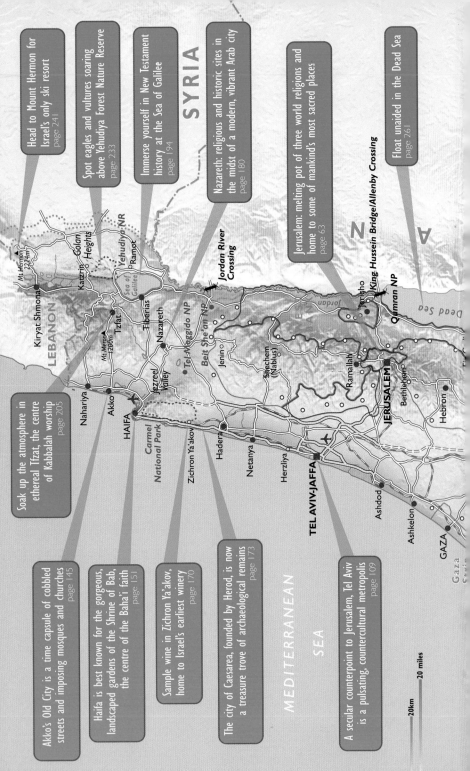

Head to Mount Hermon for Israel's only ski resort
page 241

Spot eagles and vultures soaring above Yehudiya Forest Nature Reserve
page 233

Immerse yourself in New Testament history at the Sea of Galilee
page 194

Nazareth: religious and historic sites in the midst of a modern, vibrant Arab city
page 180

Jerusalem: melting pot of three world religions and home to some of mankind's most sacred places
page 63

Float unaided in the Dead Sea
page 261

SYRIA

Soak up the atmosphere in ethereal Tfzat, the centre of Kabbalah worship
page 205

Akko's Old City is a time capsule of cobbled streets and imposing mosques and churches
page 145

Haifa is best known for the gorgeous, landscaped gardens of the Shrine of Bab, the centre of the Baha'i faith
page 151

Sample wine in Zichron Ya'akov, home to Israel's earliest winery
page 170

The city of Caesarea, founded by Herod, is now a treasure trove of archaeological remains
page 173

A secular counterpoint to Jerusalem, Tel Aviv is a pulsating, countercultural metropolis
page 109

MEDITERRANEAN SEA

Mt Hermon 2224m

LEBANON

Kiryat Shmona

Golan Heights

Kazrin

Yehudiya NR

Ranot

Sea of Galilee

Tiberias

Tzfat

Mt Meron 1208m

Nazareth

Tel Megiddo NP

Jezreel Valley

Beit She'an NP

Jenin

Jordan River Crossing

Jordan

Jericho

King Hussein Bridge/Allenby Crossing

Qumran NP

Dead Sea

Nahariya

Akko

HAIFA

Carmel National Park

Zichron Ya'akov

Hadera

Netanya

Herzliya

TEL AVIV-JAFFA

Ashdod

Ashkelon

GAZA

Gaza Strip

Shechem (Nablus)

Ramallah

JERUSALEM

Bethlehem

Hebron

0   20km
0   20 miles

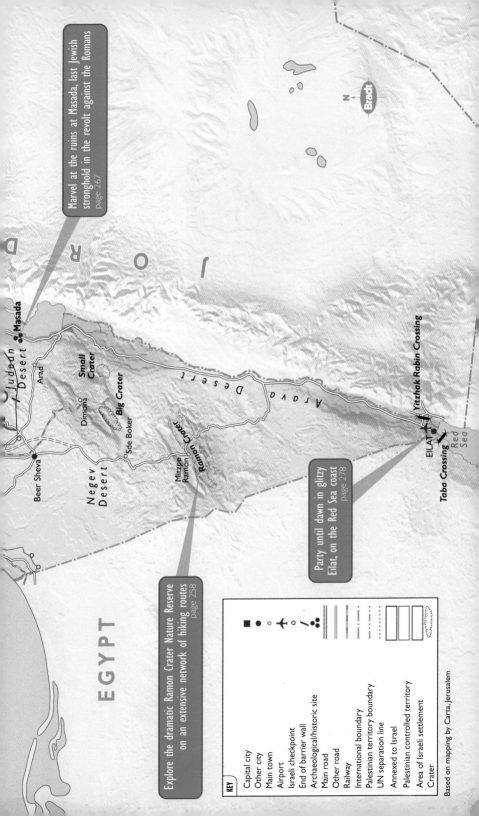

Marvel at the ruins at Masada, last Jewish stronghold in the revolt against the Romans page 267

Explore the dramatic Ramon Crater Nature Reserve on an extensive network of hiking routes page 258

Party until dawn in glitzy Eilat, on the Red Sea coast page 278

EGYPT

Beer Sheva

Negev Desert

Dimona

Small Crater

Big Crater

Sde Boker

Mitzpe Ramon

Ramon Crater

Arad

Judean Desert

Masada

Desert

Arava

Yitzhak Rabin Crossing

EILAT

Taba Crossing

Red Sea

Bradt

N

KEY

Capital city
Other city
Main town
Airport
Israeli checkpoint
End of barrier wall
Archaeological/historic site
Main road
Other road
Railway
International boundary
Palestinian territory boundary
UN separation line
Annexed to Israel
Palestinian controlled territory
Area of Israeli settlement
Crater

Based on mapping by Carta, Jerusalem

Israel
Don't
miss...

Jerusalem
The majestic golden Dome of
the Rock is the centrepiece
of the Temple Mount, the
city's holiest Islamic site
(RM) page 94

Dead Sea
The incredible buoyancy of this
large saline lake makes for a
surreal experience
(SS) page 261

Akko
This ancient port city has been continuously inhabited for 3,500 years
(SS) page 145

Sea of Galilee
The tranquil shores of this lake are steeped in New Testament history
(JA/A) page 194

Tel Aviv
Israel's fun-loving second city sets itself apart with its striking modern architecture, relaxed seafront and buzzing nightlife
(SS) page 109

above The Jewish Quarter is the most peaceful area of Jerusalem's Old City, and a living, breathing museum of ancient architecture (DM) page 91

above left The Mount of Olives is dotted with Jewish, Christian and Muslim religious sites, including the Garden of Gethsemane and the frescoed Church of All Nations (SS) page 101

left A carefully structured spice stand at the Souk Khan es Zeit, the Muslim Quarter souk (NS) page 79

below The decoration inside the Dome of the Rock is as splendid as its exterior, with coloured tiles, painted wood and carved stone (YLW/DT) page 95

right The Via Dolorosa has been a place of pilgrimage for Christians of all denominations since the Byzantine era (SS) page 88

below Orthodox Jews buying yellow citron for the festival of Sukkot, to celebrate the Exodus (SS) page 24

bottom A Bar Mitzvah ceremony at the Western Wall, the last remnant of the Second Temple and the holiest Jewish site (SS) page 91

AUTHOR

Samantha Wilson found herself in Israel quite by chance. After completing a degree in archaeology in the UK she embarked on a world trip that saw her wind up in Israel. There she spent several years travelling to every corner of Israel's little land, rescuing countless stray animals and writing for a variety of publications. She has authored or contributed to more than ten guidebooks for publishers such as Thomas Cook, Explorer Guides, Foreign Languages Press and Survival Guides, and written articles on a huge variety of topics – most focusing on Israel – for publications such as *Transitions Abroad*, *Jet2 In-flight Magazine* and *Wend*. Samantha currently lives on a tiny island off the Honduran coast, from where she can travel throughout Central America and write with views of the Caribbean. She makes regular trips back to Israel to travel, research and visit the in-laws, for a country that wasn't originally on the trip itinerary has become a second home.

AUTHOR'S STORY

Following completion of my archaeology degree at Exeter University I set off on a trip bound for South and Central America and found myself a year later living in the heart of the Middle East, a region I have grown to love for so many reasons. Perhaps it is its unconventionality, passion, staggering beauty or perhaps even its drama; I couldn't say for sure. Friends and acquaintances would ask me why I lived in such a politically sensitive and volatile country, to me a sad opening question about life in Israel. There is so much more to this small yet incredibly fascinating place and I was driven by this to share my intrigue and discoveries with others. And so I embarked on a thorough (and thoroughly enjoyable) exploration of every corner of Israel, from its snow-capped mountain peaks to its Red Sea coast and every kibbutz in between. Along the way, my project and I were greeted with an enthusiasm, gratitude and assistance I could never have predicted, the people of Israel desperate for others to share in the country of which they are so fiercely proud. In this way, while I may have put pen to paper, this is truly the work of so many who share a common love of this vibrant and colourful little land.

PUBLISHER'S FOREWORD

The first Bradt travel guide was written in 1974 by George and Hilary Bradt on a river barge floating down a tributary of the Amazon. In the 1980s and 1990s the focus shifted away from hiking to broader-based guides covering new destinations – usually the first to be published about these places. In the 21st century Bradt continues to publish such ground-breaking guides, as well as others to established holiday destinations, incorporating in-depth information on culture and natural history with the nuts and bolts of where to stay and what to see.

Bradt authors support responsible travel, and provide advice not only on minimum impact but also on how to give something back through local charities. In this way a true synergy is achieved between the traveller and local communities.

Second edition September 2011   First published January 2009

Bradt Travel Guides Ltd, IDC House, The Vale, Chalfont St Peter, Bucks SL9 9RZ, England
www.bradtguides.com
Published in the USA by The Globe Pequot Press Inc, PO Box 480, Guilford, Connecticut 06437-0480

Text copyright © 2011 Samantha Wilson
Maps copyright © 2011 Bradt Travel Guides Ltd
Where indicated, maps are based on sources provided by © Carta, Jerusalem
Photographs copyright © 2011 individual photographers (see below)
Project manager: Maisie Fitzpatrick

ISBN: 978 1 84162 362 7
British Library Cataloguing in Publication Data
A catalogue record for this book is available from the British Library

Photographers Alamy: Jon Arnold Images Ltd (JA/A), Hemis (H/A), Roger Hutchings (RH/A), Hanan Isachar (HI/A), PhotoStock-Israel (PI/A), Prisma Bildagentur AG (PB/A); Dreamstime: Shelly Agami (SA/DT), Yehuda Bernstein (YB/DT), Blaze86 (B/DT), Vladimir Blinov (VB/DT), Ellah (E/DT), Gkuna (G/DT), Rostislav Glinsky (RG/DT), Gorshkov13 (GK/DT), Yu Liang Wong (YLW/DT), Assaf Shuster (AS/DT), Yakov Stavchansky (YS/DT), Zatletic (Z/DT); FLPA: Yossi Eshbol (YE/FLPA), ImageBroker (IB/FLPA), Roger Tidman (RT/FLPA); Dinu Mendrea (DM); Radu Mendrea (RM); PhotoZion.com/John Theodor (PZ); Niv Silberman (NS); SuperStock (SS)

Front cover Children at the Jaffa Gate in Jerusalem's Old City (HI/A)
Back cover Timna Valley (PB/A), Old Jaffa port (HI/A)
Title page Goat on a desert cliff (SA/DT), Dead Sea (RT/FLPA), Dome of the Rock detail (SS)

Maps David McCutcheon

Typeset from the author's disk by Wakewing, High Wycombe
Production managed by Jellyfish Print Solutions and manufactured in India

Acknowledgements

A book like this doesn't come together without the help of many people to whom I shall always be grateful. The interest, support and encouragement that I received when researching and writing the first edition of this guide have certainly continued and I thank all my friends, in Israel and around the world, for that. I would also like to take this opportunity to thank all those who have read and used the guide, and who hopefully took away from their trip the same passion, intrigue and fun that I have always found researching and travelling in Israel.

To my family in Israel, thank you so much for all your wonderful hospitality, car loans, Shabbat dinners and of course your love and support – you have made Israel my second home. Thank you also to Allison Gosney for all her cheeriness and enthusiasm and for making all the pavement-pounding research so much fun. I would also like to thank Ami Dorfman for always giving up his time to share his knowledge and passion of the Galilee with me, Yael Armon for her input and suggestions, and the guys at Parrots Dive Centre for their daily interest and encouragement in my work (and their attempts at distractions!).

I would like to send my heartfelt thanks to my family, especially my parents, who have helped me plan a wedding at the same time as writing this book, and who are always my number one supporters. And lastly to Niv, without whom I would have never have found my way to Israel, and certainly never have had the courage to pursue a career I so love. Thank you for your selfless help, encouragement and enthusiasm. And thank you for marrying me.

Contents

A NOTE ABOUT MAPS

Several maps use grid lines to allow easy location of sites. Map grid references are listed in square brackets after the listing in the text, with page number followed by grid number, eg: [68 B2].

LIST OF MAPS

FEEDBACK REQUEST

Israel is a modern country with a fast-paced way of living and, as such, things tend to change quickly in this little stretch of land. The trendiest bar or café today is obsolete tomorrow, hotel prices fluctuate with the political situation, profound archaeological discoveries occur on a daily basis and public transport continues to improve and grow at a rate of knots. Everyone sees Israel in a different way and I would love to hear from readers about their own experiences in the Holy Land, something that would help me to prepare for the next edition of this book. If you come across something that you feel should be included, a hotel that has lost its charm or a fantastic little restaurant nestled away somewhere then please get in touch; be it good or bad it all goes towards making the next edition that much better. Write to me care of Bradt Guides, IDC House, The Vale, Chalfont St Peter, Bucks SL9 9RZ; e info@bradtguides.com; www.bradtguides.com/guidebook-updates/.

KEY TO SYMBOLS

——·—— International boundary	✡ Synagogue
——··—— Palestinian enclave boundary	☾ Mosque
▬▬▬ UN Demilitarised zone boundary	✝ Church/chapel/cathedral
National park/protected area	⊞ Ⓒ ✡ Cemetery (Christian/Muslim/Jewish)
National forest park/reserve	🏛 Tomb
✈ ✈ Airport (international/domestic)	$ Bank/bureau de change
---◄--- Ferry (pedestrian)	⚲ Statue/monument
═══ Motorway/main road	⁘ Archaeological/historic site
═══=== Other road/4x4 track	▲ Summit (height in metres)
▮▮▮▮ Pedestrianised town street	❁ Garden
‖‖‖‖‖‖‖‖ Stepped ways (paths)	🌣 Windmill
▬▬▬▬ Railway	Λ Campsite
▪=▪=▪= Underground railway/subway	🚗 Car hire
⊟—o—⊟ Cable car	♻ Cycle hire
VI V The Stations of the Cross route	🐫 Camel riding
---------- National trail/footpath	Urban park
🚌 Bus station etc	Urban market
🅿 Car park	Shopping centre/mall
⌂ Hotel/inn etc	Defined 'old town' area
☆ Nightclub/casino	Cruise ships
✕ Restaurant	⌐ ⌐ ⌐ Airport runway
⚲ Bar	Built-up area
☕ Café	Coral reef
e Internet access	✳ Viewpoint
℮ Embassy	⚱ Lighthouse
i Tourist information	o Hot springs
✉ Post office	〴 Waterfall
✚ Hospital/clinic	⌂ Cave/grotto
✚ Pharmacy/surgery/dentist	Crater edge
☗ Museum/art gallery	Salt lake/pan
☗ Theatre/cinema	⍩ Industrial complex
⊞ Important/historic building	⌉⌐ Beach
⌂ Castle/fort	⤳ Birdwatching area
⌂ Ancient city gate	⚐ Skiing
⚲ City wall	

Introduction

Israel is a land of dramatic and poignant contrasts, a land whose tumultuous existence often casts a shadow over the rich and vibrant life that beats beneath it, a land of incredible beauty, variety and character. Upon this soil have walked some of the greatest figures of our past, a ground that has seen the birth of world religions and the passionate battles that ensued to protect them.

It is a sad yet realistic state of affairs that the word 'Israel' has today become synonymous with conflict, religious tension and political debate, and historically this tiny stretch of land has formed the gladiatorial arena where empires and faiths have risen and fallen, a fact that remains today as it did 2,000 years ago.

Yet behind the television cameras and glare of the international limelight, Israel's tourist appeal is simply enormous. From the snow-capped peaks that straddle the northern border with Syria, to its barren and eerily beautiful expanse of rock deserts that form the gateway to Egypt and Africa beyond, the country leaves few landscapes unrepresented. As a meeting point between the cold steppes of Europe and the desert lands of the Syrian-African Rift Valley, Israel is a country geographically (and politically) divided. The swirl of green valleys, tree-studded hills and trickling streams that form the northern region are dotted with towns that have stood the tests of time, their inhabitants displaying a vibrant mesh of beliefs, traditions and cultures that remain proud and strong. In contrast are the arid lands of the south, vast craters, tiny isolated settlements and the inhospitable beauty of the Dead Sea swallowed up in their midst. The lively, cosmopolitan hub of Tel Aviv takes pleasure in its role as the country's economic, commercial and diplomatic centre, its wild beaches and secular way of life providing Jerusalem's diametric opposite. Jerusalem: few, if any cities on this planet can attest to the life that this incredible city has lived, its willpower, determination and passion to survive having seen it rise above all else that has come its way. Forming the cross on the map where the world's three biggest religions converge, it is a place like no other, one that leaves even the most religiously apathetic of visitors in awe.

Israel is a modern country that has created, thanks to its millions of immigrants, countless faiths and numberless cultures, a charm and uniqueness like nowhere else on earth. Combine this with its rich historic, geological and natural treasures and it is instantly apparent why so many have fought for so long to keep it.

Part One

GENERAL INFORMATION

ISRAEL AT A GLANCE

Location Middle East

Neighbouring countries Lebanon, Syria, Jordan, Egypt and the Palestinian territories of the West Bank and Gaza Strip

Area 20,330km^2 (22,145km^2 including the West Bank and Gaza Strip)

Climate Varies according to latitude: temperate in central and northern regions, hot and dry in the south

Status Parliamentary democracy

Population 7,116,700 (Central Bureau of Statistics May 2008 census)

Life expectancy Women 83.5, men 79.7

Capital Jerusalem (although most countries retain embassies in Tel Aviv)

Other main towns Tel Aviv, Haifa, Eilat, Nazareth, Tiberias, Tzfat, Netanya, Beer Sheva, Hadera, Ashdod

Economy Cut diamonds, high-technology and agricultural products are the major exports

GDP Purchasing power parity US$217.1 billion; per capita US$29,500

Languages Hebrew and Arabic are official languages. English is widely spoken.

Religion Judaism, Islam, Christianity, Druze, Baha'i

Currency New Israeli Shekel (NIS)

Exchange rate (June 2011) US$1 = 3.5NIS; £1 = 5.6NIS; €1 = 4.9NIS

National airline El Al

National airport Ben Gurion International Airport

International telephone code +972

Time GMT +2

Electrical voltage 220V/50Hz

Weights and measures Metric

Flag White and blue with the Star of David in the centre

National anthem Hatikvah

National emblem Menorah

National sport Football (soccer)

Public holidays Rosh Hashanah (September), Yom Kippur (September/October), Sukkot (September/October), Simchat Torah (September/October), Hannukah (December), Purim (February/March), Passover (March/April), Holocaust Memorial Day (April/May), National Memorial Day (April/May), Independence Day (April/May), Shavuot (May/June), Tisha Bav (July/August). Dates vary according to the Jewish calendar.

Background Information

GEOGRAPHY AND CONSERVATION

Israel is located in the western fringes of the Middle East. The long, narrow strip of land is almost diamond shaped, coming to a point at the Red Sea in the south. It borders Lebanon and Syria in the north, Jordan in the east and Egypt in the southwest, with the eastern coast fringing the Mediterranean Sea. The Gaza Strip is located on the southern Mediterranean coast and the West Bank stretches centrally from the border with Jordan. Measuring just 470km in length and 135km at its widest point the country is unique in that it has three highly contrasting geographical regions. In the west is the fertile coastal plain, home to major cities such as Tel Aviv and Haifa and the most densely populated region of the country. The forests, valleys, mountains and rivers that make up the north and east of the country incorporate the verdant Galilee region and the wild stretch of the Golan Heights, as well as the freshwater Sea of Galilee, Jordan River and Israel's highest peak, Mount Hermon (2,224m). More than half of Israel is desert, stretching all the way down to the Red Sea and the southern city of Eilat. The Dead Sea forms the eastern border with Jordan and stands as the world's lowest point at 400m below sea level. Sitting in the vast Syrian-African Rift Valley, its extreme salinity does not support any living organisms, the freshwater oases that dot the desert the only source of life to the flora and fauna of the region. Comprising the rocky Negev, Arava and Judean deserts, Israel's south is sparsely populated and transport links are few and far between.

NATIONAL PARKS Israel is today home to over 66 national parks and 190 nature reserves which are under the management of the Israel Nature and National Parks Protection Authority (INPA) (*www.parks.org.il*). In contrast to many other countries where the term 'national park' implies vast areas of open, protected land, in Israel the term is used to denote any protected area, be it a small archaeological site, vast canyon or landscaped hot spring park. Castles and fortresses, churches and synagogues, desert oases, caves, rivers, waterfalls and wildlife reserves grace the list of the country's national parks. Almost all parks charge an entry fee which goes towards continued conservation and management efforts. Discount cards can be bought at any of the park offices for 130NIS per person (the Green Card), are valid for two weeks and provide access to almost all national parks and nature reserves in the country. There is also a 90NIS pass which grants access to six national parks of your choice.

FLORA The Bible describes the Holy Land as 'a land of wheat and barley, of vines and fig trees and pomegranates, a land of olive trees and honey'. This wealth of plant life not seen in other Middle Eastern countries is down to its varied climate, geology and geographical positioning. A total of 2,380 species of flora have been

MOSHAV AND KIBBUTZ

About 8% of Israel's population lives in rural areas, divided between small towns, villages and two types of co-operative frameworks unique to the country. These co-operative frameworks, the *moshav* and the *kibbutz*, started appearing in the early part of the 20th century and today remain a key feature of the landscape and social structure of the country.

KIBBUTZ The word 'kibbutz' in Hebrew means 'gathering', and is used to describe a collective, self-contained farm settlement whereby members make decisions together for the good of the community, and wealth and property are shared out. The kibbutz appeared in Israel at the turn of the last century, created by Jewish settlers in Palestine, the first being Kibbutz Deganya Alef just south of the Sea of Galilee (see page 199). For decades, the idealistic community living attracted non-Jews who came to volunteer and live within the enclosed settlements. Parents lived in separate quarters to children, meals were eaten communally and homes were owned by the community not the individual. These days, however, the original concept has mostly been lost and while kibbutz communities are still famously tight-knit and children and dogs run freely, many meals continue to be eaten in the communal dining room and a kibbutz-run business remains in each, members in most *kibbutzim* (the plural of kibbutz) are allowed to purchase their own homes, go out to work and live more independent lives. Today around 130,000 people (less than 2% of the population) live in some 270 kibbutzim, their main economies centring on agriculture, tourism, industry and services – indeed, kibbutzim produce 38% of Israel's farm produce.

MOSHAV Created in the early 1900s, the moshav settlement was a collective village based on agriculture. Each family maintained its own farm and household, and land was divided up between family members. Today there are 451 *moshavim* (the plural of moshav) housing 3.4% of the population, and while farming businesses still form the backbone of much of Israel's agriculture (in particular cattle rearing, dairy and poultry), families maintain a more independent lifestyle and generally work outside of the settlement. The safe, homely, family-oriented environment that abounds on these settlements is today much sought after and such property rarely comes on to the market. In many parts of the country, the incredible popularity of *zimmers* (see page 53) – luxury, privately run rural accommodation – has seen tourism begin to play an important part in the economies of the moshavim and has made them yet more sought after.

recorded, many endangered or endemic to Israel. The Mediterranean region supports the densest concentrations, where alpine species thrive mainly along the Carmel Mountain ridge, in the Jezreel Valley and in the Galilee region. Plant life in the desert is sparse with the exception of small pockets of dense vegetation in oases such as Ein Gedi and Ein Avdat. In its accreditations, Israel is famed as being the northernmost limit for species such as the papyrus reed, the southernmost limit for plants such as the red coral peony and the only place where the Euphrates poplar still grows. The famed Madonna lily and Gilboa iris, rare Kermes oak trees and gnarled, ancient olive trees decorate the fertile northern terrain while towering date palms flourish in the arid, sub-Saharan soils of the desert.

WILDLIFE

Mammals Israel is home to 116 species of mammal, which, compared with the 140 species recorded in the whole of Europe, is vast. The country forms the crossroads for animals originating in the alpine European region to the north and those arriving from the desert regions of Arabia and Africa in the south. The largest inhabitants are mountain gazelles, wild boar, foxes, Nubian ibex, hyenas, jackals, wolves, onagers and the rarely seen leopards. A large conservation effort is in play to reintroduce many biblical creatures long since hunted to extinction from their natural lands. Jerusalem's Biblical Zoo and the Hai Bar nature reserves are at the centre of this scheme (see below and page 106).

Birds Sitting on the main migratory thoroughfare, Israel's skies and valleys seasonally fill with hundreds of species of birds who rest on their long journey south or north. A total of 510 bird species have been recorded, birdwatching reserves such

---

WALKING IN THE HOOFPRINTS OF ISRAEL'S BIBLICAL ANIMALS

Hai Bar is a nationwide organisation whose principal objective is to preserve the country's endangered animals and reintroduce indigenous species long since hunted to extinction back to their previous habitats. Lions, cheetahs, bears and crocodiles, some of Israel's more ferocious ancient inhabitants, are not, for obvious reasons, part of this scheme, but more mild-mannered species such as fallow and roe deer, Arabian oryx, Ethiopian ostrich and the onager (a type of wild ass) are being reintroduced to the delicate ecosystem. Several herds of onager have been released into the arid wilderness of the Arava Desert, with the Arabian oryx, whose impressive horns make them easily recognisable in the landscape, being another success story for the desert terrains. The **Yotvata Hai Bar Reserve** is home to many species which still roam the savanna-like lands of the south, and a delightful safari and conservation zoo makes a highly recommended trip. Hyenas, caracals, leopards, wolves, gazelle, sand and fennec foxes, desert hedgehogs and many birds and reptiles have all now been placed significantly lower down the endangered list thanks to ongoing efforts.

The last native roe deer was shot in the Carmel forest in 1912 and an intensive project has been under way to return them, and fallow deer, to their original habitat. Today, the **Carmel Hai Bar Wildlife Reserve** (04 832 0648; 08.00–16.00 Sat; admission car 33NIS), which hit headline news in December 2010 when a vicious wild fire reached the enclosure fences before being extinguished by hundreds of fire-fighters and volunteers, is home to the biggest population of fallow deer in the world, many of which have been successfully released. Wild sheep and goats, griffon, Egyptian vultures and Bonelli's eagles are also bred at the reserve which is located 300m south of Haifa University's main entrance on route 672. Another important griffon vulture sanctuary is located next to the hilltop fortress of **Kochav Hayarden** (see page 200).

Visitors are invited to enter the reserves to appreciate up close these biblical animals, the entry fees providing invaluable contributions to their continuing success. Many species, including the more fearsome contenders, can also been seen at the **Biblical Zoo** in Jerusalem, which is closely involved with the conservation efforts (see page 106).

as those in the Hula Valley, Eilat and Beit She'an Valley being prime places to see the splendid array of species that includes cranes, honey buzzards and pelicans. Of those who make their home in Israel are the highly endangered griffon and Egyptian vultures and imperial and spotted eagles. The Yehudiya National Park is the best place to see wild vultures soaring in the skies above, while the Israel Nature and National Parks Protection Authority has a research station and shelter next to Belvoir Castle in the Lower Galilee.

Reptiles There are 97 species of reptile and seven species of amphibian in the country, most others having disappeared because of urban and agricultural expansion and a loss of habitat. Scorpions are still prevalent in the desert while several snake species can be found across the country. Green turtles nest almost exclusively in Israel, Cyprus and Turkey, and researchers believe there are fewer than 1,000 females alive today.

The more common loggerhead turtles, most populous in Greece, Cyprus and Turkey, also nest in Israel, Syria and north Africa, although numbers are dwindling.

Marine life Eilat's Red Sea coast is home to several species of tropical marine life although the once-flourishing coral reefs have been overexploited and are now well past their prime. However, dolphins, octopuses, countless fish species and extremely occasionally whale sharks can be seen in the waters off Israel's southern coast.

CLIMATE

Israel has a 'Mediterranean', subtropical climate with hot summers and mild winters. Summer months are from April through October with temperatures peaking in July and August. Climatic conditions do, however, vary considerably. The Mediterranean coast suffers hot, humid summers and wet, mild winters, while the hilly regions of the north and east (including Jerusalem) are less humid in summer but have moderately cold winters and occasional snow. Mount Hermon is snow-capped almost year-round but snowfall has been significantly less in recent years. The desert is hot year-round, with exceptionally arid conditions. Rare flash floods can occur during heavy rains as water runs across the surface of the impermeable rock desert. Additional information and weather reports are available at the Israel Meteorological Service (*www.ims.gov.il*).

CLIMATE CHART						
	Tzfat	Haifa	Tiberias	Tel Aviv	Jerusalem	Eilat
Mean temp Jan °C	4–9	9–17	9–18	10–17	6–12	10–21
Mean temp Aug °C	19–29	24–31	23–38	24–30	19–29	26–40
Days rainfall per annum	58	51	47	46	44	5
Annual rainfall (mm)	712	540	407	524	553	32

HISTORY

IN THE BEGINNING... 'In the beginning God created the heavens and the earth.' And if you asked any observant Jew where Israel's history begins, it would be around this time. Historically, the land that is modern-day Israel has always stood on a great world crossroads, where empires, religions and cultures clashed or convened. In the 24th century BCE (Before Common Era, a term used in lieu of BC in non-Christian regions), it formed the cultural bull's-eye between Egypt, Assyria Mesopotamia and Asia Minor and in the 2nd millennium BCE various tribes began an invasion of the country, at the time inhabited by the Canaanites. Around the 17th century BCE, the Hebrew Bible's Book of Genesis records the appearance of three Jewish patriarchs: Abraham, Isaac and Jacob, the last of whom was also known as Israel. The Bible tells how Abraham was summoned to Canaan to unite a people who believed in 'One God'. When famine ravaged the land, the Israelites relocated to Egypt where, according to biblical sources, they spent 400 years in slavery. Led by Moses they escaped to freedom and spent the following 40 years wandering the desert before resettling in Canaan. Every year the Jewish holiday of Pesach (Passover) is celebrated in honour of this.

THE ISRAELITES AND THE IRON AGE (1200–586BCE)

Throughout the next two centuries the Israelites conquered the land, a time known as the Period of Judges. During this time of fierce wars people made allegiances with many of the 'judges', who emerged as leaders at that time. The divided armies were weak and suffering from incursions from the Philistines, a tribe descended from Asia Minor who had settled along the southern coast. In 1020BCE, the Israelites received the gift of unification in the form of King Saul, the Jewish people's first monarch. Upon Saul's defeat against the Philistines, David ascended to the throne and it was under his reign that Jerusalem was conquered (from the Jebusites) and declared capital of the realm. David was succeeded in 965BCE by his son Solomon who not only massively expanded the kingdom, but also commissioned the building of the First Temple. After Solomon's death civil unrest led to the division of the monarchy and the emergence of two kingdoms: Israel in the north, governed by ten tribes; and Judah in the south, led by two tribes. In 721BCE, the Assyrians conquered the Kingdom of Israel and its ten tribes fled, never to return. In 586BCE, the Kingdom of Judah suffered a similar fate at the hands of the Babylonians who destroyed Jerusalem and sacked the First Temple.

THE PERSIANS, ALEXANDER THE GREAT AND THE HASMONEANS (538–63BCE)

After the Persians conquered Babylon in 538BCE, the tribe of Judah was granted permission by the Persian king Cyrus to return to Jerusalem where in 515BCE they constructed the Second Temple. Throughout the Persian period the Jews prospered and strengthened, the Knesset Hagedolah (Great Assembly – see page 19) owing its origins to this time. In 332BCE, however, Persian rule came to an end with Alexander the Great's conquest. His death in 323BCE led to battles over his legacy and right to the throne, a struggle that was eventually won by Seleucus I who founded the Syrian-based Seleucid dynasty. This period is characterised in history as the Hellenistic, whereby the remaining descendants of Alexander's Greek kingdom and its merging with the Persians resulted in the emergence of a distinctly Greek cultural phase, even under Seleucid rule. By this time synagogues had become the centre of the Jewish community and when the Seleucid rulers began suppressing the Jewish religion, imposing upon the population Greek-oriented culture, language and beliefs, the Jews in 166BCE rose in a revolt led by the Maccabees, a Jewish family of patriots (an event celebrated today with the festival of Hanukkah). This in turn led to the establishment of the Jewish Hasmoneans, who eventually ousted the Seleucids and imposed their own religion on the land. It was during this period of Jewish rule that religious tensions caused breakaway groups to emerge, most notably the Essenes who are the believed authors of the Dead Sea Scrolls found at Qumran (see page 266).

JESUS AND THE ROMANS (63BCE–212CE) In 63BCE Pompeii captured Jerusalem, replacing the Seleucids as the region's great power, and demoting the Hasmonean king, Hyrcanus II, to acting king under Roman rule. The Jewish population was hostile to the new regime and rebellions eventually led to the final demise of the Hasmoneans, and Roman rule over the Land of Judea. In 37BCE, Herod the Great was appointed king, becoming one of the Roman Empire's most powerful leaders. Under him the great coastal city of Caesarea exploded on to the scene as one of the world's most crucial seaports, the palace of Masada (see page 267) was built as his luxury playground and the temple was given a magnificent makeover. Despite (or perhaps in spite of) these achievements the Jews were displeased, and revolts led to the destruction of the Second Temple under Titus. A last attempt in 123CE (Common Era, used in lieu of AD) to claim Jewish liberation failed after an ambitious but unsuccessful uprising led by Shimon Bar Kochba. According to Josephus Flavius, a 1st-century historian, hundreds of thousands of Jews were exiled and dispersed across the empire, an event known as the Jewish Diaspora. Jerusalem was razed to the ground and on it built a wholly Roman city named Aelia Capitolina. Judea thereafter became known as Syria-Palaestina.

Jesus of Nazareth was born in the early years of Roman rule. However, it would be a further 300 years until Christianity was legitimised by the Romans and became the official religion. Details of Jesus's life – especially his early years – are taken primarily from the Gospels, telling of his descent from the bloodline of King David, his mother Mary's Immaculate Conception and his birth in Bethlehem following a move made by Mary and Joseph in compliance with King Herod's census. The Gospels however mention nothing of Jesus from the age of 12 until he began his public ministry 18 years later, following his baptism by John the Baptist (see page 16).

For the Jews, the remainder of the Roman period is characterised by the survival of their communities, now scattered across the land and beyond. The supreme legislative and judicial body, known as the Sanhedrin (successor to the Knesset Hagedolah) reconvened in 70CE in Tiberias, reinforced over time by returning exiles. During these exiled years the great texts of Judaism were scribed, the Mishnah (a book on Jewish oral law) in 210CE by Rabbi Judah ha-Nasi, and the Talmud (a commentary on the Mishnah) in 390CE.

THE BYZANTINES (313–636) In 313CE, Constantine the Great founded the Byzantine Empire and legalised Christianity. An influx of pilgrims and a huge building phase got under way with churches and monasteries appearing all over the country, more than 450 ecclesiastical buildings having been dated to this time. In 614, the Persians invaded Palaestina, aided by the Jews who as a sign of gratitude were granted permission to once again rule Jerusalem. But it was to be a short rule as three years later the Byzantine army ousted the Persians and once again expelled the Jewish inhabitants.

ARAB RULE (636–1099) Four years after the death of the Prophet Muhammad in 632 the caliphate (Arab Islamic Empire) conquered Jerusalem under the caliph Omar along with the lands of Mesopotamia, Syria, Palestine (present-day Israel) and Egypt. According to Muslim tradition, Muhammad ascended to Heaven from Jerusalem and as such it is considered Islam's third holiest city. In 638, Caliph Omar built the first mosque on the site of the destroyed Second Temple, which was enhanced by the construction of the Dome of the Rock in 691 by the ninth caliph Abd al-Malik. In the first years of Arab rule Christians (and Jews) were allowed to enter Jerusalem, but this was stopped in the 11th century, prompting Pope Urban II to call for the crusade to free the Holy City from Muslim rule.

THE CRUSADES AND SALADIN (1099–1291) In the 200 years that followed, the country was dominated by waves of crusades that arrived from Western Europe with the aim of returning the land to Christendom. The brutal and relentless First Crusade ended in 1099 with the capture of Jerusalem and the massacre of most of the city's Jewish and Muslim residents. Throughout the succeeding decades the Crusaders extended their power across the country either by diplomacy or, more often than not, brute force directed from their fortresses and castles that formed a fortified network across the land. The result was the founding of the Latin Kingdom of Jerusalem, first under Godfrey of Bouillon and then his brother Baldwin.

In 1187 Saladin, the Muslim sultan of Egypt, recaptured Jerusalem after victory at the mighty Battle of Hittin. Although his death four years later allowed the crusades to gain another foothold in the country, they remained limited to their castles and fortifications, suffering countless incursions that ended with their defeat at Akko, their last stronghold, against the Mamluks.

THE MAMLUKS AND OTTOMANS (1291–1917) Throughout Mamluk rule the country descended into a dark era; governed from Damascus it became a peripheral province. The once-thriving port cities of Akko and Jaffa were closed through fear of more crusades and the economy suffered. By the end of the Middle Ages towns were dilapidated, Jerusalem was all but abandoned and the small Jewish, Christian and Muslim communities that remained were poverty-stricken. The dire situation was not aided by violent earthquakes and a devastating plague. Sources estimate that there were but 200,000 people left in the land by the time the Ottoman period began in 1517.

The Ottoman Turks governed Palestine from their centre of power in Istanbul for the succeeding 400 years, until the onset of World War I. Suleiman the Magnificent, the Ottoman Empire's longest-reigning sultan, is attributed with having constructed the great walls around Jerusalem. The small Jewish population that had existed in Palestine when the Ottomans arrived, expanded quickly as immigrants from north Africa and Europe began to arrive, Tzfat becoming a major centre for Jewish learning (see page 205). However, after Suleiman's death in 1566, things took a turn for the worse and the country fell once more into decline.

ZIONISM Zionism refers to the movement of Jews in the 19th century to establish a Jewish homeland. As the dark Ottoman years were finally consigned to the past, signs of progress emerged: Western powers took an interest in Palestine, opening consulates in Jerusalem; trade links were reopened; the Jerusalem to Jaffa highway was constructed; and the land once again became a continental crossroads. Subsequently Jewish numbers in the four holy cities of Jerusalem, Tzfat, Hebron and Tiberias increased, with growing anti-Semitism displayed towards Jews in European countries and the pogroms of Russia. The French Baron Edmond de Rothschild (see page 171) ploughed money into Jewish settlements founding Deganya, the first kibbutz. Hebrew was revived amidst the Jewish population, Jerusalem's new city was founded and modern Tel Aviv grew outside of Jaffa. In 1897, Theodor Herzl initiated a Zionist movement at the World Zionist Conference in Basle, Switzerland. This was aided by the signing of the Balfour Treaty in 1917 that saw the British Foreign Secretary Lord Balfour approve the establishment in Palestine of a 'national home for the Jewish people' provided it did not prejudice the religious and civil rights of the non-Jews who lived there.

BRITISH RULE AND JEWISH IMMIGRATION (1918–48) In World War I, Turkey allied itself with Germany. Having already signed the Balfour Treaty, the British were at the same time allying themselves with the Arabs, pledging to support Arab independence in exchange for them waging war against the Ottomans. In 1916, the Arab Revolt, aided by T E Lawrence (of Arabia) declared war on the Ottomans. When, in 1917, General Allenby entered Jerusalem to a warm Arab welcome, little did he know that France, Britain and Russia had signed the secret Sykes–Picot Agreement to divide up the Middle East. France administered Lebanon and Syria while Britain administered Iraq and Transjordan. Palestine remained under international administration until after World War I when the new League of Nations entrusted Britain with the Mandate for Palestine. As the area east of the Jordan River was not to be included in the new Jewish homeland, Transjordan eventually became the Hashemite Kingdom of Jordan.

The British Mandate Authorities granted the Jews – and to a far lesser degree the Arabs – the right to administer their own internal affairs. In 1922, as stipulated in the mandate, the Jewish Agency was formed. Throughout this period Jewish culture flourished and Hebrew was recognised as an official language alongside English and Arabic, much to the discontent of the Arab population, which was increasingly losing its land. Arab unrest culminated in the Jaffa Riots and the subsequent issuing of a White Paper whereby the British imposed restrictions on the numbers of Jews allowed to immigrate. By this time the country had seen two *aliyah* ('moving up' or large-scale Jewish immigration) in the early 1920s from Russia and in the late 1920s from Poland. The last major wave of immigration (some 165,000 people) before the onset of World War II occurred in the 1930s when Hitler rose to power in Germany.

PARTITION, DECLARATION AND WAR Following the Holocaust, which saw the genocide of around six million Jews and subsequent mass immigration to Palestine, the British intensified their restrictions. Between 1945 and 1948 however, underground Jewish militias smuggled in an estimated 85,000 people in spite of naval blockades and border patrols. As a result of increasing friction between the Jews and Arabs, and revolts from both sides against the British, the British government turned to the UN. On 29 November 1947, they proposed a partition whereby the land would be divided into one Jewish and one Arab country, with Jerusalem governed by the UN. The Jews reluctantly agreed to the partition but the Palestinian Arab leaders, and leaders of neighbouring Arab countries, rejected it.

On 14 May 1948, the same day the British Mandate in Palestine came to an end, Israel declared its independence. Within hours Palestinian Arabs were joined by forces from Egypt, Jordan, Syria, Lebanon and Iraq who retaliated against the declaration, and so began the 1948 Arab–Israeli War. Although Israel successfully defended most of its new country it submitted to the Egyptians in Gaza and the Jordanians in the West Bank, half of Jerusalem being absorbed into Jordan. Thousands of Palestinians stormed into these Arab-controlled areas, creating crowded refugee camps. Today, the 1948 Arab–Israeli War is referred to by many as *al-Nakba* or The Catastrophe, an estimated 15,000 Palestinians losing their lives and a further 700,000 becoming refugees. Despite Israel's ultimate victory, it came at a cost and over 6,000 Israelis died in the war.

THE STATE OF ISRAEL AND THE SUEZ–SINAI WAR After the war Israel set about building a state: the Knesset, Israel's government, was founded; it became the 59th member of the UN; David Ben-Gurion was democratically elected as the first prime minister; and between 1949 and 1951 some 700,000 Jews immigrated to Israel.

In early 1949, armistice agreements between all warring countries except Iraq confirmed the situation reached at the end of the war, whereby Jordan controlled half of Jerusalem and the West Bank.

The armistice failed, however, to achieve lasting peace and security issues in Israel heightened. In 1956, Egypt's prime minister, Gamal Abdel Nasser, retaliated against the US and British after they withdrew funding from his Aswan High Dam project following Nasser's association with the Soviet Union. In his retaliation he nationalised the Suez Canal, ousting French and British owners from its management. Blockades on Israeli-bound cargo, a massive increase in military preparations in the Sinai Peninsula, blockades in the Straits of Tiran and the signing of a tripartite military alliance between Egypt, Syria and Jordan resulted in the Israel Defence Force (IDF) allied by France and Britain initiating the Suez–Sinai War. In the course of an eight-day campaign the IDF succeeded in capturing the Gaza Strip and the entire Sinai Peninsula, stopping just 16km short of the Suez Canal. On 30 October, as planned, Britain and France issued an ultimatum demanding Israel and Egypt relinquish control of the Suez Canal. Egypt refused and on 31 October Britain and France responded by bombing Egyptian military bases, an act which put them back in charge of the canal. An urgent ceasefire demand issued by both the US and Soviet Union forced British, French and Israeli forces to relent.

THE SIX DAY WAR (1967) Enraged by the losses he suffered during the Suez–Sinai War, Nasser encouraged the Palestine Liberation Organization (PLO) to continue its raids on Jewish settlements and formed an alliance of Arab states that began preparations for war. This, combined with persistent Syrian artillery attacks in the north and the re-imposition of the Tiran Straits blockade, resulted in Israel making a pre-emptive strike against Egypt on 5 June 1967, decimating the Egyptian air force. King Hussein of Jordan was next to attack but within two days the Israelis had taken Jerusalem. The following day saw the IDF once again reach the Suez Canal and the Egyptians pushed back, essentially now out of the war. That in hand, attentions were turned to Syria which had seen the destruction of two-thirds of its air force at the hands of IDF planes. Israeli forces penetrated the Golan Heights and on 10 June Israel and Syria signed a ceasefire agreement. The result of the Six Day War was a need to redraw the map of the Middle East. Judea, Samaria, Gaza, the Sinai Peninsula and the Golan Heights were now under Israeli control and Jerusalem was once again reunited.

THE PLO After the Six Day War the Palestinian refugee situation worsened and peace in the Middle East was very far away. The UN was not comfortable with the land gained by Israel and urged its return. Israel refused, agreeing only to consider returning the land in the cause of a comprehensive peace plan. The Arab states were calling for the destruction of Israel and peace talks were by no means on any agenda. Putting their support behind the PLO (formed in 1964 at a summit meeting of the Arab League in order to provide a more organised form of Palestinian nationalism than that offered by the scattered *fedayeen* or guerrilla forces, primarily Fatah), they urged them to continue their spate of terrorist attacks on Israel, attacks that were made from bases in Lebanon, Jordan, Syria, the West Bank and Gaza Strip. In 1969, Fatah leader Yasser Arafat was elected chairman of the PLO. The raids on Israel executed from within Jordan were not only straining the fledgling secret peace talks between King Hussein and Israel, but the Palestinians had managed to create a state within a state that was becoming a threat to Jordan. In 1970, a short, bloody war between the Jordanian army and the PLO's *fedayeen* resulted in the latter fleeing to

Lebanon. The heavy losses incurred by the Palestinians have come to be known as Black September.

THE WAR OF ATTRITION (1969) In early 1969, skirmishes between Egyptian and Israeli forces erupted along the Suez Canal, which soon turned into the all-out War of Attrition. Backed by heavy military equipment from the Soviet Union the humiliated Egyptian army sought revenge for the Six Day War and undertook a campaign which inflicted maximum casualties on Israeli troops. In response, Israel's new prime minister Golda Meir retaliated with even more force. The following year Anwar Sadat succeeded Nasser and hostilities ceased, the war-weary Egyptians looking towards the possibility of a pull-out from the Sinai Peninsula.

THE YOM KIPPUR WAR (RAMADAN WAR) (1973) Peace after the War of Attrition was not to be, however, and the Egyptians, Syrians (backed by Soviet weaponry) and the Israelis (backed by military funding from the US) started to prepare their armies once again. On Yom Kippur, 6 October 1973, Judaism's holiest day, Egypt and Syria executed a surprise attack on Israeli forces along the east bank of the Suez Canal and in the Golan Heights. By mid-October however, despite heavy losses, the Israelis had pushed the Syrians back out of the Golan Heights and had come within 40km of Damascus. A similar scene was playing out in Suez, whereby Israeli forces had re-crossed the canal and were now stationed a mere 100km from Cairo. Soviet leader Leonid Brezhnev, fearing the decimation of the encircled Egyptian Third Army would have dire consequences on the stability of the country, issued a veiled warning to the US to get Israel to back off or reap the repercussions of a Soviet intervention. US secretary of state Henry Kissinger subsequently received President Nixon's permission to put the country on nuclear alert. The head to head was quickly defused and on 25 October a fragile ceasefire agreement was signed.

CAMP DAVID ACCORDS AND THE DISENGAGEMENT For two years after the war Kissinger travelled between Israel and the Arab states looking to achieve a peace accord. Egypt was seeking to reclaim the Sinai Peninsula and was starting to open to the idea of peace talks. In the Geneva Peace Conference in December 1973 the US, Soviet Union, Israel, Egypt, Jordan and Syria signed an accord agreeing to relinquish parts of Sinai. Back in Israel however, Israelis were angered by Golda Meir's disengagement decision and continued to settle in great numbers in the occupied lands. In May of the following year much of Sinai was turned over to the Egyptians, the Golan Heights border was redrawn to the pre-1967 line and Golda Meir was forced to resign. In her place Yitzhak Rabin (Labor Party) managed to halt settlement but his successor, Menachem Begin (Likud) funded and encouraged it.

By the late 1970s, Sadat was ready to talk peace and reclaim the remaining strip of Sinai coast still under Israeli control. He journeyed to Jerusalem and in what became known as the Camp David Accords, an Egyptian–Israeli peace treaty was signed in 1979. The Sinai coast was returned to Egypt and normal diplomatic relations ensued. But the rosy picture was soon to turn dark as the Arab League expelled Egypt and in 1981 Sadat was assassinated by Islamist fundamentalists (although relations did continue even after Sadat's death).

THE FIRST LEBANON WAR (1982) The Camp David Accords, while finally achieving peace between the Egyptians and Israelis, did nothing for the situation with Syria and the PLO. The PLO continued relentless terrorist activity from within Lebanon and in June 1982 Israel, under then Minister of Defence Ariel Sharon, invaded the south of the country. Throughout what was known in Israel as Operation Peace for Galilee the Israeli troops eventually occupied Beirut and drove out the bulk of the PLO who fled to Tunisia. In 1985, Israel finally withdrew from Lebanon leaving itself a small security zone in the south, one that it would hold for the next 18 years.

THE INTIFADA AND THE GULF WAR In December 1987, the first intifada ('shaking off' in Arabic) occurred when Palestinians in the West Bank and the Gaza Strip launched riots against Israel's occupation. The world once again turned its attentions to the Palestinian situation and demanded a solution. In the meantime, following Iraq's invasion of Kuwait, the Gulf War erupted. An allied coalition of Western and Arab countries led by the US managed to expel Iraq from Kuwait but in an attempt to gain support from the Arab states Iraq launched 39 Scud missiles at Israel, encouraged by Yasser Arafat and the Palestinians.

THE MADRID AND OSLO ACCORDS AND THE ASSASSINATION OF YITZHAK RABIN Following the Gulf War, what looked to be a glimmer of light in the dark clouds materialised when, in July 1991, Syria, Israel (under agreement that this did not include the PLO), the US, Soviet Union, Lebanon, Egypt and Jordan convened at the Madrid Conference to openly discuss peace. Negotiations soon broke down however with the fate of Jerusalem proving to be the breaking point. In 1993, a breakthrough was finally made when Israel – once again under Yitzhak Rabin – and the Palestinians managed to come to a secret agreement known as the Oslo Accords. The accords set the way for the newly formed Palestinian National Authority (with Yasser Arafat as its president) to take over administrative control of the Gaza Strip and West Bank. At the same time, despite opposition from other Arab countries, Jordan's King Hussein opted to sign a peace treaty with Israel, one that has remained the most stable and lasting.

The Israeli–Palestinian agreement was not well received by everyone, however, and militant extremist groups on both sides undertook a series of terrorist activities. Hamas continued attacks on Israeli civilians and, in the midst of an Israeli peace rally in Tel Aviv, Yitzhak Rabin was assassinated by Yigal Amir, an Israeli student opposed to the peace process. His death is seen by many in the country as one of the darkest events in Israel's history.

PEACE TALKS THROUGH THE 1990s Following Rabin's shocking assassination, Benjamin Netanyahu (Likud Party) ascended to the position of prime minister and peace talks took a nosedive. The tentative negotiations that had been sparked between Israel and Syria at the Madrid Accords dissolved, and despite withdrawing Jewish settlers from Hebron as part of the Oslo Accords, Netanyahu angered Arabs by encouraging settlement in Arab East Jerusalem. In turn, terrorist attacks on Israeli civilians were relentless, and peace talks once again came to an abrupt end. Netanyahu, pressured both from some home sectors (there are many who strongly oppose a land-for-peace accord) and abroad, agreed to withdraw from more of the West Bank in return for cessation of terrorist attacks. Although this went through, negotiations broke down soon afterwards and early elections saw Ehud Barak (Labor Party) rise to become prime minister.

THE NEW MILLENNIUM Despite continuing friction between Jews and Arabs, Christian pilgrims still flocked to the Holy Land, and in 2000 Pope John Paul II made a historic visit. In the same year Israel withdrew its forces from the security zone in southern Lebanon. Controversy arose, however, over the disputed 'Shebaa

Farms' a 22km² area of land both countries lay claim to. Almost as soon as the Israelis withdrew, Hezbollah, an Islamic fundamentalist group moved in, the Lebanese failing to assert their rule over the area.

In September of that year Ariel Sharon caused outrage when he visited the Temple Mount (see page 94), sparking the second (or Al Aqsa) intifada (although Israel claims the violence was pre-planned and his visit used as an excuse). Amidst a rapidly deteriorating Israeli–Palestinian situation, Barak called for elections, only to lose to Ariel Sharon.

Arafat's death and Israel's disengagement from Gaza In 2001, Sharon announced that, although he considered Arafat to be a hindrance to the peace process, he planned to execute a full withdrawal from the Gaza Strip. Later that year, following months of heavy terrorist activity, Sharon instigated the construction of a wall around the West Bank and the IDF surrounded Arafat's Ramallah home, in effect putting him under house arrest. It wasn't until 2004, shortly before his death, that he was allowed to leave to seek medical treatment in France. In November 2004, Mahmoud Abbas stepped in as leader of the Palestine National Authority (PNA). In the months leading up to the 2005 Gaza disengagement Israel found itself divided, with many residents strongly opposed. That summer the world watched as unarmed IDF soldiers dragged Israelis from Jewish settlements in Gaza and parts of the West Bank.

The Second Lebanon War In 2005, Sharon left Likud and formed the Kadima Party which, after Sharon's stroke, went on to win elections in 2006 headed by Ehud Olmert. Later that year saw continued skirmishes on the border with Gaza, which erupted into full-scale war when Hamas entered Israeli territory, killing two soldiers and kidnapping a third. In the two months that followed, Israel bombarded Gaza with heavy forces, killing over 200 Palestinians and decimating the infrastructure. At around the same time, Hezbollah militants from south Lebanon also crossed the border to kidnap two IDF soldiers, killing others and shelling northern Israeli towns and villages. An attack on southern Lebanon ensued and soon escalated, drawing condemnation from the international community, who accused Israel of excessive force. Approximately 1,200 Lebanese civilians lost their lives and thousands more were displaced. Residents of northern Israel spent the summer in bunkers as rockets rained down, most concentrated on Haifa (see page 151). In August 2006, the UN orchestrated a ceasefire and stepped in to man southern Lebanon.

The Gaza Conflict In 2006 Hamas won Palestinian elections by a wide margin and an Israeli-imposed blockade was placed on Gaza, which, at the time of writing, is still in place four years on. In response to rocket and mortar fire from Hamas, Israel launched an air strike and ground offensive on Gaza in December 2008. In the month that followed, about 1,400 Palestinians and 13 Israelis were killed before a ceasefire agreement was reached in January 2009. After a year of relative calm, tensions once again skyrocketed when Israeli naval forces boarded a Turkish flotilla bound for Gaza. Following repeated warnings not to breach the imposed blockade on Gaza being ignored the Israeli forces boarded the ships and killed nine pro-Palestinian Turkish activists. They maintain they acted in self-defence upon being attacked by those on board. Relations between Turkey and Israel remain hugely strained.

A constant and hugely sensitive subject within Israel is the kidnapping of Gilad Shalit, an Israeli soldier who was captured by Hamas in 2006 and at the time of writing remains captive.

A shy, good natured 24-year-old Israeli man today sits unwittingly in the midst of an international drama, one that has caused battles, political debate, anger, pain and intense negotiations. On 25 June 2006 Gilad Shalit, an IDF soldier, was captured just outside the Gaza Strip by Hamas militants who demanded the release of thousands of Palestinian prisoners from Israeli jails. A failed rescue attempt three days after his capture, and ignored ultimatums on both sides led to a stalemate. Over the following months, Egyptian mediators intervened (and a letter was received from Gilad confirming he was alive) plus countless foreign governments and dignitaries including Jimmy Carter and the French government (Gilad has dual French and Israeli citizenship) attempted to negotiate for his release, but to no avail.

Public opinion in Israel remains divided as to how the government should proceed. The question at the core of the debate is whether Israel should release the prisoners Hamas demands or not. A huge march across the country arranged by the Shalit family in August 2010 involved thousands of supporters, and prime minister Benjamin Netanyahu agreed to release 1,000 Palestinian prisoners, although not top Hamas leaders. Hamas rejected the negotiation. Since his capture there have been a few letters, an audio tape and in September 2009 (following the release of 25 prisoners) a video proving Gilad is still alive. Four years on and Gilad Shalit is now a household name in Israel, his capture the realisation of every Israeli parent's worst nightmare.

THE CURRENT SITUATION Following Ehud Olmert's resignation and the Kadima Party's successor Tzipi Livni's failure to form a coalition government, a general election was held in February 2009. Despite gaining a majority vote Tzipi Livni and the Kadima Party had to relinquish power to Likud with Benjamin Netanyahu at its head, again due to the inability to create a coalition. Today the situation in Israel remains sensitive, and if history has taught us anything it's that peace in the Middle East is, at best, tenuous. While Israel has received negative press over the years for being a danger zone, and countries often warn their citizens against travel there, the increase in international terrorism has seen tourists look at the country in a new light. Israel's extreme security measures and experience with terrorist attacks has seen tourism numbers rocket. With obvious exceptions throughout the Second Lebanon War, the country has seen a steady influx of tourists and pilgrims coming not only to Jerusalem and the holy sites but to take advantage of the natural and archaeological sites, health resorts, spas and beach holidays; and with home football games against England and Ireland and top musicians such as Roger Waters and Phil Collins making appearances, tourism is on the up and up.

TIMELINE

17th–6th centuries Biblical period

BCE

c17th century	Abraham, Isaac and Jacob settle in Canaan. Famine forces the Israelites to flee to Egypt.
13th–12th century	Israelites are led from Egypt by Moses and settle in Canaan
c1020	King Saul becomes the first Jewish monarch
c1000	Jerusalem becomes capital of King David's kingdom
c960	First Temple built by King Solomon

The poignant, devastating and dramatic events that have taken place on the tiny stretch of land officially known today as the State of Israel have given rise to several acclaimed motion pictures that depict their stories on the glittering silver screen. The following movies in particular will help to put into perspective some of the major events of the past.

Exodus (1960) Tells the story of Palestine under the British Mandate and the immigration of the Jews.

Mivtsa Yonatan (1977) Re-enactment of the rescue operation undertaken by the IDF following the hijacking of a flight from Tel Aviv to Paris that was forced to land in Entebbe, Uganda.

The Impossible Spy (1987) Chronicles the life of Eli Cohen, Israel's most acclaimed spy.

Schindler's List (1993) Deals with the Holocaust in Europe and the story of Oscar Schindler who saved his Jewish workers from death camps.

Kippur (2000) Israeli-produced movie depicting the Yom Kippur War.

Syrian Bride (2004) Tells the story of a young Druze bride from the Golan Heights who is sent to Syria for an arranged marriage, never to return or see her family again.

Munich (2005) Depicts the massacre of Israeli athletes at the 1972 Munich Olympics at the hands of Palestinian Black September militants.

Paradise Now (2005) A story of suicide bombings as seen through the eyes of two young Palestinian men.

Kingdom of Heaven (2005) Focuses on the crusades and the Kingdom of Jerusalem.

One Night with the King (2006) Tells the story of Queen Esther for whom the Jewish holiday of Purim is celebrated.

Beaufort (2007) Israeli-produced movie depicting Israel's withdrawal from southern Lebanon after 18 years.

Waltz with Bashir (2008) Animated movie depicting the director's memories of the 1982 Lebanon War.

Lebanon (2010) The story of four young Israeli soldiers and their experiences during the Lebanon War.

721	Israel falls to the Assyrians (Northern Kingdom)
586	Judea falls to Babylon (Southern Kingdom). Jerusalem and the First Temple destroyed.
538–142	**Persian and Hellenistic periods**
515	Jerusalem's Temple rebuilt
332	Alexander the Great conquers Persia. Hellenistic period begins.
166	Jewish revolt against the Seleucid dynasty and beginning of the Hasmonean period
63	Jerusalem captured by the Roman general Pompeii
63BCE–313CE	**Roman period**
37BCE	Herod the Great appointed King of Judea
c8BCE	Jesus born
c26CE	Jesus begins his ministry after being baptised by John the Baptist
c30	Jesus crucified

66	Jewish revolt against the Romans
70	Destruction of Jerusalem and the Second Temple
132–135	Shimon Bar Kochba leads the Jews in what becomes known as the Bar Kochba uprising against the Romans
200	New Testament fixed in current form
c210	Mishnah (book on Jewish oral law) completed
313–636	**Byzantine period**
c390	Talmud (commentary on the Mishnah) completed
614	Persian invasion
636–1099	**Arab period**
691	Dome of the Rock built by Caliph Abd al-Malik
1099–1291	**Crusades (Latin Kingdom of Jerusalem)**
1187–93	**Ayyubid period under Saladin following Battle of Hittin**
1291–1516	**Mamluk period**
1517–1917	**Ottoman period**
1537	Suleiman the Magnificent constructs Jerusalem's walls
1897	Zionist Organisation founded by Theodor Herzl
1909	Tel Aviv founded. Deganya becomes the first kibbutz.
1917	British issue Balfour Declaration to establish a 'national home' for the Jews in Palestine
1918–48	**British rule**
1922	British granted Mandate for Palestine by League of Nations
1936–39	Arab Revolt
1939	Jewish immigration limited by British White Paper
1939–45	World War II. Holocaust in Europe.
1947	UN proposes Arab and Jewish states
1948	
14 May	End of British Mandate
14 May	State of Israel declared
15 May	Beginning of Arab–Israeli War following attack by Egypt, Syria, Jordan, Iraq and Lebanon
1948–52	Huge immigration from Europe and Arab countries
1949	
July	Armistice agreements signed with Egypt, Jordan, Syria and Lebanon. Jerusalem divided between Israel and Jordan. Israel enters UN.
1956	Suez–Sinai War
1964	PLO (Palestine Liberation Organization) formed
1967	Six Day War. Israel conquers and occupies Gaza, Sinai, West Bank, Golan Heights and Jordanian-controlled Jerusalem.
1969	War of Attrition
1970	Jordan expels PLO who re-settle in Lebanon
1973	Yom Kippur War
1979	Peace treaty signed between Israel and Egypt
1982	First Lebanon War
1987	First intifada; violence between Israelis and Palestinians
1994	Israel–Jordan peace treaty signed
1995	Palestinian Authority established. Israel and PLO agree to mutual recognition (Oslo Declaration of Principles). Oslo Interim Agreement signed. Israeli prime minister Yitzhak Rabin assassinated by right-wing Jewish fanatic Yigal Amir.

2000	Israel withdraws from southern Lebanon. Second intifada.
2001	Ariel Sharon (Likud Party) elected prime minister
2002	Israel constructs wall around West Bank following series of suicide bombings
2004	Palestinian Authority president Yasser Arafat dies
2005	Israel carries out Disengagement Plan and withdraws Jewish settlers from Gaza and parts of West Bank

2006

January	Ariel Sharon suffers a stroke. Ehud Olmert becomes prime minister with new Kadima Party.
26 January	Radical Islamist Hamas movement win election in Palestinian territories
12 July–14 August	Second Lebanon War

2007

| February | Hamas and Fatah agree to share power in Palestinian Unity Agreement |
| June | Hamas ousts Fatah from Gaza |

2008

February	Hezbollah member Imad Moughniyeh killed by car bomb in Damascus
July	Israel frees five Lebanese prisoners in exchange for the remains of two soldiers captured by Hezbollah in July 2006
December	Israel embarks on heavy air and ground offensive in Gaza in response to rocket fire on southern Israeli towns

2009

January	A ceasefire between Hamas and Israel is achieved
February	Benjamin Netanyahu (Likud) becomes Israel's prime minister despite a majority vote going to Tzipi Livni (Kadima)
September	An Israeli Air Force F16 crashes in training killing pilot Assaf Ramon, son of Ilan Ramon, Israel's first astronaut who was killed in the space shuttle *Columbia* disaster
October	The first video of Gilad Shalit, an Israeli soldier captured by Hamas in Gaza in 2006 is released
December	Ada Yonath becomes first Israeli woman to win a Nobel prize (in chemistry)

2010

May	Israeli soldiers board Turkish ships attempting to break the blockade on Gaza. Nine activists are killed – both countries claim self-defence.
August	Lebanese and Israeli troops exchange fire along the border
2–5 December	The country's largest forest fire rages across Mount Carmel killing 44 prison officers in a bus and destroying hundreds of acres of land

GOVERNMENT AND POLITICS

The State of Israel was declared on 14 May 1948 as a parliamentary democracy. The state is headed by the president, whose role is essentially symbolic. It is in effect managed by three authorities: the legislative authority (the Knesset), the executive authority (the government) and the judiciary. Although portrayed as a secular government, issues of religion and politics often find themselves tightly interwoven, the Jewish and Palestinian and Israeli Arab conflict constantly giving rise to internal as well as external political tensions.

THE KNESSET AND GOVERNMENT The Knesset is the country's unicameral legislative body that took its name and declared its membership as 120 based on the Knesset Hagedolah (Great Assembly), the Jewish council that convened in Jerusalem in the 5th century BCE. The Knesset members, who represent a wide range of political parties, are chosen every four years through a nationwide election. Voters (of age 18 and over) cast ballots for political parties and not individual members (although the winning party is headed by the country's prime minister) and the entire country forms one electoral constituency. Election Day is a national holiday, and Israel has seen 77–90% of registered voters casting ballots. Israel's main parties, Likud, Labor and the most recently formed Kadima, often dominate the votes, but smaller parties representing different opinions on religion, security concerns and social issues have been making more impact in recent elections. Kadima was formed by Ariel Sharon in 2005 after he left the Likud Party and bases itself on a centrist theory whose concerns focus on civil and secular issues. Following Ariel Sharon's stroke in January 2006, Ehud Olmert became prime minister and following an election Kadima extended an invitation to Labor to form a coalition. This act saw Amir Perez, the first Mizrahi Jew to lead a major party, become defence minister.

In February 2009, following Ehud Olmert's resignation, a general election saw the country torn and frustrated as Tzipi Livni (Kadima) received the majority vote, only to be ousted by Benjamin Netanyahu and the Likud Party when she couldn't form a coalition government. It has led to questions and scepticism in Israel over the state of parliamentary voting.

THE IDF The Israeli Defence Force (IDF), often referred to simply as the Israeli army (*tzahal*) comprises conscripts, reserve and career service personnel, the bulk of which is formed by reservists. Conscription is mandatory for men and women of 18 years, men serving three years and women 21 months. Those undertaking higher education courses, in big demand by the IDF, may defer entry but will serve after qualification. After completing their service men undergo 39 days a year of reserve training until the age of 51; employers and higher education institutions are bound under law to honour positions and not penalise workers and students for missed time. Because of the long periods of compulsory conscription, the army plays a huge part in the lives of most Israelis and service is regarded as heroic and honourable. There are, however, some highly controversial exemptions from conscription, which include Orthodox Jews, Israeli-Arabs, new immigrants and Bedouin. Given the choice, Druze residents often opt to enter the IDF, as do increasing numbers of Bedouin.

Military spending forms a considerable chunk of the country's outgoings, approximately 16.5% of government expenditure, with the United States providing in the region of US$2.4 billion per year in security assistance.

ECONOMY

Since its declaration of independence in 1948 Israel has struggled to cope with several major economic challenges thrown its way: security and the IDF, the immigration of two million Jews according to the country's Law of Returns and the need to establish modern infrastructure and public services. In its earlier years, heavy financial aid from Jewish organisations across the world as well as foreign governments (principally the US) supported the country's massively expanding population and increased security issues. Despite these pressures, Israel has managed in recent years to create a stable economic foundation through extensive privatisation as well as its free-trade agreements, and today its major industrial sectors are based on the production of metal products, electronic and biomedical equipment, processed foods, chemicals, transport equipment, and software development. Two other principal exports are cut and polished diamonds (in which it is the world's leading country) and agricultural products, namely fruit and vegetables, its total export income exceeding US$54.31 billion. In recent years tourism has begun to play an important role, which despite wars and conflict recovers rapidly.

Following the Israeli–Palestinian conflicts in 2001 and 2002 and the Second Lebanon War in 2006, the country's GDP growth took a nosedive but managed to get back on course and recover quickly.

In 2010, Israel's GDP reached an estimated US$217.1 billion, with a per-capita figure of US$29,500, putting it on a par with European countries such as France and Italy. It had already experienced a 0.5% GDP growth in 2009 when many other Western countries saw a decline.

PEOPLE

Despite being founded as a Jewish state, Israel comprises a jigsaw puzzle of religions, cultures and traditions. Today the country's more than seven million-strong population is divided into 75.5% Jews, 16.8% Muslims, 2.1% Christians (mostly Arabs), 1.7% Druze and 3.9% not classified by religion (mostly from the former USSR). Within this varied framework each religion is granted judicial rights over its people as well as administration of its own holy sites. Another interesting characteristic of Israel's diverse population is its incredible growth rate, highly unusual for a developed country. Long before Israel declared independence in 1948 Jews had been immigrating to the country, and following the declaration this increased tenfold. In the last 60 years the Jewish population has grown from 650,000 to over five million.

Culturally, the country is a melting pot of different traditions where immigration has led to the emergence of strong communities even within different religious groups. European Jews (or Ashkenazi), Jews of Arab descent (or Sephardi), Russians, Ethiopians, Druze and Bedouin live within one country, yet retain their strong cultural traditions, language and way of life. For most of the Jewish population, third- or fourth-generation descendants of post-World War II immigrants, their cultural affiliation is most certainly Israeli, and while each is proud of their heritage there is an undeniable feel of nationalism and patriotism.

JEWS Since Israel's declaration of independence (and long before it) waves of immigration, known in Hebrew as *aliyah* or 'ascent', saw the country's Jewish population expand enormously. Between 1948 and 1952 it more than doubled, Holocaust survivors and refugees from Arab countries forming a large percentage of this. Subsequent major waves of *aliyah* occurred in the mid 1950s and early 1960s from north Africa and Romania (350,000 people), in the 1990s from the former USSR (900,000 people) and in 1984 and 1991 when virtually all of Ethiopia's Jews were extracted and relocated to Israel.

Today the percentage of Israeli-born Jews (Tsabar) has reached 70%, and while there are still pockets of strong culturally independent communities, intermarriage and cultural assimilation have blended the differences, whereby

'Israeli' culture most certainly prevails. Within the Jewish community, levels of religious observance form the biggest separation, and communities of like-minded residents have emerged. Orthodox (devout Jews who strongly follow religious law and tradition) form 12% of Israel's Jews, religious (who do not follow the Orthodox way of life but are devout in their day-to-day lives with respect to keeping kosher, attending synagogues, abiding by religious holidays and keeping Shabbat) 10%, traditional (who are less strict in their religious observance) 35% and secular 43%.

Israel's Jewish background reaches from the far-flung corners of the globe but the following form the greatest numbers of the population:

Ashkenazi This relates to Jews of northern or eastern European descent as well as North American, Australian and South African.

Sephardi This relates to Jews of north African or Mediterranean countries, mainly Spain and Portugal in the 15th century. After their expulsion they spread across the Mediterranean.

Mizrahi This is used to loosely define Jews of Arabic descent (mainly countries such as Yemen, Iraq and Iran) although often Sephardi is used instead.

Beta Israel of Ethiopia Ethiopian Jews today number over 100,000 in Israel, brought from their famine-ravaged country in two huge operations: Operation Moses in 1984 and Operation Solomon in 1991 that saw over 22,000 Ethiopian Jews airlifted to Israel. The term Beta Israel (meaning 'House of Israel') was a self-designated term used when they inhabited Ethiopia, preferred to the derogative Falasha, meaning exiles or stranger used by many non-Jewish Ethiopians. Since arriving in Israel, the term Ethiopian Jews has become more politically correct in recognition of their equality. Their exact ancestral link to Judaism is unknown but many believe them to be descended from the biblical Queen of Sheba and King Solomon.

ARABS The largest non-Jewish population in Israel is Arab and communities vary considerably in heritage, religious practice and cultural traditions.

Muslim Arabs Not counting Bedouin Arabs, Muslims (Sunni) make up about 70% of Israel's Arab population. Many hold close family ties with Palestinian Arabs in the West Bank and Gaza Strip and as such classify themselves as Palestinian Arabs (although they are referred to as Israeli Arabs by the Jewish community of Israel). They do not undertake military service in the IDF and live mostly in homogeneous communities in villages, towns and cities around the Galilee, eastern coastal plain and the northern Negev. There are also large communities in cities such as Haifa, Akko and Jerusalem.

Christian Arabs Christian Arabs comprise about 9% of Israel's Arab population, the largest concentration living in the Galilean city of Nazareth. Despite their differences in religion many Christian Arabs still consider themselves closely affiliated to the Palestinian people and as such rarely enlist in the IDF. However, personalities such as Salim Jubran, the first non-Jewish Arab judge to preside over Israel's Supreme Court, demonstrate a certain degree of cohesiveness between them and Jewish members of society.

Druze Druze (see also *Religion*, page 27) communities are spread mainly across the mountainous areas of Lebanon, Syria and Israel, in the last being concentrated in the northern Golan Heights and towns and villages across the Carmel Mountain range, notably Carmel City (better known as Isfiya and Daliat al-Carmel). In Israel the Druze community (which today numbers some 120,000 people) is officially recognised as a separate religious entity and although their culture and language are both Arabic, their religious beliefs and affiliation to Israel (most serving in the IDF) separate them from the nationalism of other Arab communities. It is an integral part of the Druze faith to serve the country in which they reside, a fact that has seen families separated by Israel's capture of the Golan Heights in 1967 fight for opposing countries (see *The Shouting Hill*, page 244). Their loyalty to Israel, peaceful way of life and renowned hospitality has earned them great respect amongst Jewish members of society, a fact compounded by their presence in political, public and military positions.

Bedouin The term 'Bedouin' generally applies to any member of an Arabic-speaking community of desert nomads in the Middle East. Historically these communities would migrate with the seasons, herding their cattle, sheep, goats and camels to the desert regions during the rainy season. After World War II, however, most Middle Eastern countries, Israel included, prevented this movement by consolidating their borders. Following Israel's declaration of independence and the war that ensued, most Bedouin fled or were expelled from the country, approximately 11,000 of an estimated 65,000–90,000 remaining. In the 1950s and 1960s, the Israeli government relocated almost all of the Negev's Bedouin population to an area known as the *siyag* or enclosure, a relatively infertile area in the north of the Negev Desert. Despite legally being ordered to live in assigned towns, many Bedouin still preferred to live in makeshift villages, often having permanent structures torn down. The Israeli government also imposed mandatory school attendance on Bedouin children, which led to a rise in literacy. The offshoot of enforcing this sedentary lifestyle on a nomadic people who survived on a subsistence lifestyle, however, was that unemployment rose and poverty and crime in Bedouin towns increased. They have, however, benefited from the developed medical care in the country, often serve in the IDF (renowned for their tracking skills), retain strong cultural traditions and have one of the highest birth rates in the world. There are currently an estimated 125,000 Bedouin living in the Negev.

CIRCASSIANS There are approximately 3,000 Circassians (or Cherkessians) living in Israel, all concentrated in the two Galilean villages of Kafr Kama and Reyhaniye. Although their religious affiliation is Sunni Muslim, the Circassians descend from the northwestern Caucasus (today's western Ukraine) and are not Arabs. Following the Russian–Circassian War that lasted from 1763 to 1864, large numbers of Circassians were deported to the Ottoman Empire while others settled in Russia. In the Middle East, the largest communities are found in Jordan and Syria, and throughout the French Mandate of the then Syrian Golan Heights, the members of the town of Quneitra (see page 238) sought a national homeland for themselves in the area (it was not granted). Like the Druze, Circassian leaders have asked to be included in mandatory IDF conscription (although only for men), have strong cultural traditions and are officially recognised as a separate religious entity.

SAMARITANS See *Religion*, page 28.

LANGUAGE

Hebrew and Arabic are the official languages of Israel. English is compulsory at school, which, combined with the lack of international television dubbing means most Israelis speak at least some English, mostly to a high level. As a result of the huge waves of immigration over the years French, Spanish, Russian, Yiddish (a pre-World War II European variation of Hebrew), Polish, Hungarian and German are still widely spoken. For more information see *Appendix 1, Language*, page 289.

RELIGION

JUDAISM Judaism is one of the world's oldest existing religions (see *History*, page 6), the foundations of which are based upon monotheism; specific laws and practices; ethnic and territorial identity; messianism and its belief in a special covenant with God. It began as the ancient religion of a small nation of Hebrews, and through thousands of years of suffering, persecution, diaspora and the occasional victory, has continued to be significantly influential both as a religion and a culture. Today Judaism has approximately 14 million adherents, half of whom live in Israel, the Jewish homeland.

The core belief of Judaism is that there is only one God, something that was unusual for the time the religion was born. According to tradition, God revealed this to Abraham, the founder of the Jewish people. Jewish identity arises primarily from belonging to an ancient people and an upholding of its ancient traditions, today seen as much as a culture as a religion. The following is a designed to provide a brief overview of the practices and beliefs of Jewish religion and culture, but it is important to note that rituals and practices vary within different Jewish groups (Reform, who generally have a liberal view of Judaism; Conservative, devout interpretation of Judaism; and Orthodox, rigid and fervent interpretation of Judaism, often with a negative view of modern society).

Theology
Sacred texts Textual tradition in Judaism is rich and old, the Torah (part of the Old Testament in Christianity) forming the core of this. The Talmud (the body of Jewish civil and religious law, including commentaries on the Torah), is divided into two parts: the Mishnah (the codification of laws) and the Gemara (a commentary on the Mishnah).

The covenant One of the major concepts in Judaism is that of the covenant, or agreement, between God and the Jewish people. The agreement states that the Jewish people acknowledge God as their one and only king, and he in return will acknowledge the Jews as his 'chosen people' and take special care of them.

The Messiah One of the principal goals of Judaism is the patient wait for the Messiah, who will free the Jews and restore justice and peace to the world.

Rituals
Circumcision At eight days old Jewish boys are circumcised by a rabbi as a symbol of belonging to the covenant between God and Abraham (who self-circumcised at age 99).

Upsherin This is the ritual first haircut for three-year-old Orthodox boys held on the festival of Lag Ba'omer. Their hair is cut short with the exception of two pieces at the temples known as *peyot*.

Bar and Bat Mitzvah At age 13 boys and girls celebrate their entering of adulthood (Orthodox Jews do not celebrate this).

Daily prayer Jews pray three times daily: *shaharith* in the morning, *minhah* in the afternoon and *maarib* in the evening. In Conservative and Orthodox groups synagogue prayer is attended daily.

Head coverings Jewish men and boys (in Conservative or Orthodox groups) wear a skull cap known as a *kippah* or *yarmulke* in order to demonstrate their submission to a higher being, God.

Tefillin This is a ritual practised by men only and usually only by Orthodox members. The *tefillin* consists of two small boxes containing biblical scriptures which are strapped to the forehead and left arm during weekday morning prayer.

Shabbat See page 35.

Kosher See page 54.

Major religious holidays
Yom Kippur This is the Day of Atonement when most Jews fast and attend the synagogue. It is considered the last day on which to repent any wrongdoings and change God's judgement for the upcoming year.

Rosh Hashanah This is the Jewish New Year celebrated as a day of remembrance, not celebration. On this day it is common to hear the *shofar* or horn being blown 100 times in accordance with biblical traditions.

Pesach (Passover) and Sukkot These festivals celebrate the Exodus, when Moses freed the enslaved Jews from Egypt and the subsequent 40 years of wandering in the desert. Passover is celebrated by a meal (or *seder*) during which symbolic food is consumed and recitations from the Haggadah (book telling the story of the Exodus) are carried out. To commemorate the suffering of the Jews in Egypt no leaven (bread or cake) may be consumed and as such, *matzah* (unleavened bread) is a major feature.

Hanukkah This festival is post-biblical and commemorates the victory of the Maccabees over the Seleucid rulers of Jerusalem (see page 7). It is celebrated by lighting eight candles, one on each day of the festival.

Purim This is the jolliest of Jewish festivals, celebrated in the name of Esther (see page 218). On this day people dress in costume, partake in a joyous meal, drink alcohol freely and often give gifts.

Holy places The Western Wall is the single holiest place in Judaism (see page 91) and stands as the last remnant of the Second Temple, destroyed by the Romans. The second holiest place is the tomb of Abraham in Hebron (today's West Bank). Abraham's son Ishmael is considered the ancestor of Islam, making this also a sacred site to Muslims. There are many other holy sites in Israel including the tombs of prominent rabbis and sages in Tiberias (see page 188), Beit She'arim (see page 186), Tzfat (see page 205), Meron (see page 216) and the Mount of Olives (see page 99).

CHRISTIANITY Christianity is the world's largest religion with an estimated two billion followers. Founded in the 1st century AD (CE), it has at its core the teachings, miracles, Crucifixion and Resurrection of Jesus of Nazareth (see box in *Chapter 3*, pages 88–9), and in effect started as a messianic orientation of Judaism. The principal texts in Christianity are the Old and New Testaments, the first four books of the latter being known as the Gospels, written 20 to 100 years after the death and Resurrection of Jesus. He is believed in Christian tradition to be the Messiah, the son of God, the 12 Apostles appointed by him during his ministry being the first to believe this.

Jesus was arrested, tried and crucified in Jerusalem under the orders of the Roman leader Pontius Pilate, because he was seen as a threat to Judaism and Roman rule in the city. Today the Church of the Holy Sepulchre in Jerusalem's Old City is revered as the holiest site in Christianity, this being the place of Jesus's Crucifixion, burial and Resurrection (Golgotha in the New Testament). The Via Dolorosa (see page 88) marks the traditional route taken by Jesus as he carried the Cross on his back to Golgotha and has been a site of pilgrimage for hundreds of years. Other holy sites include Bethlehem (in today's West Bank) where Jesus is believed to have been born, Nazareth (see page 180) where his mother Mary received news of the Immaculate Conception, and several sites around the Sea of Galilee (see page 194).

While the core principles remain the same, Christianity has branched off into many different denominations, the three principal ones being Roman Catholicism, Eastern Orthodoxy and Protestantism.

Roman Catholicism Perceived by many as the 'original' Christian denomination, it is today seen as separate due to the emergence (and later acceptance) of other denominations such as Eastern Orthodoxy and Protestantism. Roman Catholicism has the largest number of adherents (more than one billion) and is centred on the Vatican City in Rome. The main differences between Roman Catholicism and other denominations are its appointment of a pope as leader of the Church, the belief that saints can intercede on behalf of believers and the concept of Purgatory (a place of purification before being allowed to enter Heaven). With respect to ritualistic practices, Roman Catholicism tends to be stricter than Protestantism, with the Eucharist (also known as Mass or communion) one of the central rites, celebrated weekly. Catholic nuns, monks and priests take a vow of celibacy, and rosary beads (prayer beads), crosses and the worship of saints are other distinctive features of the denomination. Monastic orders within Roman Catholicism include Jesuits, Dominicans, Franciscans and Augustinians.

Protestantism With an estimated 500 million followers, Protestantism is the second-largest Christian denomination. Because of its numerous, wide-ranging denominations it is difficult to classify as a single religious thought. In essence, the denominations differ in how much they denounce Roman Catholicism, ranging from conservative to very liberal. Most Protestant Churches adhere to two of the biblical sacraments, baptism and communion (as opposed to seven in Roman Catholicism). Throughout history different Protestant Churches have appeared, most in the 16th century. Presbyterians owe their origins to John Calvin, John Knox and the Church of Scotland; the Church of England to King Henry VIII; the Baptists to John Smyth and the Separatists; the Anglicans and Episcopalians to the Church of England; Evangelism and Methodism to a 17th-century Protestant movement; and Lutheranism to Martin Luther.

Eastern Orthodoxy Also known as Orthodox Christianity, it began in the Byzantine Empire (see page 8) and today numbers some 225 million adherents living predominantly in Greece, Turkey and Russia. Its separation formed in the 11th century when a divide between Western and Eastern Christian churches materialised, Roman emperor Constantine moving the Roman capital to Constantinople. The main differences lay in opinions relating to political, religious and cultural matters, with the use of icons and the date of Easter two of the stumbling blocks. Despite the glimmer of reconciliation between the Eastern and Roman Catholic churches during the crusades (see page 9) there have long since been tensions between the two. Since the 1960s, however, attempts have been made to recognise and respect each other's Churches and beliefs.

Major Eastern Orthodox denominations include the Greek, Russian, Romanian and Bulgarian Orthodox churches, the Church of Alexandria, the Church of Jerusalem and the Church of America. In contrast to Roman Catholicism and Protestantism, Eastern Orthodoxy's religious authority is the Scriptures as interpreted by the Seven Ecumenical Councils, and theology and philosophical thought play a bigger role. In Israel, and particularly Jerusalem, Eastern Orthodox architecture is renowned for its beauty and ornate décor.

ISLAM Islam is the world's second-largest religion with over one billion adherents. It is based on the teachings of the Prophet Muhammad, a camel herder who, in the 7th century in Saudi Arabia, was approached by the Angel Gabriel. Gabriel delivered to Muhammad a message from God, which he spent the rest of his life spreading. Three decades after his death, Muhammad's life teachings were recorded in what became the spiritual text of Islam, the Koran. Islam, which means 'submission', is based on a submission to God's will and centres on the Five Pillars of Islam: confession of faith; daily prayer; fasting during Ramadan; pilgrimage; and charity.

The three most sacred sites in Islam focus on the activities of Muhammad. The holiest site in Islam is the Kaaba in Mecca (Saudi Arabia), which tradition dictates is the mosque built by Abraham. Muhammad declared Mecca Islam's holiest site and that it should be towards this place that all prayers should be directed (*qibla*). Performing the once-in-a-lifetime pilgrimage (*hajj*) to Mecca is one of the Five Pillars of Islam and every year thousands of Muslims congregate here. The second holiest site is Medina or 'City of the Prophet' in Saudi Arabia and marks the spot to where Muhammad fled when he was exiled from Mecca and the place where his first followers joined him. Jerusalem, or more precisely Al-Haram ash-Sharif (the Noble Sanctuary, or Temple Mount to Jews), is third in spiritual significance and, until Mecca was declared as *qibla*, it was to the mosque here that Muslims directed their prayers. Islamic tradition states that this is where Muhammad ascended to Heaven following the Night Journey, and that the rock housed within the Dome of the Rock bears his last footprint. The stone is also considered holy to Jews, who believe it was the site upon which Abraham prepared to sacrifice his son Isaac to God, and over which the two temples were built.

Sunni and Shi'a When Muhammad died, a battle for the leadership of Islam ensued, a battle that rages to this day and forms a fierce divide between the two sects that emerged. The dispute of who would become *kalifa* or leader was between those who believed that Muhammad had chosen Ali, his cousin and brother-in-law, and those who claimed allegiance to Abu Bakr, Muhammad's father-in-law and good friend. Ultimately Abu Bakr became the first of four caliphs (the anglicised version of *kalifa*) who are attributed with the great spread of Islam in the 7th century. Today the vast majority of Muslims are Sunnis, the name associated with those who followed Abu Bakr, while those who pledged allegiance to Ali are known as Shi'ites, of which there are an estimated 120 million adherents. In contrast to the denominations in Christianity and Judaism, Sunni and Shi'ite Muslims are seen more as sects, each refusing to acknowledge the other, a fact that to this day causes a rift across the Islamic Middle East.

DRUZE The Druze (see also *People*, page 22) originated from the Ismaili sect of Shi'a Islam in the 11th century and today call themselves *muwahhidun*, or monotheists for their profound belief in the one God. The Druze religion is based on the belief that al-Hakim, a caliph of the Fatimid dynasty of Egypt, was the incarnation of God. While most Muslims believe al-Hakim died in 1021, the Druze believe he merely disappeared and is waiting to return to the world in the golden age for true believers. It is these beliefs that set the Druze aside from other Muslims (compounded by the fact that the Koran does not seem to play a role in their religious life) and it is apparent that the religion was strongly influenced by Gnostic elements from Judaism, Christianity, Hindu and Greek belief. Although the new religion was proselytised after its creation in the 11th century, this was short-lived and from 1050 has been closed to outsiders, the religion kept to this day a well-guarded secret.

The Druze believe in many prophets who they consider embody the spirit of monotheism – Adam, Muhammad, Abraham, Noah, John the Baptist, Jesus and Solomon – as well as in the philosophies of Socrates, Plato, Pythagoras, Aristotle and Alexander the Great. Despite their acknowledgement of all three monotheistic religions they believe that the performing of rituals and ceremonies has caused followers to move away from what they consider the 'pure faith'. They therefore do not (with the exception of fasting during the Islamic Ramadan) undertake any ceremonies, rituals, sanctification of physical places or organised prayer sessions, believing one should pray at all times to God. That said, popular gathering places have emerged whereby members will convene to discuss matters relating to the community. In Israel there are several such places, one of the most important being Jethro's Tomb (Nebi Shu'eib) at the Horns of Hittin (see page 193), where the Druze gather on 25 April.

In keeping with the air of secrecy surrounding the Druze religion, the community itself is divided into two groups; the *al-Uqqāl* or 'knowers', and *al-Juhhāl* or 'ignorant ones'. The *al-Juhhāl*, who form about 80% of the population, do not have access to the religious literature and generally occupy political, military or administrative roles. The *al-Uqqāl* on the other hand are the keepers of the religion, and men and women are considered equal in their rights to become *al-Uqqāl*. Under Druze tradition it is forbidden to eat pork and smoking and drinking alcohol are prohibited.

BAHA'I FAITH The Baha'i faith was founded in 19th-century Persia from Babism (a religion that developed out of the Shi'a branch of Islam). It is a monotheistic religion and, although Baha'is emphasise that God is ultimately unknowable, human knowledge of God can be achieved through his messengers. In 1844, Mirza Ali Muhammad declared himself Bab, the guide to divine truth, also declaring that 19 years later an even greater manifestation would come. In 1863, Mirza Hussayn Ali Nuri, who after Bab's death in 1850 took the name Baha'u'llah, declared himself as this manifestation. Not long after, the Persians began persecuting the Babi (followers of Bab), Baha'u'llah and some of his followers being spared from death and imprisoned (to this day Baha'i followers in Iran suffer considerable persecution). Sent by the Ottomans to the Palestinian city of Akko (in modern-day Israel) he remained under house arrest until his death. After his death, however, it was Baha'u'llah's son Abdu l-Baha' who, after being released from imprisonment in 1908, travelled extensively spreading the Baha'i word. Baha'u'llah is perceived as the last in a line of messengers that include Buddha, Jesus, Krishna and Muhammad.

Today there are around five million Baha'is worldwide, most residing in non-Muslim Third World countries. The faith has no priesthood and spiritual authority rests with elected councils known as 'Spiritual Assemblies'. The ultimate authority, however, rests with the Universal House of Justice in Haifa, Israel therefore being the centre of this far-reaching religion. Taking pride of place in the country's third-largest city, Haifa's breathtakingly beautiful Shrine of the Bab and Persian Gardens (see page 161) is not only a site of pilgrimage for Baha'is but attracts admirers from all religions. While this may be the grandest Baha'i shrine, the most sacred is the Shrine of Baha'u'llah just outside Akko (see page 151).

Baha'i claims to be a universal religion based on unity. Its key principles are unity of God, religion and mankind, harmony between races and religions, equality of the sexes, world peace, the elimination of prejudice, a universal language, education for all and the elimination of extremes of wealth and poverty. Gambling, gossip, alcohol, homosexuality and sexual relations outside marriage are forbidden and members over the age of 15 should pray daily. It is claimed that the Baha'i faith is the second most widespread religion, is established in 247 countries and has religious texts translated into hundreds of languages. To find out more visit the official website of the Baha'i faith (*www.bahai.org*).

SAMARITANS The Samaritans are a small religious group who claim descent from the ancient Kingdom of Israel. While figures once numbered the Samaritans at over one million people in the 4th and 5th centuries, forced conversion to Islam and Christianity as well as persecution are just 600 left today. Of these, half live in Kiryat Luza, close to Mount Gerizim, just south of Nablus in the West Bank, the remainder residing in the Holon district near Tel Aviv. Mount Gerizim is the holiest site in the Samaritan faith and the site of their 6th-century BCE temple, constructed following their break from Judaism. The Samaritans broadly practise a religion similar to that of the biblical Jews, with some elements of Islam added in. They write and speak in ancient Hebrew, abide by thousands-of-years-old traditions, recognise Moses as the one prophet and have one holy book, the Pentateuch (handed down by Moses).

EDUCATION

The Israeli workforce is well educated, having received many trained professionals through immigration, and today has a literacy rate of 97.1%. Its citizens enjoy a high standard of living with an unemployment rate of 7.6%. Despite this, the level of education in the country has resulted in disproportionate demographics and after Israel stopped Palestinian workers entering the country found itself short of manual labourers. In recent years it has begun recruiting thousands of workers from China, Thailand, the Philippines and eastern Europe to fill the labour void.

School attendance is mandatory from age five to 16 and free until the age of 18. The school system in Israel has created its own solution to the problems of differing social and religious backgrounds by forming different institutions to suit each group: state schools which are attended by the majority; state religious schools which emphasise Jewish studies and observance; Arab and Druze schools with classes in Arabic; and private schools. Israel has many higher education institutions attended by over 200,000 students at any one time. Higher education tends to start much later than in most other Western countries on account of the prolonged time spent in the army (and subsequent year abroad that most Israelis undertake afterwards), with men often not beginning studies until their mid to late twenties.

CULTURE, ENTERTAINMENT AND SPORT

ART Organised art in Israel can be traced back to 1906 and the Bulgarian professor Boris Schatz, who established the Bezalel Academy of Arts and Crafts in Jerusalem, years before Israel's declaration of independence. It encouraged talented Jewish artists to immigrate to the country and proved to be instrumental in the development of the rich artistic culture there today. To this day colonies such as **Ein Hod** and **Rosh Pina** flourish, the artists ranging from painters, sculptors, photographers and ceramicists, to those specialising in more unusual crafts such as weaving, glassblowing and calligraphy. Israel's art museums are world class, and Jerusalem's **Israel Museum** (see page 102) and the **Tel Aviv Museum of Art** (see page 127) are held in the highest esteem internationally. Israel's multiculturalism has once more provided for a range of styles, genres and traditions few other countries can match.

MUSIC With weekly sell-out performances and record-breaking numbers of season-ticket holders, the **Israel Philharmonic Orchestra** needs little introduction. It was founded in 1936 and often plays host to guest conductors and musicians from around the world. Surprisingly, its home is not in Jerusalem as one would expect but in Tel Aviv's Mann Auditorium (see page 124). The **Jerusalem Symphony Orchestra**, while not quite on a par with the Israeli Philharmonic, is still highly regarded and its concerts are broadcast on Israel's classical music stations. Other esteemed orchestras include the **Haifa Symphony Orchestra**, the Ramat Gan Orchestra, the Beer Sheva Simfonetta and the Israeli Chamber Orchestra. The Israeli Opera Company performs in the Merkaz le-Omanuyot ha-Bama near the Tel Aviv Museum and its repertoire includes classical compositions and modern operas.

Modern music is also big business and many young Israelis have a rather deep passion for heavy trance. Rock, jazz and classic 1970s and 1980s hits also make their way into bars and clubs (with the odd Christmas song thrown in during July for good measure). For more information about music events in Tel Aviv see *Chapter 4, Entertainment and nightlife,* page 122.

THEATRE Israeli theatre comprises both large and small theatre troupes, the **Habima Theatre** in Tel Aviv forming the national core of theatrical performances (see page 124). The mesh of cultures that immigrated to the country in the early 20th century formed a unique blend of theatre that has lasted to this day. Jerusalem and Tel Aviv play host to the greatest number of theatres and productions (many of which provide English translation) whose styles and genres span a vast range.

DANCE Dance is gaining in popularity and over the last decade institutions such as the **Suzanne Dellal Centre**, **Bat Sheva Dance Troupe** and the **Israeli Ballet** have become household names. However, they are still nowhere near as well established as theatre and classical music and as such performances are less frequent.

CINEMA Israeli cinema is more developed than most would imagine and several films have made their way along the red carpets of the Cannes Film Festival

THE DARKEST DAY IN OLYMPIC HISTORY

On 5 September 1972, the Munich Olympics were well under way when gunmen from the Palestinian terrorist group Black September stormed the athletes' village, killing two Israelis outright and taking hostage a further nine. Just 27 years after the Holocaust, Israeli participation in the event was seen as a significant and important step towards rebuilding Jewish morale and attempting to repair relations with Germany, yet the event was to be marred forever, and seen as one of the darkest days in Israel's history. The terrorists demanded the release of over 200 Palestinian prisoners from Israeli jails and free passage for themselves out of Germany, throwing the body of wrestling coach Moshe Weinburg out of the building as grim evidence of their intentions should their demands not be met.

The Tunisian ambassador and members of the Arab League offered their help to the German authorities in negotiating with the terrorists, but it was to minimal avail, Israel standing firm on its policy of not negotiating with terrorists. At one stage in the negotiations, German officials offered to personally take the places of the Israeli athletes, such was their distress and horror that harm may come to the Jewish captives in their country so soon after the end of World War II. After more than 12 hours, the terrorists requested to leave the Olympic Village and were taken by helicopter to a military airport, handcuffed to the hostages. It was around this time that mounting pressure on the International Olympic Committee finally succeeded in getting the games halted, which until then had continued, seemingly oblivious to the events unfolding. At the airport, as the terrorists and their hostages walked across the runway to a waiting aircraft, German snipers attempted unsuccessfully to pick them off, an act that was to go horribly wrong and see the immediate murder of the Israeli athletes as the terrorists turned their guns on them. The remaining hostages were inadvertently killed when a German grenade was thrown into the helicopter in which they were waiting. At the end of the shocking and tragic day 11 Israeli athletes had lost their lives. In a move seen in Israel and many countries across the world as insensitive and disrespectful, just 24 hours after the shocking day had ended, the Olympics resumed.

and even received Academy Award nominations as best international films. Cinematographic topics tend to centre on issues close to the hearts of Israelis and Jews, such as the Holocaust, the Israeli–Palestinian situation and the IDF. The enormous **Jerusalem Cinematheque** (*www.jer-cin.org.il*) is the best place for film aficionados to start, with its wealth of information, eclectic programme and educational courses, while the **Spielberg Film Archive** (*www.spielbergfilmarchive.org.il*) at the Hebrew University of Jerusalem is the world's largest centre for Jewish and Israeli film material.

SPORT If you look at Israel's medal-winning record in international events, you'd be forgiven for thinking that sport doesn't feature very highly in the country. However, despite their lack of presence in any sport other than basketball, Israelis in fact love sport, most notably extreme sports. Basketball, and in particular Maccabi Tel Aviv, is very popular and during a game is the quietest the streets ever get. To add to Israel's basketball accolades, in 2009 Omri Casspi was selected by the Sacramento Kings for the NBA Draft, making him the first Israeli to play in the NBA. Israel received its first (and to date only) Olympic gold medal in windsurfing in 2004 (interestingly the medal was inadvertently stolen in a run-of-the-mill house break-in and was later found discarded in woodland and returned to the athlete). Football (soccer), judo and tennis also feature highly whilst sky diving, scuba diving, parasailing and kite surfing are the new 'in' extreme sports. Golf is limited to the Caesarea golf course (see page 176) while rather surprisingly, Mount Hermon has a semi-decent ski slope (although in recent years this has been somewhat lacking in snow).

In the same style as the Olympics and Commonwealth Games, every four years Israel hosts the **Maccabiah Games**, where Israeli and Jewish athletes from across the world compete in the country's biggest sporting event. The games were founded in 1932 and in the last games in 2009 had over 6,000 participants from across the globe.

2

Practical Information

WHEN TO VISIT

Israel's mild winter climate and brilliant sunshine mean that visiting the Holy Land at any time is possible. However, the extreme summer heat that permeates the entire country can often make sightseeing hard and exhausting work, so if you don't plan to spend a lot of your time on the beach then spring and autumn are prime tourist times (see *Climate*, page 6). It is important to note that while getting the opportunity to experience Israel's national holidays (in particular Yom Kippur – see below) is a wonderful insight into the culture of the country, the collection of holidays that fall around the end of September and into October see the country barely open for business. Between the holidays and Shabbat, working days during that time can be very limited and as such many shops, restaurants, museums, national parks and sites of interest may be closed.

HIGHLIGHTS

Israel is a small country whose treasure trove of appeal reaches from religious interest and profound historical and archaeological discoveries to cosmopolitan cities and a varied and rich nature. So where do you start planning a trip and what are the must-sees? **Jerusalem** should be the first stop on any trip, its Old City the jewel in the crown of a fascinating, dramatic and poignant city. On the shore of the Mediterranean Sea is **Tel Aviv**, whose fun-loving residents and secular, relaxed way of life are a unique contrast to the Holy City, while the country's third-largest city, **Haifa**, perched on the edge of Mount Carmel and with the Baha'i Gardens forming its centerpiece, is a pleasant place to spend a few days. In the far south of the country is the resort city of **Eilat**, a mesh of great hotels and watersports resting on Israel's tiny stretch of Red Sea coast. The centuries of conquest, rebellion and settlement are represented in the bewitching old cities of **Nazareth**, famed as Jesus's birthplace; **Tzfat**, a Jewish Holy City, centre of Kabbalah learning and home to a burgeoning artist's colony; and **Akko,** the ancient Crusader port city, with its cobbled lanes, minarets and old city walls.

Historical and archaeological sites such as **Caesarea**, the sprawling remains of the great Roman port city; **Masada**, Herod's palace perched high on a desert cliff; and **Beit She'an**, the staggering remains of a prosperous Roman city shattered by an earthquake, are but the tip of the iceberg.

Apart from the enigmatic modern cities, charming old cities and profound archaeological sites, Israel is a wonderful blend of hugely varied landscapes as it tumbles from the steppes of Europe down to the arid African deserts. The calm waters of the **Sea of Galilee** are surrounded by the lush, green fields, small kibbutzim and gently rolling hills of the **Galilee**, while the wild uplands of the

Golan Heights are dotted with Druze and Jewish communities, horse ranches, jagged peaks and gushing rivers. Forming the southern half of the country are the great **deserts,** at their midst the **Dead Sea,** the lowest point on earth and a geological marvel.

SUGGESTED ITINERARIES

WEEKEND – JERUSALEM AND DEAD SEA Spend one day getting lost in Jerusalem's Old City, a second day visiting the bustling Mahane Yehuda Market and the Yad Vashem Holocaust Memorial Museum, and a third day taking a trip down to the Dead Sea.

ONE WEEK – JERUSALEM, DEAD SEA, TEL AVIV, SEA OF GALILEE AND AKKO As above plus a day or two in Tel Aviv and Jaffa, sitting in outdoor cafés, spending an afternoon on the beach, visiting the world-class art museums and exploring Jaffa Old City. From there head northwards and spend one day in Akko Old City, the ancient Crusader port city, today home to one of the country's largest Arab populations, a famous souk and countless historical buildings, sights and museums interwoven into the maze of cobbled lanes. Spend one day visiting the beautiful lower Galilee, at its midst the twinkling Sea of Galilee whose shores are adorned with pretty villages, rolling hills and churches commemorating Jesus's miracles.

TWO WEEKS – JERUSALEM, DEAD SEA, NEGEV DESERT, TEL AVIV, SEA OF GALILEE, AKKO, NAZARETH, TZFAT, HAIFA, GOLAN HEIGHTS AND CAESAREA Begin in Jerusalem and spend three days exploring the Old City, Mount of Olives, museum and neighbourhoods before dropping down to the Dead Sea. Spend two days at the Dead Sea and visit the archaeological site of Masada and Ein Gedi national park oasis. Continue down to Mitzpe Ramon and spend a day hiking in the Ramon Crater and getting to one with nature at one of the desert eco-lodges. Make your way up to Tel Aviv and enjoy two days relaxing on the beach, exploring Jaffa Old City and visiting the art museums. Head northwards to Haifa, making a stop at the impressive remains of Caesarea Maritime Archaeological Park and overnight in the country's third-largest city with its pretty German Colony, Baha'i Gardens and museums. Spend the next day exploring the jumble of ancient lanes and buildings in Akko Old City and enjoy a fresh fish lunch and sweets from the souk. Head east into the Galilee and visit Nazareth Old City in the morning, with an afternoon by the shore of the Sea of Galilee. Spend one day hiking through the Yehudiya National Park in the Golan Heights and overnight in one of the rural villages of the highlands. Spend your penultimate day in the holy Jewish city of Tzfat Old City, where time seems to have stood still and an air of mysticism permeates. Head back to Tel Aviv for an easy connection to the airport.

THREE WEEKS – AS ABOVE ... BUT MORE With three weeks on your hands it is recommended that you follow the above itinerary (with a couple of days spent in Eilat on the Red Sea) but take your time and add in as many of the national parks, archaeological sites and array of activities as you can. Spend at least one night in a luxury rural *zimmer* (see page 53), delve into the nature of the lower Galilee such as Beit She'an, Gan HaShlosha, Belvoir and Meggido (Armageddon) national parks, visit the crumbling relics of great Crusader castles in the upper Galilee, enjoy Druze hospitality in the northern Golan Heights, or raft down the Jordan River.

With the exception of Yom Kippur, Shabbat or the Sabbath is the holiest day in Judaism, and as it comes around every seven days there are a lot of them. According to the Ten Commandments and the Old Testament it was on this day that God rested during his creation of the world, and so man too must rest. Shabbat is seen as one of the great Jewish institutions and even the most secular of Israelis will greet each other with 'Shabbat Shalom', meaning 'peace on the Sabbath'. In the Jewish calendar days begin not at midnight but at sunset, and each week Shabbat begins as the sun sets on Friday evening until one hour past sundown on Saturday. Shabbat practices vary considerably. Religious Jews abstain from most activities, including work, travel, switching electricity on or off (hence automatic elevators in some hotels), cooking or answering the telephone. For observant Jews it is a day of rest, most of which is spent praying. For the secular members of society it still entails a day off work and as public transport, offices and many businesses are closed this limits movement. In cities such as the eternally secular Tel Aviv, the dawn of Shabbat sees the bars, cafés and beaches fill to bursting as Israelis take advantage of their free time in a country that works 5½-day weeks. Jerusalem, on the other hand, sees the city all but shut down. While there are still non-Shabbat observant restaurants and bars, a large majority abide by the day of rest, and as the sun sets on Friday a calm settles over the normally bustling streets. Needless to say, in Arab communities, life continues as normal, the Muslim holy day being Friday when many services and businesses close and residents attend mosque prayer services.

PUBLIC HOLIDAYS AND FESTIVALS

The dates of Israel's national holidays change yearly according to the Jewish calendar. The following table provides the dates for the forthcoming years. It is important to note that holidays run from sunset to sunset, and as such the dates listed below will in fact begin the evening before. Holidays' eves are considered the same as Fridays (see page 36) with respect to all opening hours listed in the guide, while holidays will correspond to Saturdays.

	2011	2012	2013
Rosh Hashanah	29–30 September	17–18 September	5–6 September
Yom Kippur	8 October	26 September	14 September
Sukkot	13 October	1 October	19 September
Simchat Torah	20 October	8 October	26 September
Hannukah	21–28 December	9–15 December	28 November–5 December
Purim	20 March	8 March	24 February
Passover (Pesach)	18–26 April	6–14 April	25 March–2 April
Holocaust Memorial Day	2 May	19 April	8 April
National Memorial Day	9 May	25 April	15 April
Independence Day	10 May	26 April	16 April
Shavuot	8 June	27 May	15 May
Tisha Bav	9 August	29 July	16 July

Religious and national holidays in Israel are an emotional time, where raw passions of sorrow, celebration, faith and pride emerge. Of these, there are two particular times of the year when visitors can see Israeli patriotism and the resilience of the Jewish people come to light: the holy festival of Yom Kippur and the week in which Holocaust Memorial Day, National Memorial Day and Independence Day are celebrated. Yom Kippur, or the Day of Atonement, is the holiest day in Judaism, marking the end of the 'Ten Days of Repentance'. It is a day of fasting and prayer, for many secular Jews the only day of the year they attend the synagogue. Like a scene from a movie it is a fascinating sight to behold as not a single vehicle moves, children ride bicycles down the great motorways, the sounds of pigeons flap through the normally manic streets of Tel Aviv and the television and radio stations shut down.

In contrast to the country's most religious day, Holocaust Memorial Day and, exactly one week later, National Memorial Day are times of great sorrow, where the raw pain of the world's worst genocide and the loss of the soldiers who have died in Israel's many wars comes bubbling up. Television stations play reels of the fallen soldiers' faces, families attend memorials and the country collectively mourns. Yet come 20.00 on the eve of National Memorial Day the country erupts into an almighty celebration of independence, relief from the pain of the previous week lifted from heavy hearts. Jerusalem, Tel Aviv and towns across the country explode into a vibrant party of fireworks, folk dancing, beer swilling, dancing and raucous, family fun.

_i_ TOURIST INFORMATION AND TOUR OPERATORS

For those who want hassle-free, well-organised excursions around Israel, there are many extremely good (and plenty of extremely bad) tour companies offering a great number of trips. The Israel Tour Operators Association (_www.israeltravel.co.il_) and Israel Ministry of Tourism (_www.goisrael.com_) have a comprehensive list. In addition you can find hundreds of private licensed tour guides at www.israel-guides.net.

Bein Harim Tourism Services Ltd ✆03 5422000/5422001; e info@beinharim.co.il; www.beinharim.co.il. Big, professional multi-lingual company offering countless private vehicle tours around Israel as well as to Bethlehem & the West Bank, Petra in Jordan & Egypt's Sinai.

CNairways Tours ✆09 9520520; e info@cnairways.com; www.cnairways.com. Helicopter tours across Israel. Tours for up to 4 people include the Galilee (2hrs/US$2,800), Jerusalem & the Dead Sea (6hrs/US$5,500) which includes landing on Masada & lunch & spa at the Dead Sea & a winery tour (4hrs/US$3,500) which includes 2 landings at vineyards.

Desert Eco Tours ✆08 86326477 / 052 2765753; e angela@desertecotours.com; www.desertecotours.com. Based in Eilat, they offer a multitude of trips around the country as well as to Jordan & Egypt. Well known for their adventure excursions.

Egged Tours ✆03 5271212–14; e israel-4-u@eggedtours.co.il; www.eggedtours.com. In addition to their city tours they also arrange fantastic, reasonably priced tours around the country.

Falafel Bus ✆+962 795224378 (Jordan) or +61 390057066 (Australia); e info@falafelbus.com; www.falafelbus.com. Hop-on, hop-off bus passes aimed at backpackers & independent travellers. Passes include Israel (US$369), Egypt & Israel (US$1,099) & Jordan & Israel (US$1,099). The pass is valid for between 5 & 30 days & includes airport transfer & 1st night's accommodation.

Mazada Tours ✎ 02 6235777; e info@mazadatours.com; www.mazada.co.il. Arrange tours & transport to Jordan & Egypt. There are daily buses to Amman (300NIS) & Cairo (500NIS) & a range of tours around Israel.

Noah Tours ✎ 02 5666601; e sales@noahtours.com; www.noahtours.com. Offer day & multi-

day tours within Israel as well as to Jordan & Egypt.

Society for the Protection of Nature in Israel (SPNI) ✎ 03 6388688; e teleteva@spni.org.il; www.teva.org.il. Offer trips ranging from 1–4 days that centre on hiking, environmentally friendly outdoor activities & guided tours to sites of interest.

United Tours ✎ 03 6173333; e united1@netvision.net.il; www.unitedtours.co.il. One of the biggest tour companies in Israel offering many 1- & 2-day coach tours.

OVERSEAS TOUR OPERATORS Holidays to Israel have long been seen as specialist travel, with many operators focusing on religious groups. These days though, Israel is a hugely popular place for all types of travellers and so there is a wide selection of tour operators around. Many of the big-name operators are starting to include Israel in their packages and numerous independent or specialist agencies have years of experience in tours to the Holy Land. The Israel Ministry of Tourism has an excellent tour operator search facility (*www.goisrael.com*).

UK

El Al Superstar Holidays ✎ 020 7121 1500; e info@superstar.co.uk; www.superstar.co.uk. El Al national airlines offers packages to Israel from London & Manchester.

Issta ✎ 20 8202 0800 / 03 7777316; e admin@isstadirect.com; www.isstadirect.com. Offer holidays to Israel from the UK, Holland, France & Ireland. Also have cheap flight options & last-minute deals.

Longwood Holidays ✎ 020 8418 2516; e reservations@longwoodholidays.co.uk; www.longwoodholidays.co.uk. British tour operator specialising in Israel, Egypt, Jordan & Morocco. They have package & tailor-made holidays available.

Travelink ✎ 208 931 8000; e info@travelinkuk.com; www.travelinkuk.com. Specialist UK travel agent offering flights, holidays, tours & accommodation in Israel.

US & Canada

America Israel Travel ✎ 818 7049888; e info@americaisrael.us; www.americaisrael.us. Specialising in Christian-themed trips to Israel from North America.

Pilgrim Tours ✎ 800 3220788 (USA) 610 2860788 (Canada); e mail@pilgrimtours.com; www.pilgrimtours.com. North American

organisation offering affordable trips to Israel, Jordan & Egypt.

Shalom Israel Tours ✎ 800 7631948; www.shalomisraeltours.com. North American-based agency specialising in Jewish-themed custom tours but with many good packages available also.

RED TAPE

Citizens from the following countries will be issued with a tourist visa at their port of entry, valid for up to three months (a passport valid for six months from the date of entry will need to be provided).

EUROPE Austria, Belgium, Bulgaria, Cyprus, Denmark, Estonia, Finland, France, Germany, Gibraltar, Greece, Holland, Hungary, Iceland, Ireland, Italy, Liechtenstein,

Luxembourg, Malta, Monaco, Norway, Portugal, Romania, San Marino, Slovenia, Spain, Sweden, Switzerland, United Kingdom.

ASIA AND AUSTRALASIA Australia, Fiji, Hong Kong, Japan, New Zealand, Philippines, Singapore, South Korea.

AFRICA Central African Republic, Lesotho, Malawi, Mauritius, South Africa, Swaziland.

THE AMERICAS Argentina, Bahamas, Barbados, Bolivia, Brazil, Canada, Chile, Colombia, Costa Rica, Dominican Republic, Ecuador, El Salvador, Guatemala, Haiti, Jamaica, Mexico, Panama, Paraguay, St Kitts & Nevis, St Lucia, Surinam, Trinidad & Tobago, United States, Uruguay.

Citizens of all other countries should contact their local Israeli consulate or Israel's Ministry of the Interior (*www.mfa.gov.il*).

ISRAELI STAMP Israel does not hold diplomatic relations with most Arab and predominantly Muslim countries and therefore Israeli citizens are not permitted to travel to such places. More than that, however, foreign nationals who have an Israeli visa stamp inside their passports will be refused entry into many of these countries. As such it is a good idea to ask that the Israeli stamp does not appear on your passport if you are planning travel to any countries where this may be a problem (Egypt and Jordan are notable exceptions). Until recently this was at the discretion of the immigration office but now there is an official form you can ask them for which you complete and they stamp.

EXTENDING VISAS Most tourist visas are issued for three months but can be extended at the Ministry of the Interior offices.

Jerusalem 1 Shlomzion Hamalka St; ✆ 1700 55111
Tel Aviv 125 Menachem Begin St; ✆ 03 5193305; Ben Gurion Airport; ✆ 03 9774200

Haifa 15 Pal Yam St; ✆ 04 863333
Eilat 2nd Floor, City Centre Mall, HaTemarin St; ✆ 08 6381333
Tiberias 23 Ze'avi Elkhadif St; ✆ 04 6729111

EMBASSIES
Foreign embassies in Israel Since 1967 when Israel captured East Jerusalem (and the West Bank and Gaza Strip), the UN and much of the international community has been unwilling to recognise all of Jerusalem as Israel's capital. Almost all countries therefore maintain embassies and consulates in Tel Aviv, although a few now have consulate offices in Jerusalem.

Australia Discount Bank Tower, Level 28, 23 Yehuda Halevi St, Tel Aviv; ✆ 03 6935000; e telaviv.embassy@dfat.gov.au; www. australianembassy.org.il; ⊕ 08.00–12.30 & 13.00–16.30 Mon–Thu, 08.00–13.00 Fri
Canada Hasapanut Hse, 3/5 Nirim St, Tel Aviv; ✆ 03 6363300; e taviv@international.gc.ca; www.canadainternational.gc.ca/israel; ⊕ 08.00–16.30 Mon–Thu, 08.00–13.30 Fri

Egypt 54 Basel St, Tel Aviv; ✆ 03 5464151; f 03 5441615; ⊕ 09.00–12.00 Sun–Thu. Consulate 68 Afroni St, Eilat; ✆ 08 5976115; ⊕ 09.00–15.00 Sun–Thu
France 112 Herbert Samuel St, Tel Aviv; ✆ 03 5208300; f 03 5208340; www.ambafrance-il.org; ⊕ 09.00–12.00 Mon–Fri. Consulate 5 Paul Emil Botta, Jerusalem; ✆ 02 6259481; www.consulfrance-jerusalem.org; ⊕ 09.00–12.00 Mon–Fri

Germany 3 Daniel Frish St, Tel Aviv; ☎03 6931313; f 03 6969217; e ger_emb@netvision. net.il; www.germanemb.org.il; ⏰ 08.00–16.00 Mon–Thu, 08.00–12.30 Fri

Ireland 3 Daniel Frish St, Tel Aviv; ☎03 6964166; f 03 6964160; ⏰ 08.00–13.00 & 14.00–16.00 Mon–Thu, 08.00–13.00 Fri

Jordan 14 Aba Hilel St, Ramat Gan; ☎03 7517722; f 03 7517712; ⏰ 09.00–15.00 Sun–Thu

Netherlands Beit Oz 13th Floor, 14 Aba Hillel St, Ramat Gan; ☎03 6957377; e info@ holland-israel.com; www.netherlands-embassy. co.il; ⏰ 08.00–17.00 Mon–Thu, 08.00–12.30 Fri

South Africa Sason Hogi Tower, 17th Floor, 12a Abba Hillel St, Ramat Gan; ☎03 5252566; e diplomatie@ambafrance-il.org; www.safis. co.il; ⏰ 09.00–11.30 Mon–Fri, 09.00–11.30 & 14.00–15.00 Wed

Israeli embassies abroad

Australia 6 Turrana St, Yarralumla, Canberra; ☎+61 2 6215 4511; e info@canberra.mfa.gov.il; canberra.mfa.gov.il; ⏰ 09.30–13.00 Mon–Thu, 09.30–12.00 Fri.

Canada 1 Westmount Sq, Suite 650, Montreal; ☎+1 514 940 8500; e con-sec@montreal.mfa. gov.il; www.montreal.mfa.gov.il; ⏰ 09.00–17.00–12.30 Mon–Fri. Suite 1005, 50 O'Connor St, Ottawa; ☎+1 613 567 6450; e info@ottawa.mfa.gov.il; www.ottawa.mfa.gov. il; ⏰ 10.00–13.00 Mon–Fri. 180 Bloor St West, Suite 700, Toronto; ☎+1 4166408500; www. toronto.mfa.gov.il.

Egypt 6 Sharia Ibn-el Maleck; ☎+20 2 3332 1500; e info@cairo.mfa.gov.il; www.cairo.mfa. gov.il; ⏰ 10.00–12.30 Sun–Thu

France 3 Rue Rabelais, Paris; ☎+33 1 40 76 55 00; e info@paris.mfa.gov.il; www.paris.mfa.gov.il; ⏰ 09.00–17.30 Mon–Thu, 09.00–15.00 Fri

Germany 74–75 Auguste Victoria, Berlin; ☎+49 30 8904 5500; e info@berlin.mfa.gov.il; www.berlin.mfa.gov.il; ⏰ 09.30–13.00 Mon–Thu, 09.30–12.30 Fri

UK 192 HaYarkon St, Tel Aviv; ☎03 7251222; f 03 5271572; ⏰ 08.00–16.00 Mon–Thu, 08.00–13.30 Fri. Consulate 1 Ben Yehuda St; ☎03 5100166; e webmaster.telaviv@fco.gov.uk; http://ukinisrael.fco.gov.uk/en; ⏰ 08.00–13.00 Mon–Thu, 08.00–12.30 Fri. Consulate 19 Nashashibi St, Jerusalem; ☎02 5322368; e Britain.Jerusalem@fco.gov.uk; www.britishconsulate.org; ⏰ 07.30–15.30 Mon–Thu

USA 71 HaYarkon St, Tel Aviv; ☎03 5197575; f 03 5102444; ⏰ 08.00–16.00 Mon–Thu, 08.00–13.00 Fri. Consulate 1 Ben Yehuda St; ☎03 5175151; e nivtelaviv@state.gov; www.telaviv.usembassy.gov; ⏰ 08.00–16.30 Mon–Fri. Consulate 18 Agron Rd, Jerusalem; ☎02 6227230; e jerusalemvisa@state.gov; jerusalem.usconsulate.gov; ⏰ 08.00–16.30 Mon–Thu

Ireland 122 Pembroke Rd, Dublin; ☎+353 1 230 9400; e info@dublin.mfa.gov.il; www. dublin.mfa.gov.il; ⏰ 10.00–13.00 Mon–Fri

Jordan 47 Maysaloun St Rabiya, Amman; ☎+962 6 550 3500; e info@amman.mfa.gov.il; amman.mfa.gov.il; ⏰ 09.00–13.30 Mon–Thu

South Africa 428 Kings Highway, Pretoria; ☎+27 12 470 3500; e publicaffairs@ pretoria.mfa.gov.il; www.pretoria.mfa.gov.il; ⏰ 09.00–13.00 Mon–Thu, 09.00–12.00 Fri

UK 2 Palace Green, London; ☎+44 20 7957 9500; e info@london.mfa,gov.il; www.london.mfa.gov.il; ⏰ 10.00–13.00 Mon–Thu, 10.00–12.00 Fri. Consulate 15A Old Court Pl, London; ☎+44 20 7957 9500; e consulate@ london.mfa.gov.il; London.mfa.gov.il; ⏰ 09.45–13.00 Mon–Thu, 09.45–11.45 Fri.

USA 800 Second Av, New York; ☎+1 212 499 5000; e consular@newyork.mfa.gov.il; www.israelfm.org. 3514 International Dr, Washington; ☎+1 202 364 5500; e info@ washington.mfa.gov.il; www.israelemb.org; ⏰ 09.30–13.00 Mon–Thu, 09.30–10.30 Fri

GETTING THERE AND AWAY

BY AIR Ben Gurion International Airport (TLV) (☎ *03 9755555; www.iaa.gov.il/ Rashat/en-US/Airports/BenGurion*) is Israel's main international airport although more and more charter flights now go to Ovda Airport near Eilat (☎ *1 700 705 022; www.iaa.gov.il/Rashat/en-US/Airports/Eilat)*. Tel Aviv's velvet ropes came down in

FLYING WITH EL AL

El Al is Israel's national airline and flying with this famously security-conscious company is certainly an interesting experience. Since its conception in 1949 when it flew Israel's first president Chaim Weizmann home from Switzerland on its maiden voyage, it has had security at the forefront of its management. Post 9/11, El Al, and indeed Ben-Gurion Airport as a whole, has become a model for other airlines looking to improve their security standards. They are so confident of their security measures in fact, that after you have gone through their rigorous security checks they provide passengers with metal cutlery as a reward.

Embarking on a flight with El Al however needs some preparation, as even the most seasoned flyers will find things work a little differently. Firstly, check-in. In most airports across the world, El Al's check-in can be found at the furthest end of the terminal, cordoned off by barriers and surrounded by a selection of burly, heavily armed airport police. Only passengers may approach the cordoned-off area and passports and tickets must be shown to even get in line. At this point an Israeli El Al staff member, clipboard in hand, will approach and begin to ask rather a lot of questions. Who do you know in Israel? Why are you going there? Plus the standard 'did you pack your own bag?' questions. With the interrogation over you will then proceed to the enormous X-ray machine into which you will heave your suitcases. More often than not, your suitcase will then undergo an intensive search and rub down with a long, wand-looking object (which is in fact an explosive detector). After check-in comes phase two. As you approach the heart-sinkingly long queue to go through security you will suddenly be ushered down a different, El Al-only (and therefore considerably shorter) channel. Once through, there is another long walk to the gate, again the furthest the airport has to offer where you will finally board the plane. Most flights go by uneventfully unless you have yet to experience often large groups of Orthodox men praying fervently in the aisles, tefillin affixed to their heads and arms (see page 24). While Israelis are notorious amongst airline staff for not abiding by seatbelt signs, as the wheels of the plane touch down a round of applause normally erupts in recognition of the pilot.

2004 to reveal a plush, new terminal that Israelis are rightly proud of. There are good bus and train transport links with Tel Aviv (see page 111) and Jerusalem (see page 63) and car-rental counters can be found on the first floor of the East Gallery in the arrivals terminal (⊕ 24hrs) (see page 114).

Israel's national airline is **El Al** (☏ 03 9716854; www.elal.co.il; code LY) and it operates regular flights to destinations all around the world. Due to stringent security measures, prices were always notoriously high, although increased competition on flights to Israel has meant they are now mostly on a par with other major airlines. It is important to note that El Al does not fly on Shabbat and all meals are kosher (glatt kosher can be ordered in advance).

A huge increase in budget airlines offering flights to Israel has seen tourist numbers soar, and now city breaks to Tel Aviv or Jerusalem, until recently expensive and unrealistic trips, are becoming more and more common. Big European low-cost airlines such as easyJet, Air Berlin and Jet2 now have daily or several times weekly flights to the Holy Land.

Tickets Most airlines offer online ticket purchasing or tickets can be booked over the phone. Alternatively, travel agencies such as Issta or Ophir Tours (see page 115) offer good budget deals and last-minute flights. In 2009, the budget airline easyJet started offering daily flights from London Luton (£124 one-way), as well as a new route to Geneva, Switzerland. Travellers coming from **Australasia** and **South America** (or countries that do not have diplomatic relations with Israel) will need to change in Asia or Europe. El Al offers regular flights from **Hong Kong**, **Beijing** and **Bangkok** (approx 3,000NIS return). Delta, El Al, Israir, Continental Airlines and American Airlines run regular flights between Tel Aviv and **New York** as well as **Los Angeles** and other major airports in the **United States** and **Canada**. Air France, Iberia, Lufthansa, KLM and Alitalia offer fairly pricey tickets from **western Europe** and are the most commonly used connections to **South America**. There are now however, several low-cost airlines running between Europe and Israel including, as well as easyJet, Air Berlin, Jet2 and German Wings. Apart from **Jordan** and **Egypt**, **Turkey** is the only other Middle Eastern country with relations with Israel. Turkey was once a top Israeli holiday destination with cheap flights to Istanbul and Marmaris, but diplomatic relations have been strained since mid-2010 (see page 14). Good-priced tickets to the Greek Islands and Cyprus can easily be found, especially in summer.

Airlines

Air Berlin +49 30 41 02 10 03; www.airberlin.com. Budget airline serving Germany with European connections.
Air Canada 03 6072111; www.aircanada.com
Air France 03 7555057; www.airfrance.com
Alitalia 03 7960766; www.alitalia.com
American Airlines 03 7952122; www.aa.com
Arkia 09 8644444; www.arkia.com
Austrian Airlines 03 5115110; www.aua.com
British Airways 03 5101575; www.ba.com
Cathay Pacific 03 7952111; www.cathaypacific.com
Cimber Sterling +45 70101218; www.cimber.com. Budget airline flying from Norway and Denmark.

Continental Airlines 03 5116777; www.continental.com
Delta + 03 620 1101; www.delta.com
easyJet +44 905 821 0905; www.easyjet.com
Germanwings +49 900 19 19 100; www.germanwings.com. Budget airline flying from several European cities.
Iberia 03 7951920; www.iberia.com
Israir +03 7954038; www.israirairlines.com
Jet2 +44 203 031 8103; www.jet2.com. Budget airline operating out of Manchester, UK.
KLM 03 7967999; www.klm.com
Lufthansa 1809 371937; www.lufthansa.com
Royal Jordanian Airlines 03 5165566; www.rj.com
South African Airways 03 7951344; www.flysaa.com

BY LAND Of its neighbours Israel only has diplomatic relations with Jordan and Egypt and therefore it is only possible to travel overland (or by any other means for that matter) between these countries. While getting to either country under your own steam is perfectly achievable, Mazada Tours (see page 27) arranges buses to Amman and Cairo from both Tel Aviv and Jerusalem. The Israeli Airports Authority has detailed information on all the border crossings *(www.iaa.gov.il)*.

To/from Egypt Despite several border crossings with Egypt, only the **Taba border crossing** (08 6360999) in the south of the country near Eilat is open to tourists (the **Rafah border** is closed to foreign travellers for the foreseeable future owing to its proximity to Gaza). To travel to Sinai you don't need to apply for a visa in advance but can instead obtain one at the border crossing (46 Egyptian pounds/

US$8), which is open 24 hours, seven days a week except Yom Kippur and Eid el-Adha. There is a 101NIS exit fee from Israel. If you plan on continuing to the Egyptian mainland you will need to apply for a visa at the Egyptian consulates in Tel Aviv or Eilat (see page 38). It is a modern and well-run crossing with streams of Israelis and tourists crossing daily. Rental cars cannot be taken into Egypt. Egged bus 15 runs from Eilat bus station.

To/from Jordan There are three border crossings with Jordan and, with the exception of the King Hussein/Allenby border crossing, visas can be obtained at the border. Those using the Allenby border will need to apply for a visa from the Jordanian embassy in Tel Aviv beforehand (see page 39). Your passport must be valid for at least six months.

Yitzhak Rabin/Arava border crossing (*Eilat;* \ *08 6300555;* ⏰ *06.30–20.00 Sun–Thu, 08.00–20.00 Fri/Sat*) This was the first border between the two countries and is used mainly for day trips to Petra and Wadi Rum. While there is a lot of toing and froing, passport stamping, photographing and form filling, it is a relatively easy crossing. Exit tax is 101NIS and a two-week Jordanian visa costs 20 dirhams (US$30) (which can be extended at Jordanian police stations for up to three months). There are no buses from Eilat but it is a short taxi ride. On the way back, ask the Israeli guard at the gate to call you a taxi. There are a few taxis on the Jordanian side that will take you to Aqaba.

Allenby border crossing/King Hussein Bridge (\ *02 5482600;* ⏰ *08.00– 20.00 Sun–Thu, 08.00–15.00 Fri/Sat*) This border is used mainly for traffic to and from Amman and Jerusalem. Buses on both sides are regular and will take you to the capital cities. Exit tax is 167NIS.

Jordan River crossing (*Beit She'an;* \ *04 6093400;* ⏰ *08.00–21.00 Sun–Thu, 08.00–20.00 Fri–Sat*) This border is convenient if you're travelling in the Galilee or coming from Jerusalem and Haifa. There is a 2km no-man's-land between the two terminals but a shuttle service now operates (4.5NIS from Israeli terminal, 6NIS from Jordanian terminal). There are buses to the border from Beit She'an. Exit tax is 101NIS and two-week Jordanian visas are issued on the border (20 dirhams/US$30).

BY SEA Ferry lines have been closed due to lack of traffic for several years but it is still possible to get on one of the increasingly popular cruises departing from Haifa's port. Cruises to and from Turkey, the Greek islands and Italy can be arranged through **Mano Tours** (*2 Paliam St, Haifa;* \ *04 8606666;* f *04 8667666; www.mano.co.il*) or **Caspi Shipping** (*76 Ha'atzmaut St, Haifa;* \ *04 8674444;* e *lea@ caspi-sapanut.co.il; www.caspitours.co.il*) and leave from the rather nice **Maritime Passenger Terminal** (\ *04 8518245; www.haifaport.co.il*).

✚ HEALTH   *with Dr Felicity Nicholson*

Israel is a modern, developed country with Western standards of health, hygiene and medical facilities. Visitors do not need to have any vaccinations to enter the country although it is advisable to be up to date on tetanus, polio, rubella, mumps and diphtheria. Hepatitis A is also sometimes recommended. It is also advisable to get children vaccinated against measles as outbreaks have occurred primarily in Orthodox neighbourhoods of Jerusalem where vaccination is opted against. Israel is home to several highly reputable and internationally renowned hospitals, in particular Ichilov in Tel Aviv, the Hadassah Ein Kerem in Jerusalem and Soroka in Beer Sheva (see the relevant chapters for details). Pharmacies are commonplace, well stocked with most Western-brand medicines and have pharmacists who speak a high level of English. Superpharm is the most widely distributed chain and most cities have several branches.

HEALTH TOURISM With the increasing international popularity and awareness of the medicinal effects of the Dead Sea and its products, health tourism in Israel is growing by the year. Health clinics and spas that centre on natural resources such as the Dead Sea or hot springs have been claimed to help heal a whole host of ailments (see page 266).

INSURANCE As with all sensible travel, insurance is most certainly a requirement, but many policies do not cover injuries sustained through acts of terrorism so be sure to check the small print of your insurance company's documents. Most insurance companies only provide emergency dental treatment so if you have any concerns, get your teeth checked before leaving home. While Israel has good dental clinics, they come at a rather hefty price.

WATER Tap water is generally safe to drink in Israel and poses no health risks. It can occasionally have a rather chlorine-like taste so if your palate doesn't approve, bottled water is widely available and inexpensive.

HEALTH RISKS
Heat-related sicknesses Israel in general doesn't pose many health risks, with the exception of travel in the desert. Temperatures can reach as high as 45°C, which combined with the intense sunshine and arid conditions, poses **dehydration** risks. Be sure to always carry plenty of water when venturing into the southern desert region and stay hydrated. A hat, strong sunscreen and sunglasses are also important to minimise the effects of the relentless sun, both in winter and summer. For more details on safety around the Dead Sea, see page 261.

Mosquitoes and sand flies Israel does not suffer from malaria so no antimalarial drugs are necessary. In summer, however, mosquitoes are out in their millions and can cause infections and irritations so be sure to use strong mosquito repellent such as those containing DEET. Likewise, sand flies along coastal regions can leave sore, itchy bites so apply repellent regularly.

Stray animals and rabies Stray cats are a major problem in Israel and although most are not tame enough to be touched, some (mainly kittens) have got used to people and beg for food in outdoor restaurants. Despite their heartbreaking plight it is best not to touch them as a variety of pests, infections and funguses can be transferred to you. Rabies is also present in Israel, although contained almost wholly in rural areas, so be attentive when camping and do not touch stray animals.

Jellyfish While Israel's jellyfish do not cause any lasting harm and are not poisonous, they can leave you with a rather painful sting and red, whip-like mark. In general those who wash on to the shores of the Mediterranean do so in waves between the months of June and August and, for the most part, the coast is clear. The small jellyfish who occasionally appear along Eilat's Red Sea coast however, are sting-less and can be moved gently aside so as not to harm them while swimming.

Scorpions and snakes Scorpions are found in the desert and can have a nasty, painful bite. In general the black scorpion bites are not life-threatening but those inflicted by the yellow scorpion can be much more severe. Either way, seek medical advice if you get bitten. Be aware when moving rocks or stones and keep shoes on, especially at night. Israel is home to several species of venomous snakes but bites are rare. Don't stick your arms or hands into cracks, crevices or under rocks and if you're camping make sure you keep the tent flaps zipped closed at all times. If you do get bitten by a snake, immobilise the limb and place a bandage over the bite. Seek medical help as soon as possible.

WOMEN'S HEALTH As in any country, women travelling in warm climates or regions where sanitation levels may be low (camping in the desert, for example) should be aware of the possibility of contracting urinary tract, bladder or yeast infections, and should take necessary medication with them. Wearing loose-fitting clothing, drinking plenty of fluids and carrying toilet paper with you are preventative measures which can be taken to avoid these complications. If you do develop a gynaecological problem, over-the-counter medications are widely available and most hospitals have women's health departments. Tampons, sanitary towels and condoms are available in all supermarkets, mini-markets and pharmacies although not all brands are stocked so if you use something specific be sure to take enough with you. Contraceptive pills differ from country to country so take a supply sufficient to last you your trip.

SAFETY

In general, visitors to Israel encounter few problems. **Crime** levels are low and while petty theft and pickpocketing do occur, violent crimes are rare. The most worrying safety threat for people considering a trip to Israel is terrorism, which despite considerable improvements over recent years, is unfortunately a part of life in the country. As the security situation in Israel and the Palestinian Territories can change rapidly it is important to check with your country's foreign office (see the following list) before setting off.

Australia www.smartraveller.gov.au
Canada www.voyage.gc.ca
Germany www.auswaertiges-amt.de
Ireland www.dfa.ie
New Zealand www.safetravel.govt.nz
South Africa www.dfa.gov.za
UK www.fco.gov.uk
USA http://travel.state.gov

TERRORISM Compared with many countries, Israel has a higher risk of terrorism, although stringent security measures have resulted in fewer bombings in 2009 and 2010 than in previous years. Rocket fire from the Lebanon and Gaza borders is the biggest cause for concern, and has killed or injured several people in the past two years. Despite a decrease in indiscriminate suicide bombings it is important to understand the danger and simply be aware. Bombers target crowded areas such as transport terminals, shopping centres, restaurants, markets and nightclubs. It is important to be vigilant and stay away from establishments that do not have security guards outside (it is common to be checked with a metal detector and be asked to open bags before entering most places). As situations can change quickly it is a good idea to monitor media outlets and always follow the instructions of Israeli authorities. It is highly recommended to register at your country's consulate upon arrival as they will be able to inform you of any changes to security issues.

BORDERS It is advisable not to travel to the **Shebaa Farms area** and **Ghajar** along Israel's northern border with Lebanon because of ongoing military operations over the highly disputed land. While problems along other sections of the Israeli/ Lebanese border are rare these days, a clash between troops in August 2010 means tensions are heightened. At the time of writing all but essential travel to within 12km of the border with the **Gaza Strip** was strongly warned against by Israeli and foreign authorities. While a tentative ceasefire is in place between Hamas and Israel, tensions are high and the area is hugely sensitive. Because of a breach in the Gazan/Egyptian border in March 2008, **route 10** running along the Egyptian/ Israeli border is closed to civilian traffic until further notice. Live **minefields** along some border areas with Lebanon, the West Bank and Gaza remain in place so it is important not to venture off marked roads or tracks. The Golan Heights too has a number of live mine areas, remnants of past wars, and it is therefore imperative to stick to designated paths (see page 247).

NATURAL DISASTERS Israel is located along an active earthquake zone and while most tremors go undetected (and it has been several hundred years since the last major earthquake), scientists and meteorologists have said the country may experience larger quakes in the future. Sandstorms and flash floods in winter months can become serious dangers in the desert regions so it is important to check with local national park authorities and meteorological stations before venturing off-road.

DRIVING Statistically you are considerably more likely to come to harm driving down Israel's fast and furious motorways than in a terrorist attack, and it is important to be aware of the somewhat haphazard driving techniques many Israelis have adopted. The idea that road traffic rules only apply to others, combined with aggressive driving techniques and high speeds, sadly results in hundreds of deaths a year. Tiredness on the long, straight, monotonous roads in the desert can also lead to accidents, so pull over and rest if you feel yourself start to tire.

CULTURAL CONCERNS Religious observances can often be the cause of serious negativity so it is important to be aware of religious and cultural taboos and respect them. Serious issues include the following:

- Being inappropriately dressed in religious neighbourhoods. When entering ultra-Orthodox Jewish neighbourhoods it is important to dress conservatively. This includes women not wearing trousers. Violent reactions towards those dressed or not behaving in accordance with Orthodox Jewish traditions have been reported.
- Inappropriate conduct in religious neighbourhoods. Shabbat is devoutly observed and therefore no cars should be driven through ultra-Orthodox neighbourhoods during these hours (see page 106). The stoning of vehicles not abiding by this is commonplace. Likewise, these neighbourhoods are best avoided during the holy day of Yom Kippur.

- Public displays of affection in religious sites. This applies to Jewish and Muslim religious sites as well as ultra-Orthodox neighbourhoods, and applies to both heterosexual and (considerably more so) to homosexual couples. Appropriate dress in any religious site should be adhered to (see page 106).
- Public conduct on religious holidays. Fasting during both the Muslim holiday of Ramadan and the Jewish holiday of Yom Kippur is strictly followed and you should abstain from eating, or drinking alcohol (and in the case of Muslim areas during Ramadan, smoking) in public areas during these times.
- Taking photos of military or police installations. This is prohibited and enforced for security reasons.

WOMEN TRAVELLERS As with any country, women travelling alone can incur unwanted attention and face additional security risks. On the whole Israel is a safe country for women and violent crimes are rare, but sensible precautions should be taken to ensure you have a hassle-free trip. Wearing a wedding ring, dressing modestly, not accepting hitchhiking lifts, staying in well-lit areas at night, letting someone know where you are going, carrying cash on you for a taxi or phone call, staying in women-only dormitories and ignoring male advances can all help avoid unwanted confrontations.

GAY/LESBIAN TRAVELLERS In recent years Tel Aviv has well and truly established itself on the gay travel scene, and its residents and tourism board are fully embracing and encouraging this trend. The annual Gay Pride parade (see page 122) attracts party-goers from around the country and the world, and there is a burgeoning nightlife scene aimed at homosexual revellers. The Tel Aviv Endless Summer (*www.gayisrael.org.il*) is a weekend of parties, events and festivals aimed at the gay community and visitors. The city is liberal and secular and as such it is common to see open displays of affection.

In complete contrast is Jerusalem, whose predominantly religion-abiding residents are less used to, and therefore less tolerant of, homosexuality. While in the modern city it is sometimes fine to be openly affectionate, in religious neighbourhoods, the Old City or near any religious buildings this will not be well received and violence has been reported in the past. In 2005 an Orthodox Jew attacked marchers on a gay pride parade in Jerusalem with knives, and in 2009 a gay

TRAVELLING WITH CHILDREN

Israelis love children and having a large family is common practice, and as such your little ones will be welcomed into most venues with open arms. What many foreign parents often find a little disconcerting to begin with, however, is the tendency of complete strangers to come up and pinch cheeks, pick up, cuddle or play with children, something not accepted in many more reserved Western countries. While obvious precautions should always be taken with regards to your children, do not be alarmed by these acts as they are almost always offered in the most tender way and are purely an outpouring of affection that most Israelis, men and women alike, hold for babies and young children. Being stopped in the street and given 'helpful' advice as to whether your child should be wearing a hat, be given more water or needs a nap are also common, and while few parents appreciate advice from strangers, this is again not meant to offend.

centre was attacked in Tel Aviv by Jewish Orthodox fanatics and two teenagers were killed. These sorts of incidents are extremely rare however, and Israel's government is encouraging homosexual visitors to the country. The rest of the country can be divided into either the Tel Aviv or Jerusalem category, with cities such as Haifa, Eilat and predominantly secular cities generally more respectful of homosexuality, with religious neighbourhoods and cities such as Tzfat, Nazareth and Akko strongly and vociferously opposed.

DISABLED TRAVELLERS Israel is a modern country and as such it is well geared towards travellers with disabilities. Increasing numbers of establishments, national parks and public transport have disabled facilities, wheelchair accessibility and assistance, and the Israel government is working on schemes and projects to increase this number. Access Israel *(www.aisrael.org)* offers detailed, up-to-date information on accessible tourism sites, hotels, tours, events, restaurants and car rental, as well as ideas on touring routes.

SECURITY CHECKLIST The following are recommendations as to how best to minimise potential problems whilst travelling in Israel:
- Organise a variety of ways to obtain money, for example credit cards, cash, travellers' cheques, etc.
- Make two copies of your documents (passports, insurance details, credit cards, etc). Give one set to a relative or friend at home and keep the other set with you but separate to the originals.
- Leave expensive jewellery behind to minimise the risk of theft.
- Steer clear of political demonstrations that can occasionally turn violent.
- Be vigilant in crowded areas (see above).
- Register with your consulate upon arrival.
- Be prepared to undergo lengthy questioning and bag searches on arrival into and departure from Israel.
- Abide by cultural and religious traditions in certain areas (see above).
- Avoid travel to within a 12km radius of the border with the Gaza Strip.
- Check Foreign Office warnings before leaving home.
- Do not venture off marked roads and footpaths to avoid live minefields and army training zones.
- Beware of flash floods in desert regions. Abide by ranger instructions, avoid ravines, narrow gorges and caves and monitor weather conditions before setting off.

WHAT TO TAKE

While there are few things that you cannot buy in Israel, prices for many products are equal to, if not more expensive than, other Western countries, and considerably more expensive than in developing countries. Shopping malls, big chain stores and vast supermarkets generally stock all the necessities you may have forgotten, but while camping and outdoor shops are well stocked, they are expensive and you're best buying any equipment before leaving home. Summers are hot and humid so bring lightweight clothing and some long-sleeved shirts and trousers, or a light shawl, for entering religious sites. Sunscreen, sunglasses and a hat are essential items whatever the time of year, especially if you're travelling in the desert region. A wet-weather jacket is a good idea during the autumn, winter and even spring months when rain is likely, and if travelling during the winter months a warm jacket and winter attire will be necessary for Jerusalem and the mountainous areas. Electricity is 220V and while most power sockets have three pinholes, they will usually work with standard European two-pin plugs. Plug adapters are cheap and most mini-markets and pharmacies will stock them.

$ MONEY, CURRENCY AND BANKING

Israel's official currency is the New Israeli Shekel (₪) (NIS), referred to simply as shekels; anything under a shekel is known as an agora (plural agorot). There are coins of five, ten and 50 agorot and one, five and ten shekels as well as notes of 20, 50, 100 and 200 shekels (you can see the notes at www.bankisrael.gov.il/catal/cataloge). Standard exchange rates are usually around 3.6NIS to US$1, 5NIS to €1 and 5.8NIS to £1 but vary according to current exchange rates. Most major credit cards are widely accepted in stores, tour agencies, restaurants, hotels, etc, and ATMs are commonplace.

CHANGING MONEY AND TRAVELLERS' CHEQUES There is no limit on the amount of money allowed into Israel, be it in cash, travellers' cheques or credit cards. Most major currencies and travellers' cheques can be exchanged for shekels at the airport, banks, post offices, many hotels or licensed exchange booths dotted around most towns and cities. To exchange travellers' cheques you will need to show your passport. Exchange rates vary and you will often get the best rate from the exchange booths in city centres, but it is a good idea to shop around a little, especially if you are changing large sums. All public services such as banks and post offices are closed on Shabbat so be sure to arrange your finances before Friday evening. At the end of your trip it is possible to change money from shekels only at the airport. A maximum of US$500 (or equivalent in other currencies) can be changed, or up to US$5,000 if you have the receipt for the original conversion.

TIPPING AND BARGAINING In a country that tends to complain loudly about most things, it is a surprising fact that bad service is rarely reported and tips are still given to sullen staff. It is customary to tip about 12% in restaurants, cafés and sit-down bars as well as bellboys and other service providers. In general, taxi drivers are not tipped although it is common to tell the driver to round up the fare to the nearest appropriate round number (for example a 18NIS fare would be rounded to 20NIS). Taxi drivers are required by law to run the meter and those who refuse are highly likely to be overcharging you. Bargaining is standard procedure only in open markets.

VAT AND TAX RETURN Israel has a VAT rate of 16%, although many services aimed at tourists are not subject to VAT, including hotel accommodation. In addition, many businesses offering services to tourists are registered with the Ministry of Tourism programme to return VAT to customers. For a complete list visit the Change Place (\ 03 9754020; www.cpl.co.il/English). VAT refunds will be given on the spot at the Change Place in Tel Aviv Ben Gurion Airport, and forwarded on at a later date from Eilat Airport. To be eligible for VAT refund you must have a complete receipt list of all purchases from a vendor or vendors, the total expenditure must be more than $100 in each shop or service and the items must be in a sealed bag. VAT refunds are not given on food, drinks, tobacco, electrical appliances or photography equipment.

BUDGETING

Israel isn't a cheap country in which to travel and you'll find that without keeping a close eye on your expenditure, money can fly out of your pocket at a rate of knots. One of the biggest expenses is ultimately accommodation. Although the country has thankfully seen a big boom in hostels thanks to increasing numbers of independent travellers and backpackers, there is little in between these and the hugely pricey hotels. Prices tend to be around 100NIS for a dormitory bed and 350NIS for a private room. Outside of the big cities, zimmers (see *Accommodation*, page 53) form the core of rural accommodation and while these are small and privately owned, they come under the luxury category and are therefore at the higher end of price bracket (500–800NIS average). In the desert regions there are many eco-lodges and hostels that provide reasonably priced accommodation options. Food is less of a problem if you're travelling on a tighter or shoestring budget as Israeli/Arabic fast food is healthy, widely available, extremely cheap (falafel costs around 15NIS and a hummus meal 25–40NIS), filling and delicious (see *Eating and drinking*, page 53) so you won't be reduced to the likes of McDonald's. For self-catering, prices are comparable with western Europe, a loaf of bread costing 3.45NIS and litre of water 5NIS, for example. If you're renting a car then petrol, not the rental itself, will be your biggest expenditure as prices are around 7.10NIS per litre. Alcohol in bars and pubs is also expensive in Israel so you're best off opting for the perfectly good local Goldstar or Maccabee beers (22–25NIS for half a litre) than imported brands. Spirits are also pricey, and a single shot of Baileys will set you back 40NIS.

Many of Israel's top archaeological and natural sites are managed by the Israel Nature and National Parks Protection Authority who offer a 'Green Card' ticket that can save you huge amounts of money on entry. They can be purchased for 130NIS per person at any park ticket office and are valid for two weeks. Likewise, the Tel Aviv and Jerusalem city municipalities offer free guided tours around their cities which are a good and cost-effective way to dig deeper into the history and culture. Students and senior citizens can get discounts on entry to most sites of interest as well as on public transport (see the following section) by showing an international student card or identification respectively.

GETTING AROUND

Israel is wonderfully compact, making travel easy, affordable and free of draining, long-distance journeys. It is in fact possible to drive from Israel's northernmost point in the Golan Heights to the southernmost tip of Eilat on the Red Sea in about eight hours. While public transport is good in most urban regions, travelling around areas such as the Golan Heights and Negev and Arava deserts can be arduous and time-consuming without your own wheels, so renting a car is highly recommended to get the most out of your time in these beautiful, wild and remote regions. It is important to note that, with the exception of some services in Haifa (see page 155), none of Israel's public transport runs on Shabbat or religious holidays.

BY BUS Buses are the most commonly used form of public transport in Israel, and both inter- and intra-city networks are very developed. Egged provides the bulk of bus lines, although some areas have their own inter-city companies, such as Dan which serves Tel Aviv and surrounding urban areas. Conditions are good, and although inter-city buses can get crowded, all are air conditioned, clean and comfortable (in particular long-distance coaches for which seats need to be reserved). Tickets can be purchased either at ticket booths inside bus stations or from the driver. Discounts for students and senior citizens are available. Egged has recently translated its online timetable and it is now possible to search for routes, prices and bus numbers.

BY TRAIN Although bus travel still forms the core of public transport, Israel's train network is growing extremely quickly and, with massive rush-hour congestion problems around all main cities, it is becoming a very popular commuter option. Routes serve only main cities such as Tel Aviv, Haifa, Akko and Nahariya as well as connecting with Jerusalem, Ben Gurion Airport and Beer Sheva, but train services are particularly useful for those travelling up and down the Mediterranean coast and between Jerusalem and Tel Aviv (via the airport). Tickets can be purchased at either ticket booths or automated vending machines (also in English) at all train stations. Discounts for students and senior citizens are available. Israel Railways has complete schedules and ticket pricing (☏ 03 577 4000; www.rail.co.il/EN). A serious fire in December 2010 resulted in 100 people being taken to hospital and several trains being taken out of service, but things are again running normally.

BY METRO Israel's one and only underground system is located in Haifa, the country's third-largest city. Designed to help residents navigate the steep geography of the city, it has five stops running between Paris Square near the port and the

---

ISRAEL NATIONAL TRAIL

Stretching from Kibbutz Dan in the far north of the country to Eilat in the south, the Israel National Trail (Shvil Yisrael) was created to incorporate some of the most stunning natural landscapes, pristine countryside and national treasures that Israel has to offer. The entire trail is approximately 940km in length and winds its way through varied terrains with verdant, green hills rolling down to the Sea of Galilee, where the sandy Mediterranean coast sweeps through the metropolitan cities, which in turn explode into the vast, barren beauty of the Negev Desert. To undertake the entire trail takes seasoned hikers between 30 and 50 days, although cutting the Israel National Trail into bite-sized chunks is a more realistic choice and offers hikers the opportunity to experience some of the best sections. The trail is clearly marked by tri-colour markers (orange, blue and white) but good hiking maps are an essential piece of kit to have in your backpack before embarking on long sections. *Hike the Land of Israel* is a recently published English-language guide to hiking the trail and contains 67 topographical maps as well as places to stay, what to look for and a wealth of other information. It can be bought from major book and camping shops in Israel as well as online on sites such as Amazon (*www.amazon.co.uk*). There is currently a set of 16 maps that although in Hebrew are still usable to non-speakers, and which cost around US$20 each. There is a good forum on the official website which allows prospective hikers to chat to those who have walked the trail (*www.israelnationaltrail.com*).

In addition to this well-established hiking trail is the exciting new **Israel Bike Trail** that, with a similar idea in mind, traverses the country's varied lands from Mount Hermon in the Golan Heights to Eilat in the far south of the desert, covering 1,200km. It is already under way and due to be finished in 2013.

Central Carmel area (see page 155). Two metro systems are in their fledgling development phases in Tel Aviv and Jerusalem but it will be many years before they are fully functional.

BY TAXI All major towns and cities have large numbers of taxis which can be hailed from the street, telephoned for or found at taxi ranks. Rates start at 9.10NIS and an average inter-city ride costs around 20NIS. An additional 2.90NIS will be added for each suitcase and 3.50NIS if you telephone order. Rates increase by 25% during Shabbat and between 21.01 and 05.29. Taxi drivers almost always try and negotiate a price with foreigners and are reluctant to run the meter. Insist they use the meter or find another taxi. There is no need to tip taxi drivers although a rounding-up change is common.

Shared taxi (sherut) Shared taxis, known as *sherut*, run along the main intra- and inter-city bus routes and consist of small minibuses that generally only depart when full. Their appeal is that apart from being marginally cheaper, they can be stopped anywhere along the route and often run on Shabbat. The number of the bus route they correspond to is normally posted in the front window and fares are paid to the driver once the journey is under way (normally passed down the bus via the other passengers).

BY DOMESTIC FLIGHTS The country's diminutive size means that often internal flights are unnecessary and almost always more expensive than other forms of transport. Some companies do however offer special deals at certain times of the year so it is worth asking if you're pushed for time. It is really only worth flying between Eilat and Tel Aviv or Haifa. The following companies offer internal flights between Tel Aviv (Sde Dov and Ben Gurion airports) and Eilat and between Haifa and Eilat.

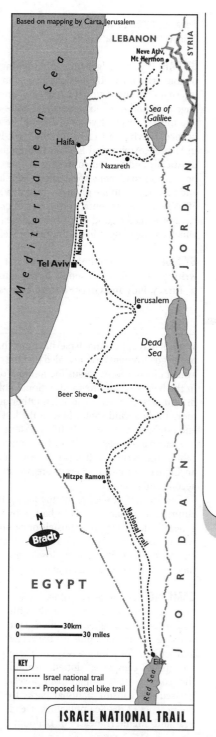

Based on mapping by Carta, Jerusalem

LEBANON

SYRIA

Neve Ativ, Mt Hermon

Sea of Galilee

Mediterranean Sea

Haifa

Nazareth

JORDAN

National Trail

Tel Aviv

Jerusalem

Dead Sea

Beer Sheva

Mitzpe Ramon

National Trail

EGYPT

N

Bradt

JORDAN

0 ⸻ 30km
0 ⸻ 30 miles

Eilat

Red Sea

KEY
······· Israel national trail
- - - - Proposed Israel bike trail

ISRAEL NATIONAL TRAIL

Practical Information GETTING AROUND

2

Arkia ☎ 03 6902222; www.arkia.co.il. Offer flights only between Eilat & Haifa.

Israir ☎ 03 7955777; www.israirairlines.com
El Al ☎ 03 9716111; www.elal.co.il

BY CAR If your budget runs to it, renting a car is the best way to get the most out of your trip to Israel, especially in regions where public transport is sparser. Most international and national rental companies have offices at Ben Gurion Airport (see page 112) and in major towns and cities (see the relevant chapters). To rent a car you must be over 21 years of age and be in possession of an international driving licence. Driving in Israel is on the right-hand side of the road and most signs are in Hebrew, Arabic and English (although the quality of English spelling can vary drastically and be a bit confusing at times, a classic example being Tzfat, which can be seen on road signs spelt Safed, Tsfat and Zefat). It is the law to wear seatbelts and talking on mobile phones whilst driving is strictly illegal and subject to fines of 500NIS (some car-rental companies offer hands-free sets). Carta (*www.carta.co.il*) have produced a good English-language road map designed especially for tourists which can be bought in any branch of Steimatsky bookshops or from their website.

BY SEA Israel's ferry links are sadly not what they used to be and at the time of writing there are no passenger ferries into and out of Israel, but it is possible to get to Turkey, Italy and Greece aboard cruises that depart from Haifa (see page 151).

ACCOMMODATION

While it may appear that Israel has more than its fair share of hotels, statistics released by the government have revealed that the country is close to bursting with respect to availability of rooms versus the number of visitors. Needless to say, booking ahead in the height of summer and national holidays is highly recommended, especially in Jerusalem, Tel Aviv and Eilat. Other areas are slightly less pressured so you are more likely to find somewhere at the last minute. In general, however, the higher-end establishments seem to fill up fastest.

Israel has a sweeping array of accommodation types, and although luxury hotels, cabins and resorts still form the vast majority of accommodation options, with an increase in backpackers there are slowly appearing more hostels and budget accommodation.

One of the greatest problems facing travellers is the policy held by almost all zimmers and many hotels to have a two-night minimum stay on weekends (this generally doesn't apply to hostels or campsites). It is worth taking this into account when making travel plans. Having said that, there is no public transport on Shabbat and services and attractions close early or don't open at all, so settling somewhere nice for the weekend is a good idea.

CAMPING Camping is an extremely popular activity in Israel, both with youngsters and families who pitch giant tents, set up the compulsory barbecue and settle in for a long weekend. There are many campsites dotted around the country that range from lovely grassed areas inside national parks to the beaches of the Sea of Galilee, Dead Sea and Mediterranean to Bedouin-

HOTEL PRICE CODES	
Price of a double room per night in high season:	
$$$$$	801NIS +
$$$$	601–800NIS
$$$	351–600NIS
$$	201–350NIS
$	0–200NIS

style encampments in the desert. Some beaches, particularly in Eilat and along the Mediterranean where turtles nest, do not allow camping, but these will be signposted. While Israelis love being pampered, they are essentially outdoor types and all big towns and cities have camping shops aplenty and equipment is easy to come across (although expensive). Safety issues arise when pitching tents outside designated campsites, which while it is possible and legal, needs to be approached with caution. Beware of army training zones (in the desert and Golan Heights) and minefields (in the Golan Heights), which pose obvious dangers. Rabies and poisonous snakes exist in Israel, which are important safety considerations when camping.

HOSTELS For many years hostels and decent budget accommodation were extremely limited, but in recent years an increase in the number of foreign backpackers and budget travellers has resulted in countless new hostels being opened. Israel's hostels can be divided into those belonging to Hostelling International (HI) (*1 599510511; www.iyha.org.il*) and privately run establishments. HI hostels can be somewhat sterile and attract large groups of teenagers on organised trips but do offer good value for money and are undoubtedly clean. A 50NIS membership card needs to be purchased from any hostel or the HI website to be able to stay. Private hostels are more hit and miss but on the whole are full of character, reasonably priced and friendly. ILH Israel Hostels (*www.hostels-israel.com*) is a group of 30 independent hostels dotted around the country that offers great budget accommodation, a great ambience and host of other facilities.

ZIMMER Israel has, over recent years, been overtaken by zimmer fever. The zimmer (based on the German word for room and pronounced 'tzimeh') is essentially a luxury rural cabin built in the owner's back garden or on their land. There are quite literally thousands of them found in every part of the country and while some can be slightly questionable, most are beautifully decorated, set in stunning locations and run by friendly owners as a little side earner. One of the main features is the jacuzzi baths and no self-respecting Israeli would pay for one without such a feature. Prices can range between 400NIS per night for a standard zimmer up to 800NIS (or more) for something more luxurious during peak season. It is important to note that prices quoted in this guide are based on weekend rates, which during the week are up to 200NIS less per night.

HOTELS Hotel standards in Israel are high and most major international chains are represented. National chains such as Fattal, Dan and Isrotel also have numerous high-quality hotels dotted around the country, while the European chain Leonardo has opened or taken over dozens of hotels in the last couple of years. In addition, spa resorts have become big business in the Holy Land, especially along the Dead Sea, as well as 'boutique hotels' found mainly in Tel Aviv that blend modern Art Deco with classy (if sometimes a little pretentious) service.

✕ EATING AND DRINKING

FOOD With such a diverse population, there is not really such a thing as 'Israeli food'. Culinary styles have blended together from all across the world to leave a rather eclectic mix of cuisines. Apart from the insuppressibly popular Middle Eastern fast foods such as hummus and falafel (see box, page 55), both kosher and non-kosher restaurants are well and equally represented. Tel Aviv is undoubtedly the culinary centre of the country, and is home to the bulk of non-kosher restaurants. Seafood, fish and French-style gourmet are found alongside traditional Indian food, steakhouses and Japanese sushi bars. That isn't to say that Jerusalem doesn't offer good food, as it most certainly does. While it may be considered a little more conservative than experimental, secular Tel Aviv, it has a wonderful mixture of cuisines,

including some creative vegetarian places. Haifa too has benefited from its varied population and offers a wealth of great eateries. For rustic country food, juicy, succulent steaks and age-old, traditional Druze dishes the wilds of the Golan Heights, with its cattle ranches, farming communities and sweeping lands, is the best bet, while Eilat offers the complete opposite with themed restaurants and beach bars. The website www.restaurants-in-israel.co.il often has vouchers and discounts for many restaurants throughout the country so it is worth checking beforehand.

DRINKS Israelis love their coffee so you will find cafés in the most unlikely of places. Apart from the European brews, be sure to try the strong, aromatic Arabic coffee that is hugely popular in Israel. A word of warning, however: avoid drinking the entire contents of the cup as a thick layer of coffee sediment sits at the bottom, which is rather unpleasant to swallow. In the height of the sweaty summer fruit-juice bars will freshly squeeze you your own fruity concoction and most kiosks sell inexpensive, creamy iced coffee. While Israelis aren't particularly big drinkers they love the whole bar scene and most alcohols are represented. The local beers are Goldstar and the more famous but less popular Maccabee, which are both more than respectable.

KOSHER When asked the reason behind kosher laws most Jews will reply that it is for health issues. While several of the laws do indeed seem to have positive health effects, there are others that do not appear to have relevance. In fact, the reason behind kosher laws (or *kashrut*) is that the Torah says it should be so. It doesn't however elaborate as to reasons why these laws were put in place, but for devout Jews there doesn't need to be. Kosher is upheld to varying levels of strictness in Israel, the secular barely abiding by it all, or simply eliminating pork from their diet. There is no law in Israel that restaurants need to be kosher and as such a large proportion of those in secular cities such as Tel Aviv choose the 'not' option. While seafood and meat and dairy dishes are widely available on non-kosher menus, pork is the lasting taboo and doesn't often feature in Israel.

General rules
- Certain animals cannot be eaten. Of mammals, only those that chew their cud and have cloven hooves are considered kosher. Pigs, camels and rabbits are not kosher. Marine life must have fins and scales, therefore shellfish is not *kashrut*. The Torah mentions only birds of prey as not being edible along with rodents, reptiles, amphibians and insects.
- Of permitted animals, they must be slaughtered in accordance with *kashrut* (the laws of kosher). This includes not consuming animals that have died of natural causes.

MCFALAFEL – FAST FOOD, MIDDLE EASTERN STYLE

Israel is a virtual casserole dish of cultures, traditions, culinary styles, religions and nationalities yet if you were to pinpoint the single unifying ingredient, one that has become the unofficial national symbol of the country, it would undoubtedly be the modest chickpea, or more specifically hummus and falafel. Israelis eat these two inexpensive, fast food-style dishes by the bucket load and there is unlikely to be a fridge in the country that doesn't have an emergency pot of hummus inside. The good news for visitors is that the country's cheapest food is also some of its best and no trip would be complete without several helpings of creamy hummus, puffy pitta, moist falafel, crunchy salad, crisp aubergine, roasted lamb or seasoned goat's cheese. Below is a guide to the best of Israel's fast-food dishes:

HUMMUS A thick, creamy mixture of chickpeas, tahini, oil, lemon juice and garlic served with pitta. It can be eaten hot or cold, lumpy or smooth, and with a variety of toppings.

FALAFEL Ground, spiced chickpea balls deep-fried and served piping hot in fresh pitta with hummus, tahini and a selection of salads.

SABICH Believed to have come to Israel with Iraqi Jews it is a big favourite, more so in Israel than any other Middle Eastern country. Pitta is stuffed with fried aubergine, a hard-boiled egg, hummus, tahini and a variety of salads.

SHAWARMA Known in other countries as doner kebab, gyros and a whole host of other names, it consists of slow-roasted, spiced lamb on a large skewer, finely sliced and eaten in pitta with a choice of sauces and salads.

BUREKAS AND SAMBUSAK Thin pastry parcels stuffed with a variety of fillings such as spinach, potato, cheese, mushroom or meat. *Sambusak* are in effect big *burekas*.

LABANE Soured, creamed, goat's cheese usually eaten by scooping with pitta alongside salad, hummus and chips.

TAHINI A thick sauce made from sesame seeds that is a crucial ingredient of hummus. It can also be eaten on its own with pitta.

SHAKSHOOKA While not exactly considered fast food, this cheap, filling dish is a big Israeli favourite and was brought to the country by Sephardic Jews from north Africa. It involves a big mash of eggs, tomatoes, onions, green and red peppers and garlic cooked in a frying pan and eaten by scooping it onto bread.

- No blood of any animal must be consumed. Slaughtered animals must be drained of blood so as to ensure none of the animal's spirit is left.
- Certain parts of an animal may not be eaten including certain fats and nerves.
- Meat and dairy must be separated. Not only can they not be eaten together but they cannot be cooked or come into any contact with each other. A time period of three to six hours must elapse between consuming the two foods.

2

- Cooking utensils must be kept kosher. This involves reserving one set for cooking with dairy ingredients and another for preparing meat. Kitchen work surfaces, towels and even dishwashers are included in this rule.
- Wine must be made only by Shabbat-observant male Jews and all preparatory instruments must be kept kosher.

SHOPPING

One of the favourite Israeli pastimes is shopping, and more specifically shopping in malls. In fact, Israel has one of the highest mall-to-population ratios in the world. Malls and high-street shops are comparable to any western European country and you can find pretty much anything you can at home, with many major international brands represented, particularly in Jerusalem and Tel Aviv. For many tourists however, the vibrant markets are one of the main shopping appeals, where bargaining, noise, hustle and bustle and Middle Eastern charm are the main draws.

MEDIA AND COMMUNICATIONS

POST The Israel Post Office has several branches in all major cities and towns which are denoted by their red sign with the white logo of a gazelle inside. While branches do differ slightly, most are open 08.00–12.00 and 15.30–18.30 Sunday, Tuesday and Thursday, 08.30–12.30 Wednesday and 08.00–12.00 Friday (the last includes the eve of holidays). Postal services include express, registered mail and EMS. EMS is a quick, international service that allows for tracking of parcels and includes insurance. All post offices in Israel offer a poste restante service to tourists for up to three months. They will hold post for up to 30 days and identification needs to be shown to collect mail.

TELEPHONE Telephone connections in Israel are reliable, convenient and modern, and international calls can be made with ease. Most hotel rooms come with direct-dial telephones, but be aware that prices can be grossly over-inflated. Public phones can be found widely distributed in towns and cities and operate with telephone cards that can be purchased in post offices, kiosks and supermarkets. Alternatively, many kiosks offer coin-operated phones or pay after you use-style phones, but these are normally more expensive than the pre-paid cards. Mobile phones are big business in Israel and you are unlikely to find an Israeli, young or old, who doesn't have one. Indeed, there are more phones per capita in Israel than anywhere else in the world. Pelephone, Cellcom and Orange mobile phone companies will rent you phones for the duration of your stay (their rental offices are located in the airport). Expect to pay around US$0.65 per day for rental and US$0.24–0.33 per minute for calls locally and to North America and western Europe.

Most phone numbers include an area code (02 for Jerusalem or 03 for Tel Aviv, for example) but there is also a smaller telephone company called Hot that issues numbers that don't require a code (Hot is also the main internet and cable television provider in the country). All telephone numbers in this guide are supplied with their code if necessary – if there is no code listed then there is no need to add one.

INTERNET AND FAX Most businesses and homes are connected to the internet and as such internet cafés are fairly easy to find, offering inexpensive, fast connection (you will pay more for fancy cafés offering drinks and snacks so if it's just the internet you're after look for somewhere less glitzy as it will certainly cost less). In more rural areas internet connection is generally limited to hotels. Faxes can be sent from post offices, hotels or internet cafés for the price of an international call.

MEDIA In a country with such a tumultuous existence it is perhaps unsurprising that most Israelis are fanatical about reading, watching, listening to and talking about current affairs and the news. Because of the country's wide-ranging cultural and linguistic differences, television and newspapers offer a plethora of languages and topics to suit the eclectic mix of the population. There are currently seven daily **newspapers** published in Hebrew, the one with the highest circulation being *Yediot Aharanot* (Latest News), with approximately two-thirds of all newspaper readers in the country, closely followed by *Israel HaYom* (Israel Today). *Ha'aretz*, which is also published in English, is the country's oldest daily, founded in 1919, and it enjoys a wide circulation. In addition there are several publications printed in Russian and French as well as the internationally renowned *Jerusalem Post* (formerly the *Palestine Post*), which is published in English in Israel and North America, and French in western Europe. *Al-Ittihad* (The Union) is the main Arabic-language daily and there are also several periodicals.

Despite the sweeping popularity of cable **television**, which has found its way into approximately 70% of Israeli homes, the three Israeli television channels (Channels 1, 2 and 10) still enjoy high viewing figures and cover a wide range of topics from news broadcasts to entertainment to Arabic- and English-language programmes, from Latin American soap operas to children's programmes and live sporting events. Likewise, **radio** is an integral part of Israeli life and Kol Yisrael (Voice of Israel) is responsible for eight stations, broadcasting in countless languages and covering a wide range of genres. One of the most popular stations is Gal Galatz, a predominantly music and news headline station run and hosted by the IDF.

While freedom of the press is an important institution in Israel, military censorship is in place that deals with stories considered a threat to national security, and some stories undergo governmental screening before release.

BUYING PROPERTY

The religious significance of land in Israel, combined with a rapidly growing economy, has seen a large demand for land acquisition. Indeed, when many countries were suffering a huge economic crisis, apartment prices in Israel went up by 5% in 2009. The majority of opportunities for property purchase tend to be new constructions, as families often live in the same house for their lifetime and pass it on to children. This is especially the case in the pretty *moshavim* (see page 4) where property rarely comes on the market.

When buying property in Israel expect to pay around 8% in fees divided into 2% commission (which the buyer and seller both have to pay), 1% lawyer's fees and purchase tax of 3.5–4.5%. Foreign non-residents can apply for mortgages, 60% being the norm for resale properties and up to 80% on new constructions. It is important to note that advertised homes are described on the basis of number of rooms, which includes bedrooms and living rooms, and areas are expressed in dunams, one dunam being equivalent to 1,000m^2.

CULTURAL ETIQUETTE

With such a diverse population it is unsurprising that customs and etiquette are also hugely diverse within Israel. Most customs arise from religious significance but within secular society there is no strict etiquette and Israelis are, for the most part, well travelled and knowledgeable of others' customs and cultures. The following points will help you understand the culture of the country and be respectful towards its residents:

- **Greetings** Handshakes are common, although observant male Jews are not permitted to touch women; men should wait for a hand to be extended to ensure no awkward situations. *Shalom* is the usual greeting, although on Shabbat *Shabbat Shalom* is used.
- **Communication** Israelis can be very loud, direct and to the point, which other nationalities can occasionally interpret as rude or aggressive. It almost always isn't intended that way and they will appreciate honesty and directness. Touching on the arm is common and a sign of friendliness, and the use of hands and hand gestures is a major part of communication.
- **Men and women** With the exception of religiously observant communities, men and women have equal rights in Israel and women hold equal roles in government, the IDF and business. Religiously observant women rarely work outside of the home.
- **Taboos** Within the Muslim culture it is offensive to show the sole of your foot. The left hand is considered unclean so only shake hands or eat with your right hand. Dressing appropriately in religious neighbourhoods and sites (see page 47) is important and strictly adhered to.

BUSINESS ETIQUETTE

Israel's business etiquette can be described as casual and relaxed. Meetings are often held over food and involve a lot of chatting beforehand to get to know one another. Dress is usually casual, trousers and shirt for men, and a suit or blouse and skirt for women. Ties and suits are worn only in formal situations. If engaging in business with observant Jews, women are best advised to wear less revealing attire. Most business people speak English, first names are used, and Israeli hosts often like to take their clients or guests on a short tour of the country or at least Jerusalem.

As Hebrew is read right to left, books, leaflets or folders will also open in reverse (from the back cover). The working week is from Sunday to Thursday, although many businesses will open Friday morning. Shabbat (see page 35) which runs from Friday sunset to Saturday sunset is observed broadly depending on the level of religious adherence, but no business will occur during that time. In Muslim communities the holy day is all of Friday.

TRAVELLING POSITIVELY

SUSTAINABLE TRAVEL AND ECOTOURISM In a world that is seeing a huge boom in all things 'eco', where green travel and responsible holidays are a growing trend, Israel stands as one of the foremost countries in this arena. For decades schemes and projects have been in place to return the land to its former, pre-Ottoman glory and natural abundance. Today this cascades from the higher echelons of government, through the Israel Nature and National Parks Authority and their ongoing conservation efforts down to the tiny kibbutzim and moshavim that dot the countryside and which are embracing organic farming, recycling projects and a communal way of life. Israel is fast becoming one of the most popular, genuine eco-vacation spots in the world (*www.ecotourism.org.il*).

The rural regions are undoubtedly the most ecologically aware, and tourism infrastructure, both for Israelis and foreigners, is plentiful. The wild desert lands, Galilee and the Golan Heights play the most pivotal roles, and small, family-run ecological cabins have become a super-trend across rural Israel, where organic food is served and horseriding and hiking opportunities are plentiful. In the deserts, several kibbutzim including Lotan (see page 278), Yahel and Ketura practise sustainable living, farming and building practices as well as offering workshops, guest accommodation, meditation and massage. Likewise, the eco-lodges that dot the desert lands (see *Negev* and *Arava* chapters) have been created from organic, locally sourced materials and aim to enlighten visitors about the fruits of the desert and how to live sustainably. Even in big cities, giant hotel chains are subject to strict environmental policies and engage in the use of solar power, low-flush toilets, grey water and recycling programmes. In 2010, the Israel Ministry of Tourism launched the '100 Years of Green' campaign (*travelgreenisrael. com*), which aims to promote this unique side of Israel, including activities from hiking to cycling to rafting and horse- and camel-trekking. Indeed, thanks to efforts by the Keren Keyemet L'Israel (KKL) – the Jewish National Fund – the Israel National Trail (see page 50) is soon to have a cycling version running the entire length of the country.

The infrastructure is in place, the knowledge is there and the potential enormous to make Israel a true example of sustainable travel, from luxury to budget trips. The author urges you to take full advantage of these resources, to consider your options and select carefully, and to make your trip count both personally and environmentally. Tell others of your experiences, suggest ideas to hostel and restaurant owners and let them, and the tourism bureau, know what you enjoyed or would have preferred on your trip to help them in future endeavours.

CHARITIES

Meir Panim (*www.meirpanim.org*) Israel's ongoing conflict, political problems and the cost of supporting the IDF has led to government cuts in social welfare, payments, health and education: and as such the lowest-paid and unemployed members of society suffer most. Meir Panim is a national organisation dedicated to providing a range of welfare care including food handouts, free kitchens, meals on wheels to elderly members of the community, youth clubs, vocational training, homes for abused women and centres for the elderly. Volunteers are always needed, to help prepare and hand out food at the 30 free restaurants dotted around the country, as are donations.

Cat Welfare Society of Israel (*www.cats.org.il*) Feral street cats are a major problem in Israel's cities and their numbers increase exponentially every year. The CWSI is one of the biggest animal welfare institutions in the country committed to educating people, rescuing, neutering and caring for feral or unwanted cats. In 2004, during Israel's disengagement from Gaza and parts of the West Bank, thousands of street cats that survived on handouts or scavenging in rubbish bins were left as Jewish settlers moved out. The CWSI lobbied the government for access to the Gaza Strip and went in to capture hundreds of animals. Today they reside in a shelter in Hadera, and as most cannot be re-homed, will remain cared for there. Visitors can volunteer their time at the shelter, raise awareness in their home countries, donate blankets and equipment or sponsor a cat for US$25 per month. They also have an internet shop where you can buy a 'I helped save a Holy Cat!' T-shirt.

Safe Haven for Donkeys (*www.safehaven4donkeys.org*) In many rural areas of Israel working donkeys are still very much a part of life. Yet because of their cheap purchase price, those that get sick or old are just left abandoned, many to suffer considerably. British-born Lucy Fensom arrived in Israel many years ago and vowed to do something to help these 'beasts of burden'. Today she runs an enormous shelter for abused and abandoned donkeys that is home to over 100 animals. The enormous costs of running the shelter, located between Netanya and Hadera, are difficult to maintain and donations are always needed.

Part Two

THE GUIDE

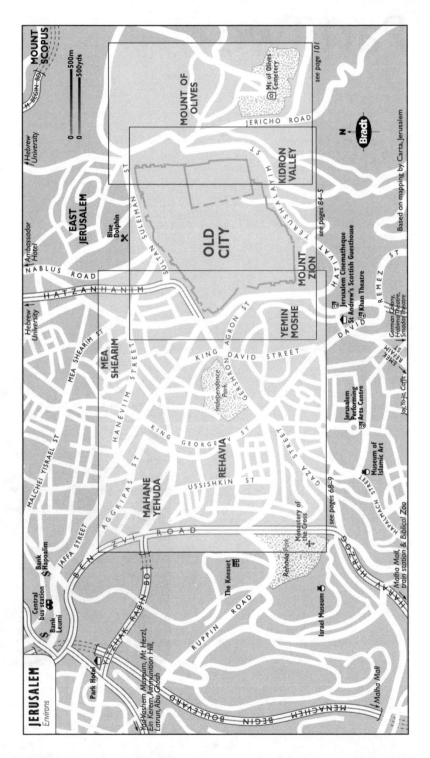

JERUSALEM
Environs

MOUNT SCOPUS

MOUNT OF OLIVES

Mt of Olives Cemetery

see page 101

JERICHO ROAD

KIDRON VALLEY

see pages 84–5

OLD CITY

MOUNT ZION

EAST JERUSALEM

Blue Dolphin ✕

Ambassador Hotel

NABLUS ROAD

Hebrew University

Hebrew University

HATZANHANIM

SULTAN SULEIMAN ST

YERUSHALAYIM ST

MEA SHEARIM

MEA SHEARIM ST

HANEVIIM STREET

HANEVIIM ST

MALCHEI YISRAEL ST

AGGRIPAS STREET

Bank Hapoalim $

Central bus station

$ Bank Leumi

Park Hotel

JAFFA STREET

BEN ZVI ROAD

YIZHAK RABIN BD

MENACHEM BEGIN BOULEVARD

HERZL

HATAYASIM HERZOG

RUPPIN ROAD

The Knesset 🏛

Israel Museum 🏛

Rehavia Park

Monastery of the Cross ✝

see pages 68–9

MAHANE YEHUDA

REHAVIA

USSISHKIN ST

KING GEORGE STREET

GERSHON AGRON ST

KING DAVID STREET

GAZA STREET

HATAMACH STREET

Independence Park

YEMIN MOSHE

Jerusalem Cinematheque 🎬

St Andrew's Scottish Guesthouse

Khan Theatre

DAVID REMEZ ST

Museum of Islamic Art 🏛

Jerusalem Performing Arts Centre 🎭

German Colony; Habima Theatre; Smadar Theatre

EMEK REFAIM ST

Joy, Yo-ja, Coffit →

HATIVAT YERUSHALAYIM

Malha Mall, train station & Biblical Zoo →

Yad Vashem Museum, Mt Herzl, Ein Kerem, Ammunition Hill, Latrun, Abu Ghosh →

Malha Mall →

N

Bradt

500m
500yds
0
0

Based on mapping by Carta, Jerusalem

3

Jerusalem

Telephone code 02

As the sun sets over Jerusalem's white-stone buildings, it is impossible to imagine the millions of people who have stood and witnessed the very same event. For centuries Jerusalem has stood as the single most revered, contested and loved city in the world. Its many different inhabitants have given it a cultural and religious make-up like no other place on earth, a place pilgrims flock to and residents defend to the bitter end. To define the city is impossible, as it is above all else a city of contrasts. A city where Judaism, Christianity and Islam meet; where ancient neighbourhoods tumble into shiny new ones; where both the devout and the secular find their own place; and where modern and traditional somehow flourish together.

At its core sits the Old City, a remarkable and awe-inspiring area that has come to define the Holy Land's capital. Yet despite its historic, archaeological and religious treasures, its centuries of turmoil and conflict, and its political tensions, Jerusalem is first and foremost a vibrant, living city. Outside its walls, Jerusalem is a mesh of modern neighbourhoods, efficient transport networks, bustling souks, world-famous museums and high-class universities. Jewish Orthodox, secular and Arabic neighbourhoods each maintain their own traditions, for the most part respecting each other's day-to-day lives.

Visitors to the city find they leave changed. For the spiritually minded, the almost overwhelming wealth of holy sites is humbling and moving, while the more religiously apathetic find themselves stirred. A history that seemed so distant is now as real as the present. For Jerusalem has always marked the final battle for the land, a fact that remains as true today as it did thousands of years ago. The stumbling block over which peace negotiations fall, Jerusalem sits unwittingly in the midst of an international drama, the world watching every move out of the corner of its eye. Yet for those who live there, and for those who get the chance to visit, the tensions and turmoil are put to the back of the mind as they witness first hand the reasons so many want to call it home.

HISTORY

THE CANAANITES AND THE ISRAELITES Although evidence points to occupation in the Stone Age, by c4000BCE the more technologically advanced Canaanites had taken over the area we now know as Jerusalem. In the 15th century the Egyptians conquered, ruling until the Israelites took control of the region in 1250BCE. While they managed to capture most of the realm, the fortified Jerusalem didn't fall for another 200 years. During this time David was declared the first King of Israel and in 1004BCE he finally stormed the city, declaring it capital of his kingdom and renaming it the City of David.

THE FIRST TEMPLE PERIOD (1006–586BCE) Following David's conquest, the city soon became the political, religious and cultural centre of the kingdom. He constructed a great palace, installing in it the sacred Ark of the Covenant. The construction of the First Temple is attributed to Solomon, David's son, who at the same time enlarged the city. Soon after Solomon's death the kingdom split in two, the northern Kingdom of Israel forming a new capital, while the southern Kingdom of Judah retained Jerusalem as its centre. In 586BCE, however, Jerusalem fell to the Babylonians who exiled the Jews and destroyed the temple.

THE SECOND TEMPLE PERIOD (536BCE–70CE) Shortly afterwards, the Persians came to rule and the Jews were once more allowed to return. During the following years they constructed the Second Temple and reignited the religious and spiritual fervour that had been flourishing before the Babylonian incursion. When Alexander the Great conquered the Persian Empire and, in 333BCE Jerusalem with it, the city entered a period of Greek and Hellenic cultural influence. Upon Alexander's death a fervent battle for the great city took place, the Syrian ruler Antiochus IV emerging as victor and installing Seleucid rule over the land. Subjugation of the Jews and the destruction of the Second Temple instigated a great revolt under the leadership of the Maccabees, a Jewish family of patriots. This in turn led to the establishment of the Hasmoneans, who eventually ousted the Seleucids, beginning an 80-year period of Jewish independence.

THE ROMANS AND THE HERODIAN ERA (63BCE–96CE) In 63BCE, Roman general Pompeii conquered Jerusalem and in 37BCE Herod ascended the throne. His reign saw the city expand northwards and a massive phase of building get under way. Herod constructed the second wall of the temple, today part of which is the Western Wall. He is also attributed with giving the temple a magnificent makeover and constructing the Antonia Fortress, Citadel, numerous palaces, markets, a theatre and a hippodrome.

It was during this time that Jesus of Nazareth was also active. After gathering support and naming his Apostles in the Galilee, Jesus made his way to Jerusalem where, according to the New Testament, he was tried and crucified by Pontius Pilate as a threat to Roman rule and religious order for his increasing numbers of followers. Herod's death and the subsequent iron-fisted rule of the Romans led to a Jewish revolt, which ended in Roman victory. The Jewish residents were once again expelled, the Second Temple destroyed and Jerusalem burnt to the ground.

THE ROMAN BYZANTINE PERIOD (135–638CE) In 135CE, Emperor Hadrian named his new conquest Aelia Capitolina, a new city layout was installed (the main streets of which still form the central cross-section through the Old City), Roman buildings mushroomed, paganism prevailed, Jerusalem became a backwater city and Jews and early Christians were forbidden to enter. Until, that is, Constantine assumed power in 303CE. Constantine was the first Roman ruler (by this time Byzantine after the break-up of the western Roman Empire) to be converted to Christianity, and throughout his rule Jerusalem exploded on to the scene as a pilgrimage destination, hundreds of churches, including the Church of the Holy Sepulchre, owing their origins to this time. Over the next three centuries Christianity became the official religion of the Byzantine Empire, marking a crucial chapter in Jerusalem's history. In 614, Jerusalem fell to the Persians who massacred the city's inhabitants and decimated many of the holy sites. Although the Emperor Herclius managed to reclaim the city six years later, it was not to last and Jerusalem fell once again, this time to the rising force of the Arab Islamic Empire.

THE EARLY MUSLIM PERIOD (638–1099) In 638, Jerusalem came under Muslim rule following Calpih Omar's conquest of the kingdom. Although the Koran does not mention Jerusalem by name, the Hadith (a collection of sayings and traditions of Muhammad) specifies that it was from here that the Prophet ascended to Heaven in the Night Journey. The conquest was bloodless and Christians and Jews were granted permission to continue practising their faiths unhindered. By the end of the 7th century Jerusalem was recognised as the third holiest site in Islam (after Mecca and Medina) and, shortly afterwards, Abd Al-Malik built the Dome of the Rock above the stone said to be both where Muhammad ascended to Heaven, and the site of the former First and Second Temples. A short distance away the grand Al-Aqsa Mosque was also built.

THE CRUSADES AND SALADIN (1099–1250) In the 11th century the city came under the harsh rule of the Turkish Seljuks, an event that saw Pope Urban II call for the Crusades. Led by Godfrey of Bouillon, European Christians travelled to Jerusalem with the aim of liberating it from Islamic control. In 1099, they captured the city, naming it the capital of the Latin Kingdom of Jerusalem. It was a vicious and bloody conquest and most of Jerusalem's Jewish and Muslim residents were slaughtered. Jerusalem entered a new cultural phase whereby European customs and language became commonplace and where Christianity prevailed. Churches were restored and the holy sites on the Temple Mount (see page 94) became Christian, the Knights Templar (an order of monastic knights) installing their headquarters there. Even though the Kingdom of Jerusalem lasted until 1291, the capital fell to Saladin, a powerful Islamic hero, in 1187. Saladin allowed worship by all religions and during this time many exiled Jews returned. Despite attempts by Richard the Lionheart to recapture the city in the Third Crusade, it remained under Saladin's control until the Mamluk conquest in 1260.

THE MAMLUKS AND OTTOMANS (1250–1917) A somewhat peripheral city, Jerusalem fell into a period of decline and poverty. A respite from the dire situation was offered when the city was incorporated into the Ottoman Empire and Sultan Suleiman took the reins. Under his rule the great Old City walls were erected along with gates and an aqueduct. Following his death however, things took a turn for the worse and the succeeding 300 years are seen as a dark era in Jerusalem's past. Poverty, neglect and a static population blighted the once great city and it wasn't until exiled Jews fled to the land in the 15th and 16th centuries that things began to improve. By the 19th century, as the Ottoman Empire weakened, Jerusalem was taking on a more Europeanised outlook. Foreign consulates were established, trade links flourished, the population grew rapidly and neighbourhoods burst out of the Old City walls. The population at the time was divided into four major communities: Jewish, Christian, Muslim and Armenian, each concentrated around its respective religious shrine.

THE BRITISH MANDATE, THE ARAB–ISRAELI WAR AND A CITY DIVIDED (1917– 1948) Towards the end of World War I and the collapse of the Ottoman Empire, Jerusalem surrendered to British forces and on 11 December 1917 General Allenby marched through Jaffa Gate as a sign of respect to the holy city. By this time the patchwork of cultures and religions dotted across the Old and New cities had expanded considerably, but was lacking any sort of planning. With the advent of the 1922 mandate granted to the British by the League of Nations, they set about developing plans for its growth. The use of the white sandstone façades that are today one of the city's most endearing features was made law, while buildings such as the Hadassah Medical Centre, Hebrew University, King David Hotel and Jewish Agency headquarters owe their origins to this period. Yet as the city expanded, the separation between Jews and Palestinian Arabs once observed in the Old City again began to materialise. The struggle for religious and political control escalated and tensions heightened. This culminated in the 1920s riots and the Arab Revolt of 1936–39. Following the departure of the British (and the dissolution of the Partition Plan), Israel declared independence on 14 May 1948. Less than 24 hours later, neighbouring Arab nations invaded the fledgling country and so ensued the 1948 Arab–Israeli War. The end of the war found the city divided: Jordan had control of East Jerusalem and the Old City, Israel of West Jerusalem. From this time until the Six Day War in 1967, fences and land mines separated the two halves of the city.

A UNITED CITY OF DIVIDED PEOPLE The 1967 Six Day War saw Israel capture the Jordanian-controlled half of Jerusalem and in 1980 the Knesset officially declared the united city its capital, a declaration highly contested by the UN and international community to this day. The Moroccan area of the Old City was demolished, and in its place the Western Wall Plaza was built. The Waqf (the Supreme Muslim Religious Council) was granted administration of the Temple Mount and Jews forbidden (both by Israel and the Waqf) from praying there. Over time clear divisions appeared between West and East Jerusalem, both culturally and economically. Money was poured into West Jerusalem and the Old City given a makeover, yet East Jerusalem, now populated by almost equal numbers of Jews and Arabs, was suffering. To this day the UN and much of the international community do not recognise the annexation of East Jerusalem (and the West Bank and Gaza Strip) and nearly all countries maintain embassies in Tel Aviv.

JERUSALEM TODAY Under Israeli control, members of most religions are granted access to their holy sites, the exceptions being those Palestinians living in the West Bank and Gaza Strip. Jews are also forbidden to pray or study inside the Temple Mount although entrance is permitted. Inside this fragile and highly sensitive city, where political and religious tensions are on a knife-edge, conflicts do arise. Events such as the arson attack on the Al-Aqsa Mosque in 1969 by a Christian fundamentalist; rioting following the digging of an exit to the Western Wall tunnels in the Muslim Quarter; Jewish opposition to the Waqf's excavations inside the Temple Mount, and the igniting of the second intifada by Ariel Sharon's visit to the Islamic holy site in 2000 being but some examples. Jerusalem has always been the stumbling block over which any form of peace negotiations break: Israel lays claim to the entire city; the Palestinians to at least the eastern half including the Old City. As the conflict continues with little sign of a solution on the horizon, it must be said that for travellers, the Old City at least displays a remarkable aura of calm. While this cannot be classified as unity, day-to-day tolerance of one another is a good enough step for now.

GETTING THERE AND AWAY

BY BUS AND SHARED TAXI (SHERUT) Jerusalem's **central bus station** (*Jaffa St;* 5304704; ⊕ *06.00–21.30 Sun–Thu, 06.15–15.45 Fri*) has buses running all over the country.

BY TRAIN The **Jerusalem Malha train station** (*Yitzhak Moda'i;* 5770/03 6117000; *www.rail.co.il*) is located in the southwest of the city near the Jerusalem Malha

ROUTES TO AND FROM JERUSALEM CENTRAL BUS STATION

To	Frequency	Bus number	Duration	Price
Tel Aviv	20mins	405	1hr	20NIS
Haifa	30mins	947/940	2hrs	45NIS
Tiberias	hourly	961/962/963	3hrs	48NIS
Nazareth	16.00/18.00	955	2hrs 25mins	48NIS
Kiryat Shmona	06.30/10.30/ 13.30/23.30	963	4hrs	63NIS
Beer Sheva	20mins	446/470	2hrs	32.5NIS
Ein Gedi (Dead Sea)	9 daily	486/421/487	1hr 20mins	37NIS
Ben Gurion Airport	30mins	947+train	30mins	23NIS+5.3NIS for train
Eilat	07.00/10.00 14.00/17.00	444	5hrs	75NIS
Katzrin	08.15/17.15	966	4hrs	59NIS

Mall. Western Israel's train network is still in its fledgling stage and you therefore need to change once in Beit Shemesh on the way from Tel Aviv's Hahagana train station. Trains depart hourly (1hr 30mins/21.5NIS). There is also a station at the Biblical Zoo, a few minutes from the main station. Buses 4, 5, 6, 18, 24 and 160 stop outside.

BY AIR Jerusalem is one of the few capital cities in the world that hasn't got its own international airport. That said, Tel Aviv's Ben Gurion Airport (see page 112) is located in between the two cities and can be accessed easily from the capital (approximately 30mins) by car or a combination of bus and train (change to the train at El Al Junction).

GETTING AROUND

BY BUS The Holy City has yet to see underground trains, trams or metros, so buses connect Jerusalem's mountainous, higgledy-piggledy neighbourhoods quite efficiently. A one-way ticket to anywhere costs 5.30NIS. Useful bus routes are as follows:

- **#1 & #1a** Run from the central bus station along Sarei Yisrael, down Malchei Yisrael and past Mea Shearim before running clockwise around the walls of the Old City and returning to the central bus station.
- **#4 & #4a** Run from Malha along Yohanan Ben Zakai, Emek Refa'im in the German Colony and on to King David where it then proceeds to Keren Hayesod, King George V, Nathan Strauss, Yehezkel and then continues to French Hill. The 4a continues to Mount Scopus.
- **#6** Runs from French Hill, along Bar Lev Boulevard to the New Gate. From there it heads down Jaffa Street, along Herzl Boulevard, Shmuel Beyt and on to Herzog (for the Israel Museum). It terminates (or begins) at Malha train station.
- **#18** Runs from the central bus station along Jaffa Street, stopping at the New Gate of the Old City and then heading down to the German Colony.
- **#19** Runs from Ein Kerem along Malcha, Harav Herzog and Gaza before heading along King George V, Yehekel, Hativat Har'el and onto Levi Eshkol (for Ammunition Hill). It terminates at Mount Scopus before turning back.

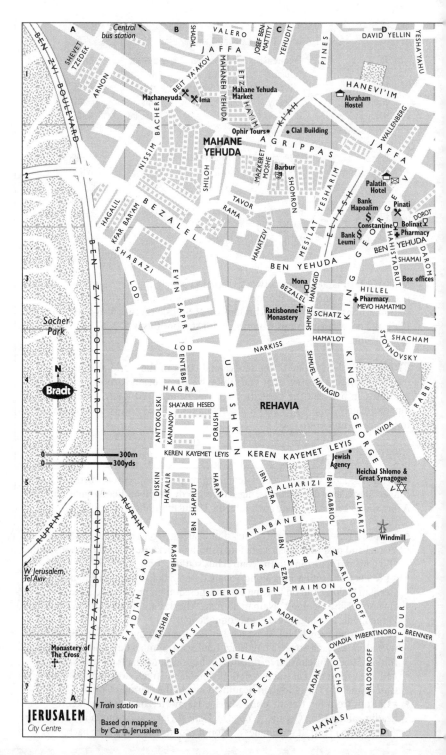

JERUSALEM
City Centre

Based on mapping
by Carta, Jerusalem

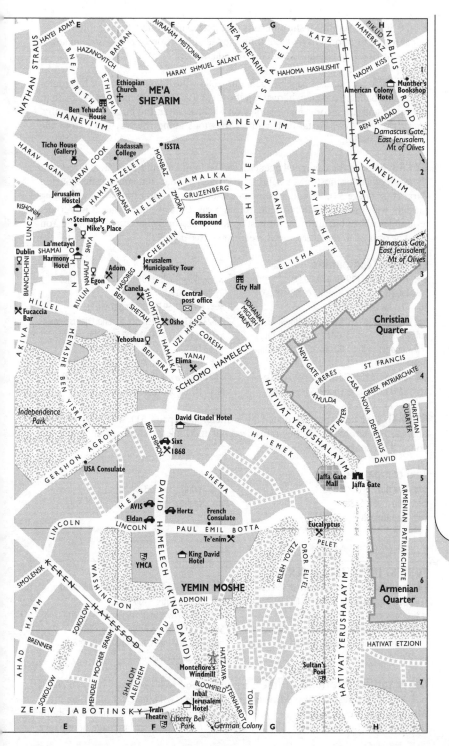

- **#20** Starts in Yemin Moshe and runs past Jaffa Gate, along Jaffa Street to the central bus station and then continues to Herzl Junction (for Yad Vashem and Mount Herzl), passing the Mahane Yehuda market.

BY SHERUT *Sheruts* (see page 51) generally follow the lines of the major bus routes but can be hailed from anywhere along those routes. They cost marginally less than the buses and are a convenient option on Shabbat when the buses stop running. *Sheruts* to Tel Aviv, Haifa, Eilat and all the stops along the way leave from the central bus station.

BY CAR Most of the car-rental agencies can be found along King David Street and there are offices of most major national and international companies at Ben Gurion Airport (see page 39). Parking in the city can be difficult and expensive and parking illegally will result in your car being towed away. Cars are not an ideal way to get around Jerusalem but are by far the best option for exploring the country at large. You must be over 21 to rent a car anywhere in Israel (see page 52).

Car rental companies

🚗 **AVIS** [69 F5] 19 King David St; ☎6249001; www.avis.co.il; ⏰ 08.00–18.00 Sun–Thu, 08.00–13.00 Fri

🚗 **Budget** [69 F6] King David Hotel, 23 King David St; ☎03 9350015; f 03 9350115; www.budget.co.il; ⏰ 08.00–18.00 Sun–Thu, 08.00–14.00 Fri

🚗 **Eldan** [69 F5] Eldan Hotel, 24 King David St; ☎6252151/2; e jer_hotel@eldan.com; www.eldan.co.il; ⏰ 08.00–17.00 Sun–Thu, 08.00–13.00 Fri

🚗 **Hertz** [69 F5] 18 King David St; ☎6231351; www.hertz.co.il; e hertzjerusalem@hertz.co.il; ⏰ 08.00–18.00 Sun–Thu, 08.00–14.00 Fri

🚗 **Sixt** [69 F5] 8 King David St; ☎6250833; f 6248205; www.sixt.com; ⏰ 08.00–18.00 Mon–Fri, 08.00–18.00 Sun

BY TAXI Taxi fares are calculated by a meter (see page 51) which drivers are obligated by law to run. If they refuse, get out and look for another one, otherwise you will no doubt be overcharged.

Taxi companies

🚗 **Bar Ilan** ☎05866666
🚗 **Gilo** ☎6765888
🚗 **Hapalmach** ☎6793333

🚗 **Israel** ☎6252333
🚗 **Nesher** ☎6257227

TOURIST INFORMATION

TOURIST INFORMATION CENTRES

ℹ️ **Christian Information Centre** [84 C5] Jaffa Gate, opposite the Citadel; ☎6272692; e cicinfo@cicts.org; www.cicts.org; ⏰ 08.30–17.30 Mon–Fri, 08.30–12.30 Sat. Offers information on Christian sites in & around the Old City.

ℹ️ **Jaffa Gate Tourist Information Office** [84 C5] Jaffa Gate; ☎6271422; f 6271362; www.tourism.gov.il; ⏰ 08.30–17.00 Sun–Thu. Offers a wealth of information including free maps, hotel reservations & tour guide recommendations.

Other tourist information There are some good web resources you can check out before setting off: the **Ministry of Tourism** (*www.tourism.gov.il*) and the **Municipality of Jerusalem** (*www.jerusalem.muni.il*), which also has a 24-hour hotline 106 (from land lines). The *Jerusalem Post* is an English-language newspaper that has lots of practical information and entertainment listings about Jerusalem and Tel Aviv for tourists and foreign residents. *Haaretz*, Israel's leading newspaper, is also printed in English daily. Another good publication to pick up is the *Tours and Sites* booklet produced by the Municipality of Jerusalem Tourism Department. *Time Out* magazine now has a Jerusalem edition to add to its popular Tel Aviv publication.

LOCAL TOUR OPERATORS The sheer volume of things to see in Jerusalem, from its wide-ranging history, means that taking guided tours is a good way to get orientated and expand your understanding. Apart from those listed below, the tourist information office (see above) can supply a list of licensed tour guides. The **Jerusalem Municipality** offers three-hour free themed tours on Saturdays starting from the main entrance to the Russian Compound [69 F2] (*32 Jaffa St; ⊕ tours begin at 10.00*). Tours change on a weekly basis so for more information call 5314600 or visit www. jerusalem.muni.il. Sandeman's New Europe is also offering a hugely popular free tour, which leaves daily from Jaffa Gate (*www.newjerusalemtours.com; ⊕ 11.00 daily & 14.30 Sun–Thu; 3hrs; free*). Reservations must be made on their website.

Egged City Tour ☎05 08422473; www.city-tour.co.il. Run by Egged Bus Co. Line 99 offers red, open-top double-deck buses that do a circuit of Jerusalem's major sites (adult/ child 80/68NIS or 2hr tour 60/48NIS) or you can hop on & off at any one of 24 stops. There are 4 buses daily (Sun–Thu) & tickets can be purchased on board. Buses stop at the Jaffa Gate at 09.45, 11.45, 14.15 & 16.30. Commentary in 8 languages via headphones.
Knesset Guided Tours (see page 103).
Mazada Tours (see page 37).
Segwayz ☎052 8119996; www.segwayz.co.il; e info@segwayz.co.il. Offering a variety of unusual tours, this is a unique & eco-friendly

way to see the city (Botanical Garden tour 180NIS pp; Cross Jerusalem Tour 440NIS inc lunch 4hrs). Tours include a 20min lesson on using the 2-wheeled Segway bikes.
Zion Walking Tours Jaffa Gate; ☎6277588/ 6289524; e zionwt@dsites1.co.il; ⊕ 09.00– 14.00 Sun–Fri. Zion are 30-year veterans of tours around the Old City. Don't let the dusty little shop put you off – these guys know their way around. 3hr tours cost 110NIS pp & leave at 10.00 & 14.00 daily. They also offer tours to the Mount of Olives (10.00 Mon & Wed), Judean Desert (book in advance) & Western Wall Tunnels (10.00 Mon & Wed).

For national tour operators, see page 000.

TRAVEL AGENCIES
Issta [69 F2] 31 Hanevi'im St; ☎6213600; www.issta.co.il; ⊕ 09.00–18.00 Sun–Thu, 08.30–13.00 Fri. Israel's biggest agency. Specialises in budget travel.

Ophir Tours [68 C2] 42 Agrippas St; ☎5398666; e henriette_h@ophirtours.co.il; www.ophirtours.co.il; ⊕ 08.30–18.00 Sun–Thu, 09.00–12.30 Fri

⌂ WHERE TO STAY

CITY CENTRE
⌂ **David Citadel Hotel** [69 F4] (384 rooms) 7 King David St; ☎6211111; e reservations@tdchotel.com; www.thedavidcitadel.com. One of Jerusalem's hotel greats it is 2nd in line to the throne after the King David Hotel (see box, page 000). It combines Old City views, traditional Jerusalem

architecture, plush, modern facilities (inc a swimming pool) & fresh, contemporary décor. *Rooms start at 2000NIS*. **$$$$$**
⌂ **Harmony Hotel** [69 E3] (50 rooms) 6 Yoel Moshe Salomon St; ☎6219999; www.atlas.co.il/harmony-hotel-jerusalem. Kitsch chic makes for a different stay in the Holy City.

MP3 tours are growing in popularity across the world, and Jerusalem is an excellent candidate for these do-it-yourself walking tours. By simply downloading the tour on to your iPod, iPhone or mp3 player and printing out the associated map, you can tour the city's maze of cobbled lanes in your own time, stopping to take photos or take a coffee break without the rush of an organised tour. MP3 tour downloads are growing at a rate of knots, but the following are a good start:

Jerusalemp3 www.jerusalemp3.com; free. Excellent tour offered by the Jerusalem Municipality.

Trek Exchange www.trekexchange.com; 45NIS. Four hours of recorded tour information covering the whole of Jerusalem.

TourCaster www.tourcaster.com; 55NIS. Six hours of tours ranging from the Old City to the Ein Kerem neighbourhood.

Tower of David www.towerofdavid.org.il; free. The museum now offers the chance to download their 90min tour for free before your visit, saving you money on renting the audio headsets.

GPSMyCity.com www.gpsmycity.com; 18NIS. This iPhone application provides 20 separate walking tours with maps & photos.

Spacious, funky rooms, Wi-Fi, an excellent b/fast & 10min walk to the Old City make it a great package. **$$$$$**

⌂ **Inbal Jerusalem Hotel** [69 F7] (283 rooms) Liberty Bell Park, 3 Jabotinsky St; ✆6756666; www.inbalhotel.com. Sophisticated, understated elegance & wonderful new or old city views from every room. Israeli b/fast buffet is inc & there is a choice of world cuisine restaurants as well as a luxury spa. *Rooms start at 1400NIS.* **$$$$$**

⌂ **Palatin Hotel** [68 D2] (200 rooms) 4 Agripas St; ✆6231141; e info@palatinhotel. com; www.palatinhotel.com. Excellently located between the sights of the Old and new cities, it offers Jerusalem family-run charm, quality & comfort. **$$$**

⌂ **Park Hotel** (210 rooms) 2 Vilnay St; ✆6582222; e reservation@park-hotel-jerusalem. com; www.park-hotel-jerusalem.com. Fantastic value hotel offering comfort & style & a range of facilities inc AC, Wi-Fi, an Israeli b/fast & big, open-air dining room. **$$$**

⌂ **St Andrew's Scottish Guesthouse** (19 rooms) 1 David Remez St; ✆6732401; e info@scotsguesthouse.com; www. scotsguesthouse.com. One of the few buildings constructed by the British during the Mandate period, St Andrew's Guesthouse and Church stand on the Valley of Hinnom; a beautiful, castle-like building offering refined elegance & a taste of classic Jerusalem. **$$$**

⌂ **Abraham Hostel** [68 D1] (40 rooms) 67 Hanevi-im St; ✆6502200; e reservations@ abrahamhostels.com; www.abrahamhostels. com. Excellently geared towards budget independent travellers, it offers big communal areas, Wi-Fi throughout, single-sex & mixed dorms & private rooms. Great location next to the bustling Mahane Yehuda Market. *Dorm 85NIS.* **$$**

⌂ **Jerusalem Hostel** [69 E2] (14 rooms) 44 Jaffa Rd, Zion Sq; ✆6236102; e reservation@ jerusalem-hostel.com; www.jerusalem-hostel.com. What the rooms lack in character the hostel makes up for in cleanliness & great location. Well-equipped kitchen, roof terrace & internet access. *Single-sex dorms 70NIS.* **$$**

⌂ **Mount of Olives Hotel** (61 rooms) 53 Mount of Olives Rd (Rab'a El-Adawiyeh Rd); ✆6284877; f 6264427; www.mtolives.com. Its proximity to the Christian sites on the Mount of Olives has made this simple but comfortable family-run hotel a favourite with small pilgrim groups. It offers great views over the Mount & Old City. **$$**

EAST JERUSALEM

⌂ American Colony Hotel [69 H1]
(92 rooms) 23 Nablus Rd; ☏6279777;
e reserve@amcol.co.il; www.americancolony.
com. The breathtakingly beautiful building &
grounds exemplify the elegant, classic charm
that Jerusalem stands for. Its long history has
seen it rise in the ranks of prestige from the
home of a Turkish pasha to today acting as
the temporary home of visiting diplomats,
journalists & UN officers. It was from this
building that the 'white flag' now housed in
London's Imperial War Museum was flown, an
act signifying Jerusalem's surrender in World
War I. The epitome of elegance, service & top-
of-the-range facilities. *Rooms start at 1800NIS.*
$$$$$

⌂ Jerusalem Hotel [84 C1] (14 rooms)
Nablus Rd; ☏6283282/toll-free USA +1 800 657
9401/UK 0800 328 2393; e raed@jrshotel.com;
www.jrshotel.com. Run by the same family since
1960 & rebuilt following its devastation in 1967,
this traditional Arabic mansion hotel has retained
its age-old Palestinian charm & character.

OLD CITY

⌂ Gloria Hotel [84 C5] (100 rooms) 33 Latin
Patriarchate St; ☏02 6282431–2;
e gloriahl@netvision.net.il. Opened in 1957, it
has retained all its Old City charm combined with
modern facilities. A rustic, stone-arched lounge

Decorated with Islamic & Andalucian furniture &
antiques throughout & boasts an indoor dining
room & the beautiful Kan Zeman restaurant
(35–60NIS). Facilities inc AC, balconies, TV, Wi-Fi,
travel arrangements & classical Arabic music
evenings. **$$$$$**

⌂ Ambassador Hotel (120 rooms)
Nablus Rd; ☏5412222; e reservation@
jerusalemambassador.com; www.
jerusalemambassador.com. Bright, spacious,
recently renovated rooms with AC, TV, minibar,
hairdryer & phone. The hotel is well located
15mins' walk from the Old City. **$$$$**

⌂ Faisal Hostel [84 C1] 4 Hanevi'im St;
☏6287502; e faisalsam@hotmail.com;
www.angelfire.com/vt/faisalhostel. Although
a little rough around the edges, this is a great
place to chill out with a *sheesha*, game of
backgammon & black coffee. Located a few
mins' walk from Damascus Gate. Staff can
help arrange trips to sites around Israel & the
Palestinian Territories. *Dorms 20NIS & simple
private rooms available.* **$**

& bar is the perfect place to rest after a day of
sightseeing. Rooms have AC & TV. **$$$$**

⌂ Knight's Palace [84 B4] (50 rooms) Freres
St; ☏6282537; e kp@actcom.co.il;
www.knightspalace.com. Nestled in a quiet

A ROYAL HOTEL

The **King David** [84 A6] (*23 King David St;* ☏ *6208888;* e *kingdavid@danhotels.
com; www.danhotels.co.il*) stands as Israel's most prestigious and luxurious
hotel, frequented by politicians and royalty from across the globe. With five
restaurants, a fitness centre, swimming pool, tennis courts and flawless,
elegant rooms it doesn't get much better than this. More than just a hotel
however, the King David is a Jerusalem landmark, with a tumultuous and
dramatic history. The hotel was founded in 1931 and afforded asylum to King
Alfonso VIII of Spain, Emperor Haile Selassie of Ethiopia and King George II of
Greece who were all exiled from their countries. The British Mandate period
saw the King David act as the headquarters of British rule in Palestine until it
was bombed by the Irgun Zionist group in July 1946. Throughout the 1948
Arab–Israeli War the hotel became a Jewish stronghold, only to find itself
poignantly isolated between Israeli- and Jordanian-controlled lands. When
Israel recaptured Jerusalem in 1967, the hotel was restored to its former
grandeur and elegance and has since stood as the jewel in Jerusalem's royal
crown. Rooms start at 2000NIS. **$$$$$**

corner of the Muslim Quarter is this charming hotel steeped in Old City elegance with vaulted ceilings & arched windows. It has comfortable rooms, a nice restaurant & bar, Wi-Fi throughout, AC & cable TV. **$$$$**

🏠 **Austrian Hospice** [85 E3] (34 rooms) 37 Via Dolorosa; ✆6265800; e office@ austrianhospice.com; www.austrianhospice. com. Beautiful building in the beating heart of the Muslim Quarter. Impressive collection of modern & classical art plus high ceilings, a rich history & antique furniture. There is also a lovely café (see *Where to eat*, page 000), garden & great view from the roof terrace. Rooms are simple but enormous & the b/fasts (inc) are wonderful. *Dorm beds available 110NIS.* **$$$**

🏠 **Hashimi Hotel & Hostel** [84 D3] (65 beds) 73 Souq Khan es Zeit St; ✆6284410; e hashimi123@gmail.com; www. alhashimihotel-jerusalem.com. Nestled in the Muslim Quarter markets, it offers single-sex dorms with fans & private rooms with AC. There

is a TV lounge, internet access, money-changing facilities & rooftop restaurant. The hotel abides by Islamic law where unmarried couples are not permitted to share rooms & no alcohol is permitted on the premises. *Single-sex dorms 125NIS.* **$$**

🏠 **Jaffa Gate Hostel** [84 C5] Jaffa Gate; ✆6276402; e jaffa_gate_hostel@yahoo.com; www.jaffa-gate.hostel.com. Simple hostel rooms with a great location & set of facilities inc internet facilities, BBQ areas, lockers & a big terraced area. *Dorm 75NIS.* **$$**

🏠 **Petra Hostel** [84 C5] (40 rooms) Omar Bin Khatab St; ✆6286618; e petrahtl@ netvision.net.il; www.newpetrahostel.com. Bohemian backpacker hostel in the Christian Quarter market. Dorms are good value for money with small balconies overlooking the Old City although private rooms are a bit shabby. Located upstairs past a money-change kiosk as you enter the market street from Jaffa Gate. *Single-sex or mixed dorms 85NIS.* **$**

✖ WHERE TO EAT

Israelis love to eat out and accordingly the country is awash with fabulous restaurants serving more cuisines than you'd find at a UN dinner party. Whilst Tel Aviv is accepted as Israel's culinary centre, Jerusalem does its best to keep up. In contrast to its secular neighbour, Jerusalem's restaurants are generally kosher and abide by Shabbat opening hours, although it is possible to find plenty that are open during this time, notably in East Jerusalem and the Muslim Quarter of the Old City. Outside Shabbat, restaurants, cafés and fast-food joints stay open until the small hours and serve a myriad of international styles. Restaurants tend to cluster in certain areas and neighbourhoods so the following, like the hotels above, have been divided into broad geographical zones.

CITY CENTRE

✖ **Canela** [69 F8] 8 Shlomzion Hamalka St; ✆0579443636; canela.rest-e.co.il; 🕐 12.00–15.30 & 18.00–23.00 Sun–Thu, end of Shabbat–23.00 Sat. Kosher. Elegant décor, delicate Continental cuisine & a big wine selection. Mains inc prime beef, fresh fish & lamb. **$$$$$**

✖ **Adom** [69 E3] 31 Jaffa St; ✆6246242; 🕐 18.30–03.00 Sun–Fri, 13.00–03.00 Sat. Elegant yet unpretentious French-style bistro set in a beautiful stone bldg. The gourmet menu inc lamb chops on aubergine in chimichurri sauce, shrimps in saffron cream & entrecôte in mustard & cream sauce & a simpler bar menu (**$$**). **$$$$**

✖ **Fucaccia Bar** [69 E3] 4 Rabbi Akiva St; m 0579443123; 🕐 10.00–02.00 daily. Kosher. Italian-influenced food & ambience. Housed in a stone cottage with a lovely garden, its *pièce de résistance* is its oven-baked pizzas & breads. Pastas, hearty sandwiches, noodles & meat dishes are all featured at decent prices. As the sun goes down this is a great place to chill out with a glass of wine & good music. **$$$**

✖ **Sushi Bar Rechavia** 29 Aza St; ✆5667477; 18.00–02.00 Sun–Thu; 11.30–16.30 Fri, 21.30–02.00 Sat. Regarded as the city's best sushi bar it offers a tantalising selection of fresh sushi rolls (15–30NIS for

8 pieces), noodles, Japanese salads, soups & chicken dishes. $$$

✗ **Elima** [69 F4] 16 Shlomo Hamelech St; ☎5371122; ⏰ 12.00–late Sun–Thu, end Shabbat–late Sat. Kosher. Modern, minimalist décor with a menu chock-full of hearty, vegetarian Italian-style foods ranging from huge bowls of pasta to focaccia to fish. Excellent value. $$

✗ **Little Jerusalem Restaurant at Ticho House** [69 E2] 9 Harav Kook St; ☎6244186; ⏰ 10.00–00.00 Sun–Thu, 09.00–15.00 Fri, end of Shabbat–24.00 Sat. Kosher. Vegetarian café set inside the delightful Ticho House (see page 106). Sandwiches, baked potatoes, soups & a creative selection of salads make a great light lunch while pastas, stuffed artichoke or grilled fish are more filling. The outdoor courtyard is shady & quiet. $$$

✗ **Pinati** [68 D2] 13 King George St; ☎6254540/0579438531; ⏰ 07.00–19.00 Sun–Thu, 07.00–before Shabbat; kosher. Considered one of, if not the, best falafel joints in Jerusalem as attested to by the queues of salivating customers lining the street outside. $

GERMAN COLONY

✗ **Joy** 24 Emek Refaim St; ☎1599530033; ⏰ 12.00–late Sun–Thu, 12.00–Shabbat Fri, end of Shabbat–late Sat. Kosher. Housed in a typical 19th-century German Colony stone building this is a delightful place to enjoy some prime, juicy meat with an oriental twist. Renowned for its steaks & beefburgers. $$$$

✗ **Caffit** 35 Emek Refaim St; ☎5635284; ⏰ 08.00–01.00 Sun–Thu, 07.00–14.00 Fri, end of Shabbat–01.30 Sat. Kosher. Although it may appear under the title 'café' this is a great option for a relaxed meal (the b/fasts are particularly good). The menu inc fresh sandwiches, pies, salads, grilled fish & gooey desserts & there is a breezy little terrace on which to enjoy them. $$

✗ **Yo-ja** 25 Emek Refaim St; ☎5611344/0579439500; ⏰ 12.00–23.00 Sun–Thu, 12.00–15.00 Fri, end of Shabbat–23.00 Sat. Kosher. Noodles served with a variety of Asian sauces can be vegetarian or with chicken or beef. Chinese spicy Szechuan dishes are a big favourite & Peking duck can be ordered in advance. $$

MAHANE YEHUDA MARKET The market and Aggripas Street outside have dozens of tiny eateries and cafés nestled amidst the bustling stalls. Most are as old as the market itself serving traditional Middle Eastern foods, but there is a new influx of trendy yet relaxed places too.

✗ **Machaneyuda** [68 B1] 10 Beit Yaakov St; ☎5333442; ⏰ 18.30–late Sun–Thu, 21.00–late Fri & Sat. This is the trendiest new place on the block & has young Jerusalemites talking. The menu changes every day & reflects all manner of international cuisine from gazpacho soup to amberjack fish to oxtail & Jerusalem artichoke. $$$$

✗ **Ima** [68 B1] 189 Agripas St; ☎6246860; ⏰ 11.00–23.00 Sun–Thu, 11.00–Shabbat Fri. Kosher. Ima translates as 'mother', & this is exactly the sort of hearty food Jewish mamas cook up for their offspring: salads, soups, stuffed vegetables & a variety of meat dishes. Big portions of Israeli/Middle Eastern food at decent prices. $$$

✗ **Azura** Inside the Iraqi Market section; ☎6235204; ⏰ 09.00–16.00 Sun–Thu, 08.30–Shabbat Fri. Kosher. Situated in the delightful Iraqi area of the market, where old men while away the hours playing backgammon, this is a true local joint where you are unlikely to get a seat & even unlikelier to get one with your companions. *Kube*, hummus, stuffed vegetables & lentil dishes are cheap & authentic. $–$$

YEMIN MOSHE

✗ **1868** [69 F5] 10 King David St; ☎6222312; www.1868.co.il; ⏰ 12.00–15.00 & 17.00–23.00 Sun–Thu, end of Shabbat–23.30. Kosher. Prime ingredients are cooked to perfection in succulent traditional French cuisine. Meals don't come cheap but you pay for top quality & an atmosphere of elegance & sophistication. $$$$$

✘ **Eucalyptus** [69 G6] 14 Hativat Yerushalayim St; ☎6244331; ⏰12.00–00.00 Sun–Thu, 10.00–Shabbat Fri, end of Shabbat–late Sat; www.the-eucalyptus.com. Chef Moshe Basson has spent over 20 years resurrecting traditional biblical foods & has been awarded many times for his contribution to the culinary arts. Try starters such as stuffed figs or eucalyptus salad & mains such as lamb with green fava beans in almond milk, or the famous taster menus (167–225NIS). $$$$$

EAST JERUSALEM

✘ **Ambassador Hotel Restaurant** 23 Nablus Rd; ☎5412213; ⏰ 11.00–23.00 daily (tent 20.00–23.30). Located in the irrefutably charming Ambassador Hotel (see page 000), you can choose from European-style food in a sleek, indoor setting or an enchanting garden Bedouin tent complete with water pipes, thick red cushions & sizzling Middle Eastern dishes. Live music on Thu & Sat nights. $$$$$

✘ **Blue Dolphin** 7 Shimon HaTzadik St; ☎5322001; ⏰ 12.00–midnight daily. Lebanese-influenced Mediterranean restaurant renowned for its incredible fresh fish. Local catches such as

St Peter's fish, sea bream, sea bass & mullet are particularly good. $$$$

✘ **Askadinya Restaurant Bar** [84 C1] 11 Shimon HaTzadik St; ☎5324590. ⏰ 12.00–00.00 Wed–Mon, 19.00–00.00 Tue. An old East Jerusalem favourite; it is easy to see why people come again & again. A comfortable family atmosphere, hearty Italian & Middle Eastern food all set in a traditional cobbled stone building. There is live music on Thu. $$$

✘ **Kan Zeman** [84 C1] See Jerusalem Hotel, page 73.

OLD CITY The Old City specialises in traditional, home-cooked food that reflects the origins of those who make and serve it. Aromas of warm, fresh hummus, falafel, *shwarma*, spices, nuts, aromatic coffee and sticky pastries waft down the narrow streets of the **Muslim Quarter souks**, while the Jewish Quarter sports the more sedate cafés and bakeries along the leafy **Tiferet Yisrael Boulevard**. There are also some cheap eateries around **Muristan Square** in the Christian Quarter.

✘ **Armenian Tavern** [84 C6] 79 Armenian Orthodox Patriarchate St; ☎6273854; ⏰ 11.00–22.00 Mon–Sat. One of the most atmospheric places to enjoy a meal in the Old City. Housed inside a Crusader-era cellar with rustically elegant décor, traditional Armenian dishes & comfortable ambience. $$$

✘ **Papa Andrea's** [84 D4] 64 Aftemeos St; ☎6284433; ⏰ 08.00–midnight daily. Open-air terrace on the 3rd floor (well signposted). While the food is nothing spectacular, the view across the rooftops of the Old City most certainly is. $$$

✘ **Amigo Emil** [84 D4] El Khanka St Bazaar; ☎6288090; ⏰ 10.00–21.00 Mon–Sat. A nice mix of international & Middle Eastern dishes. The décor is traditionally Old City, & it has a quieter ambience than the busy market hummus joints. $$

✘ **Keshet HaHurva** [84 D5] 2 Tiferet Y'Israel; ☎5380150; ⏰ 07.30–22.00 Sun–Thu, 07.30–15.00 Fri, end of Shabbat–23.00 Sat; www.keshethahurva.com. Kosher. With little tables nestled in the corner of Hurva Sq, this is a wonderful spot to sit & soak up the atmosphere of the Jewish Quarter. Omelettes, salads, filled bagels & soup form the heart of the menu. $$

✘ **Nafoura** [84 B5] 18 Latin Patriarchate St; ☎6260034; ⏰ 12.30–23.00 daily. Middle Eastern & Mediterranean meats are served in this delightful Christian Quarter restaurant. The stone courtyard is particularly pleasant & there is a good-value buffet. $$

✘ **Versavee Bistro, Bar & Café** [84 C5] Greek Catholic Patriarchate Rd, Jaffa Gate; ☎6276160; www.versavee.com. A much-needed addition to the Old City is this classy yet unpretentious bistro, bar & café. Steeped in Old City charm & set inside a 2,000-year-old building it is fast-becoming the favourite haunt of international journalists & tourists. Meals consist of salads, hot & cold sandwiches (20–25NIS) & simple but filling mains. $$

✘ **Abu Shukri** [85 E3] 63 Al Wad Rd; ☎6271538; ⏰ 08.30–18.00 daily. Located where the Via Dolorosa crosses Al Wad Rd this is one of,

if not the, best hummus joints in the city. It is easy to spot by the throngs of people queuing for their turn at the little plastic tables inside. $

✘ **Viennese Café** [85 E3] Austrian Hospice, 37 Via Dolorosa; ☎6265800; ⏰ 07.00–22.00 daily. Take afternoon tea away from the hubbub of the Muslim Quarter in the tranquil gardens of the Austrian Hospice. Traditional, delicate Viennese cakes, teas, coffees & liqueurs are all home baked & superb. $

ENTERTAINMENT AND NIGHTLIFE

BARS AND CLUBS Jerusalem's bars are not quite on a par with its naughty neighbour Tel Aviv, but then again, they don't try to be. Watering holes tend to be more refined and less rowdy, attracting those who want to enjoy some sociable drinks with friends in pleasant surroundings, and many double as restaurants. There are, however, several places where you can let your hair down to live music, have one too many and enjoy a good dance. The Zion Square/Nahalat Shiva area is teeming with small bars, cafés, pubs and restaurants and is a good place to head for a night out. Ben Yehuda Street is another popular area.

♀ **Bar 17** 17 Haoman St; ☎6781658. Formerly Haoman 17 this is considered the best club in the city attracting international DJs & playing house & techno. Its Facebook page details upcoming events & times.

♀ **Bolinas** 6 Dorot Rishonim St; ☎6249733; ⏰ 24hrs daily. Friendly, relaxed bar & restaurant that attracts the 20-something Jerusalemites. Music styles vary but you are unlikely to hear Abba on the stereo here. Rich, feel-good meals are another big draw.

♀ **Cellar Bar** 23 Nablus Rd; ☎6279777; ⏰ 19.00–midnight daily. Housed within the famous American Colony Hotel, this is a favourite watering hole of foreign journalists. The intimate, charming ambience is perfect for sipping a glass of smoky red wine & discussing the current situation in the Middle East.

♀ **Constantine** [68 D2] 3 Hahistadrut St; ☎6221155; ⏰ 21.00–late daily. The enormous bar/club has been decked out in flashy modern décor & offers live performers, a huge drinks menu & a selection of bar food. Themed nights all week.

♀ **Egon** [69 E3] 9 Nahalat Shiva St; ☎6222458; ⏰ 24hrs daily. Relaxed, cosy bohemian haunt where Indian prints hang from the walls & ceilings, a mishmash of bottom-friendly seating is scattered across the floor &

an open-air courtyard allows for dancing under the stars.

♀ **Mona** [68 C3] 8 Shmuel HaNagid St; ☎6222283; ⏰ 17.00–02.00 Sun–Thu, 12.00–02.00 Fri & Sat; www.monas.co.il. Mona's is predominantly a restaurant specialising in fish & meat but its rustic charm & wide bar has seen it become popular with those looking for a comfortable place to enjoy a cool beer. Popular also with journalists. Located inside the Jerusalem Artists' House.

♀ **Osho** [69 F3] 3 Shlomizion Hamalka St; ☎6251666; ⏰ 19.00–late daily. Trendy, modern fusion restaurant known for its quality meats, fresh fish & seafood ($$$). As the sun goes down it turns into a rather swanky wine bar.

♀ **Smadar Theatre Bar** 4 Lloyd George; ☎5617819; 08.00–00.30 Sun–Fri, 11.00–00.30 Sat; www.lev.co.il. Situated in the artsy Smadar Theatre which shows films (one at a time) it attracts a bohemian crowd who come as much for the bar/café as the films.

♀ **Yehoshua** [69 F4] 3 Ben Sira St; ☎6246076; ⏰ 20.00–late Mon–Sat. A more refined watering hole, Yehoshua's elegant interior & modern décor tends to attract a slightly older crowd of Jerusalemites in their 20s & 30s.

♀ **Versavee Bistro, Bar & Café** [84 C5] See restaurants, page 76.

3

LIVE MUSIC

☆ **Dublin** [69 E3] 4 Shamai St; ✆6223612; ☺ 17.00–03.00 Sat–Thu, 17.00–05.00 Fri. Friendly, relaxed Irish-style pub. Modern Hebrew & Irish music, rock performances & DJ nights all week.

☆ **Mike's Place** [69 E3] 37 Jaffa St; ✆054 9292551; www.mikesplacebars.com; ☺ 16.00–late daily. This quintessential British pub has branches in Jerusalem & Tel Aviv & has managed to remain firmly popular over its years of existence. Live rock, jazz, blues & acoustic performances & open mic night every night.

☆ **Yellow Submarine** 13 HaRechivim Rd, Talpiot; ✆6794040; www.yellowsubmarine.org. il; ☺ shows get going late (after 22.00) & finish early; admission 30–90NIS. Known across the country for its live rock, punk, jazz & acoustic performances, this is Jerusalem's hottest spot to catch up-&-coming artists (despite its rather inconvenient location in the Talpiot Industrial District).

FESTIVALS

Israel Festival (May–Jun) Theatre, dance & classical music performances in theatres & concert halls around Jerusalem.

Jerusalem Film Festival (Jul) International, avant-garde, Israeli directed & modern films & documentaries shown in theatres & cinemas around the city.

Jerusalem International Book Fair (Feb) Browse, buy & read hundreds of genres of books at this internationally respected book fair.

Latin Patriarch Procession (Dec) The procession heads from Jerusalem to the Church of the Nativity in Bethlehem.

International Puppet Festival (Aug; Train Theatre) Jerusalem has become the international centre for puppetry & this week-long festival is the culmination of the most colourful performances of this rare art form.

Taste Festival (Te'ami) (During Sukkot; Old Train Station, German Colony) The city's best restaurants lay out their finest meals for 20NIS per dish. It is a great way to taste the best of the city's cuisine.

PERFORMING ARTS Israel has long been high in the world rankings of classical music, producing a continuous stream of top-class musicians and orchestras. The arts remain incredibly popular and getting tickets to many of the concerts and theatre performances can be difficult (see page 81 for box offices).

Barbur [68 C2] 6 Shirizli St; www.barbur. org. A non-profit space created by artists for artists offering regular concerts & showings of differing music genres, art, architecture, dance & cinema.

Habima Theatre Floor 4, 4 Yad Harozim St; ✆6254463; www.habima.org.il. Shows avant-garde & experimental pieces in the small studio. Performances are in Hebrew only.

Jerusalem Cinematheque 11 Hebron Rd; ✆6724131; www.jer.cine.org.il. Shows a mixture of classical, avant-garde, Hollywood & experimental films. For more mainstream films your best bets are the grandiose cinema complexes of Rav Hen (*19 Ha'uman St;* ✆*6792799*) & Gil (*Jerusalem Mall, Malha St;* ✆*6788448*).

Jerusalem Performing Arts Centre 20 David Marcus St, German Colony; ✆5605755; www. jerusalem-theatre.co.il. Houses the Jerusalem Theatre, Henry Crown Auditorium & Rebecca Crown Hall that show a collection of Israeli plays, Hebrew translations of classic plays & concerts by the Jerusalem Symphony Orchestra, the Israel Chamber Ensemble, & occasionally the world-renowned Israel Philharmonic Orchestra whose permanent home is in Tel Aviv.

Khan Theatre 2 David Remez Sq; ✆6718281; www.khan.co.il. One of the most popular venues for new Hebrew theatre performances ranging from Israeli pieces to translations of international classics. There are also regular chamber & jazz concerts, Israeli folklore nights & occasional English performances.

Sultan's Pool [69 G7] Between Jaffa Gate & Mount Zion. Often acts as the beautiful & dramatic setting for modern rock, classical, jazz & theatre performances in the summer months.

Ticho House [69 E2] (see page 106) Has regular music performances, art exhibitions & poetry readings. There is a jazz, wine & cheese night every Wed at 20.00.

Train Theatre [69 F7] Liberty Bell Pk; ✆5618514; www.traintheater.co.il. The home of the world puppetry centre & has regular performances (see *Festivals* above).

YMCA [69 F6] 26 King David St; ✆5692692. Has a regular stream of Israeli music concerts & folk dancing performances. Seats cannot be reserved in advance so get there early.

SHOPPING

West Jerusalem's modern shops and malls are comparable to those found in western Europe, with their marble-floored glitzy walkways, fashionable clothes shops and plethora of eateries. **Malha Mall**, also referred to as 'the Kanyon', is located in Jerusalem's southern Malha neighbourhood and stands as the country's biggest shopping centre. If time is of the essence then you're best advised to give this a miss for there is little to distinguish it from any other mall. **Ben Yehuda Street** in the city centre is a pedestrianised hub of fun, albeit with mainstream commercial activities: bustling cafés; ice-cream parlours; fast-food kiosks; overpriced souvenir and Judaica shops; high street-type chain stores; and, come summer evenings, a carnival of festivals and street entertainment (particularly in Zion Square).

For more cultural shopping experiences you can't beat the colourful **Old City souks** (see page 96) and **Mahane Yehuda Market** [68 C1] (see page 75). Despite the souks' obvious tourist appeal they are undoubtedly among the main attractions of the Old City, each quarter selling wares that reflect the ethnic origins of the vendors. The **Cardo** [84 D6] in the Jewish Quarter is one of the best places to buy quality Judaica, jewellery and Israeli art, although it is important to note that most Judaica stores do not give refunds, so make sure you compare prices first. Bargaining is not the done thing here but you can politely ask for a 'discount'. Other good areas for buying Judaica include **Yochanan Migush Halav Street**, the **Mea Shearim neighbourhood** and for more modern styles, the **German Colony**. The Muslim Quarter souks are known for their vibrant, bustling atmosphere and are certainly more 'alive' than their Christian Quarter counterparts, which cater wholly to tourists. At the bottom of Armenian Patriarchate Road in the Armenian Quarter are some good, little-known-about **craft and pottery stalls** that sell handmade products for a fraction of the price of the Muslim Quarter. To buy the unique turquoise and blue-patterned tiles and ceramics like those adorning the Dome of the Rock look no further than **Armenian Ceramics-Balian** (*14 Nablus Rd*; ✆*6282826; www.armenianceramics.com*) or **Jerusalem Pottery** (*15 Via Dolorosa, Old City*; ✆*6261587; www.jerusalempottery. biz*; ⊕ *09.30–17.00 Mon–Sat*) that specialise in authentic, hand-painted wares in a range of geometric patterns, floral motifs and animal designs. Outside **Damascus Gate** [84 D2] is East Jerusalem's busiest shopping area, where local residents come to buy and sell a wide range of products, from food to home wares to Arabic-style embroidered clothes.

Outside of Jaffa Gate is the newly opened **Jaffa Gate Mall**, which houses a modern selection of cafés, high street shops and facilities. It has some rather fancy public toilets if you get caught short whilst touring the Old City.

As with the rest of the country, shopping hours in West Jerusalem are 08.30–13.00 and 16.00–19.00 Monday to Thursday and 08.30–14.00 Friday. Stores tend to reopen on Saturday evenings after Shabbat. In Muslim areas such as East Jerusalem and the Muslim Quarter of the Old City many shops will be open during Shabbat but will often close or have shorter working hours on Fridays, the Muslim holy day. Likewise shops in the Christian or Armenian quarters will likely close on Sundays. When you are making purchases bear in mind that it may be possible to get a tax refund on items over US$100 so be sure to ask the vendor for a special receipt or voucher which can be submitted upon departure from Israel at Ben Gurion Airport.

BOOKSHOPS

The Book Gallery 6 Schatz St; ☎6231087; www.bookgallery.co.il; ⏰ 09.00–19.00 Sun–Thu, 09.00–14.00 Fri. A treasure-trove of secondhand, rare & antique books in many languages.
Munther's Book Shop [69 H1] Nablus Rd; ☎6279777; ⏰ 09.00–21.00 daily. Friendly, fascinating little bookshop opposite the American Colony Hotel. Stocks many English books inc maps, bestsellers, history & politics.
Steimatsky [69 E3] 33 Jaffa St; ☎6250155; ⏰ 08.00–19.00 Sun–Thu, 08.00–14.00 Fri. This was the flagship shop in this now incredibly popular nationwide chain & has been open since 1925. Big selection of English novels, non-fiction, maps & travel guides.

CAMPING AND OUTDOOR EQUIPMENT

La'metayel [69 E3] 5 Yoel Salomon St; ☎0773334509; ⏰ 10.00–20.00 Sun–Thu, 10.00–14.00 Fri. Big outlet branch of nationwide chain of camping & travel shops. Good range of outdoor equipment, travel books, road & hiking maps & travel information.

OTHER PRACTICALITIES

EMERGENCY

Fire ☎102
Magen David Adom ☎101. This is the Israeli equivalent of the Red Cross.

Tourist Police Jaffa Gate ☎100 or 6226222

MONEY Branches of major banks can be found all over the city but should not be your first choice for changing money. Change bureaux – kiosks denoted by the word 'Change' above them – may look shifty but are reputable and offer commission-free currency exchange at pretty much the same rate as each other but at better rates than the banks, have shorter queues than the banks and the post office and are open longer hours. Zion Square, Ben Yehuda Street shopping centre and in the Old City (particularly around Jaffa Gate) have concentrations. Travellers' cheques can be changed at most banks and at the post office for no commission.

$ **Bank Hapoalim** 216 Jaffa St; ☎03 6532407; ⏰ 08.30–13.15 Sun, Tue, Wed, 08.30–13.00 & 16.00–18.30 Mon & Thu. There are other useful branches at 1 Zion Sq, 16 King George St & 1 Malchei Yisrael St.

$ **Bank Leumi** 234 Jaffa St; ☎03 9544555; ⏰ 08.30–14.00 Sun, Tue & Wed, 08.30–13.00 & 16.00–18.15 Mon & Thu. This is the main branch but other convenient branches can be found at 19 King David St (⏰ *08.30–17.00 Sun–Thu, 08.30–12.00 Fri*), 22 King George St, 4 Hananya St & Herod's Gate, Saladin St.

POST Most major post offices are open 08.30–18.00 Sun–Thu, 08.00–12.00 Fri, although some now close on Wednesday afternoons. The postal authority's website can provide a list of all branches in the city (☎ *03 5385909; www.israelpost.co.il*). Courier services such as FEDEX (☎ *6512693; www.fedex.com*), DHL (☎ *03 5573557; www.dhl.com*) and UPS (☎ *6541880; www.ups.com*) are commonplace in Israel and Jerusalem.

✉ **Central post office** [69 F3] 23 Jaffa St; ☎6290676; ⏰ 08.00–18.00 Sun–Thu, 08.00– 12.00 Fri. There are other useful branches at 6 King George St, Jaffa Gate, & Klal Bldg, 42 Agrippas St.

MEDICAL

✚ **Hadassah Hospital** Ein Kerem; ☎6777111
✚ **Shaare Zedek Medical Centre** 12 Beit Shmuel St; ☎6666666

✚ **Newpharm pharmacy** 27 King George St; ☎6259999; ⏰ 08.30–19.30 Sun–Thu, 08.30–14.00 Fri
✚ **Superpharm pharmacy** 3 Hahistadrut St; ☎6246244; ⏰ 08.00–midnight Sun–Thu, 08.00–15.00 Fri, 19.00–00.00 Sat

INTERNET Internet cafés are commonplace around Jerusalem and most offer a fast internet service, new computers and refreshments. Prices vary between 10NIS and 25NIS per hour. Almost every such café will offer free wireless internet connection.

🅔 **Ali Baba Internet** [84 D3] Via Dolorosa, Old City; ☎5271959; ⏰ 09.00–23.00 daily; 10NIS/hr.
🅔 **Café Net** 3rd Floor, New Central Bus Station, 232 Jaffa St; ☎5379192; www.cafenet.co.il; ⏰ 05.30–midnight Sun–Thu, 05.30–16.00 Fri, 20.00–0.00 Sat. 15NIS/hr. Fast internet, excellent equipment & an extremely cheap selection of hot & cold drinks & snacks. 15mins free internet with a food or drink purchase.
🅔 **Old City Net** [84 B5] Latin Patriarchate St; ☎6275799; ℮ oldcitynet@hotmail.com; ⏰ 11.00–23.00 daily. High-speed services, local & international calls & photo downloading services.

LAUNDRY

Superclean 16 Hapalmach Rd; ☎5660367; ⏰ 07.00–19.00 Mon–Thu, 07.00–17.00 Fri, 07.00–14.00 Sat

BOX OFFICES

Bimot 8 Shamai St; ☎6237000; www.bimot.co.il
Klaim 12 Shamai St; ☎6231273

WHAT TO SEE

OLD CITY In a city of such religious and historic poignancy, Jerusalem's Old City sits like the jewel in the crown. Within the grand city walls, a living, breathing museum of sacred buildings, fervent worshippers, ancient architecture and centuries-old traditions abounds. The Old City is but 1km² in size, yet its reach extends across the world, Jews, Christians and Muslims worshipping here with passion and zeal. The Western Wall, Church of the Holy Sepulchre and Temple Mount may stand as the three most ideologically and conceptually opposing religious sites, yet they are by no means the extent. A jumble of buildings fall into four rough quarters: Christian, Armenian, Jewish and Muslim, forming an array of ornate architectural styles from every century of the city's long life. Holy men, pilgrims, tourists and street vendors together wander the cobbled alleyways, bazaars and souks, their customs and dress adding yet more colour to this eclectic mini city.

Christian Quarter Located in the northwest quadrant of the Old City, the Christian Quarter is characterised by its ancient churches, bustling bazaars and representation of most Christian denominations. Its centrepiece, the Church of the

Holy Sepulchre [84 D4], is the holiest place in Christianity and marks the final stop on the Via Dolorosa pilgrimage walk, an approximation of the footsteps of Jesus on his path to Golgotha (see box, pages 88–9). The quarter is accessed by the New and Jaffa gates, the latter being the Old City's busiest visitors' entrance. Of the 4,200 people who reside within the Christian Quarter, the vast majority belong to the Greek Orthodox Church, its architectural and cultural influence being clearly visible, while Arabic remains the predominant language.

Jaffa Gate The Jaffa Gate [84 C5] is located on the border between the Armenian and Christian quarters to the left of the Citadel of David. At the time of its construction it marked the beginning (or end) of the highway leading to the thriving port city of Jaffa. The gate has gone by a number of names over the years, notably the Arabic Bab al-Halil (Hebron Gate), named after the road leading to the city of Hebron. A closer inspection reveals two entrances: one an arched L-shape and next to it a wider one created in 1898 to allow Kaiser Wilhelm II to enter the city without alighting from his carriage. Today the gate is accessed from the main Jaffa Road, and steps on the left lead up to the beginning of the Ramparts Walk (see page 98).

Church of the Holy Sepulchre [84 D4] (⊕ *04.30–19.00 daily*) This awe-inspiring church is the traditional site of Jesus's Crucifixion, burial and Resurrection and is the single most important shrine in Christendom. From the exterior, the church looks rather shabby, its scaffolding a long-lasting remnant of the conflict of ownership between the countless religious sects that have laid claim to it. Today, the church is divided amongst the Greek Orthodox, Armenian Orthodox and Roman Catholic denominations, their different ecclesiastical styles and ornate methods of worship forming a fascinatingly beautiful blend within the ancient church.

History Following Constantine the Great's adoption of Christianity, his mother Queen Helena arrived in the Holy Land in search of Jesus's site of Crucifixion and burial. She is attributed with having discovered what is believed to be the rock of Golgotha and nearby tomb, known as Anastasis (Greek for resurrection). Constantine commissioned a shrine above the site in 330CE later destroyed by the Persians in 614. Most of the building we see today dates to the 12th-century Crusader period as well as later renovations following a series of earthquakes and fires.

MODEST DRESS

Jerusalem is first and foremost the religious centre of three world faiths, and walking around the Jewish, Christian and Muslim sites it is important to respect dress codes. Wearing revealing clothing such as sleeveless shirts, shorts or skirts above the knee will result in you not being allowed entry into any religious buildings. In Jerusalem's cold winters this isn't a problem but come the stifling hot summer months dressing up can be more uncomfortable. Loose, baggy clothing is recommended, or alternatively carry a shawl or shirt with you to put on as you enter religious buildings. Men must wear *yarmulkes* (Jewish caps) on entering synagogues and to approach the Western Wall, but paper versions are provided on entry free of charge.

Unlike Israel's second city Tel Aviv, Jerusalem strictly abides by Shabbat rules and come Friday afternoon most places in the city shut down. Public institutions, shops, offices and public transportation do not operate during Shabbat hours (Friday sundown to Saturday sundown) and there is a palpable feel of calm during these times. Inside the Old City and more religious neighbourhoods there is a mad dash to get home and settled before the sun goes down, a fascinating experience to witness. Some restaurants, cafés and bars, however, are open during Shabbat particularly in the downtown area, around the Russian Compound and in Ein Kerem (with the exception of Yom Kippur – see page 36). Inside the Old City, different institutions are open depending on their religious connotation. The Muslim holy day is Friday and therefore Saturdays see cafés, religious sites, restaurants and markets open as usual (Friday has more limited opening hours). While Christianity's day of rest is Sunday, most sites within the Old City are open for prayer services.

What to see The **Unction Stone** is located immediately inside the entrance and commemorates the preparation of Jesus's body for burial. The ornate lamps that hang over the stone belong to each of the different denominations that are represented within the church.

Calvary (Golgotha) is the traditional site of Jesus's Crucifixion and is accessed by narrow steps to the right of the entrance. It is the most extravagantly decorated area of the church and comprises three parts: the Chapel of the Nailing of the Cross (station 11 along the Via Dolorosa) to the left of the altar, the Statue of Mary (station 13) marking the spot where Jesus's body was removed from the cross and given to his mother and, next to this, the Rock of Calvary (station 12). It was around this rock that the church was built and is today encased in glass, a small hole allowing visitors to touch it.

The **Rotunda (Anastasis)** is the church's *pièce de résistance*, located to the west of the entrance beneath the vast dome. In the centre sits the edicule, revered as the tomb of Christ. It is housed within a rather unsightly wooden structure, supported by scaffolding to protect it against earthquakes. Inside, the Chapel of the Holy Sepulchre (station 14) contains the tomb of Jesus, marked by a marble slab.

Other notable sights within the church include the **Chapel of Adam**, which houses the cracked rock said to have been caused by the earthquake that occurred at the moment of the Crucifixion; the **Holy Prison** where tradition has it Jesus was kept before the Crucifixion; and **St Helena's Church**, a vast underground complex containing the Chapel of the Finding of the Cross. Also of note is the small **tomb of Joseph of Arimathea**, whose discovery proved this area was once used as a burial site and, according to Christian tradition, that it was the site of Jesus's death, burial and Crucifixion (although the Garden Tomb is another, later contender – see page 104).

Church of St John the Baptist [84 D5] (*Muristan Sq*) The silver-domed Church of St John the Baptist stands as the oldest in Jerusalem, and is the original 'Hospital of St John' after which the Knights Hospitaller were named. The present church was built on the site of a 5th-century chapel, possibly because of the presence of the relics of St John the Baptist, and belonged to a pilgrim hospice. In 1099, Christian knights wounded in the battle for Jerusalem were cared for in the church, many of whom, upon recovery and

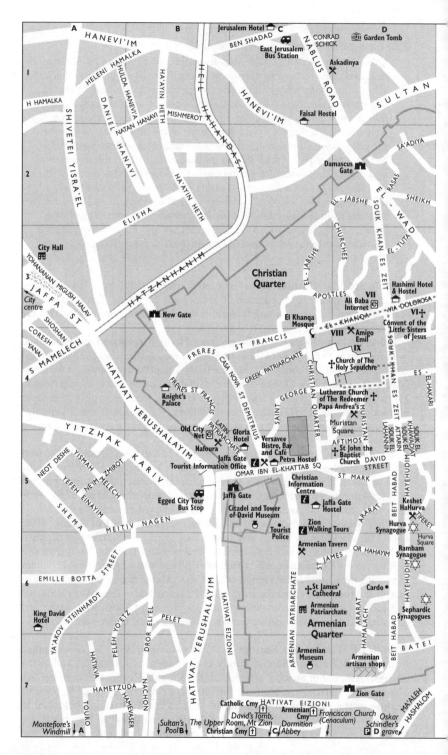

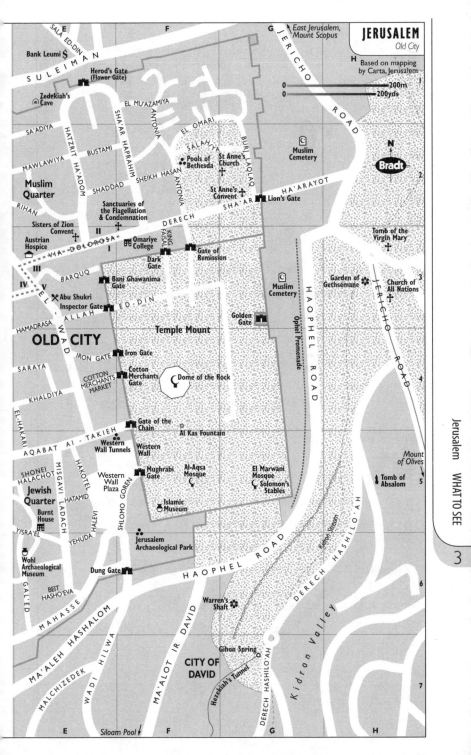

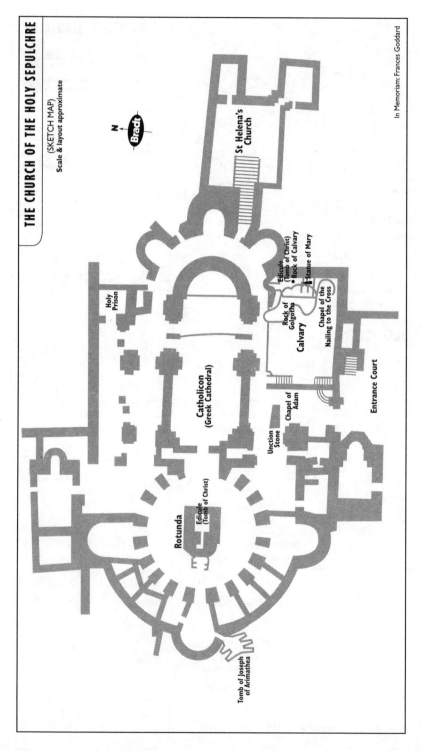

THE CHURCH OF THE HOLY SEPULCHRE

(SKETCH MAP)
Scale & layout approximate

N

Bradt

St Helena's Church

Holy Prison

Edicule
(Tomb of Christ)
• Rock of Calvary
↑ Statue of Mary

Rock of Golgotha
Calvary

Chapel of the Nailing to the Cross

Catholicon
(Greek Cathedral)

Chapel of Adam

Unction Stone

Entrance Court

Rotunda

Edicule
(Tomb of Christ)

Tomb of Joseph of Arimathea

In Memoriam: Frances Goddard

subsequent defeat of the Crusaders, dedicated themselves to caring for the sick and protecting pilgrims of the Holy Land. They called themselves the Knights Hospitaller, and so the order was formed. They later developed into the military order that played a crucial role in the defence of the country. The church can be seen from the fountain in the middle of **Muristan Square**, *muristan* an Arabic word meaning 'hospital'. With the exception of the simple façade and its two bell towers, the church remains as it has for 1,000 years, and is an integral part of Jerusalem's Christian history. The entrance is located along Christian Quarter Street in Muristan Square. It is signposted in Greek only but a small blue painting of St John indicates you are in the right place. The church doesn't keep regular opening hours but you can ask the Greek Orthodox priest who resides in the adjacent monastery to open it for you.

Lutheran Church of the Redeemer [84 D4] (*Muristan Sq;* \ *6276111;* ⊕ *09.00–13.00 & 13.30–15.00 daily; guided tours are available for 10NIS*) The current Protestant church, consecrated by Kaiser Wilhelm II on 31 October 1898, was built upon land granted to the German emperor by the Ottomans as a symbol of alliance. It has formed the seat of the Lutheran sect in Jerusalem ever since. While the history of the site is undoubtedly significant, the view from the top of the bell tower (3NIS) is most certainly its most charming feature. Climb the narrow, circular stone steps past the vast bell to the top of the tower for a 360° panoramic view over the Old City. While it is rather demanding, those who undertake the hike will reap the rewards of Jerusalem's best viewpoint. The bell rings daily at 12.00 so visitors (in the interest of preserving their eardrums) cannot ascend between 11.45 and 12.20. English services are held on Sundays at 09.00.

Bazaars (*generally* ⊕ *09.00–19.00 Mon–Sat with limited opening on Sun*) In contrast to the Muslim Quarter souks that remain an active part of local daily life, those in the Christian Quarter cater only for the throngs of visitors who pour in through Jaffa Gate. Packed into the narrow, cobbled alleys stores sell an interesting mix of religious items, the vendors happy to promote rosary beads alongside *yarmulkes* with a few novelty T-shirts thrown in for good measure. Handicrafts, jewellery, pottery, Arabic-style home decorations and spice stalls compete for space amidst the crowds that weave through the alleyways, and yet somehow, despite its obvious tourist appeal, the souk is a fascinating and lively place to explore. Prices are predictably over-inflated so if you wish to buy authentic handicrafts, the Armenian workshops along **En Nebi Dawoud** near the Zion Gate are a better bet. Alternatively, bargain hard! Stores are generally open 09.00–19.00 Monday–Saturday with limited opening on Fridays.

From Jaffa Gate walk straight ahead and enter **David Street**, the busiest Christian Quarter souk. At the end, three streets lead off to the left: **Souk el Lahannin**, **Souk el Attarin** and **Souk el Khawadjat**.

New Gate [84 B3] New Gate was not one of Suleiman's original seven gates (hence the name) but was built in 1887 by Sultan Abdul Hamid to link the houses in the northwest with the Old City. The adjacent Tancred's Tower, named after the Latin Kingdom ruler who is believed to have commissioned it, is built from stones originally prepared for Herod's palace. During the Crusader period, the stones were removed and used to build the tower. The tower is known in Arabic as Qasr Jalud (Goliath's Castle) after a legend that it was near here that David killed Goliath.

The Via Dolorosa (Way of Sorrow or Suffering) is one of Christianity's most celebrated devotional routes and follows what tradition states was Jesus's path from his condemnation to his Crucifixion in Golgotha. Today the route begins near the Lion's Gate in the Muslim Quarter and ends in the Church of the Holy Sepulchre in the Christian Quarter. Every Friday at 15.00 Christian pilgrims, led by Italian Franciscans, walk the course, which is marked by 14 Stations of the Cross (nine located along the route and four within the Church of the Holy Sepulchre). Stations III, IV, V, VI and VII are open only on Friday afternoons. During Holy Week, thousands of pilgrims join the procession that winds down the narrow alleys of the Old City, a moving and impressive sight to behold.

HISTORY Pilgrims began to trace the route taken by Jesus when open Christian worship became permitted during the Byzantine period. Over the years the route has changed along with the Old City's jumbled façade, and would have looked very different during Jesus's time. From the 14th to 16th centuries, pilgrims followed what was known as the Franciscan route, which began in the Church of the Holy Sepulchre and included eight stations. At the same time, the tradition of 14 stations was emerging in Europe, and so as not to disappoint European pilgrims, six more were included. Although members of different denominations follow their own routes, the most widely accepted is that of the early Byzantine Christians. Eight of the 14 stations along the Via Dolorosa are described in scriptures, while the other six are traditional. It is important to note that the stations are not historical sites but commemorate religious events.

STATION I – JESUS IS CONDEMNED TO DEATH Located on the left, 300m from Lion's Gate is the large courtyard of the **Omariye College** [85 F3] (⏀ *14.30–18.00 Mon–Thu & Sat, 14.30–16.00 Fri*) that marks the beginning of the Via Dolorosa. The minaret that stands in the distance is traditionally named the 'Antonia Tower' after historian Josephus's description of the ancient Roman fortress where Jesus was condemned to death by Pontius Pilate. The college is still used as a school and can be visited at limited times.

STATION II – JESUS TAKES UP THE CROSS Across the street in a large courtyard are the **Sanctuaries of the Flagellation and Condemnation** [85 F2] (⏀ *08.00–11.45 & 14.00–18.00 daily*) where according to tradition, Roman soldiers flogged Jesus and placed a crown of thorns on his head. A few metres further along is the **Sisters of Zion Convent** [85 F3] where steps lead down to what has long been claimed to be the **Lithostratos (Pavement of Justice)** (⏀ *08.30–17.00*), the section of paving stones where Pilate condemned Jesus (it has since been dated to the 2nd century CE). A little further on, and spanning the route, is the **Ecce Homo Arch** named after Pilate's words 'Behold the man!' upon Jesus being presented to the crowd. The arch is a traditional symbol, having also been built in the 2nd century CE.

Armenian Quarter The Armenian Quarter is the smallest area of the Old City and is today home to some 2,200 residents. The area centres on the ornate Armenian cathedral and has its own schools, seminary, library and residential areas, all occupying what was once the site of Herod's great palace. The Armenians

STATION III – JESUS FALLS UNDER THE CROSS FOR THE FIRST TIME This traditional station is marked by a small 19th-century **chapel** that was funded by Catholic soldiers of the Free Polish army during World War I. Walk to the corner of El-Wad Road and turn left. The chapel is immediately on the left with a relief of Jesus falling, above the door.

STATION IV – JESUS MEETS HIS MOTHER The station is marked by a small Armenian chapel located a few metres along from Station III. Blue iron doors, above which is a bas-relief of the Virgin Mary comforting Jesus, mark the entrance.

STATION V – SIMON OF CYRENE IS FORCED TO CARRY THE CROSS The event, where Simon of Cyrene (a north African pilgrim) was compelled by Roman soldiers to help Jesus carry the Cross, is mentioned in three of the Gospels. The station is marked by a **Franciscan oratory** and is located on the corner of El Wad Road and the Via Dolorosa.

STATION VI – VERONICA WIPES THE SWEAT FROM JESUS'S FACE A hundred metres further up is the chapel of the **Convent of the Little Sisters of Jesus** [84 D3]. The chapel is the traditional house of Veronica from where she emerged to wipe the sweat from Jesus's face.

STATION VII – JESUS FALLS FOR THE SECOND TIME This station traditionally marks the place where Jesus passed beneath the Gate of Judgement on his way to Golgotha. Today a large Roman column housed within a **Franciscan chapel** commemorates the event. Walk to the crossroads at the end of the Via Dolorosa. The chapel is located on the northwest corner where Souk Khan es Zeit Street and El Khanqa Street meet.

STATION VIII – JESUS CONSOLES THE WOMEN OF JERUSALEM A stone embedded in the outer wall of the **Greek Monastery of St Haralambos** commemorates the point where Jesus met the daughters of Jerusalem, who wept over his fate. According to Luke's Gospel he replied: 'Do not weep for me; weep for yourselves and for your children.' In Jesus's time this would have been an open field between the city wall and Golgotha. The monastery is located 30m up El Khanqa Street on the opposite side to Station VII.

STATION IX – JESUS FALLS FOR THE THIRD TIME Walk back to Souk Khan es Zeit Street and turn right. After 50m a stairway on the right leads to a Coptic church within which is a Roman column painted with a Latin cross. This marks the traditional spot where Jesus fell for the third time. A doorway to the left of Station IX leads on to the roof of the Chapel of St Helena, where an Ethiopian church is located.

STATIONS X–XIV The final five stations are located within the Church of the Holy Sepulchre. From the Ethiopian chapel walk down the stairs, which will bring you out in the courtyard of the church (see page 82).

have formed part of the city's demographic make-up since the 1st century when the Roman emperor Titus brought Armenian traders, artisans and soldiers to the Holy Land. They were the first to adopt Christianity in the 4th century and within 100 years, following an influx of pilgrims, had erected over 70 monasteries in Jerusalem. The Armenians are an ancient people whose history dates back over 4,000 years, their rich cultural value and dramatic history often being overlooked in favour of their more vocal Old City neighbours. As an exiled people who have suffered great persecution and a devastating genocide, the small community in Jerusalem has a strong sense of cultural identity and independence, and has largely managed to avoid the battles and wars that have ravaged the rest of the Old City.

Citadel and Tower of David Museum The Tower of David Museum [84 C5] occupies the imposing citadel that forms one of the Old City's most recognisable landmarks. Throughout Jerusalem's tumultuous past, the citadel stood as the main line of defence to the north and west, being reinforced and rebuilt by each generation of invaders. The area was hugely fortified by the Hasmonean kings and, in 24BCE, refortified by King Herod. Throughout the ages the citadel was used as a garrison for Roman soldiers and, with the adoption of Christianity, a quasi-monastery. It once again resumed its military role throughout the Muslim conquest and Crusader rule, during which time its large moat was constructed. It also became the seat of the Crusader king of Jerusalem. The fortress in its present form dates from the Mamluk period, and later underwent changes during the Ottoman period when a large mosque was built, its towering minaret later dubbed the 'Tower of David' by 19th-century European travellers (which has caused considerable confusion over the years). When the British army entered the city in December 1917, it was from the platform outside the citadel that General Allenby addressed the people of Jerusalem, declaring freedom of worship.

The museum (6265333; www.towerofdavid.org.il; 10.00–17.00 Sat–Thu, 10.00–14.00 Fri; admission adult/child 30/15NIS) Today the citadel is home to the Tower of David Museum, one of the city's top attractions and a valuable tool in piecing together Jerusalem's past. Displays are spread throughout the network of guardrooms and cover the 5,000 action-filled years of Jerusalem's history. Exhibits present the city's chronological story with the aid of models, visual aids and multimedia displays. The walls and ramparts of the citadel provide some fantastic views of both the Old City and modern city.

Show and tours Every evening (except Fri) the citadel hosts the son et lumière show, a light display depicting the city's history (adult/child 55/45NIS). Free guided tours in English leave the main entrance at 11.00 Sunday to Thursday and a free downloaded mp3 tour is available on the website. A multiple-entry ticket is available (adult/child 80/50NIS).

St James Cathedral [84 C6] (08.00–17.00 daily) Amidst such an abundance of ecclesiastical buildings within the Old City, St James Cathedral is sadly often overlooked. Tradition has it the cathedral was named after both Jesus's brother and James the Apostle, both of whom are said to be buried within. Jesus's brother is believed to be buried within the central nave, while St James the Apostle rests under the exquisitely decorated shrine behind large wooden doors. Hundreds of gold and silver lanterns hang in the cathedral illuminating the domed ceiling. If possible, try to visit during Armenian Orthodox mass. Afternoon mass is signalled by the priest clanging wooden bars in the porch. The entrance to the monastery is located approximately 200m along Armenian Patriarchate Street from Jaffa Gate on the right.

Museum of Armenian Art and History [84 C7] (*Armenian Orthodox Patriarchate St;* ✆ *6283331;* ⊕ *09.30–16.30 Mon–Sat; admission 5NIS*) Heading south towards the Zion Gate, pass under the narrow bridge and turn left after 30m. The museum is located on the right of a large, 200-year-old courtyard. Displays are simple yet informative, depicting the lives, history, culture and art of the Armenian community in Jerusalem. The most moving and horrifying exhibit depicts the Armenian genocide in Turkey during World War I, a graphic and powerful display of photographs and personal descriptions.

Zion Gate [84 D7] The gate leads out of the Armenian Quarter and provides access to and from Mount Zion. It remains in the original 'L' shape, designed to prevent horse-mounted soldiers from charging, and to slow the battering rams used in attacks during the Ottoman period. Cars slowly weave their way through the awkwardly shaped pass and a resident camel often sits in the corner. The gate bears the scars from the 1948 Arab–Israeli War in the form of bullet marks on its outer edge. It is known in Arabic as Bab el Nabi Daoud (Gate of the Prophet David) because of the traditional site of David's tomb just outside (see page 000).

Jewish Quarter The Jewish Quarter is undoubtedly the most serene area of the Old City, where Jerusalem's oldest synagogues stand, where bougainvillea flowers creep over brick walls, and where an air of religious learning permeates the quiet cobbled alleys. During Herod's reign, this was the city's most affluent neighbourhood, inhabited mainly by aristocratic and priestly families. It also formed the core of the Roman city of Aelia Capitolina with the grand Cardo, the city's main thoroughfare, beginning here. The quaint Hurva Square sits at the centre of the quarter and is fringed by outdoor cafés and bakeries. At the eastern edge of the Jewish Quarter, the vast plaza stretches the length of the Western Wall, the last remaining icon of the Second Temple, and the holiest Jewish site.

Western Wall [85 F5] The Western Wall is the single most sacred site in Judaism. It stands as the last remnant of the Second Temple and has been a site of pilgrimage for Jews from all over the world since the Ottoman period, who come to lament over the loss of their temple, their emotional and sorrowful prayers awarding it the name 'The Wailing Wall'. Today it remains the heart of the Jewish faith and one of the most religious and politically sensitive sites on the planet.

History The wall, or HaKotel, was built by King Herod in 20BCE as part of the Temple Mount complex and is all that remains from the Roman destruction of the temple in 70CE. From the Ottoman period, Jewish pilgrims flocked to the wall, at the time accessed by a narrow alley – 3.6m wide and 28m long – embedded in the surrounding Muslim neighbourhoods. Throughout the 19th century, conflict hummed around the wall and several prominent Jews, including Baron Rothschild (see page 171) and Sir Moses Montefiore, attempted unsuccessfully to gain control of it. During the British Mandate period there were numerous clashes between Jews and Muslims and from December 1947 Jews were banned from approaching the wall, a restriction which, following the capitulation of the Jewish Quarter in May 1948, lasted 19 years. After the 1967 Six Day War the wall once again fell into Jewish hands and was greatly expanded to create the vast plaza that we see today.

The wall and tunnels The Western Wall lies at the end of the 56m long, sloping **Western Wall Plaza** [85 E5] and is the principal site of Jewish pilgrimage, where worshippers come to slip prayer notes in between the ancient stones. The plaza itself is a great place to people-watch, especially during religious celebrations or the Shabbat prayer sessions. Inside the men's area the cavern-like **Wilson's Arch** serves as the main place of prayer (particularly in summer when it is air conditioned). It once formed part of the great bridge linking the upper city and temple. To the left of the men's prayer area is the beginning of the **Western Wall Tunnels** [85 E5] (✆ 6271333; www.thekotel.org; ◷ 07.00–last tour booking Sun–Thu, 07.00–12.00 Fri; admission adult/child 30/15NIS), excavated to reveal buried sections of the original temple wall and stretching as far as the Via Dolorosa. Guided tours (in English, 1¼hrs, must be booked in advance) are a fascinating insight into the wall's complex layers of history. Tours take visitors along the narrow **Secret Passage** to the Herodian Wall, once a beautiful public building. The **Large Hall** leads to the **Largest Stone**, a 570-ton building stone that is the last remaining foundation block and the largest stone to be unearthed in the country. **Warren's Gate** (there are also three other ancient gates: Wilson's, Barclay's and Robinson's) is named after the prominent 19th-century researcher of Jerusalem and leads to a **small alcove** that is part of the wall closest to the temple. Known as 'the holy of holies', it is separated from the foundation stone (located beneath the Dome of the Rock) by a mere 100m. From here the tunnels lead to the **Herodian Wall**, which during temple times was a bustling shopping street, past a **quarry** and **aqueduct** and emerge along the **Via Dolorosa** in the Muslim Quarter. The **Chain of Generations Centre** (✆ 6271333; www.thekotel.org; ◷ 08.00–last tour Sun–Thu; admission adult/child 25/15NIS) is a good accompaniment to the tunnel tour, relating the story of the Jewish people throughout the past 3,500 years using a combination of music, sculpture, archaeology, glass, light effects and holographic images. It was seven years in the making and is a revolutionary museum experience.

The Cardo [84 D6] The Cardo formed the main north–south thoroughfare of Roman Jerusalem, which was modelled on the structure of typical Roman cities. The street was excavated for 200m and today a small section at its southern end has been restored to reveal the parallel columns that ran its length and would have supported a wooden roof. The 22.5m-wide thoroughfare was flanked by shops, but later had a row of buildings erected down the centre. The street now comprises two lanes: Chabad and Hayehudim. The street is bordered by cafés, art galleries and age-old bakeries and is one of the busiest areas of the Jewish Quarter. A section of the Cardo has been rebuilt as a modern shopping area comprising mainly pricey Judaica stores and art galleries, and is a far cry from the original shops selling grain, spices and olives, but it is nevertheless a pleasant place to stroll around.

Synagogues The **Hurva Synagogue** [84 D5] (*hurva* meaning 'ruins') was originally commissioned by Rabbi Yehuda HaNassi who arrived in Jerusalem in 1701 with 500 Ashkenazis. Following his death, the synagogue fell into disrepair and wasn't fully rebuilt until 1856. From then until its destruction during the 1948 war it acted as the spiritual core of Jerusalem's Ashkenazi Jews. After the Israeli capture of Jerusalem in 1967, plans were discussed to rebuild the ancient synagogue, but weren't put into action until 2006 when its signature arch was dismantled. A US$6.2 million budget saw it rebuilt it to its former neo-Byzantine splendour, and it was completed in early 2010.

The **Rambam Synagogue** [84 D6] is named after Rabbi Moshe ben Nachman (the Rambam) who arrived in Jerusalem in 1267 following the decimation of the city in the battle between the Crusaders and the Mamluks. He established a synagogue amidst the destruction, a poignant event seen by Jews as the beginning of the reconstruction of Jerusalem. In the 16th century, the Muslims commandeered the building, and between 1949 and 1967 it was used to house livestock. Only after Israel gained control of the city was it returned to its original purpose. Since then it has superseded the Hurva Synagogue as the most important Jewish house of worship within the Old City. It has been well restored and marks a key point on the Jewish history trail.

The **Four Sephardi Synagogues** [84 D6] (✆ *6280592;* ☉ *09.30–16.00 Sun–Thu, 09.30–12.30 Fri*) is a complex of four Jewish houses of prayer, each representing different histories, religious requirements and prayer practices. Following the arrival of Sephardic Jews expelled from Spain in the 17th century, a new synagogue was built, becoming the first since the Ottoman period. It was named the **Yochanan ben Zakai Synagogue** after the notable sage who is attributed with later establishing the Sanhedrin (Jewish school of biblical studies). Another wave of Sephardic immigrants arrived from Istanbul, Turkey, later in the 17th century who constructed the adjacent **Istanbuli Synagogue**. Named after Elijah the Prophet, the third, **Eliyahu Ha'navi Synagogue** was used solely for Torah study. In the centre of the three buildings a courtyard formed, which during the 18th century was converted into the **Emtsai (or Middle) Synagogue**. The complex is also attributed with being the last position held by Jewish defenders before the fall of the Jewish Quarter to the Jordanians in 1948.

The Herodian Quarter During the Second Temple period the Upper City (the present-day Jewish Quarter) housed the most affluent of Jerusalem's residents and was the last section to be razed to the ground by the Romans in 70CE. The **Burnt House** [85 E5] (✆ *6287211;* ☉ *09.00–17.00 Thu–Sun, 09.00–13.00 Fri; admission adult/child 25/12NIS*) stands as a testament to the day the Upper City was burnt and those within lost their lives. Finds discovered in the house include an arm bone seemingly reaching for a nearby spear, coins, and many household objects including a set of weights inscribed with the name 'Bar Kathros'. This find proved to be the most telling, possibly identifying the occupants as being of the priestly family known from the Talmud to have lived at the time of the Second Temple. Inside the house there is a short film (every 40mins) that delves into the history of the site and Upper City. A visit to the house is more interesting for what it represents than for the finds inside.

The **Wohl Archaeological Museum** [85 E6] (*1Hakara'im St;* ✆ *6283448;* ☉ *09.00–17.00–Thu, 09.00–13.00 Fri; admission adult/child 35/15NIS, combined* *with Burnt House*) contains remains of Jewish mansions and houses from the affluent Upper City, which was mostly occupied by Jewish Temple priests. On display are luxury relics ranging from mosaic floors to expensive glassware that provide an insight into the Herodian Quarter and its wealthy residents. The quarter lies today 3–7m below street level, a staircase leading up from the submerged museum ending abruptly and providing a clear reminder of the devastation caused by the Roman destruction. The museum contains three sections, the most impressive being the **Palatial Mansion**, the most complete of the Herodian houses on display.

Jerusalem Archaeological Park [85 F5] (✆ 6277550; www.archpark.org.il; ⌚ 08.00–17.00 Sun–Thu, 08.00–14.00 Fri; admission adult/child 30/16NIS) This covers the area surrounding the Western Wall Plaza and southern wall of the Temple Mount complex, and has been extensively excavated to reveal substantial remains from the Second Temple period. Jumbled remains from the Byzantine, early Islamic, Crusader and Mumluk periods provide an interesting glimpse into Jerusalem's layers of occupation and are best appreciated by first paying a visit to the Davidson Centre which displays historic exhibits and virtual reconstructions. A one-hour guided tour costs 160NIS and must be booked in advance.

Dung Gate [85 F6] The Jewish Quarter is accessed by the Dung Gate located on its southern wall. A bus stop at the top of Shlomo Goren Street that passes through the gate is directly outside the southern entrance to the Western Wall Plaza. It also provides access to the visitors' entrance to the Temple Mount and Jerusalem Archaeological Park. There are conflicting theories as to the origins of the name of the gate, the most plausible being that it was where rubbish was brought out of the city from the 2nd century onwards.

Muslim Quarter
What the Christian, Jewish and Armenian quarters have in historic buildings, state-of-the-art museums and ecclesiastical marvels, the Muslim Quarter has in vivacity. It is undoubtedly the liveliest of the four quarters, the Damascus and Herod's gates opening into the thriving Arab neighbourhood of East Jerusalem. Its markets are incomparable: a hub of activity, noise, aromas and traditional Arabic merchandise, a wonderful contrast to the more serene streets elsewhere in the quarter. But the area is not without its historic gems: the vast, walled Temple Mount complex occupies the most prized piece of real estate in the country, its majestic golden Dome of the Rock forming the centrepiece of the Old City. As the call of the muezzin echoes across the city signalling the beginning of Friday prayer sessions, swarms of worshippers pour down the lanes towards the mount, while from its easternmost gate begins the Via Dolorosa, Christianity's holiest processional.

Temple Mount (✆ 6283292; ⌚ 07.30–10.00 & 12.30–13.30 Sun–Thu; admission free) Rising above the city, the golden Dome of the Rock forms the centrepiece of Jerusalem's holiest Islamic site, the Temple Mount. Known to Muslims as Haram Es Sharif (Noble Sanctuary) it is believed to be the site from where Muhammad began his Night Journey to Heaven and today ranks as the third holiest Islamic site in the world after Mecca and Medina. To Jews, this is also the pinnacle of holiness, the site where the First and Second temples stood, where the Foundation Stone upon which the world was built stands, where Adam was created and where Isaac was almost sacrificed by Abraham. In a city that has seen more than its fair share of turmoil and tension, the Temple Mount is today still a raw and sensitive point, often acting as the centre of unrest between Jews and Muslims. For the most part, however, the area is a peaceful and tranquil place of worship and as you wander around the wide, open complex, it is hard to envisage the 3,000 years of turmoil that have surrounded it.

History The history of the Temple Mount spans 3,000 years, seven periods of time, three world religions and five cultures. Upon land bought by King David, Jerusalem's First Temple was built by his son King Solomon and stood until the Babylonians destroyed it in 586BCE. Not long after, Jews returning from exile rebuilt it and so the Second Temple came into being. Following the Roman destruction of the city in 70CE, the temple (bar the Western Wall) was left in ruins until the Muslim conquest in 638 when Caliph Omar built the first mosque upon the site. Fifty years later, during the reign of Caliph Abd al-Malik, the Dome of the Rock and Al-Aqsa Mosque were erected.

In 1099, the Crusaders captured Jerusalem whereby holy sites on the Temple Mount were declared Christian and the area became the seat of the Knights Templar. In 1187, Saladin put an end to Crusader rule, reconverting churches to mosques.

Safety issues Following the 1948 Arab–Israeli War, Jerusalem remained divided, with the Old City and Temple Mount under Jordanian rule. After Israel captured the city during the 1967 Six Day War, the Waqf was allowed to retain administration of the site on the proviso that non-Muslims be allowed to enter. In order to prevent rioting and religious unrest, the Israeli government has banned any non-Islamic praying on the site. Modest dress is compulsory and open displays of affection are not appreciated. At the time of writing, the Dome of the Rock, Al-Aqsa Mosque and Islamic Museum are closed to all non-Muslims. Some Jews do enter the Temple Mount but often limit themselves to the perimeter wall. During times of political unrest it is best to check government warnings on the advisability of visiting the complex, although entry is generally prohibited if threats arise. During the relatively short opening times, queues for entry can be long so it is best to arrive early.

What to see While the most impressive and alluring structure within the Temple Mount is undoubtedly the Dome of the Rock, the 144,000m² **Al-Aqsa Mosque** is the holiest part of the complex. It was the earliest mosque constructed in Palestine and is today one of Islam's most important houses of prayer, believed to be the place referred to in the Koran as '*al-aqsa*' (the furthermost). Although the mosque has suffered great tragedy over the last century, being inter alia the site of King Abdullah of Jordan's 1951 assassination, it is today a mostly peaceful and active centre of prayer holding up to 4,000 worshippers at any one time. In the southeast corner of the temple esplanade are the scanty remains of **Solomon's Stables,** which contrary to their name were not in existence in Solomon's time but acted as stables during the Crusader occupation. Just north of the mosque, the circular **Al Kas Fountain** dates to 709 and is used by Muslims for the ritual washing prior to prayer sessions. Directly ahead lies the octagonal **Dome of the Rock**, crowned by its gold-leafed dome, a million-dollar gift from Saudi Arabia in 1965. It stands as the oldest Islamic shrine in the world dated to 688 and also boasts the world's oldest-surviving *mihrab* (niche indicating the direction of Mecca). Extensive decoration from a variety of periods including mosaics, painted wood, marble, coloured tiles, carpets and carved stone covers both the interior and exterior of the building, most of the blue and gold exterior tiles laid under Suleiman the Magnificent. Muslim pilgrimage to Jerusalem is known as *taqdis* and marks the final destination on the main pilgrimage (*hajj*). The **Islamic Museum** [85 F5] (⊕ *08.00–11.30 Sat–Thu*) although currently not open to non-Muslims, has interesting displays on Islamic art, Koran books and architectural items.

Bazaars (⊕ *09.00–19.00 daily*) The Muslim Quarter bazaars are among the most fascinating places to visit in the Old City, a clear demonstration of the thriving Arab communities who call this area (and the neighbourhoods in East Jerusalem) home. Beginning at the swarming Damascus Gate two market streets branch off southwards: **El Wad Street** and **Souk Khan es Zeit**. A third street, **Souk el Qattanin (Cotton Market)**, is located at the southern end of El Wad Street, and is probably the most ancient and intriguing market, with its stone-arched roof and rudimentary stalls. An atmosphere of effervescent hubbub surrounds the markets where colourful shops, cafés and food stalls squeeze into any available space. Compared with the Virgin Mary statues and Stars of David that attract tourists and pilgrims in the Christian Quarter markets, the Muslim markets form the centre of daily life in the Arab community. Spices, leather goods, Arabic-style clothes, carpets, butchers, bakers and candlestick makers all have their place.

Bargaining is customary in all of the markets so don't be shy or you'll pay over the odds. Expect to pay in the region of three-quarters of the vendor's opening price (you can offer half and go from there). It is a lively and fun activity and a smile goes a long way. You will no doubt get offered strong Arabic coffee or mint tea so take it – it's a great way to get to know the people and a more relaxing way to bargain.

Church of St Anne and the Pool of Bethesda [85 F2] ℘ *6283285;*
⊕ *08.00–12.00 & 14.00–17.00 Mon–Sat; admission 10NIS*) The vast church complex is located on the right of Sha'ar Ha'arayot Street 30m from Lion's Gate. Entering through the large wooden gate, the Church of St Anne is located at the rear of a small garden (on the right) and the excavations of the Pool of Bethesda lie opposite.

The Pool of Bethesda was documented in John's Gospel account as the site where Jesus healed a man who had suffered illness for 38 years (John 5:2–9). Until 1871 proof was based on faith alone, until excavations unearthed remains of a colonnaded pool matching John's description. It is now considered by archaeologists and Christians to be the exact site described in the Gospel. The Pool of Bethesda is today a series of impressive submerged dry relics, but during Jesus's time was a site of healing, where legend had it an angel moved the waters and cured the sick.

The Church of St Anne and ruins are located within peaceful, quiet gardens that are often thronged with pilgrims who come to sing hymns in the beautiful 12th-century Crusader church renowned for its acoustics. The church was erected over the traditional site of the birthplace of St Anne, the mother of Mary. The Crusader church that stands today was built over an earlier Byzantine church, which was later converted by Saladin into a Muslim theological school (an inscription above the church commemorates this). The church was eventually abandoned until, in 1856, the Ottomans donated it to France who restored it to its former beauty (although most of what you see today is in fact original). From within the church stone steps lead down to the cavern, traditionally regarded as St Anne's birthplace.

Zedekiah's Cave [85 E1] ℘ *6277550;* ⊕ *09.00–17.00 Sat–Thu*) Located 100m east of Damascus Gate, Zedekiah's Cave (also known as Solomon's Quarries) is believed to be the vast quarry from which the building blocks of the First Temple were unearthed. While there isn't an awful lot to see inside, the cave's interest lies in

its history and as the site of ritual ceremonies of the Freemasons, the order claiming spiritual ancestry from the founders of Jerusalem's Temple.

Gates

Damascus Gate [84 D2] At the northern end of the main Muslim Quarter souk and leading on to Sultan Suleiman Street, the Damascus Gate is in fact known by three names: the Christians refer to it as Damascus as it marks the beginning of the highway that led through Israel to Syria; it is known in Hebrew as Sha'ar (gate of) Shechem after the biblical city (modern-day Nablus) that was accessed by a road crossing the Damascus route; Arabs refer to it as Bab al 'Amud (Gate of the Pillar) after the remains of the 2nd-century wall discovered beneath. The gate is the main entrance into and out of the Muslim Quarter and a constant buzz of activity surrounds it, where merchants and worshippers stream through on their way to the souk or Al-Aqsa Mosque. There is a great view of the Muslim Quarter from the top of the gate, which can be accessed by steps on its eastern side.

Golden Gate (closed) [85 G8] The sealed gate that is today located along the eastern wall of the Old City in the Temple Mount complex dates to 640CE and was built either by the last Byzantine rulers or the first of the Arab conquerors. Jews claim that it is through this gate that the Messiah will pass on his way to the Old City and it is said to have been sealed by the Muslims during Suleiman the Magnificent's reign in an attempt to prevent the Messiah from entering. Today the closure of the gate is not considred by most Jews as a sensitive point. Many jokingly claim that if the Messiah can get this far, he will find a way to get in.

Lion's Gate [85 G2] Tradition states that Sultan Suleiman the Magnificent dreamed of being eaten by lions, and that to prevent this the walls of Jerusalem had to be rebuilt. On either side of the gate are reliefs of leopards, which are mistakenly referred to as lions. The gate also goes by the name St Stephen's Gate, as, according to tradition, this was the site where the first Christian martyr Stephen was stoned to death. In Arabic the gate is known as Bab Sitti Maryam, Gate of the Virgin Mary. The gate once again entered the history books when, during the Six Day War, Israeli soldiers from the 55th Paratroop Brigade marched through and raised the Israeli flag, signalling the conquest of the Old City.

Herod's Gate [85 E1] Located on the northern side of the city, Herod's Gate faces the vibrant Arab area of East Jerusalem. During the British Mandate period it became the principal entry point to the Old City and had its L-shape removed to allow for an easier flow of traffic. It was called Herod's Gate by 16th- and 17th-century pilgrims who mistakenly believed a house located just inside it was that of Herod Antipas, Herod the Great's son. It was also at Herod's Gate that at midday on 15 July 1099 the Crusaders breached the wall and took Jerusalem, declaring it part of the Latin Kingdom.

Mount Zion Accessed by the towering, bullet-ridden Zion Gate that leads from the Armenian Quarter, Mount Zion's wealth of religious and historic relics sees it incorporated into any tour of the Old City. It is a small, easily navigable area but often crowded with Jewish and Christian tour groups who make the pilgrimage to the holy sites concentrated here.

Dormition Abbey (℡ *5655330;* ⊕ *08.30–12.00 & 12.40–18.00 Mon–Fri, 08.30–12.00 & 12.40–17.30 Sat, 10.30–11.45 & 12.40–17.30 Sun; information leaflet 1NIS*)

To get a completely different view of the Old City, a wonderful walk around the great stone walls that encompass the maze of alleys and jumble of buildings is a lovely way to spend an afternoon, or indeed evening when the walls are illuminated. Begin at the **Jaffa Gate** and climb the steps on to the ramparts and head northwest (right if you're facing out of the gate). The wall leads around the quiet corner of the Christian Quarter, over the New Gate and continues along the north wall to the bustling Damascus Gate, which is a great place to stop and watch the milling throngs of market-goers below. Continue along the ramparts where you'll have the busy Sultan Suleiman Street of East Jerusalem on one side and the quieter parts of the Muslim Quarter on the other. At the corner of the wall is an impressive lookout over the Mount of Olives and Kidron Valley. Head down the east wall until you reach Lion's Gate and the beginning of the Temple Mount complex, and descend the steps. Exit the gate and carry on along the outside of the east wall on the **Ophel Promenade** [85 G4] that runs through the Muslim cemetery. At the end of the Temple Mount wall the promenade stops and you will need to walk along the road for about 350m until you reach the Dung Gate. Ascend the steps back on to the ramparts, which will then lead you past the tumble of white stone buildings of the Jewish Quarter and then past the quiet lanes of the Armenian Quarter.

Easily recognisable by its blue conical roof, this beautiful church was commissioned in 1906 by Kaiser Wilhelm II, its robust architecture and conical corner towers evoking images of medieval European castles. According to the Roman Catholic and Eastern and Oriental Orthodox churches, this is the site where the Virgin Mary fell asleep and was taken to Heaven (the Assumption of Mary). In the basement of the cavernous church is a statue of the Virgin. The church is frequented by hordes of tour groups so be prepared for a squeeze.

King David's Tomb and the Upper Room These two holy sites, located one above the other, attract vast crowds of quite varying religious backgrounds. To the Jews this is the site of King David's cenotaph, located on the ground floor of the building complex. It is one of the most venerated Jewish sites in the world and high on the pilgrimage list, particularly on Shavuot, the traditional day of David's death. The vast ornate sarcophagus is located within a stone-cut tomb. To Christians, the **Upper Room** (or Coenaculum) (⊕ *08.00–17.00 daily*) is the site of Jesus's Last Supper, the establishment of the rite of the Eucharist and the location of his last appearance to the Apostles. The room, today accessed by a flight of steps, was once a part of the Crusader Church of Our Lady of Mount Zion but is now located above various Jewish *yeshivas* (schools of Torah study). There isn't a lot to see inside the room bar some sparse examples of Crusader architecture. Guides direct visitors to one or other of the rooms, managing to successfully ascertain their religious preference by a mere glance.

Montefiore's Windmill [69 F7] Born in Italy, Moses Montefiore (1784–1885) was a British Jewish businessman, renowned for his Zionist dreams, Jewish philanthropy and establishment of the Yemin Moshe neighbourhood to the west of the Old City walls. Today, the unmistakable **Montefiore's Windmill** is a lasting legacy to his tireless efforts (although it was never actually used on account of a distinct lack of wind in this area).

Mount of Olives and the Kidron Valley

City of David (6262341; www.cityofdavid.org.il; ☉ 08.00–19.00 Sun–Thu, 08.00–14.00 Fri; admission adult/child 25/13NIS) The City of David referred to in the Bible lies outside the modern-day walls in the Kidron Valley. In the area between the Temple Mount and Mount of Olives, excavations have revealed the original capital of Jerusalem, built by King David more than 3,000 years ago to unify the tribes of Israel. For most, the highlight of a trip to the archaeological park is taking a 30-minute wade through the 2,700-year-old **Hezekiah's Tunnel** that leads from the **Gihon Spring** to the **Siloam Pool** further down the valley (although there is a dry route for those less disposed to getting wet). The spring was the principal water source of the city and its waters are mentioned in countless events in the Bible. In the 8th century BCE, under Assyrian threat, King Hezekiah had the water flow diverted underground in an attempt to protect this important source. Today, the 533m-long tunnel can be traversed (be sure to wear appropriate clothing as water reaches knee height). Other important sites include the extensive **Area G** excavation zone and **Warren's Shaft**. A guided tour is well worth it to gain a better understanding of the complexities of the site (adult/child 60/45NIS), which includes the **3-D Movie** depicting the history of the City of David (normally 10NIS

OSKAR SCHINDLER

Oskar Schindler (28 April 1908–9 October 1974) was a German businessman and member of the Nazi Party who is renowned for saving his Jewish workers from entering concentration camps during the Holocaust. He established a factory as a sub-camp of the Plazow labour camp, employing his Jewish workers and keeping them safe from execution. In 1944, he relocated his factory, opening it under the ruse of manufacturing tank shells. Through contacts and bribery he instead spent his fortune buying medicine and food for his Jewish workers. Following the war, Schindler found himself ostracised from his native homeland and moved to Argentina. In 1962 he was invited to plant a tree in the Avenue of the Righteous in Jerusalem, an act that brought his World War II acts to light and subjected him to abuse and harassment from Nazi sympathisers. He became the only member of the Nazi Party to be recognised as a 'righteous gentile' in Israel and shortly before his death in 1974 he declared his wish to be buried there. He died a poor man in Germany and his remains were transported to Jerusalem where his coffin was carried through the streets and buried in the Catholic Cemetery on Mount Zion. He is attributed with having saved 1,200 Jews from persecution and was venerated in the Booker Prize-winning *Schindler's Ark* by Thomas Keneally and later Stephen Spielberg's Academy Award-winning movie *Schindler's List* (1993), in which he was played by Liam Neeson.

Today the cemetery appears long forgotten. Overgrown and dishevelled, its tombstones are untended and have fared badly with the passage of time. At the bottom of the cemetery Oskar Schindler's grave stands out, tiny white stones lined along its clean slab. The custom of piling stones dates to biblical times when they were used to mark graves. Today they represent a more permanent symbol than flowers to show love and respect.

with entry ticket). A night tour of the illuminated gardens complete with harp music and a cup of coffee is a different way to see the site (✆ 6268700; 21.00 in English; 1½hrs; adult/child 35/25NIS).

Church of All Nations and the Garden of Gethsemane

[85 H3] At the foot of the Mount of Olives is the garden (✆ 6283264; ⊕ 08.30–12.00 & 14.00–17.30 daily), known in Christian tradition as the site of Jesus's agony, prayer, betrayal by Judas and subsequent arrest. The name Gethsemane derives from the Hebrew 'gat shemen' meaning 'oil press', a reference to the ancient olive trees that remain standing to this day, believed by botanists to pre-date Christianity. Within the tranquil, shady garden stands the magnificent **Church of All Nations** (also known as the Basilica of the Agony). The church, with its vast fresco adorning the façade, was rebuilt in 1924 on the site of earlier Byzantine and Crusader churches, thanks to contributions from Catholic communities all over the world. Inside the church mosaic symbols of each of these communities are present in the domes. Inside, the **Rock of the Agony** is said to be the stone where Jesus prayed. Services in English are on Sundays 11.00.

Tomb of the Virgin Mary

[85 H3] (⊕ 06.00–12.30 & 14.00–18.00 daily) The cavernous church, which dates to the Crusader period, is the traditional burial site of Jesus's mother. While this event is unrecorded in the Bible, belief in this site dates back to the 2nd or 3rd century CE. Muslims also worship this spot in the belief that the Prophet Muhammad saw a light shine over Mary's tomb on his Night Journey from Mecca. A wide marble staircase leads down to the eerily beautiful, grotto-like church, the ceiling of which is adorned with hundreds of ornate lanterns. Mary's tomb is located at the bottom of the steps to the right past a Greek Orthodox altar. To the right of the tomb is a Muslim prayer arch dating to medieval times. The church is the Greek Orthodox rival to the Dormition Abbey on Mount Zion as the site of Mary's assumption.

Dominus Flevit

(⊕ 08.00–12.00 & 14.30–17.00 daily) To find the church, turn left off Jericho Road and then right up the extremely steep and narrow lane that runs along the edge of the cemetery. Continue almost to the top and the entrance to the church is on the left through a large gate. Inside is a small, well-kept garden within which is a teardrop-shaped chapel, designed to represent the tears shed by Jesus as he lamented over the future destruction of Jerusalem.

Dome of the Ascension

(admission 5NIS) This small octagonal chapel is the traditional site of Jesus's Ascension to Heaven. A church once stood on the site but today a mosque covers the rock believed to be indented with Jesus's last footprint, the church taken and destroyed by Saladin in 1187 (Islam recognises Jesus as a prophet although does not accept the Christian belief that he was the son of God). It is but one of the contenders for Jesus's ascension, the Russian Orthodox Church and the Church of the Pater Noster also being in the running. Opening hours vary but access can normally be gained during the mornings (ring the doorbell outside to gain entry).

Mount of Olives Cemetery

(⊕ 08.00–16.00 Sun–Thu, 08.00–13.00 Fri) The Jewish cemetery that blankets the side of the Mount of Olives resides on some of the country's prime real estate, and for good reason. According to Jewish belief, the resurrection of the dead will begin here upon the coming of the Messiah. Although the cemetery dates to the First Temple period, most of the tombs that

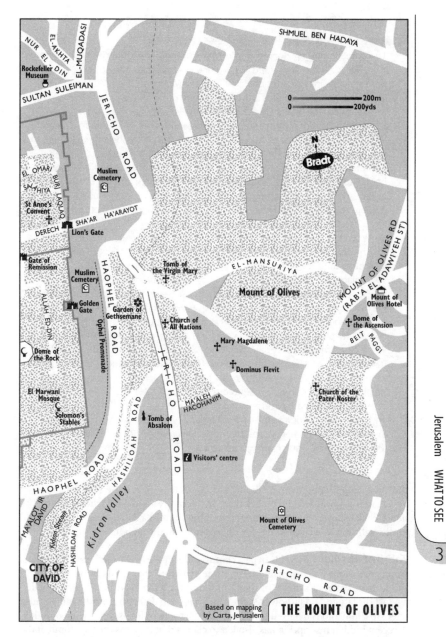

Based on mapping by Carta, Jerusalem

THE MOUNT OF OLIVES

we see today are from the 15th century. During the Jordanian rule, a road leading to Jericho was built over the graves, many gravestones being smashed, destroyed or used in construction. Following the 1967 Six Day War and Israel's conquest of Jerusalem, the government went to great lengths to restore the tombstones to their original positions. The refurbished **visitors' centre** (*Jericho Rd*; ✆ *6275050*; *www. mountofolives.co.il*; ⊕ *09.00–17.00 Sun–Thu*) is located on Jericho Road, 200m from the Lion's Gate traffic lights and provides information on finding some of the most prominent graves, including amongst many, Eliezer Ben-Yehuda, Shmuel Yosef Agnon (awarded the Nobel Prize in literature) and Menachem Begin. The new website shows an aerial photograph of the site and a database of all graves and tombs within it as well as routes for unguided tours through it.

Tomb of Absalom [85 H5] In past centuries devout Jews, Muslims and Christians would pelt stones at the magnificent stone structure that holds pride of place in the Kidron Valley, a symbol of their contempt for King David's son who rebelled against his father. Today, however, the tomb has been dated to almost a millennium after Absalom and is believed by some to be the tomb of Jehosophat, King of Judah. A recent hidden inscription has also led to claims that this was the true tomb of the priest Zachariah, father of John the Baptist, although this is hotly contested. Rather confusingly, the rock-cut **tomb of Zachariah** is located a few metres away.

CITY CENTRE
Israel Museum (*Ruppin Rd;* ✆ *6708811; www.imj.org.il;* ⊕ *10.00–17.00 Sun/Mon, Wed/Thu & Sat, 16.00–21.00 Tue, 10.00–14.00 Fri; admission adult/child 48/24NIS; free to under 17s Tue & Sat*) This is Israel's largest, and one of the world's leading,

archaeology and art museums. Its exhibits cover a wealth of topics, housed within the vast complex, interconnected pavilions and surrounding gardens. The Judaica and Jewish Ethnography Wing consists of the world's largest collection of Jewish religious objects gathered from communities across the globe. The Shrine of the Book and Model of Jerusalem in the Second Temple period is the museum's most famous exhibit, housing the Dead Sea Scrolls (see page 266). The onion-shaped roof of the pavilion was designed to reflect the jar in which the scrolls were discovered. On the lower level of the building are displays of the letters written by Simon Bar-Kochba during the Second Jewish Revolt and artefacts discovered in Masada (see page 267). The Art Pavilion proudly displays works by artists such as Corot, Monet, Renoir, Degas, Gauguin and Matisse, along with the beautifully landscaped Billy Rose Art Garden containing classical and modern pieces by, amongst others, Rodin, Picasso, Henry Moore and Chana Orloff. The newly renovated archaeology wing houses significant artefacts spanning all of the land's countless time periods, eras and invasions. Free tours are arranged in English starting at the Entrance Pavilion (6708811; *reserve in advance*). Alternatively, free audio guides are available from the entrance.

Knesset (*Rothschild St;* 6753420; *www.knesset.gov.il*) The Knesset is the seat of Israel's parliament, a vast building holding pride of place in Jerusalem's centre. An interesting tour can be arranged illuminating not only the workings of the country's political centre but also offering a fascinating insight into the history, culture and heritage of the Jewish people. Tours include architecture, art, the magnificent menorah (which can be seen outside the main complex), divisions of the Knesset, the library, archives and synagogue. Guided tours must be booked in advance (in English at 08.30, 12.00 & 14.00 Sun & Thu), while sessions can be viewed with no need for advance reservation (16.00 Mon/Tue, 11.00 Wed). The Knesset operates a strict dress code and no jeans, shorts, skimpy tops and sandals for men are permitted. Passports must be shown on entry.

Museum of Islamic Art (*2 HaPalmach St;* 5661291; *www.islamicart.co.il;* ⊕ *10.00–15.00 Sun, Mon & Wed, 10.00–19.00 Tue, 10.00–14.00 Fri, 10.00–16.00 Sat; admission adult/child 40/20NIS*) This privately owned museum houses a varied selection of Islamic artistry from every corner of the globe and depicts the history and religious beliefs of Islam. Exhibits include weaponry, glass, jewellery, pottery and carpets from the last 1,400 years. Guided tours can be arranged in advance in Hebrew, English and Arabic.

Monastery of the Cross [68 A7] (6790961; ⊕ *10.00–16.30 Mon–Sat*) This beautiful, castle-like church sits in the middle of what is today referred to as the Valley of the Cross (Rehavia Park) near the Knesset. According to biblical belief, Lot planted branches from pine, fir and cypress trees, which grew into one tree, later used to make the Cross upon which Jesus was crucified. The monastery dates to the Byzantine period, built by Greek Orthodox monks with funding from the King of Georgia. Almost all the complex is open to the public, the kitchen in particular providing a rare and insightful view of daily monastic life.

Mahne Yehuda Market [68 B1] This covered food market is one of the city's liveliest spots, especially on a Friday before Shabbat when all and sundry come to buy their weekend groceries. Everything from fruit and vegetables to meats, cheeses, spices, olives and nuts are sold as well household items and clothes. It also contains some tiny, rustic, traditional eateries serving Middle Eastern dishes that have become some of the 'in' places in Jerusalem. The market as we see it now dates to the British Mandate era, although its roots go back much further to 1887 when the neighbourhood was first established. It is a hugely worthwhile trip both for the excellent food and to gain a real insight into local daily life, and a chance to get away from museums and history for a while.

Me'a She'arim Neighbourhood The ultra-Orthodox neighbourhood was founded in 1875 by eastern European Jews. Easily recognisable in their traditional black clothes, felt hats (*streimel*) and side curls (*peyot*), most speak Yiddish, an old Jewish variant of German, reserving Hebrew only for prayer. Signs plaster the walls surrounding the neighbourhood's entrances requesting those entering to dress appropriately (those who don't heed the warnings often find themselves at the receiving end of verbal abuse and anger). Short sleeves or the baring of legs is not allowed at any time, women are advised to wear long skirts and not trousers, and photographing the residents is also not permitted. Within the area are numerous synagogues, ritual baths, Talmudic schools and Judaica stores. The neighbourhood is also home to the Neturei Karta, a group which does not recognise the state of Israel as it was not founded by the Messiah. A visit to the neighbourhood is unarguably fascinating, and provides a deeper understanding of devout Judaism, and it should be treated with the utmost respect. While it is possible to visit during Shabbat, it is advised not to for religious laws are many, and the chances of those not familiar with them getting it wrong are high. Visiting midweek still demands a level of awareness and religious respect, but is less sensitive than on Fridays and Saturdays.

German Colony After creating an impressive and – for the time – developed neighbourhood in the heart of Haifa (see page 162), the German Templars moved to Jerusalem where, in the late 1800s, they settled in the Emek Refaim area of the city. Built in the styles reminiscent of their homeland, the Christian Templars, who had moved away from the Protestant Church, were later ousted from Jerusalem during the British Mandate period, but left in their wake a pretty neighbourhood of much sought-after real estate. Today the main street through the neighbourhood is Emek Refaim, home to countless popular restaurants, cafés and bars, and is home to a big English-speaking population.

EAST JERUSALEM
Rockefeller Museum (*Sultan Suleiman St;* ✆ *6708011; www.imj.org.il;* ☉ *10.00–15.00 Sun/Mon & Wed/Thu, 10.00–14.00 Sat; admission adult/child 26/12NIS*) Located opposite the northeast corner of Herod's Gate, the Rockefeller Museum is easily recognisable by its massive, limestone tower. It was commissioned by John D Rockefeller in 1927 following a growing need for an appropriate home for finds being unearthed throughout Palestine at the time. For those embarking on a trip around the country, the museum is best saved as a finale, where finds from great sites such as Caesarea, Akko, Beit She'an, the Carmel and the Galilee can be envisioned in their original context. Amongst the most impressive exhibits are the relief carving from the Church of the Holy Sepulchre, the 200,000-year-old skull excavated from the Carmel Caves, wooden beams from the Al-Aqsa Mosque and Egyptian and Mesopotamian material unearthed from Beit She'an.

The Garden Tomb [84 D1] (*Conrad Schik St;* ✆ *6272745; www.gardentomb.com;* ☉ *09.00–12.00 & 14.00–17.30 Mon–Sat; admission free*) The Garden Tomb is the second contender for the site of Golgotha, and couldn't be further removed from the grand Church of the Holy Sepulchre. Tombs discovered by the British general Charles Gordon in 1883 have led many to believe this is the spot mentioned in the Bible. Some archaeologists, however, date the tombs to Old Testament times. Today it is a pretty place of quiet, simple prayer and reverence visited predominantly by Protestant pilgrim groups.

GREATER JERUSALEM

Yad Vashem The Holocaust was one of, if not the most, horrific and devastating events in human history. Over six million Jews lost their lives in unthinkable ways and many more suffered unimaginable trauma and loss. In Israel, remembrance of the Holocaust is as raw today as it was post-World War II, and drives the underlying strength and social unity of the country. The **Yad Vashem Holocaust Museum** (☏ *6443420; www.yadvashem.org;* ⊕ *09.00–17.00 Sun–Wed, 09.00–20.00 Thu, 09.00–14.00 Fri; admission free (under 10s not allowed)*) was created to keep alive the memory of those who suffered, and to tell the story through their eyes. The museum, which was inaugurated by Israeli heads of state and attended by those of 40 other nations, depicts the human story behind the Holocaust. The triangular-shaped, concrete museum hall takes visitors on a walk-through of history, each room depicting a different stage in the events leading up to and during the Holocaust. Displays, which include authentic artefacts, testimonies, personal letters, documentary evidence, films, art and, chillingly, mountains of hair and shoes, are pieced together to tell the wider picture through the personal stories that emerged.

At the end of the museum, the **Hall of Names** has been given a new home. The circular hall is covered with the faces of those who perished and is a moving finale. In a separate room, the **Central Database of Shoah** (Holocaust) **Victim's Names** can be accessed, allowing visitors to search for relatives. It can also be accessed through the website (see above). An audio guide can be rented from reception (20NIS).

Ein Kerem A 20-minute bus ride from the hustle and bustle of central Jerusalem is the picturesque, tranquil village of Ein Kerem, tucked into the green hills, terraced hillsides and olive groves southwest of the city. Famed in Christian tradition as being the birthplace of John the Baptist, Ein Kerem is home to impressive churches, a burgeoning artists' colony and a few cafés and restaurants. Ein Kerem, whose name literally means 'Spring of the Vineyard', also appears in the Mishnah as being the site from where the stone for the altar of the First Temple was taken.

The Franciscan **Church of St John** (☏ *6323000;* ⊕ *08.00–12.00 & 14.30–18.00 daily*) is said to have been built over the grotto in which John the Baptist was born to Elizabeth and Zachariah. The church (not to be confused with the Eastern Orthodox church of the same name) was built in the 19th century over the remains of earlier Byzantine and Crusader churches. At the far end of the village, the beautifully tended **Church of the Visitation** (⊕ *08.30–12.00 & 14.30–18.00 daily*) was originally built by the Crusaders to commemorate the pregnant Mary visiting her cousin Elizabeth. On one wall of the church are the words of the Magnificat, the hymn Mary traditionally sang at the time, in 62 languages. The gates are closed on Saturdays so ring the bell for entry. Not far from the church is **Mary's Spring**, the traditional site of Mary and Elizabeth's meeting and from where the village received its name.

Ammunition Hill (*Givat Hatachmoshet;* ☏ *5828442; www.givathatachmosht.org. il;* ⊕ *09.00–18.00 Sun–Thu, 09.00–13.00 Fri; admission adult/child 16/12NIS*) The Ammunition Hill memorial site stands as a long-lasting reminder and tribute to

Formed out of Jerusalem's oldest neighbourhoods that grew outside the Old City walls, the centre of the new city covered in this walk is today a fascinating example of the unique atmosphere that characterises the city, where ancient and modern have continued to develop alongside one another. From the ultra-Orthodox neighbourhood of Me'a She'arim where biblical times have stood still, to the vibrancy and noise of the Mahane Yehuda food market, a day's walk leads you through the present and past of the city centre.

Start in the irrepressibly fascinating ultra-Orthodox neighbourhood of **Me'a She'arim** (see page 104).

Leave the neighbourhood and walk down the narrow Ethiopia Street towards Hanevi'im Street. On the left of the narrow road, lined with stone mansions you will find the lovely, circular **Ethiopian church** [69 F1] (⏱ *07.00–18.00*). Built in 1896, it is believed to have been a gift to the Ethiopian Queen Sheba from King Solomon. Directly opposite the large church and marked by a plaque on the wall outside is **Ben Yehuda's House** [69 E1], where he lived and did much of his work on the revival of the Hebrew language.

At the bottom of Ethiopia Street cross Hanevi'im Street and walk down Harav Kook Street. On your left is the **Rothschild Hospital**, today the Hadassah College, which was built in 1888 by funds from the baron (see page 171) and became the first Jewish hospital to be built outside the Old City. Across the street is the delightful **Ticho House** [69 E2] (↳ *6244186; www.go-out.com/ticho;* ⏱ *10.00–17.00 Sun/Mon & Wed/Thu, 10.00–22.00 Tue, 10.00–14.00 Fri*), one of Jerusalem's earliest buildings outside the walls. It belonged to Dr Avraham Ticho, a German optometrist and his wife Anna who in 1924 opened an eye clinic, which operated until his death in 1960. Anna worked as both his assistant and landscape artist

members of the IDF Paratrooper Regiment who died in one of the Six Day War's bloodiest battles. The hill, a Jordanian army stronghold, was seen as a crucial strategic point in the battle for Jerusalem and, on 6 June 1967 in a battle that lasted four hours, 36 men lost their lives in the capture of the hill. Visitors can join the throngs of young IDF soldiers who frequent the site in exploring the battleground, which includes a tour of the tunnels and bunkers.

Castel National Park and Fortress (*Mivasseret Zion;* ↳*5330467;* ⏱ *08.00–17.00 daily; admission adult/child 13/7NIS*) Although its history stretches from biblical times to the Crusades, the Castel Fortress is most poignantly remembered for its role in the 1948 Arab–Israeli War when the crucial route leading to Jerusalem was being fiercely contested. For five days, Jewish forces fought off attacks from Arab troops, and, despite drastic and almost total loss of life, gained an eventual victory. Models, exhibits and a great view from the fortress's 790m elevation make it a worthwhile trip. The park is located 15 minutes from the city centre near the village of Mivasseret Zion on route 1.

Biblical Zoo (↳ *6750111; www.jerusalemzoo.org.il;* ⏱ *09.00–17.00 Sun–Thu, 09.00–16.30 Fri, 10.00–17.00 Sat; admission adult/child 46/36NIS*) Complete with its very own Noah's Ark, the Biblical Zoo aims to preserve and rare animals from across the world. The non-profit zoo concentrates mainly on animals from Israel's past, most especially those mentioned in the Bible.

until she passed away in 1980. Upon her death, the house was converted into a museum, library, art gallery and café (see page 75). Walk to the end of Harav Kook Street and turn right on to Yafo Street. Take a mildly strenuous 25-minute uphill walk until you reach the unmistakable **Mahne Yehuda Market** (see above). Exit the market at the southern end on to Agrippas Street and turn right on to Eliash Street. Follow the road until you get to Shmuel Hanagid Street (crossing Ben Yehuda Street). Follow it to where it meets Bezalel Street, where you will see the **Ratisbonne Monastery** [68 C3] (⏱ *08.00–16.00 Mon–Thu, 08.00–14.00 Fri*). Founded in 1876 by Father Ratisbonne, a Jewish aristocratic banker turned monk, the monastery was built as a French Catholic monastery and vocational school. Today, the building remains as impressive as when it was first erected, its tower believed to be one of 16 that stretched from Jaffa to Jerusalem, each acting as part of a chain of smoke signals announcing the arrival of merchant ships. Continue walking to the end of Shmuel Hanagid Street and right on to King George V Street. A short distance away, on the left, is the **Heichal Shlomo and Great Synagogue** [68 D5], the former seat of the Israeli Rabbinate and Supreme Rabbinical Court. The magnificent synagogue next door was designed to reflect architectural features of the First Temple. From here continue across **Independence Park (Gan Ha'atzma'ut)** [69 E4], the eastern part of which is a pre-1948 Muslim cemetery. Graves can still be spotted amongst the shrubbery. Exit on to Shlomitzion Hamalka Street and turn left. At Yafo Street turn left and immediately right on to Cheshin Street. At the top is the **Russian Compound** [69 F2], whose green-domed cathedral takes pride of place. The compound was built in 1860 to accommodate the thousands of Russian pilgrims flocking to Jerusalem up until World War I. Today most of the buildings are occupied by various government institutions.

AROUND JERUSALEM

LATRUN The area of Latrun most likely owes its name to the almost completely dilapidated remains of a **Crusader fortress** 'Le Toron des Chevaliers' (The Tower of the Knights), an integral part of the many battles that took place here during the Crusades. Latrun is an area of the Ayalon Valley stretching between Tel Aviv and Jerusalem that, for hundreds of years, has formed one of the country's most important strategic routes. Running alongside today's route 1 and 15km outside the capital, there are several attractions worth stopping for. Much of the fortress is still underground and awaiting excavation so tread with care as some areas can be unstable and dangerous. It is located behind the monastery.

The **Latrun Monastery** has over recent decades become known for its wine and its thriving vineyards sweeping up the valley to the doorstep of the beautiful building inhabited by monks of the French Trappist order. In 2006, the monastery shot into a different spotlight as the unlikely setting for the much-anticipated Roger Waters concert, which attracted thousands of Pink Floyd fans from around the country. Opposite the monastery is the **Armoured Corps Museum** (*Yad La'Shiryon, Latrun;* ⍞*08 9246722;* ⏱ *08.30–16.30 Sun–Thu, 08.30–12.30 Fri, 09.00–16.00 Sat; admission adult/child 30/20NIS*), a British-built police fort used to control the passage between Tel Aviv and Jerusalem. After the British Mandate period, control of the fort passed to Arab forces, an act that resulted in a siege of Jerusalem during the 1948 Arab–Israeli War. After Israel declared independence, forces led by ex-Prime Minister

Ariel Sharon stormed the stronghold, suffering two brutal and bloody defeats. Today the police fort and its environs act as a tank museum and memorial site.

Just up from the police station is the **Mini Israel Park** (✆ *08 9130000/10; www. minisrael.co.il;* ⊕ *summer 10.00–22.00 Sat—Thu; winter 10.00–17.00 Sat–Thu, 10.00–14.00 Fri; adult/child 79/59NIS*) where visitors can feel like Gulliver in the Holy Land. Impressive reconstructions of the country's most prolific religious, architectural and geographical places occupy an area designed to resemble the Star of David.

Getting there Buses 433, 434 and 414 from Jerusalem central bus station will stop at the Hativah Sheva junction from which all sites are within walking distance (30mins/17.20NIS).

SOREQ CAVE The Soreq Stalactite Cave Nature Reserve (*near Beit Shemesh;* ✆ *9911117; www.parks.org.il;* ⊕ *08.00–17.00 daily; admission adult/child 25/13NIS*) is unique in that its relatively small area (the cave measures 82m by 60m) is home to the vast majority of cave formations known throughout the world. As old as five million years, some of the formations measure up to 4m in length, occasionally meeting up with their stalagmite counterparts rising off the cave floor. A visit to the cave involves a guided tour and slide show. Photography is permitted only on Fridays when there are no tours.

Getting there The cave is located 2km east of Beit Shemesh. From Jerusalem buses 415 and 417 run hourly to Beit Shemesh from where you can take a taxi for the final short stretch. The train from Jerusalem Malha also stops in Beit Shemesh.

ABU GHOSH About 20 minutes' drive from Jerusalem, located just off route 1, is the little Arab town of Abu Ghosh, best known across Israel for its Middle Eastern restaurants. Indeed, in 2010 it got itself into the *Guiness Book of Records* for producing the world's largest plate of hummus weighing over 4,000kg (since topped by Lebanon). One of the best restaurants is **Lebanese Restaurant** (*88 HaShalom St; Abu Ghosh;* ✆ *5702397;* ⊕ *09.00–23.00 daily; $$*), the queues of people waiting for a seat in the enormous, rustic restaurant testify to its incredible popularity. This most certainly isn't a quiet meal in the countryside, as children race about, the chatter reaches high decibels, running waiters fling piles of fresh hummus, pitta, salads, grilled skewered meats and ice-cold lemonade on to tables, and pans clatter in the busy, open kitchen.

The grand, sturdy **Crusader castle** that stands in the village dates back to the 12th-century and displays traditional architecture of that time with thick, strong walls and castle-like appearance. In 1899 it was bought by the French government who gave it to the Benedictine order. It makes a nice visit to walk off a hearty hummus lunch.

4

Tel Aviv-Jaffa

Telephone code 03

Tel Aviv is the black sheep of the family. In a country of such profound historical importance, passionate religions, political struggles and strict traditions, Tel Aviv stands out and knows it. Where Jerusalem is proud of its biblical history, architectural beauty and devout religiousness, Tel Aviv's pride is found in the opposites. This colourfully loud and vibrant city has an almost hedonistic atmosphere, where the main concerns are what to wear, where to be seen and where to party.

Tel Aviv, whose name translates as 'Spring of Hill' or 'Spring Mound', is the second-largest city in Israel with an ever-growing population of currently 394,000. While Jerusalem is the capital, it is not recognised as such by much of the international community, and so Tel Aviv steps in to fill the shoes as the economic, financial and commercial capital. A recent boom in international business has seen the city flourish, a big international airport, seafront overlooked by large five-star hotels, a highly profitable diamond exchange and the emergence of modern high-rise buildings standing as testament to this. While few would describe Tel Aviv as beautiful, a closer look will reveal the world's largest collection of Bauhaus buildings, a pre-Nazi German architectural style, granting it UNESCO World Heritage status in 2004.

In a country steeped in centuries-old history, Tel Aviv has managed to make its mark on the country in just six decades. Today it epitomises the average Israeli. The fast-paced, hard-working and fun-loving way of life has drawn people from all over the country and abroad to make money and have plenty of fun spending it. While it may be easy for visitors to overlook Tel Aviv, using it as a gateway to the more traditional sights in Jerusalem, the Dead Sea and Galilee, a trip to Israel would most certainly be a biased one without a stop in this, the most Israeli of Israel's cities.

Merely a few kilometres down the coast sits **Jaffa**, one of the most beautiful, charming and ancient places in Israel. Jaffa's Old City and port form the historic core of this predominantly Arab neighbourhood, its artists' houses, cobbled alleys, breathtaking views and old-worldly atmosphere having become a magnetic draw for visitors to the country. The once-thriving fishing port, in bygone days one of the most crucial seaports in the world, is today a tranquil area where small boats chug in and out of the harbour, old men sit patiently fishing and aromatic smells waft out of the countless restaurants. In 'modern' Jaffa the streets are abuzz with everyday hustle and bustle, the flea market, Middle Eastern eateries, mosques and Arabic culture providing a contrast with Tel Aviv so stark you would be forgiven for thinking you had crossed a border into another country.

While the town is undoubtedly steeped in charisma, crime rates tend to be higher than in neighbouring Tel Aviv so it is important to be aware of pickpocketing, especially at night. Violent crimes are rare but solo women travellers are not advised to wander the streets after dark, especially outside the Old City.

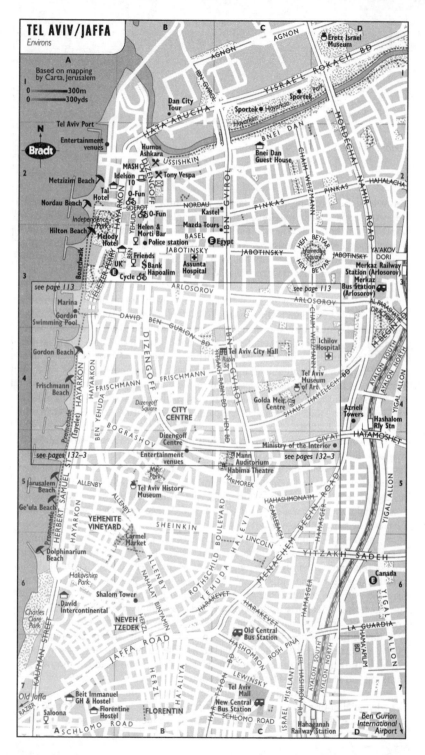

TEL AVIV/JAFFA
Environs

Based on mapping
by Carta, Jerusalem

0 ————— 300m
0 ————— 300yds

Bradt

N

AGNON

AGNON

Eretz Israel Museum

YISRAEL ROKACH BD

IBN GVIROL

HATA'ARUCHA

Dan City Tour

BNEI DAN

Sportek

Hayarkon Park

Sportek

Hayarkon

CHAIM WEIZMANN

MORDECHAI NAMIR ROAD

Tel Aviv Port

Entertainment venues

Humus Ashkara

USSISHKIN

DIZENGOFF

MASH

Idelson 10

× **Tony Vespa**

Bnei Dan Guest House

HAHALACHA

Metzizim Beach

Tal Hotel

O-Fun

BEN YEHUDA

SDEROT

O-Fun

NORDAU

Kastel

PINKAS

PINKAS

HEH BE'IYAR

Nordau Beach

Independence Park

Helen & Morti Bar

Mazda Tours

BASEL

JABOTINSKY

JABOTINSKY

Hamedina Square

HEH BE'IYAR

JABOTINSKY

YA'AKOV DORI

Hilton Beach

Melody Hotel

BEN YEHUDA

Police station

E Egypt

IBN GVIROL

HEH BETYR

Boardwalk

ELIEZER PERRY

Friends

UK

S **Bank Hapoalim**

Assunta Hospital

Merkaz Railway Station (Arlosorov)

Merkaz Bus Station (Arlosorov)

E Cycle

ELIEZER PERRY

see page 113

ARLOSOROV

see page 113

AL PARASHAT DRACHIM

M BEGIN RD

Marina

DAVID BEN GURION BD

ARLOSOROV

Gordon Swimming Pool

DIZENGOFF

IBN GVIROL

CHAIM WEIZMANN

Ichilov Hospital

Gordon Beach

Tel Aviv City Hall

Yitzakh Rabin Sq

AVALON SOUTH

AVALON NORTH

YIGAL ALLON

HAYARKON

FRISCHMANN

FRISCHMANN

Rabin Sq

Tel Aviv Museum of Art

Frischmann Beach

BEN YEHUDA

YITZAKH RABIN BD

HEN BD

Golda Meir Centre

SHAUL HAMELECH BD

Azrieli Towers

Hashalom Rly Stn

BOGRASHOV

Dizengoff Square

CITY CENTRE

Dizengoff Centre

GIV'AT

Ministry of the Interior

HATAMOSHET

Promenade (Tayelet)

see pages 132-3

Entertainment venues

Mann Auditorium

Habima Theatre

see pages 132-3

Meir Park

MARMOREK

Jerusalem Beach

ALLENBY

ALLENBY

Tel Aviv History Museum

HAHASHMONA'IM

YIGAL ALLON

Ge'ula Beach

HERBERT SAMUEL ST

HAYARKON

YEMENITE VINEYARD

SHEINKIN

CARLEBACH

HALEVI

LINCOLN

HAMASGER

MENACHEM BEGIN ROAD

Dolphinarium Beach

Carmel Market

NAHALAT BINYAMIN

ROTHSCHILD BOULEVARD

YEHUDA

YITZAKH SADEH

Hakovshim Park

ALLENBY

HERZL

HARAKEVET

HARAKEVET

Canada **E**

Shalom Tower

David Intercontinental

NEVEH TZEDEK

JAFFA ROAD

HASHOMRON

ROSH PINA

HAMASGER

LA GUARDIA

Charles Clore Park

KAUFMAN STREET

Old Central Bus Station

AVALON SOUTH

AVALON NORTH

YIGAL ALLON

HAYARKIN APLUM BD

RAZIER

Old Jaffa

Saloona

Beit Immanuel GH & Hostel

Florentine Hostel

HERZL

HA'ALIYA

FLORENTIN

HASHOMRON

LEWINSKY

Tel Aviv Mall

ISRAEL MISALANT

New Central Bus Station

ASCHLOMO ROAD

JAFFA ROAD

SCHLOMO ROAD

Hahaganah Railway Station

Ben Gurion International Airport

A   B   C   D

HISTORY

Modern Tel Aviv was officially founded by 66 Jewish families in 1909. The idea was to create a Jewish commuter suburb on the outskirts of Jaffa, the 4,000-year-old fortified port city located approximately 3km from Tel Aviv's centre. Jaffa was mentioned several times in the Bible but flourished during the 19th century when its city walls were built, trade markets established, its main mosque was erected and the great trunk road to Jerusalem constructed. It grew into a major trading port city through the Egyptian and Ottoman rule, and after the opening of the Suez Canal in 1869 saw the appearance of vast cargo ships from Europe. The clock tower face was even set to European time so as to aid merchants arriving in the port. Yet it wasn't just trade that disembarked in Jaffa. Scores of early pilgrims trudged up and down the road to Jerusalem's holy sites and German Templar and American colonies were established near the Old City.

By 1914, the population had expanded to 40,000, 15,000 of whom were Jews, and the city became the centre for waves of Jewish immigrants moving to the Holy Land until the creation of Tel Aviv. Following near abandonment during World War I, Jaffa recovered to become an almost wholly Palestinian city with Tel Aviv housing most of the Jewish population. It flourished until the 1936–39 rebellion which saw the closure of the once-prosperous port in favour of the new one in Tel Aviv. In 1948, Arab forces in Jaffa shelled nearby Tel Aviv, an attack quickly countered by Jewish forces who captured the Old City, poignantly two days before Israel's independence was declared. After Jaffa fell to the Jews in 1948 most of the 65,000 Palestinians left the city and in 1950 Jaffa was incorporated into the Municipality of Tel Aviv.

GETTING THERE AND AWAY

Tel Aviv forms the hub of Israel's transport network, with good-quality bus and/or train links to most places in the country.

BY BUS Tel Aviv has two main bus stations: the **central bus station** [133 G7] (*106 Levinsky Rd;* \6948888); and **Merkaz bus station** [110 D3] which is adjacent to the train station (both are often referred to as Arlosorov stations). Most buses arrive and depart from the central bus station although many of them will also stop at Merkaz bus station. Egged and Dan *(www.dan.co.il)* bus companies form the core of bus travel, Egged *(www.egged.co.il)* providing most of the long-distance services.

ROUTES TO AND FROM TEL AVIV CENTRAL BUS STATION				
To	**Frequency**	**Bus number**	**Duration**	**Price**
Jerusalem	20mins	405	1hr	20NIS
Eilat	1hr 30mins	394	5hrs	75NIS
Haifa HaCarmel	hourly	910	1hr 30mins	26.50NIS
Nazareth	5 daily	823	3hrs	42NIS
Kiryat Shmona	20mins	841/842/845	4hrs	61NIS
Katzrin	16.00	843	3hrs 50mins	59NIS
Tiberias	15mins	830/835/841	2hrs 45mins	48NIS
Tzfat	17.00	846	3hrs 30mins	59NIS
Golani Junction	15mins	830/835/841	2hrs 15mins	45NIS
Beer Sheva	30mins	370	1hr 30mins	16.50NIS

4

BY SHERUT Shared taxis run from most major cities in the country (following regular bus routes) and will stop anywhere along the way to pick up or drop off passengers, usually finishing at the central bus station. Some *sheruts* run on Shabbat.

BY TRAIN Tel Aviv forms the centre of Israel's growing train network and is an affordable, comfortable and convenient way of avoiding the coastal traffic. The city has four train stations running from south to north: HaHaganah [133 H7], HaShalom [110 D4], Merkaz [110 D3] (often referred to as Arlosorov) and Universita. There are regular services to and from Nahariya (1hr 50mins/43.50NIS), which stop at Atlit (55mins/29.50NIS), Haifa Hof HaCarmel (1hr/29.50NIS), Haifa Bat Galim, Haifa Merkaz HaShmona, Haifa Lev HaMifratz, Haifa Hutzot HaMifratz and Akko (1hr 40mins/38NIS) along the way. A shorter line runs as far as Caesarea (which is in Binyamina), stopping at Herzliya (20mins/8NIS), Netanya and Hadera (40mins/22.50NIS). A direct line now runs to and from Jerusalem (1½hrs/22NIS) and services south run as far as Beer Sheva (1hr 20mins/29NIS) and Dimona. Trains running between Tel Aviv and Ben Gurion Airport (12mins/14.50NIS) depart every half-hour 24 hours a day.

BY AIR Tel Aviv is home to Israel's only international airport, Ben Gurion (see page 39). **Israir** (℡ 7955777; *www.israirairlines.com*) runs regular flights between Tel Aviv and Haifa and Eilat for around 250NIS and 400NIS each way while **Arkia** (℡ 6902222; *www.arkia.co.il;*) offers flights only to and from Eilat for approximately 275NIS each way. El Al have also recently started the route and their prices average around 150NIS but can be as low as 100NIS each way.

GETTING AROUND

BY BUS Dan (*www.dan.co.il*) operates Tel Aviv's intra-city buses and fares around town cost 5.20NIS. The following bus routes run along most major streets and stop at the main attractions:

- **#4** Every five minutes from new central bus station up Allenby and Ben Yehuda streets and past the Carmel Market.
- **#5** Every five minutes from new central bus station up Rothschild and Dizengoff streets to the Dizengoff Centre then turns right and goes down Nordau, Pinkas and Weizmann streets and finishes at the central train station.
- **#10** Every 15 minutes from the central train station along Arlozorov Street, turns left to go down the coast along Ben Yehuda, Herbert Samuel and Kaufman streets to Jaffa.
- **#11** Every 15 minutes down Dizengoff Street turning right on to Ben Gurion Boulevard. It then turns on to Ibn Gvirol Street before turning left on to Shaul Hamelech Boulevard, then on to Weizmann Street past the Ichilov Hospital and on to the central train station along Arlosorov St.

BY SHERUT *Sherut* taxis (see page 51) operate along the main Dan bus routes and will have the same bus number in the front window. The fare is marginally lower than that of the buses and you can get on or off anywhere you choose. Routes 4, 5 and 16 (amongst others) also run on Shabbat. Inter-city *sherut* taxis to Jerusalem, Haifa, Eilat, Nazareth and all stops along the way leave regularly from the central bus station.

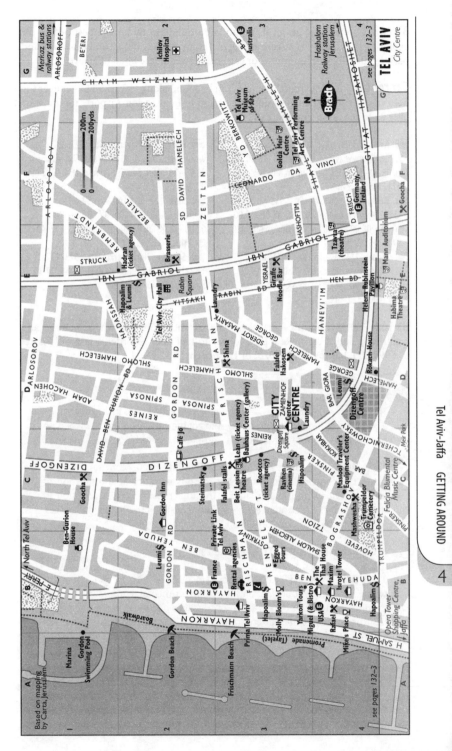

BY CAR Cars are not an ideal way to get around but by far the best option for exploring the country at large. Parking in the city can be difficult and expensive and parking illegally will result in your car being towed in the blink of an eye.

Car rental Most car-rental agencies can be found along Hayarkon Street near the bottom of Frishman and Gordon streets and in Ben Gurion Airport. You must be over 21 to rent a car anywhere in Israel.

🚗 **Avis** 113 Hayarkon St; ☎5271752; f 5223649; www.avis.co.il; ⏰ 08.00–18.00 Sun–Thu, 08.00–14.00 Fri. Ben Gurion Airport; ☎9712315; ⏰ 24hrs

🚗 **Budget** 99 Hayarkon St; ☎9350012; f 5245234; www.budget.co.il; ⏰ 08.00–18.00 Sun–Thu, 08.00–14.00 Fri. Ben Gurion Airport; ☎9712315; ⏰ 24hrs

🚗 **Eldan** 114 Hayarkon St; ☎5271166; f 5271174; www.eldan.co.il; ⏰ 08.00–18.00 Sun–Thu, 08.00–14.00 Fri. Ben Gurion Airport; ☎9773400; ⏰ 24hrs

🚗 **Hertz** 144 Hayarkon St; ☎5223332; www.hertz.co.il; ⏰ 08.00–18.00 Sun–Thu, 08.00–14.00 Fri. Ben Gurion Airport; ☎9772444; ⏰ 24hrs

🚗 **Sixt** 122 Hayarkon St; ☎5244935; www.sixt.co.il; ⏰ 08.00–17.00 Sun–Thu, 08.00–12.00 Fri. Ben Gurion Airport; ☎5244935; ⏰ 24hrs

🚗 **Suncar** 200 Hayarkon St; ☎5237017; f 5223828; www.suncar.co.il; ⏰ 08.45–17.30 Sun–Thu, 08.45–13.30 Fri

BY TAXI Tel Aviv has no shortage of taxis, except on Shabbat when the buses and trains stop and it can take a little longer to hail one. To order a taxi call **Kastel** (☎ 6993322), **Ichilov** (☎ 6967070) or **Hashekem** (☎ 5270404).

FREE GUIDED TOURS

The Tel Aviv Municipality has set up several free guided tours in English that are a great and cost-effective way to see some of the city's main sights. There is no need to reserve a spot in advance, just show up at the meeting point and join in.

1 TEL AVIV UNIVERSITY: ART AND ARCHITECTURE 11.00 Mondays. Meeting point: Dyonon bookstore, university campus entrance at the junction of Haim Levanon and Einstein streets. The tour provides an introduction to the university's Israeli architecture including styles, international influences, history, environmental sculpture and landscape designs.

2 BAUHAUS: 'THE WHITE CITY' (See page 128)

3 TEL AVIV BY NIGHT 20.00 Tuesdays. Meeting point: on the boulevard where Rothschild Boulevard and Hertzl Street meet. Incorporating a bit of everything, this tour details some of the city's history as well as shedding light on its restaurant, bar and café scene. It centres on the lively and hip southern Rothschild Boulevard and Nahalat Binyamin Street and is a great way to find out what's 'in' and trendy in the city that never sleeps.

4 OLD JAFFA 09.30 Wednesdays. Meeting point: clock tower, Yefet Street, Jaffa. The tour takes in the best of the quaint Old City of Jaffa including the flea market, cobbled alleyways, views of Tel Aviv from Hapigsa Gardens and the area's archaeological sites.

BY BICYCLE There are a few places in the city where you can rent a bicycle. Prices are usually around 60NIS per day but less if you hire them for longer.

۶**Cycle** [110 B4] 147 Ben Yehuda St; \5293037; www.cycle.co.il; 10.00–19.00 Sun–Thu, 10.00–15.00 Fri

۶**O-Fun** [110 B2] 197 Ben Yehuda St; \5442292; www.rentabikeisrael.com. Scooters also available for 150NIS per day.

TOURIST INFORMATION

ℹ Tourist information centre Tel Aviv Promenade; 46 Herbert Samuel St (corner of 2 Geula St); \5166188; e tamia@tourism.gov.il; www.visit-tlv.com; ⊕ 09.30–17.00 Sun–Thu, 09.30–13.00 Fri

ℹ Mobile Segway Information Centre Can be found throughout major tourist areas; ⊕ Jul, Aug & Sep 13.00–19.00 daily.

LOCAL TOUR OPERATORS For Bauhaus tours, see pages 128–9. For nationwide tours, see page 36.

Dan City Tour \6394444; e information@ dan.co.il; www.dan.co.il; adult/child 45/36NIS. Runs an open-top tourist sightseeing bus around Tel Aviv & Jaffa taking in the major sights from the port area to Jaffa's Old City. Buses run hourly (09.00–19.00 Sun–Thu, 09.00–14.00 Fri) & it is possible to hop & off throughout the day. Audio information is in several languages. The tour begins at the Dan bus station on Hata'arucha Street but you can join at any point.

Egged Tours 59 Ben Yehuda St; \03 9203992; f 5272020; www.eggedtours.com. Operates a system of well-run tours around Israel ranging from 1 day to over a week.
Mazada Tours 141 Ibn Gvirol St; \5444454; e mazada@mazada.co.il; www.mazada.co.il (see page 000)
Yarkon Tours 4 Bograshov St; \7965020; f 5176849; www.yarkon.co.il. Specialise in Jewish & Christian pilgrimage tours.

TRAVEL AGENCIES

Issta Dizengoff Centre, 50 Dizengoff St; \6216100; e customerserv.issta@issta.co.il; www.issta.co.il; ⊕ 09.00–20.00 Sun–Thu, 09.00–13.00 Fri. Part of Israel's biggest travel agency chain. Staff can be decidedly officious so try not to take it personally.

Ophir Tours Tel Aviv University, Music Academy Bldg; \6429001; e s@ophirtours.co.il; www. ophirtours.co.il; ⊕ 09.00–18.00 Sun–Thu, 09.00–13.00 Fri. Friendly, budget-oriented agency.

WHERE TO STAY

🏠 **David Intercontinental** [132 B4] (555 rooms) 12 Kaufman St; \7951111; f 7951112; www.ichotelsgroup.com. Renowned as being Tel Aviv's most prestigious & luxurious hotel. Located equidistant from Jaffa & central Tel Aviv, beautiful beachfront location & views, immaculate rooms & an indulgent b/fast. $$$$$
🏠 **Melody Hotel** [110 B3] (55 rooms) 220 Hayarkon St; \5215300; f 5215301; reservations@atlashotels.co.il www.atlas.co.il. Part of the growing chain of Atlas hotels, the Melody is fresh, clean & modern. Each brightly

decorated room has tv, dvd, mp3 & Wi-Fi facilities, lovely sea views & breezy rooftop terrace & free bicycle rental. $$$$$
🏠 **Center Hotel** [115 D3] (54 rooms) 2 Zamenhof St; \5266100; e reservations@ atlashotels.co.il; www.atlas.co.il. Fashionable & trendy boutique hotel in Bauhaus architecture. Fresh, minimalist décor with each room sporting a different painting by up-and-coming artists. B/fast inc & free bicycle rental Wi-Fi are offered. $$$$
🏠 **Isrotel Tower** [115 B4] (90 rooms) 78 Hayarkon St; \5113636; f 5113666;

www.isrotel.co.il. This cylindrical 30-storey hotel is one of the most eye-catching buildings in the city. Located in the heart of the city centre it affords great views of the sea & is within walking distance of most attractions. Its rooftop swimming pool is fabulous, but perhaps not if you're afraid of heights. **$$$$**

🏠 **Prima Tel Aviv** [115 B3] (60 rooms) 105 Hayarkon St; ✆ 5206666; e primatlv@prima.co.il; www.prima.co.il. Tel Aviv's representative in this nationwide chain of reputable hotels is located on the seafront in front of Frishman beach, 15mins' walk from the city centre. The recently renovated rooms are elegant, breezy & modern & have the complete range of facilities. B/fast inc & there is a swish bar & lounge area. **$$$$**

🏠 **Tal Hotel** [110 A2] (120 rooms) 287 Hayarkon St; ✆ 5425500; e reservations@atlashotels.co.il; www.atlas.co.il. Another of the Atlas chain it is a modern boutique hotel with bright, fresh rooms & plenty of facilities. **$$$$**

🏠 **Bnei Dan Guest House (HI)** [110 C2] (45 rooms) 36 Bnei Dan St; ✆ 02 5945655; e telaviv@iyha.org.il; www.iyha.org.il. A member of the Hostelling International group this large hostel is located near the Hayarkon Park & River. Immaculately clean rooms have AC & bathrooms. Kosher b/fast is inc. Often frequented by large groups. *Dorms (70NIS) & private rooms available.* **$$$**

🏠 **Eden House** [132 C2] (12 rooms) 27 Kehilat Eden St; ✆ 052 7469842;

WHAT'S IN A NAME?

Beneath Tel Aviv's cosmopolitan, bustling streets lie the silent heroes of its creation. Almost without exception, the city's street names are dedicated to those who remain close to the hearts of Israelis and Jews the world over. As you explore the city, take the time to notice the street names; it's a great way to put some of the country's complex history into context.

ALLENBY Sir Edmund Henry Allenby (1861–1936) was a British World War I commander who is best known for his Middle East campaign. He battled the Turks in Palestine, capturing Gaza and Jerusalem in 1917. In 1918, he won the vicious battle on the plain of Meggido and later took Damascus and Aleppo.

ARLOZOROV Haim Arlozorov (1899–1933) was a Ukrainian-born Zionist who represented the *yishuv* at the League of Nations in Geneva and who rose to become head of the political party of the Jewish Agency. He was assassinated in 1933, two days before he was to negotiate the Ha'avara (transfer) agreement with the Nazi government.

BEGIN Menachem Begin (1913–92) was Prime Minister of Israel from 1977–83.

BEN-GURION David Ben-Gurion (1886–1973) was Israel's first prime minister following the formation of an independent state in 1948 (see page 10).

BEN-YEHUDA Eliezer Ben-Yehuda (1858–1922) was one of the first Zionists, and was responsible for reintroducing the Hebrew language as the spoken tongue of Israel.

DIZENGOFF Meir Dizengoff (1861–1936) was the first mayor of Tel Aviv from 1911 until his death in 1936.

FRISCHMANN David Frischmann (1859–1922) was one of the first major writers of modern Hebrew literature. His most famous work is the *Bar Midbar* (1923), a series of fictional biblical tales.

e edenhousetlv@gmail.com; www.edenhousetlv.com. Lovely little guesthouse with spacious rooms, free Wi-Fi, shady outside areas & the touch of a family-run place. Rooms and self-catering apts available. **$$$**

🏠 **Hayarkon 48 Hostel** [132 B1] (36 rooms) 48 Hayarkon St; 📞 5168989; e info@hayarkon48.com; www.hayarkon48.com. This is undoubtedly Tel Aviv's best hostel & is unsurprisingly often booked to capacity. Located a few mins' walk from the beach, this immaculately clean hostel offers a fabulous array of services & facilities inc a well-equipped kitchen, lively lounge complete with pool table & TV, free safe, b/fast & a breezy rooftop balcony overlooking the Mediterranean.

Dbl rooms with AC, with or without en-suite available. *Dorms 105NIS*. **$$$**

🏠 **Hotel de la Mer** [132 B1] 2 Nes Tziona St, corner of 62 Hayarkon St; 📞 5100011; www.delamer.co.il. Elegant boutique hotel, with tasteful, unpretentious décor designed using the principles of feng shui. Rooms are spacious and comfortable (some with jacuzzi) and there is a lovely spa. Excellent value. **$$$**

🏠 **Maxim Hotel** [115 B4] (71 rooms) 86 Hayarkon St; 📞 5173721; f 5173726; www.maxim-htl-ta.co.il. Well-priced hotel with fantastic location on Hayarkon St. Comfortable, well-equipped rooms are exceptionally well priced. Israeli b/fast, laundry service & wireless internet in all rooms. **$$$**

HERZL Theodor Herzl (1860–1904) was the founder and first president of the World Zionist Organisation.

IBN GABIROL Solomon Ibn Gabirol (1021–58) was a Hebrew poet and Jewish philosopher.

JABOTINSKY Vladimir Evgenevich Jabotinsky (1880–1940) led the Revisionist Zionist Party and in 1920 organised and led the Hahaganah, a Jewish militia.

NAMIR Mordechai Namir (1897–1975) was a Knesset member, government minister, one of the heads of the Labor Zionist Movement and Mayor of Tel Aviv.

ROTHSCHILD (see page 171)

SAMUEL Sir Herbert Samuel (1870–1963) was the British High Commissioner for Palestine from 1920–25. He became the first Jew to govern the land in 2,000 years.

SHAUL HAMELECH Saul the King was the first king of the ancient Kingdom of Israel as recorded in the Old Testament and Koran. He reigned from c1020–1000BCE.

WEIZMANN Chaim Weizmann (1874–1952) was the first president of Israel from 1949–52, President of the World Zionist Organisation and founder of the Weizmann Institute of Science.

RABIN (see page 13)

SADEH Yitzhak Sadeh (1890–1952) was Commander of the Palmach and one of the founding members of the Israel Defence Force.

🏠 **Miguel Hotel and Bistro** [115 B4] (21 rooms) 88 Hayarkon St; ☎5107744; www.miguel.co.il. Resembling the elegant, family-run hotels of France & Italy, Miguel's abounds in character & finesse. On the seafront 10mins from the city centre. Rooms are equipped with AC, TV & Wi-Fi. Downstairs is a gourmet French-style restaurant & bar (🕐 *12.00–17.00 Sun–Thu;* 80NIS) serving fresh fish & meat dishes. **$$$**

🏠 **Gordon Inn Hotel and Guesthouse** [115 C2] (27 rooms) 17 Gordon St; ☎5238239; e gordonin@gmail.com; www.gordoninn.hostel.com. A welcoming & friendly little guesthouse located a few mins' walk from the beach. Dbl rooms (shared bathroom or en suite) have TV, coffee facilities & are pleasantly decorated & extremely clean. Guests receive 10% discount in the Gordon Inn pub next door & there is free Wi-Fi throughout. *Dorms 90NIS.* **$$$** (en suite), **$$** (shared).

🏠 **Mugraby Hostel** [132 C1] (14 rooms) 30 Allenby St; ☎5102443; e mugraby-hostel.com; www.mugraby-hostel.com. Simple backpacker hostel located above a newly renovated internet café. The hostel is clean but basic. Single-sex & mixed dorms available as well as dbl rooms with or without en-suite facilities & AC. Facilities inc a kitchen, free lockers & lounge. *Single-sex & mixed dorms 78NIS.* **$$**

🏠 **Sub Kuch Milega** [132 D6] (16 beds) 22 Hamashbir St; ☎6813412; e sub_kuch_milega@yahoo.com; www.subkuchmilega.com. Attracting the young, bohemian backpacker types this 4-storey guesthouse & restaurant (🕐 *12.00–late*) is as laid back as they come. Facilities inc a bar, gaming area, laundry machine, free internet access, pool table, rooftop lounge & bicycle hire. The Indian cuisine is authentic & filling & really good value (**$$**). Big screens & a party atmosphere can be found on the roof terrace in summer. AC, en-suite & fan, shared bathroom dbl rooms available. *Dorms 70NIS.* **$–$$**

🏠 **Florentine Hostel** [132 B7] (4 rooms) 10 Elifelet St; ☎5187551; e Rafi@ FlorentineHostel.com; www.florentinehostel. com. Great location in the increasingly trendy Florentine neighbourhood, it is an easy walk from Tel Aviv & Jaffa. Family-run guesthouse offering budget beds to those aged 18–40 (no children). Free Wi-Fi, communal kitchen, bicycle rental, big open terrace, BBQ area & washing machine/dryer. Dbl with shared bathroom. *Dorms 66NIS.* **$**

JAFFA

🏠 **Andromeda Hills** 3 Pasteur St; ☎6838448; e apt_rent@netvision.net.il; www.andromeda.co.il. Newly built holiday apts in a prime location in Old Jaffa. Beautiful, luxury studios & apts with access to swimming pool, gym, jacuzzi, solarium, games room & café. Less for longer rentals. **$$$$**

🏠 **Beit Immanuel Guest House and Hostel** [132 B7] (15 rooms) 8 Auerbach St; ☎6821459; e welcome@beitimmanuel.org. www. beitimmanuel.org. This cosy & family-oriented pilgrim's guesthouse has captured the serenity & atmosphere of Old Jaffa with its leafy garden & sunny balcony. The décor is a little old-fashioned but seems somehow apt for this part of the city and rooms are clean & comfortable. Private rooms available. Dorms 100NIS. **$$**

🏠 **Old Jaffa Hostel** (29 rooms) 8 Olei Zion St; ☎6822370; e ojhostel@shani.net; www.telaviv-hostel.com. Oozing Old Jaffa's rich character, the hostel is located within an ancient stone house just mins from the harbour & beach. Facilities inc a roof terrace with wonderful views of the sea & cobbled streets below, TV room, cosy kitchen, internet access & bicycle rental. *Dorms 75NIS; studio with kitchenette, TV & AC 300NIS.* **$$**

✂ WHERE TO EAT

In recent years Tel Aviv has managed to well and truly assert itself on the international cuisine map and today takes pride in its culinary prowess and thriving restaurant scene. In total contrast to Jerusalem, few restaurants are kosher and all are open straight through Shabbat, which is generally their busiest time. Prices in Tel Aviv seem to increase by the day and you can expect to pay European prices for a meal in any restaurant or indeed café throughout the city. The standard is also very high and you will rarely leave dissatisfied, although the customer service often leaves a little to be desired. Mediterranean-influenced food is the most popular, generally cooked in a gourmet, fusion style, but many Israelis are also big meat-lovers so there are plenty of steakhouses too. Sushi has seen an enormous boom so you don't have to look far for a salmon roll.

The best budget options are the Israeli staples of hummus, falafel, *shawarma* and *sabich* but if you've had enough of chickpeas for a few days there are also plenty of small pizza places (although some are decidedly shabby so choose carefully), sandwich bars, *burekas*, bakeries and cheaper-end restaurants. Most bars and pubs also serve cheap snacks for a late-night meal.

✖ **Miguel Hotel & Bistro** [115 B4] (see page 118)

✖ **Sub Kuch Milega** [132 D6] (see page 118)

✖ **Catit** [132 C5] 4 Heichal Hatalmud St; ☏5107001; ⏰ 12.00-15.00 Sun–Fri &19.00–23.00 daily. One of the most acclaimed restaurants of the moment run by Chef Meir Adoni. Mediterranean flavours are combined in new ways, turning fish ceviche, calamari & veal tartar into something truly unique. Business lunch menu available. $$$$$

✖ **Herbert Samuel** [132 B4] 6 Koifman St; ☏5166516; ⏰ 12.30–00.30 Sun–Wed, 12.30–01.30 Thu–Sat. Elegant wine bar facing the sea, considered one of the city's top. It serves a blend of Mediterranean-style cuisines, & most starters are available as smaller 'tapas' portions allowing you to try several. Daily business lunches are available. $$$$$

✖ **Manta Ray** Alma Beach; ☏5174773; www.mantaray.co.il; ⏰ 09.00–12.00 & 12.30–00.00 daily. Wonderful fresh fish & seafood cooked in a Middle Eastern style. They also serve big, hearty b/fasts in a setting of laid back beach charm. $$$$$

✖ **Onami** [133 C1] 18 HaArba'a St; ☏5620981; ⏰ 12.00–late Sun–Fri, 13.00–late Sat. One of the city's best & longest established sushi spots. The restaurant consists of a sushi bar, Yakituri grill & Japanese dishes. The business lunches are a good way to sample the variety (12.00–18.00 Sun–Fri; $$$$). $$$$$

✖ **Rafael** [115 B4] 87 HaYarkon St; ☏5226464; ⏰ 12.00–15.00 & 19.00–late daily. This is often considered Tel Aviv's best restaurant, producing food cooked by one of Israel's top chefs. The chic restaurant is located inside the Adiv Hotel & sports a rustic French-style menu infused with Moroccan & Middle Eastern spices. Great sea views so be sure to reserve a seat by the window. A lunch menu (95NIS) if offered 12.00–15.30 Sun–Thu. $$$$$

✖ **Brasserie** [115 E2] 70 Ibn Gvirol St; ☏6967111; ⏰ 24hrs daily. Chic, French bistro facing Rabin Sq. This has long been a huge favourite in the city serving elegant, hearty dishes of good Mediterranean food. Different b/fast, lunch & dinner menus have a wide choice of meals & prices. $$$ (less for lunch menu)

✖ **Max Brenner** [133 E4] 45 Rothschild Bd; ☏5604570; www.maxbrenner.com; ⏰ 09.00–late Sun–Thu, 08.00–late Fri/Sat. Chocolate is the name of the game at Israel's sweetest restaurant. It has become one of the country's most popular exports, making chocolate waves in the US, Australia, Philippines & Singapore. Outlandish, gooey recipes have been created that are rich & calorie-laden but any sweet tooth's dream come true. A good selection of salads, sandwiches, chicken dishes, pasta & crêpes form the savoury menu, but be sure to leave room for dessert. $$$

✖ **The Thai House** [115 B4] 8 Bograshov St; ☏5178568; www.2eat.co.il/eng/thai; ⏰ 12.00–23.00 daily. Authentic, traditional Thai food cooked by Thai chefs. The décor is simple, with bamboo, trees & candles adding a flavour of the oriental. Regional dishes range from hot & fiery to coconut creamy. $$$

✖ **Giraffe Noodle Bar** [115 E3] 49 Ibn Gvirol St; ☏6916294; ⏰ 12.00–01.00 daily. Noodles from all over the world converge in this trendy, laid back, quick-eat bar. They have a range of rice, dumplings & sushi but it's the noodles that give it its reputation. The French-style desserts are also highly recommended. $$

✖ **Goocha** [115 C1] 171 Dizengoff St; ☏5222886 & 14 Ibn Gvirol St; ☏6911603; ⏰ 12.00–02.00 daily. Having earned its reputation for fresh fish, seafood & pasta at unusually reasonable prices they have now opened 2 new branches, one on Ibn Gvirol. The paper cone of calamari & shrimp is a great take-out. $$

✗ **Orna & Ella** [133 E2] 33 Sheinkin St; ✆6204753; ⊕ 10.00–midnight Sun–Fri, 11.00–midnight Sat. Easy to find by the queues of young Tel Avivians waiting their turn inside one of the city's most well-known & long-lasting café/restaurants. There are plenty of vegetarian options inc a selection of quiches & sandwiches, & they serve great coffee. Meals are light so not the place to go for a big slap-up dinner. $$

✗ **Tony Vespa** [133 F1] 267 Dizengoff St; ✆5460000 & 140 Rothschild Blvd; ✆6858888; ⊕ 12.00–03.00 Sat–Wed, 12.00–04.00 Thu–Fri. Fast becoming the city's favourite pizza haunt, they now have 2 branches open late in the city centre. Pizzas are priced by weight (88NIS per kilo) & there is a huge variety of toppings. $$

✗ **Sandwich bars** Ben Gurion Bd, Rothschild Bd (southern end); ⊕ 08.00–23.00. Made-to-order sandwiches, cheap sushi, coffee & b/fast bars have popped up along Tel Aviv's wide, leafy boulevards & have become the 'in' place to see & be seen. $

JAFFA Jaffa's restaurants are known for their freshly caught fish and Middle Eastern-influenced dishes. The port area is teeming with good restaurants of varying price so have an early evening stroll around and see what catches your eye. There are also several small restaurants nestled into the ancient buildings around Kedumim Square which, come summer, lay tables outside.

✗ **Abu Hassan** (see page 121)
✗ **Puah** (see page 122)
✗ **Cordelia Restaurant** 30 Yeffet St; ✆5184668; ⊕ 12.30–15.30 & 19.00–midnight Mon–Sat. A rustically romantic place, housed in a Crusader-era building where chandeliers hang from the vaulted ceiling, serving French gourmet cuisine. Along with the Noa Bistro, Napoleon & Yaffa Bar, it is under the direction of nationally famed Israeli TV chef Nir Zook. A real treat & the most luxurious of the 4. $$$$$

✗ **Yoe'ezer Wine Bar** 2 Ish Habira St, off Yefet St opposite Clock Tower Sq; ✆6839115; ⊕ 13.00–01.00 daily. Fine wines, delicate liqueurs & rich delicacies are the signatures of this classy wine bar. Nestled in an ancient Crusader building it has a prize-winning wine list with patés, cheese & bread platters, & oysters forming the appetiser menu. Mains inc veal tartar with truffles, beef bourguignon & prime rib. $$$$$

✗ **Noa Bistro** 14 Hatzorfim St; ✆5189720; ⊕ 09.30–late Sun–Thu daily; mains. More

laid back than Cordelia's, with unique décor and interesting menu. The b/fast is certainly a highlight. $$$$

✗ **Yaffa Bar** 30 Yefet St; ✆5184668; ⊕ 20.00–late daily. Relaxed & comfortable with big, funky sofas, indoor & outdoor seating areas & a good selection of reasonably priced foods & snacks. $$$

✗ **Said el Abu Lafia Bakery** 7 Yeffet St; ✆6834958; ⊕ 08.00–22.00 Mon–Sat. This was Jaffa's 1st bakery, opened in 1880 & remains today one of the country's most famous & well-loved snack shops. Arabic-style pizza, pittas, fluffy *burekas*, freshly baked breads & sticky *baklava* are cheap, delicious & filling. There are plenty of bakeries around so make sure you find the right one. $

✗ **Napoleon Patisserie** 15 Kedumim Sq; ✆0774030258; ⊕ 07.00–late daily. Gourmet patisserie & bakery with a mouth-watering selection of sweet & savoury snacks & treats. Next to the Ilana Goor Museum (see page 000). $

CAFÉS Café culture is huge in Tel Aviv and come Friday morning every seat in the city will be full, with chic Tel Avivians sipping cappuccinos, wearing big sunglasses and soaking up the sun. You don't have to look very far to find a decent café serving good-quality coffee, Israeli breakfast (eggs, salad, bread, muesli, fresh fruit and yoghurt) and a range of salads and sandwiches. The biggest concentrations can be found along the sides of Rabin Square and along Ibn Gvirol Street, down the length of Rothschild Boulevard and along Sheikin and Bograshov streets.

I KNOW THE BEST FALAFEL …

Hummus and falafel are a godsend to those on a budget or those who simply want to savour the staple foods of the Middle East. Tel Aviv is teeming with small, cheap restaurants and kiosks selling freshly cooked falafel, pitta, hummus, salads, *shwarma* and *sabich* but the following are particularly recommended:

Abu Hassan (Ali Karavan) 1 Dolphin St; ✆6820387; 14 Shivtai Y'Israel St; ✆6828355; & 18 Shivtai Y'Israel St; ⏰ 07.45–14.45 Sun–Fri. Renowned as the best hummus in the Tel Aviv area, these rudimentary eateries are packed day in & day out. Hummus is the extent of the menu, but that's all you need. The 18 Shivtai St branch is open all day (or until the hummus runs out).$

Falafel HaKosem (The Wizard) [115 D3] 174 HaNevi'im St; ✆5252033; ⏰ 10.00–23.00 Sun–Thu. This is the best falafel you will find in Tel Aviv. Be prepared to queue but expect rare customer service from the lively owner. *Shawarma*, schnitzel & *sabich* also served. $

Haj Kahil Shawarma Clock Tower Sq, Jaffa; ✆03 6812947; ⏰ 09.00–midnight daily. Turkey, beef & lamb *shawarma* you can eat safe in the knowledge they haven't been sitting there all week. Great fillings to go on top. $

Humus Ashkara 45 Yermiahu St; ✆5464547; ⏰ 24 hours. 30-year-old veteran of the Tel Aviv hummus circuit serving lightly spiced hummus &, in winter, soups.$

Humus Shlomo HaCarmel Market; ⏰ 08.00–14.30 Sun–Fri. 50-year-old hummus hideaway in the depths of the HaCarmel Market – ask any vendor to point you in the right direction. $

Mashwesha [110 C4] 40 Pinsker St; ✆6293796; ⏰ 11.00–23.00 Sun–Thu, 11.00–17.00 Fri, 12.00–23.00 Sat. Rudimentary little eatery just off Bograshov St; get there early before the hot, chunky hummus runs out. $

Stalls on the corner of **Dizengoff & Frishman streets** are open all day, some selling *sabich* while others have stuck to the traditional falafel. $

🍴 **Orna & Ella** [133 E2] (see *Where to eat* page 120)

🍴 **Arcafe** [133 E4] 31 Rothschild Bd; ✆5660259; 35 Basel St; ✆5467001; ⏰ 07.00– midnight daily. Branches of this popular chain are dotted all over the city. Their delicate pastries, fresh baguettes & sweets are what pull the crowds.

🍴 **Café Bialik** [132 D1] 2 Bialik St; ✆6200832; ⏰ 08.00–late Sun–Fri, 11.00–late Sat. Well-loved & well-established café on the trendy Bialik St. It has a full menu ranging from b/fasts to sandwiches to full meals & often hosts live music.

🍴 **Café Hillel** [133 E4] 65 Rothschild Bd; ✆5288666/777; ⏰ 07.00–01.00 Sun–Thu, 07.00–Shabbat Fri, end of Shabbat–01.00 Sat. Ideally situated for people-watching on Rothschild Bd, you'll be lucky to get a seat on

w/ends. Part of an extremely successful nationwide chain. A selection of sandwiches, pies, quiches & cakes are available for around 25NIS each.

🍴 **Café Jo** [115 C2] 130 Dizengoff St, . corner with Gordon St; ✆5272533; ⏰ 24hrs daily. Great place to sit outside & watch the world go by.

🍴 **Garden Café Sonia** [132 D2] 1 Almunit Way; ✆057 9442801; ⏰ 09.00–00.00 daily. Located on the corner of 18 King George this bohemian-chic café has a delightful garden patio covered with plants & flowers. There is a well-stocked menu of light meals.

🍴 **Shine** 38 Shlomo HaMelech St; ✆5276186. Ultra trendy café attracting the brunch-eating, soya latte-drinking crowd. If you can get a seat, sit outside for the real chic Tel Aviv experience. Selection of salads, sandwiches & light meals served.

☕ **Tazza d'Oro** [132 C4] 6 Ahad Haam St; ⏱ 07.30–00.00 Sun–Thu, 07.30–01.00 Fri, 08.30–0.00 Sat. A lovely little patio is jam-packed come w/ends with loyal regulars, but during the week is much quieter. Prime imported Italian coffee, a varied menu & a real taste of traditional Tel Aviv makes this Neve Tzedek café a huge hit.

☕ **Tika** [133 E2] 41 Sheinkin St; ✆ 5284997; ⏱ 07.30–midnight Sun–Thu, 07.30–20.00 Fri. Rustic & comfortable, this is one of the most fashionable cafés along Sheinkin St without the pretension of some of its neighbours. A small wooden balcony provides the perfect stance for people-watching while you enjoy an iced coffee & sandwich.

ENTERTAINMENT AND NIGHTLIFE

FESTIVALS Tel Aviv is a cultural hub of the country and as such there are countless festivals and events throughout the year, from modern and classic music to theatre, film and food. Tel Aviv City (*www.telavivcity.com*) has a review of all festivals.

Taste of the City (Ta'am Ha'ir) May; Hayarkon Exhibition Centre. The city's best restaurants cook up & serve their finest dishes for 20NIS each in this festival of food. A true culinary bonanza.

Gay Pride Parade Rabin Sq. Tel Aviv's gay pride is a fun & raucous procession attended by thousands that leads through the streets to Hayarkon Pk.

BARS While in most countries it is easy to differentiate between a bar and a nightclub, in Tel Aviv the line seems to have become a little blurry. Come 01.00 dance fever will have overtaken most bars and there will be people packed into every space bopping away. Bars generally get going late and stay open until the last person staggers out.

They tend to cluster in Tel Aviv and the list below is merely a taste of what Tel Aviv has to offer night-owls. Simply head to one of the popular areas – **Dizengoff Street, Lilinblum, Jaffa Flea Market** or the **old port**, for instance – and see what's on offer.

The flea market has become one of the hangouts in the city and is a really wonderful experience for visitors to the city who get to appreciate the trendy side of young Tel Avivians in the setting of a funky, authentic old market. In summer the bars and cafés that surround the central market area come alive with antique-hunters, the young and chic and the bohemian and on Thursdays the market stays open until midnight. There are countless places to get a cold beer, cheap meal or cup of coffee but **Puah** (✆ 6823821; ⏱ 10.00–01.00 Sun–Wed, 24hrs Thu–Sat), **Sharkuteri** (3 Rabbi HaNina; ✆ 6828843; ⏱ 12.00–17.00 & 19.00-late Mon–Sat) and **Shafa** (2 Nahman St; ✆ 6811205; 17.00–02.00 Mon–Thu, 12.00–17.00 Fri) are particularly popular.

♀ **Armadillo** [133 E3] 51 Ahad Haam St; ✆ 6205503; ⏱ 18.00–02.00 Sun–Thu, 20.00–03.00 Fri, 19.00–03.00 Sat. Casual, neighbourhood bar. This is the place to go for a few drinks, some good, unpretentious food & chat with friends in the trendy Sheinkin area.
♀ **Erlich** Tel Aviv Port; ✆ 5466728; ⏱ 21.30–late daily. Chic, trendy bar, this is the place where young Israelis strut their stuff & the barmen are straight off the pages of *GQ* magazine.

♀ **Friends** [110 B3] 186 Ben Yehuda St; ✆ 054 8035757; ⏱ 20.00–late daily. One of the most popular places to go to meet members of the opposite sex. Dark & noisy it resembles more of a club but is a great late-night alternative to one.
♀ **Helen and Morti Bar** [110 B3] 196 Ben Yehuda St; ✆ 0772177766 (no area code); ⏱ 19.00–late daily. This is a comfortable, neighbourhood-type bar where anything goes. Lively music, a friendly atmosphere & plenty of flowing drinks make it a good option.

♀ **Levontin 7** [133 E5] 7 Levontin St; ☎ 5605084; ⏰ 19.00–late . Funky music bar in the charismatic Levontin neighbourhood. They often host live music nights, usually of the indie genre, & it is frequented by a relaxed, casual crowd.

♀ **MASH** [110 B2] 275 Dizengoff St; ☎ 6051007; www.mash.co.il; ⏰ 17.00–04.00 daily. MASH has been attracting sports buffs & expats for over 25 years & while it can get decidedly rowdy during televised sporting events is a far cry from the rest of the city's glitzy, chrome-decorated bars.

♀ **Mike's Place** [115 B4] 86 Herbert Samuel St; ☎ 054 9292551; ⏰ 16.00–late daily. Although from the outside it may look better suited to a Costa del Sol holiday resort, the inside actually has quite a lot of charisma. It hit international headlines when it was the target of a suicide bombing in 2003 but was subsequently rebuilt. It is a great place to see live sporting events & they have live music most nights of the week.

♀ **Molly Bloom's** [115 B3] 32 Mendele St; ☎ 5221558; www.molly-blooms.com; ⏰ 16.00–late Sat–Thu, 12.00–late Fri. Eternally popular, Tel Aviv's first Irish pub is a little rough around the edges but manages it in a charming kind of way. Not a lot of seating room on w/ends. Beers include draught Guinness & Kilkenny. Selection of good, simple pub foods.

♀ **Rothschild 12** [132 D5] 12 Rothschild Bd; ☎ 5106430; ⏰ 19.00–late Sat–Thu. Popular night-time bar in the style of a French saloon. It is a chic place, where the glitz-&-glamour set come to socialise.

NIGHTCLUBS AND LIVE MUSIC Israelis have a penchant for hardcore trance music, and raves and one-off parties are big business, although in the city centre you're more likely to find a mixture of rock, techno, dance and plenty of 1980s hits. Tel Avivians have a lot of partying stamina (mainly because of the small amount of alcohol they consume) and go out late, so don't even consider a nightclub before midnight. Live music clubs range from rock to alternative to South American drums to jazz and R&B. Admission charges tend to vary depending on who's playing.

☆ **The Barbie** 40 Salame Rd; ☎ 5188123; admission varies with performer. This is the place to see big-name rock musicians & bands in concert. The bunker-like club is generally packed with crowds of eccentrically dressed youngsters spilling on to the street.

☆ **Café Barzilay** 13 HaRachav St; ☎ 6878090; ⏰ 21.00–late daily; admission 20–80NIS. Small, alternative club featuring live performances of Israeli rock & international DJs. More comfortable than some of the big beasts of the nightclub scene.

☆ **Fifth Dimension** Tel Aviv Port; ☎ 6024559; www.mimad.co.il; ⏰ 22.00–late daily; admission 50NIS. Aptly located in one of the port's big hangars, this is a sweaty, noisy, pumping club that has been host to bands such as The Prodigy. The nearby Hangar 11 is also home to big names when they come to town.

☆ **Goldstar Zappa** 24 Raul Wallenberg St; ☎ 7674646; ⏰ daily for evening performances; admission 50–150NIS. One of the city's leading live music venues, it hosts Israeli & international artists covering a wide spectrum of music genres.

☆ **Haoman 17** 15 Abarbanel St; ☎ 6813636; ⏰ 23.00–late daily; admission 70–140NIS. This is the younger sibling of the immensely popular Haoman/Bar 17 club in Jerusalem. Equally popular in Tel Aviv, this is the place to blow your budget in one evening (drinks are exorbitant) & have a hell of a time doing it.

☆ **Shablul Jazz** Hangar 13, Tel Aviv Port; ☎ 05461891; ⏰ 20.00–late daily; admission free–80NIS. Swanky jazz bar with regular jam sessions & open mic nights as well as an impressive wine list & gourmet menu.

CINEMAS The **Tel Aviv Cinematheque** [133 G1] (*Ha'arba'a St; ☎ 6060800; www.cinema.co.il; admission 36NIS*) shows an arty selection of films, ranging from classics to avant-garde to experimental pieces. Annual film festivals are shown so check at the box office for upcoming events. The cinema is often at the centre of

Israeli debate thanks to its decision to show politically sensitive films. For new releases and blockbusters (subtitled in Hebrew) try the **Lev Cinema** [115 D4] (*Ground Floor, Dizengoff Centre;* ✆ *6200485; admission 36NIS*) or **Ravhen Movie Theatre** [115 C3] (*Dizengoff Sq & Azrieli Towers;* ✆ *5282288; admission 37NIS*).

PERFORMING ARTS Theatre has had a long and rich history in Tel Aviv and even today still enjoys regular sell-out performances. The **Habima Theatre** [133 F1] (*Habima Sq, Tarshat Av;* ✆ *6295555; www.habima.co.il*) is not only Israel's national theatre but also the one that has made the greatest contribution to Israeli and Jewish theatrical culture over the past century. It was founded in 1918 in Moscow and relocated to Tel Aviv in 1931 and today comprises 80 actors who perform four plays daily. Plays are in Hebrew but there is simultaneous English translation available. The **Cameri Theatre** [115 F3] (*Golda Meir Centre, 19 Shaul HaMelech Av;* ✆ *6060900;* e *ifat@cameri.co.il; www.cameri.co.il*) also offers English translation and has a good website for upcoming events. The smaller **Beit Lessin** [115 C3] (*101 Dizengoff St;* ✆ *7255333; www.lessin.co.il*) has performances most weeks although mostly in Hebrew, while the **Tzavta** [115 E4] (*30 Ibn Gvirol St;* ✆ *6950156*) swings between avant-garde theatre performances, Israeli folk music nights and classical performances (Hebrew only). **Tmuna** [133 H3] (*8 Shontzino St;* ✆ *5611211;* e *kupa@tmu-na.org.il; www.tmu-na.org.il*) is a small performing arts centre, where you can sit back with a drink and watch up-and-coming young musicians, actors, dancers and singers. In Jaffa, the **Arab-Hebrew Theatre** (*10 Mifratz Shlomo St;* ✆ *5185563;* e *info@arab-hebrew-theatre.org.il; www.arab-hebrew.theatre.org.il*) is housed inside an ancient stone building and comprises two groups that produce plays in both Hebrew and Arabic.

The **Suzanne Dellal Centre** [132 B5] (*6 Yehi'eli St;* ✆ *5105656; www.suzannedellal.org.il*) is the country's foremost dance centre and home of the nationally acclaimed Bat-Sheva Dance Group. Check their website for upcoming shows and ticket booking. The **Israel Ballet** (✆ *6046610; www.iballet.co.il*) company also has regular performances of the great classics.

For classical music the **Mann Auditorium** [110 C5] (*1 Huberman St;* ✆ *6211777; www.hatarbut.co.il*) is home to the world-renowned **Israeli Philarmonic Orchestra** while the **New Israel Opera** now performs at the **Tel Aviv Performing Arts Centre** [115 F3] (*19 Shaul Hamelech Bd;* ✆ *6927777; www.israel-opera.co.il*). There are also regular classical music performances at the **Felicja Blumental Music Centre and Library** [132 C1] (*26 Bialik St;* ✆ *6201185; www.fbmc.co.il*).

SHOPPING

Tel Aviv is a shopper's paradise and pretty much anything you're looking for can be found in the city's malls, shopping streets, boutiques and markets. For more mainstream shops, the huge **Azrieli** and **Dizengoff centres** (see page 127) are the places to head to, while the funky **Sheinkin Street** (see page 130) offers a range of one-of-a-kind boutiques and a variety of shoe shops. And if it's shoes and boots you're after, **Dizengoff Street** is teeming with a rather strange combination of cheap and expensive shoe shops, and a gaudy selection of wedding dresses. At the other end of town, **Allenby Street** is a fun, if rather shabby street of cheap shoes and clothes, although you might have to look a bit harder for the good stuff. Where Allenby Street meets the seafront is the plush **Opera Tower Shopping Centre** [132 B1] (*1 Allenby St;* ✆ *510796;* ⊕ *10.00–22.00 daily*). For a totally different experience, the **HaCarmel Market** [132 C3] (see page 134) is a feast of super-cheap clothes, home wares, fresh produce and sweets and is a must-see in the city. Souvenir shopping can be slightly harder in Tel Aviv and one of the best places to visit is the small **Spring** shop (*65 Ben Yehuda St;* ✆ *5223759*) which sells a good selection of Ahava Dead Sea products as well as nice gift ideas, souvenirs, novelty T-shirts and postcards. Alternatively, the twice-weekly **Nahalat Binyamin Market** (see page 134) has a great selection of arts and crafts and it is always possible to pick up a bargain or two at Jaffa's **flea market** (see page 136). In addition, many of the museum gift shops sell high-quality souvenirs and crafts. The area known as the **Electric Garden** (Gan Hahashmal) [133 E5] is an up-and-coming zone in which trendy boutiques are opening by the dozen and vying for space in the much sought-after neighbourhood.

BOOKSHOPS There are plenty of big chain stores and small secondhand shops selling Hebrew and English books as well as books in French, German and Russian.

Bibliophile [132 D4] 87 Allenby St; ✆ 6299710; ◷ 09.00–19.00 Sun–Thu, 09.00–14.00 Fri. This warren-like used bookstore has a big selection of tatty books in a variety of languages.
Sipur Pashut Book Shop [132 B5] 31 Shabazi St; ✆ 5107040; ◷ 10.00–20.00 Sun–Thu, 09.30–14.00 Fri. Small, stylish

bookshop, worth a visit for something a bit different.
Steimatzky [115 C2] 109 Dizengoff St; ✆ 5233415; ◷ 08.30–21.30 Sun–Thu, 08.30–15.00 Fri. Has a big English-language section inc the Carta map series. There is also a smaller branch in the Dizengoff Centre.

CAMPING SHOPS
LaMetayel 3rd Floor, Dizengoff Centre; ✆ 0773334508; ◷ 10.00–21.00 Sun–Thu, 10.00–14.30 Fri. Big selection of camping gear at reasonable prices, plus a great selection of maps & travel guides.

Maslool Traveller's Equipment Centre [115 C4] 47 Bograshov St; ✆ 6203508; www. maslool.com; ◷ 09.00–23.00 Sun–Thu, 09.00–17.00 Fri, 19.30–22.30 Sat. Huge variety of camping, backpacking & outdoor equipment. Sleeping bags & boots downstairs.

OTHER PRACTICALITIES

EMERGENCY
Ambulance ✆ 101
Fire ✆ 102
Police 221 Dizengoff St; ✆ 5454210, & 14 HaRakevet St; ✆ 100 or 5644458

Tourist police [132 B2] Corner of Herbert Samuel St and Ge'ula St; ✆ 5165382

MONEY There are countless currency-exchange booths around the city centre that offer commission-free money exchange. While some of them may look a little shifty they all offer pretty much the same rate, are above board and have shorter queues than in the post office and banks, and are open later. There are several branches along Hayarkon and Ben Yehuda streets and King George Street near the Dizengoff Centre and some offer Moneygram or Western Union facilities, as does the post office. Travellers' cheques can be changed at most banks and at the post office for no commission. There are branches of all the major banks dotted around the city but the following are the most convenient.

$ Bank Hapoalim [115 E2] 71 Ibn Gvirol St; ✆ 6532407; ◷ 08.30–14.00 Sun, Tue/Wed, 08.30–13.45 & 16.00–17.00 Mon & Thu. Other

useful branches can be found at 5 Dizengoff Sq; 205 Dizengoff St; 19 Ben Yehuda St; 19th Floor, Round Bldg, Azrieli Centre; 217 Ben Yehuda St.

$ Bank Leumi [115 D4] 50 Dizengoff St; ✎9544555; ⏰ 08.30–14.00 Sun, Tue, Wed, 08.30–13.00 & 16.00–18.30 Mon & Thu. Other useful branches are on 1 Jerusalem St, Jaffa; 87a Ben Yehuda St; 71 Ibn Gvirol St; 43 Allenby St.

POST
✉ **Post office** [115 E1] 108 Ibn Gvirol St; ✎5228009; ⏰ 08.00–18.00 Sun–Thu, 08.00–12.00 Fri. This is the main branch but there are also useful branches on 60 King George St; 286 Dizengoff St; and 12 Jerusalem St, Jaffa.

MEDICAL
✚ **Assuta Hospital** 58–60 Jabotinsky St; ✎5201515
✚ **Ichilov Hospital** [115 C2] 6 Weizmann St; ✎6974444

✚ **Superpharm** Ground Floor, Dizengoff Centre; ✎6203798; ⏰ 09.30–22.00 Sun–Thu, 09.00–15.30 Fri, 06.30–23.00 Sat

INTERNET Internet cafés can be found strewn all over the city and most offer new computers and fast internet connection plus hot and cold drinks. Almost all cafés, hotels and hostels offer free Wi-Fi.

🌐 **Interfun** [132 B1] 20 Allenby St; ✎5171448; ⏰ 10.00–midnight daily

🌐 **Private Link Tel Aviv** [115 B3] 78 Ben Yehuda St; ✎5299889; ⏰ 24hrs daily; 10NIS/30mins, 28NIS/2hrs.

LAUNDRY Almost all automatic laundries are open 24 hours and charge around 12NIS to wash and dry one load. **Hamahbesa** has branches at 102 Ben Yehuda Street; 95 Yehuda Halevi Street; 109 Ibn Gvirol Street; 88 Frishman Street; and 6 Dizengoff Square.

BOX OFFICES To find out what's on in the city's theatres, galleries and concert halls and to buy tickets for upcoming events visit the box offices below or visit their websites (note that some are in Hebrew only).

Hadran 90 Ibn Gvirol St; ✎5279797; www.hadran.co.il
Kastel 153 Ibn Gvirol St; ✎6045000; www.tkts.co.il (Hebrew)

Lean 101 Dizengoff St; ✎5247373; www.leaan.co.il (Hebrew)
Rococco 93 Dizengoff St; ✎5276677

MEDIA The *Jerusalem Post* is an English-language newspaper that has lots of practical information and entertainment listings about Jerusalem and Tel Aviv for tourists and foreign residents. *Haaretz*, Israel's leading newspaper, is also printed in English daily. The monthly *Time Out Tel Aviv*, which is produced in English and Hebrew, also lists what's on in the city.

WHAT TO SEE

CITY CENTRE
Rabin Square [115 E2] Few people around the world will have escaped seeing Rabin Square on the news at sometime in its 40-year history. For it is in Tel Aviv's largest public square that celebrations, festivals, rallies, protests and exhibitions are held. The most shocking event to take place here, however, was the assassination of Israeli prime minister Yitzhak Rabin in 1995 by a Jewish student, Yigal Amir.

Today a small memorial to the right of the rather unsightly City Hall (when facing it) marks the spot upon which he was killed. Following his assassination the square, then known as Kings of Israel Square, was renamed in his memory (see page 13). Yitzhak Rabin is buried in the Mount Herzl Cemetery in Jerusalem and his funeral was attended by over 80 heads of state. At the time of writing Yigal Amir was serving his life sentence in Ayalon Prison, which from 2006 included conjugal visits with his wife, something seen by most Israelis as a sore and angering concession.

While there isn't an awful lot to see when there isn't an event taking place, the square can nonetheless be a good people-watching spot where people come out to play Frisbee, walk their designer dogs or just sit and chat. During events however, this is the place to see some real Israeli patriotism, memorial and mourning, gay pride, artistic flair or political aggression.

Dizengoff [115 C3] Dizengoff is the name given to both central Tel Aviv's main thoroughfare and the country's first **shopping mall** (*corner of Dizengoff & King George sts;* \ *6212416; www.dizengof-center.co.il;* ⊕ *09.00–midnight Sun–Thu, 09.00–16.00 Fri, 20.00–midnight Sat*). Spread across both sides of the constantly busy **Dizengoff Street**, the mall is a throwback to the early 1970s when it was built. The maze-like centre seems to be designed to provide shoppers with the maximum amount of walking, and is decidedly confusing. It is still, however, one of the busiest shopping spots in the city and is home to most of Tel Aviv's big-name stores (see *Shopping*, page 124) and countless food outlets. The weekend **food market** (⊕ *16.00–22.00 Thu, 10.30–16.00 Fri*) sees the walkways of the mall fill with stalls selling home-cooked, reasonably priced food, including meatballs, couscous, stuffed peppers, cakes, pies and a whole host of traditional fare.

The long, narrow Dizengoff Street that stretches from the Azrieli buildings to the Hayarkon Park is one of the main arteries of central Tel Aviv. From the mall northwards once ultra-trendy shops line the pavements, today selling mainly shoes and gaudy, Cinderella-style wedding dresses. Just north of the mall is **Dizengoff Square** with its kitsch, all-singing, all-dancing water fountain, decidedly unattractive but something of which the locals are strangely proud. The square is home to several new boutique hotels, a few cafés, a cinema and plays host to an **antique market** (⊕ *14.00–16.00 Tue, 09.00–16.00 Fri*).

Azrieli Centre [110 D4] (*123 Menachem Begin St;* \ *6081179; www.azrielicenter.co.il;* ⊕ *10.00–22.00 Sun–Thu, 09.30–17.00 Fri, 20.00–23.00 Sat*) The Azrieli buildings have quickly become one of Tel Aviv's most recognisable landmarks. The round, square and triangular buildings are home to not only one of the Middle East's biggest business centres but also the country's largest mall. The Disneyland of shopaholics, the centre is home to an enormous selection of moderate and expensively priced stores (see page 124). One of its key attractions is the **Azrieli Observatory** (*49th Floor, Round bldg;* \ *6081179;* ⊕ *winter 09.30–18.00 daily; summer 09.30–20.00 Sat–Thu, 09.30–18.00 Fri; admission adult/child 22/17NIS*), which offers, without a shadow of doubt, the best view of the city. A 3D movie on Tel Aviv and an audio guide to help you pinpoint the major sites on the horizon will certainly aid you in getting your bearings.

Tel Aviv Museum of Art [115 G3] (*27 Shaul Hamelech Bd;* \ *6077020; www.tamuseum.com;* ⊕ *10.00–16.00 Mon, Wed & Sat, 10.00–22.00 Tue & Thu; admission adult/child 42NIS/free*) Having been in its current location since 1971, the museum started from humble beginnings in 1932 in the home of Tel Aviv's first mayor Meir Dizengoff, several years before the State of Israel was founded. It was in that first building that the signing of the Declaration of Independence took place and is today known as **Independence Hall**. The museum's collection is impressive even to an art novice, its permanent collection proudly displaying pieces by Picasso, Miro, Monet, Renoir, Cézanne, Matisse and Chagall to name but a few. Standing as one of the world's foremost art museums, it is the *pièce de résistance* of Israel's art scene and an integral part of the country's cultural heritage. Be sure not to miss the photography department, which has some beautiful photographs of 19th-century Palestine, and the temporary exhibitions that often display works based upon contemporary Israeli issues such as the disengagement of Gaza in 2005.

Helena Rubinstein Pavilion [115 E4] (*6 Tarsat Bd;* \ *5287196;* ☉ *10.00–16.00 Mon, Wed & Sat, 10.00–22.00 Tue & Thu; admission free*) The pavilion displays works by well-known Israeli artists who have made their niche in both the international and national art scenes. The gallery was established in 1959 to serve as an overflow of the Tel Aviv Museum of Art (see page 128), but has developed into a highly reputable space in its own right. Exhibitions change regularly, some of which are free while others can be accessed using the Tel Aviv Museum entrance ticket (see page 127).

Rubin Museum [132 C2] (*14 Bialik St;* \ *5255961; www.rubinmuseum.org.il;* ☉ *10.00–15.00 Mon, Wed, Thu & Fri, 10.00–20.00 Tue, 11.00–14.00 Sat; admission adult/child 20NIS/free*) One of Israel's most acclaimed artists, Reuven Rubin (1893–1974) bequeathed his house to the city upon his death and it has now been converted into a gallery displaying many of his famous works. His pieces stand alongside other works by Israeli artists and there is an audio-visual presentation on his life.

Bialik House (Beit Bialik) [132 C2] (*22 Bialik St;* \ *6042222;* ☉ *11.00–17.00 Mon–Thu, 10.00–14.00 Fri & Sat; adult/child 20/10NIS*) This is the nicely restored former home of the much-acclaimed Jewish poet Chaim Bialik who lived here until his death in 1934. All the information inside the house is in Hebrew but many of his personal rooms have been restored or recreated and are interesting in themselves.

Museum of History of Tel Aviv & Jaffa (Beit Ha'ir) [132 C1] (*27 Bialik St;* \ *5253403;* ☉ *09.00–17.00 Mon–Thu, 10.00–14.00 Fri & Sat; admission adult/child 20/10NIS, varies throughout high season*) Located in the old town hall building, this museum is a white, modernist, impressive piece of architecture. Dedicated to the history of the city it has permanent exhibitions on Meir Dizengoff, the city's first mayor, as well as temporary exhibits of photos and art. An interactive display showcasing the city's timeline is a good way to gain some historical insight.

Bauhaus architecture In 2003, Tel Aviv was awarded UNESCO World Heritage status because of its abundance of buildings built in the Bauhaus architectural style. Today, the more than 4,000 Bauhaus buildings are the pride and joy of an otherwise architecturally drab, grey city and have earned Tel Aviv the nickname 'the White City'.

The pre-Nazi Germany school of Bauhaus architecture produced several renowned architects who later settled in Tel Aviv before the founding of the State of Israel and who put their names to the buildings that many years later have come to define the city. As an architectural form, Bauhaus is simple, striking and unadorned and is based on functionality rather than glamour. Signature features of the style are its small, elongated balconies and rounded corners. While Bauhaus buildings can be found dotted all over the city centre, there are well-preserved concentrations along the length of Rothschild Boulevard, Dizengoff Square, Bialik Street and Kalisher Street as well as some buildings around the Sheikin Street area. The Tel Aviv Municipality organises a free **walking tour** in English (11.00 Sat, starting from 46 Rothschild Bd). Alternatively, the **Bauhaus Centre** [115 C3] (*99 Dizengoff St;* ✆ *5220249;* ⊕ *10.00–19.30 Sun–Thu, 10.00–14.30 Fri, 12.00–19.30 Sat*) offers a weekly two-hour guided walking tour (10.00 Fri; 50NIS). They also have MP3 recordings of the tour if you prefer to go on your own. For more information on Tel Aviv's Bauhaus buildings visit the municipality's website (*www.white-city.co.il*).

Ben-Gurion House [115 B1] (*17 Ben Gurion St;* ✆ *5221010; http://ben-gurion-house.org.il;* ⊕ *08.00–15.00 Sun & Tue–Thu, 08.00–17.00 Mon, 08.00–13.00 Fri; admission free*) Israel's first prime minister once stated: 'I bequeath to the State of Israel my home in Tel Aviv', and to this day that home stands as it did when David and Paula Ben-Gurion lived there. They alternated between this abode and their later home in Sde Boker (see page 253), which is also a museum. In the house adjacent are exhibitions about the life, history and achievements of Ben-Gurion.

Trumpeldor Cemetery [115 C4] Hidden away amidst the city centre's buildings is the old cemetery. The final resting place of countless Tel Avivan greats, it is a quiet place to reflect on those who contributed to the creation of the country and added their stamp on this enigmatic city. Haim Bialik, Shimon Rokach, Haim Arlozorov and Max Nordau are amongst just some of the notable graves.

NORTH CITY CENTRE

HaYarkon Park [110 C1] Tel Aviv's biggest park spreads out from the HaYarkon River that pours into the Mediterranean at the northern end of the city. The park is in effect divided into two sections, the larger and more developed being to the east of the Ayalon Highway where, in addition to the river, a manmade lake has been dug and the grounds nicely landscaped. It is a lovely place to go and escape the urban buzz, especially in the warmer months, but be warned – half of Tel Aviv will also have the same idea. For children in particular the park has a wealth of activities including boating (150NIS/hr) or canoeing (70NIS/hr) on the lake, countless playgrounds and activity parks and sprawling lawns on which to set up an afternoon picnic. If it's sports you're after head down to the area directly to the east of the Ayalon Highway bridge where locals will be happy to let you join in with football, basketball, table tennis or tennis; a great way to see real Tel Avivian life and a step off the tourist trail. Alternatively, on the northern side of the river in the west of the park is the **Sportek** [110 C1] (✆ *6990307; www.park.co.il*). A **climbing wall** (*www.kir.co.il;* ⊕ *17.00–22.00 Sun–Thu, 14.00–20.00 Fri, 11.00–21.00 Sat; day admission 55NIS*), **skateboard park** (⊕ *16.00–20.00 Sun–Thu, 11.00–20.00 Fri/Sat; admission 28NIS*) can all be found in the area as well as plenty of packed grassy areas to throw a ball or Frisbee around.

Eretz Israel Museum [110 D1] (*2 Hayim Levanon St;* ✆ *6415244; www.eretzmuseum.org.il;* ⊕ *10.00–16.00 Sun–Wed, 10.00–20.00 Thu, 10.00–14.00 Fri/Sat; admission adult/child 42NIS/free*) Spread across the greenery of the HaYarkon Park, the museum is a tell-all of Israel's history and culture. Permanent and temporary exhibits range from archaeology and ethnography to Judaica, folklore

and traditional crafts, and these are presented in a multitude of different ways. Impressive collections of ancient glass, coins and metallurgical pieces can be found in the permanent collection as well as the highly interesting Ethnography and Folklore Pavilion at the southern end of the museum complex. Mosaics, a 1945 New York fire engine and a full reconstruction of an ancient olive oil plant are also amongst the huge variety of exhibits. The Planetarium has several daily showings (in Hebrew only).

Old Port Long since closed to sea traffic, the Old Port has been remodelled and reshaped into a hub of recreation, good food, nightclubs, wooden promenades and great views. Located in the north of the city near the HaYarkon River estuary, the area benefits from being situated away from urban areas, its pumping clubs able to make as much noise as they wish all night long. During the daytime the port is a pleasant place to come for a stroll, light lunch or relaxing afternoon in one of the countless cafés. A nice walk starts in the centre of the port and heads southwards past the old warehouses and workshops to the old pier where there is a lovely view south. Likewise, views from the stone pier are worth seeing. For something a bit different, the **Antique Fair and Organic Market** (⊕ *10.00–20.00 Fri, market 10.00–18.00*) makes for a pleasant couple of hours perusing old knick-knacks and a whole range of organic foods. At night the area really comes into its own, with more bars and clubs than you can shake a cocktail stick at (see page 123). While there is a good selection of music genres and types of bar, the majority tend to be 'pick-up' bars attracting the young and good-looking in all their Lycra finery.

Diaspora Museum (Beit Hatefusot) (*Tel Aviv University;* ✎ *6408000; www. bh.org.il;* ⊕ *10.00–16.00 Sun–Tue, 10.00–20.00 Wed & Thu, 09.00–13.00 Fri; admission adult/child 70/55NIS*) Located in the southeast corner of the university grounds, the museum has risen to international renown as the first and largest museum dedicated to Jewish history. The permanent exhibition depicts the story of the Jewish people through video clips, drawings, reconstructions, models and computer generations. Exhibits include 'The Jews', 'The community', 'Faith' and 'The return to Zion'.

SOUTH CITY CENTRE
Great Synagogue [132 D4] (*110 Allenby St;* ✎ *5604905*) Just east of the Shalom Tower on Allenby Street is the Great Synagogue which, as its name implies, is the largest of Tel Aviv's 350-odd synagogues. Built in 1926, it underwent a major overhaul in the 1970s in an attempt to recreate the former glory of the ornate pre-Holocaust synagogues of Europe. Relative to the distinctly unadorned, plain synagogues that are a feature of Judaism, a huge domed roof and stained-glass windows have given some beauty to the building. Shabbat services are open to the public but appropriate modest dress must be worn for both men and women.

Sheinkin Tel Aviv has many areas frequented by those who think they're a cut above the rest and there is nowhere more so than Sheinkin Street. This ultra-trendy, yet slightly bohemian street, is the place to go during the week to buy the boutique fashion that you will then wear on a Friday whilst sunning yourself outside one of its countless cafés. Many Israeli designers have set up shop here selling pricey but highly individual outfits, and there are more shoe shops than you could shake a stiletto at.

Neve Tzedek This is one of Tel Aviv's most delightful neighbourhoods, unfortunately often overlooked in favour of more commercial areas. The neighbourhood was the first to appear outside the Old Jaffa walls in 1887 and formed the centre of Tel Aviv as the city grew up around it. It eventually fell into decline and became a dilapidated and tired area full of run-down, shabby buildings. A major overhaul in the 1980s however put Neve Tzedek back in the fashionista limelight, and it is now one of the city's trendiest and most enchanting areas. It was originally settled by many Jewish artists and today its heritage has been honoured by the galleries that line the main streets, as well as the famous **Suzanne Dellal Centre** [132 B5] (see page 124). The small streets that weave through the area are packed with a fascinating selection of shops selling art, designer clothes, pottery and jewellery, as well as countless cafés and restaurants when you feel the need to recharge your batteries. On your wanderings look out for the **Rokach House** (*36 Shimon Rokach St*), which was one of the first houses built in the area. Also of interest is the newly opened **Nahum Gutman Museum of Art** [132 C5] (*21 Shimon Rokach St;* ✆ *5161970; www.gutmanmuseum. co.il;* ⊕ *10.00–16.00 Sun–Wed, 10.00–20.00 Thu, 10.00–14.00 Fri, 10.00–15.00 Sat*). Located in one of Neve Tzedek's traditional buildings, the museum displays works by Gutman, a renowned Jewish artist who immigrated to the country in 1905. His works range from oil paintings to sculpture to mosaics and engravings, as well as writing and illustrating children's books.

Rothschild Boulevard Running from the Habima Theatre in the north to the Neve Tzedek neighbourhood in the south, the leafy, tree-lined Rothschild Boulevard is Tel Aviv's pride and joy, and rightly so. It forms not only the heart of Bauhaus architecture but the heart of weekend recreation and leisure. The long, wide boulevard with its central pedestrian walkway and bicycle lane is dotted with sandwich bars that have formed an unlikely super trend. Come Friday, young, chic Tel Avivians (and their designer dogs) come to strut their stuff, lounge on the grass or pull up a chair at one of the street's innumerable open-air cafés. The entire length of the street is a mass of restaurants and cafés (see page 118) ranging from the moderately pricey to the downright extortionate, but then you pay for the location.

Located at number 16 is **Independence Hall** [132 D4] (✆ *5173942;* ⊕ *09.00– 14.00 Sun–Fri; admission adult/child 20/16NIS*), the site where Israel's declaration of independence was signed. The museum hall has been left as it was on 14 May 1948 with cameras, flags and broadcasting equipment *in situ* and is a poignant and stirring dedication to Israel's heritage. On the wall is the famous photograph of Ben-Gurion reading the declaration to a large crowd above which is a photograph of Theodor Herzl, the grandfather of Zionism. The building later became the home of Tel Aviv's first mayor, Meir Dizengoff, and the first site of the Tel Aviv Museum of Art (see page 127). The small, one room-museum is surprisingly simple for a country so fiercely proud of its ancestry but worth a visit if you're passing by.

There are several Bauhaus walking tours that operate in this area (see page 128) but if you want to just take a stroll and enjoy the relaxed, carefree atmosphere and do some Bauhaus spotting of your own, look out for the following buildings: numbers 61, 66, 67, 73, 83, 84, 87, 89–91, 93, 99, 100, 117, 118, 119, 121, 123 and 126–128.

Yemenite Vineyard (Kerem Hateimanim) The tiny web of streets that form the Yemenite Vineyard (which actually isn't a vineyard in any shape or form) is one of the most rustically charming neighbourhoods in the city. It was established at the turn of the last century by immigrants from Yemen, and until its huge facelift in the early 1990s was little more than yet another run-down neighbourhood. Since

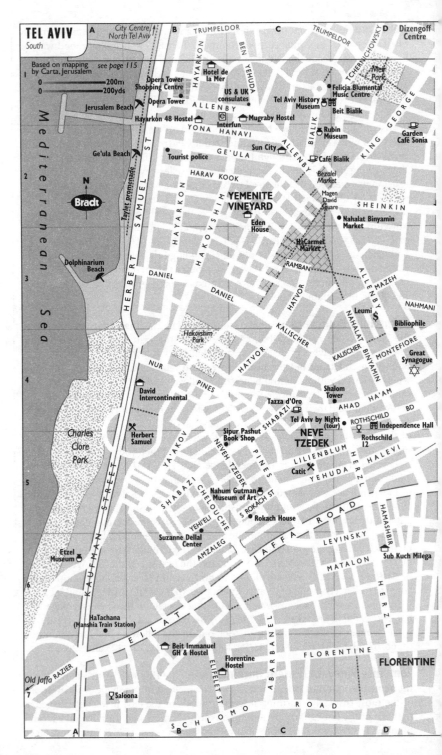

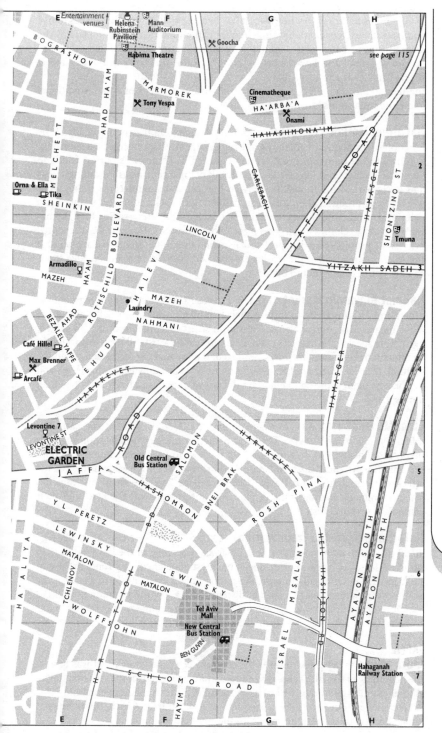

E Entertainment venues
Helena Rubinstein Pavilion
Mann Auditorium
F
G
H

BOGRASHOV
✕ Goocha
Habima Theatre

MARMOREK
see page 115

ELCHETT
AHAD HA'AM
✕ Tony Vespa
Cinematheque
HA'ARBA'A
✕ Onami

HAHASHMONA'IM

CARLEBACH
JAFFA ROAD
HAMASGER
SHONTZINO ST

2

Orna & Ella Σ
🍴 Tika
SHEINKIN
LINCOLN
YITZAKH SADEH
😃 Tmuna

3

Armadillo
MAZEH
ROTHSCHILD BOULEVARD
HA'AM
HALEVI
MAZEH
Laundry
NAHMANI

Café Hillel
Max Brenner
✕
🍴 Arcafé
BEZALEL YAFFE
AHAD
YEHUDA
HARAKEVET

HAMASGER

4

Levontine 7
LEVONTINE ST
ELECTRIC GARDEN
JAFFA
JAFFA ROAD
Old Central Bus Station 🚌
SALOMON
HARAKEVET
ROSH PINA

5

YL PERETZ
LEWINSKY
MATALON
TCHLENOV
HA'ALIYA
HASHOMRON
BNEI BRAK
LEWINSKY
MISALANT
HEIL HASHIRON
AYALON SOUTH
AYALON NORTH

6

WOLFFSOHN
MATALON
Tel Aviv Mall
New Central Bus Station 🚌
BEN GUVIN
ISRAEL
SCHLOMO ROAD
HAYIM
Hahaganah Railway Station

7

E
F
G
H

its major cosmetic surgery however, it has become one of trendiest places to live and its restored houses are now much sought after (and increasing in price by the day). The narrow streets are laid out in a gridiron pattern unusual to the city, and houses are small and low-rise. Its proximity to the seafront and the HaCarmel Market makes it the ideal place to set up home, while for visitors to the city the neighbourhood offers a pleasant stroll and a selection of small, traditional Yemenite restaurants.

HaCarmel Market [132 C3] (⏰ *08.00–17.00 daily*) On the southern side of the junction where Sheinkin, Allenby and King George streets converge is the northern entrance to the tunnel-like HaCarmel Market. This is the city's busiest fruit and vegetable (and everything else you can think of) market, and is a bustling, noisy and lively part of traditional Tel Avivian life. All and sundry come to buy their weekly fresh produce, shop for cheap trinkets and stock up on socks, and it is a delightful insight into the less chic side of the city. Apart from selling food, home-ware and cheap clothes it is a good place to buy Dead Sea products for discounted prices, but be prepared to haggle. Hidden behind the clothes stores that are found at the Allenby Street end of the market are some fantastic *burekas* and *baklava* shops so look carefully so as not to miss out.

Nahalat Binyamin Market [132 D2] (*10.00–17.00 Tue & Fri*) On market days artists and artisans come to display their handmade works on small stalls set up along the paved section of Nahalat Binyamin Street near Allenby Street. To make it even more special, the market's council handpicks the artists allowed to partake, in an attempt to keep away the mass-produced, money-making pieces and retain the cultural diversity of the market. In addition to the stalls, clowns, fortune tellers and performers often show up to entertain the crowds, creating a lively and bohemian atmosphere.

Etzel Museum [132 A6] (*15 Goldman St;* ☎ *5177180;* ⏰ *08.00–16.00 Sun–Thu; admission adult/child 10NIS*). Etzel was a Zionist military organisation that was involved in the fight for free immigration for Jews to Palestine, battling with both the Palestinians and British Mandate Authorities. They were responsible for the attack on Jerusalem's King David Hotel (see page 73). The small museum has artefacts, movies, photographic displays and information on the Etzel and their campaigns within Palestine.

HaTachana (Manshia Train Station) [132 A6] ☎ *609995; 10.00–22.00 Sat–Thu, 10.00–17.00 Fri; admission free.* The long-awaited opening of the city's oldest train station is set to see it rise to being one of the most popular cultural zones in the city. Built in 1892 in Ottoman-era style, the station linked Jaffa with Jerusalem. For the past 60 years is has been in a state of disrepair, but a major renovation project has seen it returned to its former glory, and now an entire complex of buildings boasts galleries, boutiques, cafés, weekly markets, jazz concerts, art exhibitions and festivals.

JAFFA

Clock tower Jaffa's clock tower is the centrepiece of the Old City. It was built at the beginning of the 20th century to commemorate the reign of the Ottoman sultan Abd al-Hamid II and returned to its former glory after a major overhaul in 2006. A free, guided tour leaves every Wednesday at 09.30 from **Clock Tower Square**, which borders the al-Mahmudiyya Mosque (see below).

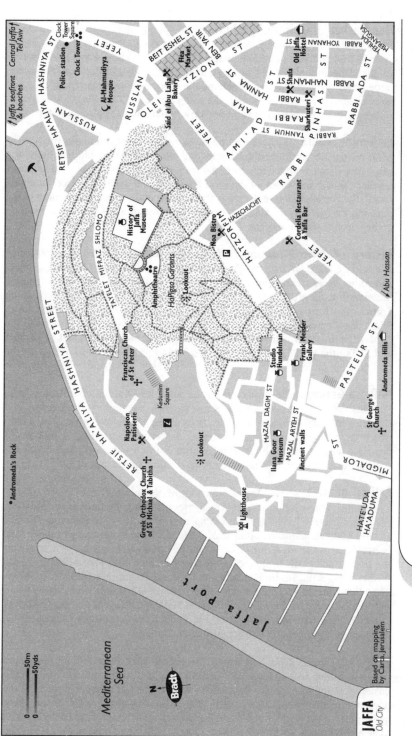

135

JAFFA
Old City

Mediterranean
Sea

Based on mapping
by Carta, Jerusalem

0 ——— 50m
0 ——— 50yds

Bradt

Andromeda's Rock

Jaffa Port

Lighthouse

Greek Orthodox Church
of SS Michael & Tabitha

Napoleon
Patisserie

Lookout

Kedumim
Square

Franciscan Church
of St Peter

TAYELET MIFRAZ SHLOMO

RETSIF HA'ALIYA HASHNIYA STREET

RUSSLAN

RETSIF HA'ALIYA HASHNIYA

RUSSLAN

HASHNIYA ST

Police station

Clock Tower

Clock
Tower
Square

Al-Mahmudiya
Mosque

Jaffa seafront
& beaches

Central Jaffa
Tel Aviv

YEFET

YEFET

OLEI TZION

Said el Abu Lafia
Bakery

BEIT ESHEL ST

Flea
Market

BEN YAIR

ST

HANINA ST

AMI'AD

RABBI TANHUM ST

RABBI PINHAS

RABBI

RABBI

RABBI ADA ST

Shafa

NAHMAN ST

Sharkuteri

Cordelia Restaurant
& Yaffa Bar

YEFET

Abu Hassan

RABBI YOHANAN

Old Jaffa
Hostel

YEHUDA
MERKAGUSA

History of Jaffa
Museum

HAZECHUCHIT

HAZOREFIM

Noa Bistro

HaPisga Gardens

Amphitheatre

Lookout

PASTEUR ST

Studio
Hundelman

Frank Meisler
Gallery

Andromeda Hills

St George's
Church

MIGDALOR ST

HATE'UDA
HA'ADUMA

MAZAL DAGIM ST

Ilana Goor
Museum

MAZAL ARYEH ST

Ancient walls

Flea Market (Shuk HaPishpeshim) Although the name conjures up images of cheap tack, Jaffa's flea market (*between Olei Tzion & Beit Eshel sts*) is in fact a great place to find yourself an antique bargain (and a lot of cheap kitsch). Wandering amongst the mountains of furniture, cloth, knick-knacks, Judaica, brassware, carpets and *nargilah* pipes and enjoying the lively, Middle Eastern ambience and noisy chatter, is a world away from the chic cafés in Tel Aviv. Haggling is a must and you're more likely to get a good deal on a Friday when the place is at its busiest.

Kedumim Square This is the central square of Old Jaffa and marks the starting point for the labyrinth of cobbled lanes and alleys amidst the old buildings. The wide square is surrounded by artists' galleries, expensive restaurants and craft and jewellery shops, and is one of the most charming and delightful places in all Tel Aviv-Jaffa. The alleys weave their way through the maze of houses downhill to the **port** and the best way to explore is to simply get lost amongst them. You'll end up in the port one way or another.

History of Jaffa Museum and Visitors' Centre (⊕ *10.00–18.00 daily; admission adult/child 8/6NIS*) The long history of Jaffa is told through displays and audio-visual presentations. They also hand out free maps. On your way to the museum from the artists' quarter you will pass the imposing, but sadly deteriorating **Franciscan Church of St Peter** (⊕ *08.00–11.45 & 15.00–17.00 daily; modest dress*), said to have been visited by Napoleon during its years as a hostel. Just off to the right of the square a small alley leads to the **Greek Orthodox Church of St Michael and St Tabitha** (⊕ *08.00–11.45 & 15.00–17.00 daily; modest dress*) displaying the traditional bright colours and architecture of Greek ecclesiastical buildings.

HaPigsa Gardens The gardens form the summit of the hill upon which Jaffa's Old City sits, and countless small paths weave their way through the greenery and rockeries. A small wooden bridge leads from the square to the gardens, within which is an amphitheatre where summer concerts are held, and a monument depicting scenes from the Bible. This is a beautiful viewpoint northwards along the coast of Tel Aviv worth visiting once during the day and again at night.

Artists' quarter Mazal Dagim Street forms the heart of the artists' quarter along which you will find several art galleries including the **Ilana Goor Museum** (*4 Mazal Dagim St;* ✆ *6837676; www.ilanagoor.com;* ⊕ *10.00–16.00 Sun & Tue–Fri, 10.00–18.00 Sat; admission adult/child 24/14NIS*). The museum and gallery have been created in a space within Goor's beautiful home and is worth a visit, partly for the artwork and partly to appreciate the classic architecture of the building. A little further along is the **Studio Handelman** (*14 Mazal Dagim St;* ✆ *6819574;* ⊕ *10.30–22.30 Sun–Thu, 10.30–Shabbat Fri, end of Shabbat–22.30 Sat*) which designs and sells silk paintings, while the **Frank Meisler Gallery** (*25 Mazal Arie St;* ✆ *5123000;* ⊕ *09.00–23.00 Sun–Thu, 09.00–16.00 Fri, 18.00–23.00 Sat*) displays a memorable, expensive selection of metalwork figurines and Judaica.

Port As the waves gently lap against the ancient rock walls and old men stand patiently, fishing rods in hand, it is hard to imagine that this was once one of the busiest ports in the country. The fact that fishing boats still chug in and out of the port on a regular basis has awarded it the distinction of being one of the oldest active ports in the world. Just beyond the sea wall are several rocks, the darkest said to be **Andromeda's Rock**. According to Greek mythology Andromeda was chained

The **Tayelet** (promenade) that runs the length of Tel Aviv's coastline (whose official name is **Herbert Samuel Promenade**) is one of the top additions to the city and the wide, paved pedestrian walkway is one of the best spots in the country to witness the true cross-section of Israeli culture. In the hot and humid height of summer the beach is standing room only, where Tel Avivians and tourists take refuge from the smoggy heat and congestion of the day. From the young groups of teenagers to families and the old, the white sands lining the clean waters of the Mediterranean are bursting at the seams. Probably the most prominent group, however, is the young 20-somethings. This is where Israeli men come to strut their stuff and young women revel in watching them do it. *Matkot* (bat and ball) has become a very popular, highly competitive game where egos are made and destroyed. Bronzed Israeli girls wearing next to nothing parade the promenade in a catwalk fashion to rival the south of France. But somehow Tel Aviv has almost managed to escape the arrogance of other cities with such a strong beach culture. Here 'each to their own' seems to be the motto, a place where people from all walks of life converge. From the glamorous and fashionable, the large gay population, the religious and the Orthodox, to families, tourists and businesspeople, foreign immigrants and students, they curiously and surprisingly live harmoniously in a city they have grown to love for its freedom and tolerance.

to this rock by her father King Cepheus as a sacrifice to Poseidon's sea monster. As the legend goes she was saved by the hero Perseus who slayed the monster and took her hand in marriage.

Great Mosque (Muhamidiya Mosque) (*Between Yefet St, Olei Tzion;* \ *5272691; closed to non-Muslims*). Built in 1810 during the Ottoman period, the mosque's minaret is a Jaffa landmark. The buildings have grown around it and while the architecture is impressive (there are columns from Caesarea), it takes a little investigating to see it fully.

BEACHES Tel Aviv's beaches are wonderful. Wide and sandy, they are clean, relaxed and thanks to coastal barriers, much calmer than some of the wild stretches further up the coast. If there is a downside it is the sheer number of people who flock to the beaches on summer weekends, when you will be hard pushed to find a square metre of sand on which to lay your towel.

Tel Baruch Beach This is Tel Aviv's most northerly beach and is actually well beyond the urban areas. Located just north of Dov Airport it is a bit of a schlep from the city centre, but worth it for the wild sands, natural feel and isolation. Once notorious for prostitution, it has been cleaned up in recent years and is now a wholesome family beach. Plans to extend the nearby airport may scupper the tranquillity of the area in the future but for now it is a great expanse of soft white sand and rolling waves.

Metzizim Beach While it would be difficult to call the view from Metzizim Beach beautiful, it is in fact one of the funkiest places to hang out both during the day and at night (when it's even harder to see the power station and old port works). The

As the sound of loud, pumping music permeates the relaxed, summery atmosphere of Tel Aviv's seafront you would be forgiven for rolling your eyes and looking around for the local boy-racer, his small hatchback and oversized stereo interrupting everyone's leisurely day. Yet, upon turning around you will find that the noise culprit is not a testosterone-fuelled youngster but in fact a minivan full of bearded, white-robed Hassidic Jews. These fun-loving men of God are members of an Orthodox Hassidic group known as Breslov, who originated from the Ukraine and are today a joyous addition to Israeli life. Founded by Rebbe Nachman of Breslov (1772–1810), their ethos is to create an intense relationship with God through happiness, joy and living life to its fullest. Equipped with loud stereo systems, groups of Breslov drive around the streets in white vans, some sitting cross-legged on the roof, their long hair and beards blowing in the wind. As the van comes to a halt at traffic lights, the back doors swing open in a style reminiscent of the A-Team and out burst Breslov men, who proceed to dance enthusiastically until the lights change and they tumble back in and move on. The Breslov are received in Israel with amusement and affection, their contagious happiness bringing smiles to the faces of those around.

wide beach, chilled bars and relaxed atmosphere are a refreshing change from some of the younger, more raucous beaches further south.

Hilton Beach Named unsurprisingly after the nearby Hilton Hotel, this beach is frequented predominantly by three very different groups of sun-seekers. The northernmost end is the only section of Tel Aviv's coastline where dogs can run free. While it is a heart-warming sight to see over-excited pups chasing each other and crashing in and out of the waves, it isn't as much fun if you're lying on a beach towel as they do it. Further down from the doggy area is a patch of sand that has become the unofficial gay beach of the city, mainly with men. Tight swim shorts, hunky bodies and a lively atmosphere are its key characteristics. The Hilton Beach is also famed as being the city's best surfing beach. An offshore reef causes waves to break nicely on their way towards the coast and surfers of all ages flock to the seas. The **Sea Centre** surfing club (✆ 6503000) operates from here.

Nordau Beach Known as the Religious Beach, this is Tel Aviv's contribution to single-sex swimming. The beach is surrounded by a high wall and is more often than not near deserted. Women looking for that all-over tan have been known to come on women's days without the fear of being leered at, something that doesn't seem to bother the conservatively dressed religious women. Women's days are on Sunday, Tuesday and Thursday while men's days are Monday, Wednesday and Friday.

Gordon and Frishman beaches These are the quintessential Tel Avivian beaches, where muscular bronzed soldiers, tiny tots in rubber rings, sunburnt foreigners and everyone in between come to enjoy the summer sun and refreshing Mediterranean waters. Their central location means they are never empty, but midweek is certainly less crowded than summer weekends. Lifeguards, shower and bathroom facilities, huge beach bars and cafés and plenty of shade add to their appeal. At the northern end of Gordon Beach is the city's marina, a small, rather quaint area that incorporates the delightful **Gordon Swimming Pool** (↻ 7623300; ⊕ 13.30–20.00 Sun, 06.00–21.00 Mon & Thu, 06.00–20.00 Tue & Wed, 06.00–19.00 Fri, 07.00–18.00 Sat; admission adult/child 60/50NIS midweek, 72/65 w/end), which was fully renovated in 2009. Like the beaches, the big, refreshing saltwater pools attract hundreds of Israeli families on weekends, but weekdays are considerably quieter.

Jerusalem Beach This is another wide, pleasant beach with several cafés, plenty of space to throw a Frisbee around and shallow, clean water. Across Herbert Samuel Street are countless ice-cream parlours, fast-food joints and the beginning of the enigmatic Allenby Street.

Ge'ula Beach Unofficially and more commonly known as Banana Beach after the highly popular bar/restaurant/café located here, this is one of the funkiest and most bohemian beaches along the coast. The **Banana Beach** (↻ 5107958; ⊕ 24hrs) is a great place to enjoy a meal at any time of the day or simply cool off with an iced coffee or fruit smoothie. The food is relatively simple but does the trick if your budget runs to it – you're paying for the location and experience anyway. During the summer, big screens often show live sporting events or movies, which is a fun and chilled-out evening's entertainment in true Tel Aviv style.

Dolphinarium Beach Named after the old dolphin tank that used to be here, the beach attracts the hippy set who come to smoke *nargilah*, juggle fire balls, play the guitar or meditate. Friday afternoons see the beach turned into the setting for a huge jam session where budding musicians come to drum out a beat in the open air. There is also a watersports club, Surfpoint (↻ 1 599567888; 09.30–dark daily) where you can rent equipment for (or do courses in) windsurfing, scuba diving, kite-surfing, surfing and kayaking.

AROUND TEL AVIV

SAFARI PARK (ZOOLOGICAL CENTRE) (Ramat Gan; ↻ 6313531; www.safari.co.il; ⊕ 09.00–19.00 Sun–Thu, 09.00–14.00 Fri; admission adult/child 57NIS) On the outskirts of the city, this is a zoo in a safari park. Visitors (who in summer arrive in their thousands) drive through the African savanna-like lands past big herds of animals and then park up and enter the main part of the zoo. There is a safari bus if you don't have your own transport. The admission charges are used to promote and develop new conservation techniques and the safari park is involved with several programmes that aim to reintroduce endangered species back into the wild. The area outside the zoo is a big weekend favourite with hundreds of barbecuing Israeli families, giving it a nice, if extremely crowded, ambience. Buses 45 and 60 from central Tel Aviv stop near the park.

5

Mediterranean Coast

Israel's western coastline marks the end of the shimmering Mediterranean waters that stretch from the border with Lebanon to the Gaza Strip and Egyptian border. Great port cities have flourished along these shores for centuries, ancient Caesarea and Akko's Old City gracing the history books and providing a glimpse into the turbulent, magnificent and dramatic past, where empires were won and lost. In modern times, Haifa, Israel's third-largest city, has bloomed into a découpage of colourful neighbourhoods that tumble down Mount Carmel's northern slopes. The undulating hills of the Carmel mountain range are blanketed with a carpet of green, as they roll alongside the coast. Upon these hills where the Prophet Elijah battled the priests of Baal, ancient biblical deer once again roam freely and the irrepressibly picturesque town of Zichron Yaakov stands as a living memorial to Edmond de Rothschild, the grandfather of Zionism.

For visitors to the country the Mediterranean coast offers sweeping sandy beaches, majestic archaeological sites and a mesh of Jewish, Druze, Baha'i, Christian and Muslim traditions. Combine this with a wealth of tourist facilities and the best of the country's public transport, and you get Israel's most relaxed, sun-soaked and culturally rich region.

NAHARIYA   *Telephone code 04*

The northern coastal town of Nahariya holds claim to a rich history. On these soils Canaanites stamped their mark, Byzantine finds were unearthed, Romans marched along their paved roads, and it was a crucial stop along the great Via Maris highway. Unfortunately, little of Nahariya's ancient glamour has managed to find a place in the modern version of the town, and today this rather gaudy seaside resort is characterised by neon-lit eateries and cafés, a developed beachfront and groups of holidaying families. Outside the summer season there is not a lot to entice anyone to Nahariya, but the warmer weather allows for plenty of sporting and water activities, and visitors are attracted by its hotels and decent restaurants. A long seaside promenade stretches to the fringes of Akko and makes for some lovely cycling or walking opportunities. The clean, sandy but often overcrowded Municipal Beach forms the hub of summer activities, where beach volleyball, a large playground and a whole host of standard seaside activities are enjoyed.

Most facilities in Nahariya can be found along the main Sderot HaGa'aton Street which runs from north to south. The train station, the last stop along the Tel Aviv line, is at the northernmost end of the street alongside the central bus station.

GETTING THERE AND AWAY
By train Trains run from Tel Aviv (1hr 50mins/43.50NIS), Akko (8mins/8NIS) and Haifa (30mins/19NIS) to Nahariya train station (*1 HaGa'aton St;* ✆ *8564446*)

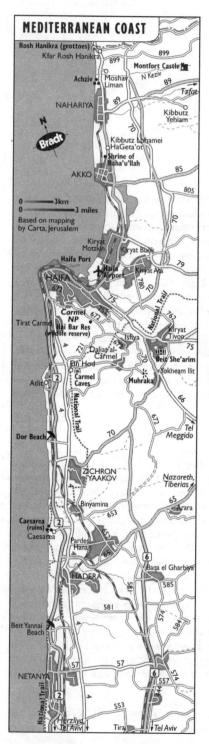

MEDITERRANEAN COAST

Based on mapping by Carta, Jerusalem

and is the final stop on the line. Trains run to and from Nahariya approximately every hour 05.20–20.20 Sunday–Thursday, 06.10–14.10 Friday and 09.15–12.00 Saturday.

By bus Buses arrive at and depart from Nahariya central bus station (*3 HaGa'aton St*; 9923434) every 15 minutes to and from Akko (15mins/7.60NIS) and Haifa (1hr/14.80NIS).

By car
Car rental
🚗 **Avis** 46 Hertzl St; 9511880; www.avis. co.il; ⏲ 08.00–18.00 Sun–Thu, 08.00–14.00 Fri. Cars from 130NIS per day.

GETTING AROUND Nahariya is a small town and it is an easy 10 minute walk down central HaGa'aton Street from the train or bus station to the seafront. Taxis can also be hailed from outside the stations.

TOURIST INFORMATION
🛈 **Tourist information centre** 19 HaGa'aton St; 9879800; ⏲ 08.00–13.00 & 16.00–19.00 Sun–Wed, 08.00–13.00 Thu/Fri. Located on the square near the Municipal Bldg. Most of the big hotels offer tours to surrounding areas so it is worth enquiring at their receptions.

WHERE TO STAY Nahariya doesn't have a lot in the way of mid-range accommodation so it's a choice between the four-star complexes or shabby, family-run guesthouses. Prices tend to be inflated, especially during peak seasons and the surrounding moshavim and kibbutzim offer lovely zimmer which are much better value for money.

🏠 **Carlton Nahariya** (200 rooms) 23 HaGa'aton St; 9005511; www.carlton-nahariya.com. Recently renovated with a good range of services inc large swimming pool, sun terrace, spa, restaurant, bar & children's club. 4x4 & boat tours can be arranged through their travel service. **$$$**

Hotel Frank (49 rooms) 4 Haalia St; 9920278; www.hotel-frank.co.il. Spacious, tidy rooms are clean and well equipped with TV, AC & big windows. A bar, outdoor terrace & buffet b/fast are also offered. **$$$**

Hotel Rosenblatt (14 rooms) 59 Weizmann St; 9920051; e jael@walla.co.il. While in dire need of a makeover, the hotel is clean, well located, & even has an outdoor swimming pool (in summer only). Rooms have AC & TV. **$$**

✗ **WHERE TO EAT** HaGa'aton Street is teeming with eateries, cafés and bars. Pizza joints and *shawarma* stands are your best budget options.

✗ **El Poncho** 33 HaGa'aton St; 9928635; 11.00–23.00 daily. This Argentinian restaurant is decked out in traditional gaucho-style décor, mimicking the cowboy saloons of the rural homeland. **$$$$**

✗ **Penguin Restaurant** 21 HaGa'aton St; 9928855; 08.00–00.00 Sun–Fri, 09.00– 00.00 Sat. The ever-popular Penguin Restaurant & attached Penguin Café serve a rather theme-less selection of meals, but all are well cooked & portions are generous. Salads, hamburgers, chicken, soups, pasta & Chinese dishes can be followed by a great choice of shakes & ice creams. **$$**

OTHER PRACTICALITIES
Emergencies
Police station 5 Ben Zvi St; 9920344
Fire 102
Ambulance 101

Money HaGa'aton Street has several branches of all Israel's major banks, all with ATMs.

$ **Bank Hapoalim** 37 HaGa'aton St; 03 6532407; 08.30–13.15 Tue/Wed, 08.30–13.00 & 16.00–18.30 Mon & Thu, 08.15–12.30 Fri

$ **Change Spot** 36 HaGa'aton St; 9921079; 09.00–19.00 Sun–Thu, 09.00–14.00 Fri

Post
✉ **Post office** 40 HaGa'aton St; 9920180; 08.00–18.00 Sun & Thu, 08.00–12.30 & 15.30–18.00 Mon & Tue, 08.00–13.30 Wed, 08.00–12.00 Fri

Medical
✚ **Hospital** Ben Zvi St; 9850505

✚ **Szabo pharmacy** Central bus station; 9920454; 08.00–13.30 & 16.00–19.30 Sun–Thu, 08.00–14.30 Fri

WHAT TO SEE AND DO
Municipal museum (*Floors 5, 6 & 7, Municipal Bldg, Ha Iriya Sq;* 9879863; *10.00–12.00 Sun–Fri, 16.00–18.00 Sun & Wed; admission free*) The simple Municipal museum contains several displays including a substantial collection of locally discovered fossils and shells. An art exhibit is housed on the fifth floor while the seventh floor is dedicated to the history of the town.

Canaanite temple (*Ha Ma'apilim St; admission free*) Located a few metres from the Municipal Beach are the remains of a Cannanite temple. It is believed the temple was dedicated to Astarte, goddess of the sea, and dates to around 1500BCE. The ruins form part of the municipal museum, so ask at the reception if you wish to have a look around.

Byzantine church (*Bielefeld St;* ℡ *9879800; admission free; call ahead to arrange entry*) Beautifully preserved mosaics make visiting the church a worthwhile activity. The 4th- to 7th-century mosaic floors are some of the best examples of their kind in the country discovered to date.

Scuba diving As far as Mediterranean dive sites go there are a few interesting ones around Nahariya. The most well known is the intentionally sunk Ahi Kidon Military Craft, which acts as a memorial site for members of the IDF water commando unit. Dive trips to the Rosh Hanikra Grottoes and Achziv Cave can also be arranged through the dive centres. A good choice is the **Diving Centre Nahariya** (*5 HaMa'apilim St;* ℡ *9511503/9929334;* e *club@putsker.co.il; www. putsker.co.il;* ⊕ *08.00–13.00 & 16.00–19.00 Sun–Thu, 08.00–17.00 Fri/Sat; 2-tank dive 170NIS, equipment rental 130NIS per dive*).

Galei-Galil Beach (⊕ *May–Oct 08.00–18.00 daily; admission 20NIS*) Renowned for its cleanliness and safety, it offers many sporting activities, eateries and cafés. The outdoor and indoor pools are included in the entry price.

AROUND NAHARIYA

ROSH HANIKRA At the northernmost point of Israel's Mediterranean coast, the large chalk grottoes and emerald waters of Rosh Hanikra (℡ *9857108–10; www.rosh-hanikra.com;* ⊕ *summer 09.00–18.00 daily; winter 09.00–16.00 daily; admission adult/child 43/35NIS*) are today a top tourist destination. As the crashing waves eroded the soft rock over thousands of years, they formed a series of large, watery caves at the base of the high cliff. Today visitors can experience these unusual geomorphological structures via a short, steep cable car that leads down to the entrance of the grottoes, providing magnificent views over the sea and along the jagged coastline.

Historically, Rosh Hanikra's prime location straddling the border with Lebanon made it an important strategic thoroughfare. During the 3rd and 4th centuries BCE, it marked the extent of the Israelite tribes and later became a crucial point along the trade route between Lebanon and Syria, and Palestine, Egypt and north Africa. In 333BCE, Alexander the Great entered the country here, supposedly leading his Greek army through tunnels dug out of the chalk. During the world wars, the British army invaded Lebanon, digging a railway tunnel between Haifa and Europe via Beirut and Turkey. The 250m-long tunnel and connecting bridges provided a means of transport for supplies and troops, and also created access for the Ha'apala (immigration) of Jews fleeing Nazi Europe. During the 1948 Arab–Israeli War, Israeli forces destroyed the bridges, fearing an insurgence from Arab forces through Lebanon.

Today, the southern tunnel and half of the middle tunnel are in Israeli territory, the remainder in Lebanon. A 15-minute sound and light show on the site provides some further insight into the history and geology of the area. The 'Small Train' (*operating 11.00—17.00 Sat & holidays*), follows the route taken by British Mandate trains, and connects Rosh Hanikra with Achziv National Park (40mins) (see below).

Getting there From Nahariya, buses 32 and 33 go to Rosh Hanikra and back several times a day (20mins/7NIS).

ACHZIV NATIONAL PARK (℡ *9823263;* ⊕ *Apr–Jun & Sep/Oct 08.00–17.00; Jul/Aug 08.00–19.00; admission adult/child 30/18NIS*) The ancient town of Achziv has had a long and prosperous past. An Old Testament settlement, it belonged to the tribe of Asher, and was also mentioned in the Talmud and Mishnah. The Phoenicians produced a vibrant and much sought-after purple dye from the marine snails that inhabit the coast, and enjoyed a flourishing economy. During the Crusader period, Achziv was known as Castle Imbert after the Crusader knight Hombertus de Pacci, until it was conquered by the Mamluk sultan Baibars in 1271.

Today, however, the park is loved not for its historical distinction, but for its shimmering turquoise waters that attract bathers and sea turtles alike. From the rocky coast, wide sandy beaches lead towards the sheltered bays and deep natural pools that have formed along the length of the coast. Sweeping manicured lawns are bordered by colourful flowers and plants, in the midst of which sit the remains of part of the ancient city. Needless to say this is a big favourite with families of summering Israelis and in holidays; loud and rambunctious sums it up fairly accurately. During the week, however, you're likely to have this little coastal paradise all to yourself.

The nearby **Moshav Liman** provides good food and zimmer accommodation. Although prices are a little steep compared with nearby Nahariya, you certainly get what you pay for and these are a much nicer alternative to the rather shabby choices in the city. The **Shpan Motel B&B** (9822255) offers a lesser degree of luxury than some of its neighbours at more affordable prices. Pretty gardens and outdoor eating areas make it a pleasant spot and self-catering apartments are good for families or couples (**$$$**).

At the northern end of the moshav is the kosher **Morgenfeld Steak House** (9524333; ⊕ 12.00–23.00 Sun–Thu, 12.00–15.00 Fri, end of Shabbat–23.00 Sat; **$$$$**), which combines hearty chunks of prime meat with à la carte fine dining. Entrecôte, Argentinian *asado*, juicy ribs and a mouth-watering selection of desserts are just some of the treats on offer in a romantic, candlelit atmosphere.

Getting there and away The park is located on route 4 between Nahariya and Rosh Hanikra. From Nahariya buses 32 and 33 go to Rosh Hanikra and back several times a day and will stop on request outside the park. Alternatively the little 'noddy' train at Rosh Hanikra trundles backwards and forwards to Achziv during peak seasons.

AKKO *Telephone code 04*

Within the ancient walls, sheltered from modernisation, development and change, Akko's Old City remains today as it has done throughout its long years of existence. The Old City is undoubtedly one of Israel's most picturesque and historically fascinating places to visit, and a must-see on any itinerary. A jumble of cobbled lanes snake around, through and past ancient stone buildings, piled one upon another; majestic, vibrant mosques and churches stream with devout worshippers; immaculately preserved relics remain, left by the city's passionate invaders; people crowd into the aromatic souks; and the tranquil waters of the ancient sea port lap against the old sea walls. It was on this small peninsula where empires were battled over, where religions clashed and where cultures merged. Akko was one of the most crucial cities of ancient times on a par with Alexandria and Troy, a fact difficult to envisage whilst wandering the lively yet peaceful alleys that today house large Muslim, Christian, Druze and Baha'i populations. The UNESCO-designated Old City is a veritable maze, and while maps are handy, your time would be better spent relaxing into the ambience around you than trying to follow one. Be sure not to miss the wonderful bazaars and souks, where you would be forgiven for thinking you were in the heart of Marrakesh's Medina.

HISTORY It was on these shores that west met east, and few towns can attest to the turbulence and passion that passed inside Akko's walls. The Canaanites, Greeks, Romans, Byzantines, Crusaders, Mamluks, Turks and the British have all left their mark, however large or small, on this stretch of land. The city's most impressive and prominent relics date to the Hellenistic–Roman periods and Crusader and Ottoman rules, and it will forever be remembered as the furthest extent and subsequent demise of Napoleon's Middle Eastern campaign.

Akko is one of the world's oldest continuously inhabited cities, dating back as far as 1504–1450bce. It was mentioned only once in the Old Testament as one of the few places where the Israelites did not succeed in ousting the Canaanites, and suffered three centuries of torment in the years leading up to the Christian era.

Akko, at the time a part of the Kingdom of Israel, was incorporated into Alexander the Great's empire following his conquest in 332bce. In 638ce the Arabs captured Akko and ruled until the Crusaders arrived. The crucial port city was named the Crusaders' headquarters in Palestine and was witness to violent and devastating battles. In 1187, Saladin managed to take Akko, only to be ousted by Richard the Lionheart's troops in 1191. Under his rule, the city became the capital of the Kingdom of Jerusalem and was placed under the directorship of the Knights Hospitaller.

In 1291, the Mamluks embarked on their bloody invasion of Akko, killing every last remaining Crusader and thus putting an end to the Latin Kingdom. The once-powerful city fell into disrepair and remained virtually ruinous for the following 500 years. It wasn't until the Bedouin sheikh Daher el-Omar made Akko his capital in the 18th century that the city once again began to breathe with life. Between the years 1775 and 1804, the Turkish governor Ahmad Pasha al-Jazzar fortified the city, the great Al-Jazzar Mosque that has become the symbol of Akko owing its origins to this time. Crusader remains became the foundations for the new phase of construction and Muslim buildings still rest on top of the near-perfect relics. Napoleon landed in Akko in 1799 as part of his widespread conquest, but Akko was to be the beginning of his Middle Eastern demise, and after two months of heavy and unsuccessful battling he withdrew to France.

Akko fell under Ottoman rule until their defeat by the British in 1918, thus placing the city under the British Mandate. Akko's Citadel fortress became a prison to house and execute political prisoners, mainly from Jewish underground organisations. Akko was captured by Jewish forces on 17 May 1948 during the Arab–Israeli War. Almost 75% of its Arab inhabitants fled the city.

GETTING THERE AND AWAY The **central bus station** is on HaArba'a Street in the New City adjacent to the **train station** (which is on David Remez St). While buses arrive from Tel Aviv, Haifa and Nahariya regularly, trains are considerably faster and more convenient. Buses 271, 272 and 361 leave and arrive every five minutes to and from Haifa's Lev HaMifratz bus station (50mins/13.50NIS). Trains from Haifa Carmel station (35mins/15NIS) , Tel Aviv (1hr 28mins/38NIS) and Nahariya (13mins/8NIS) run every 30 minutes.

GETTING AROUND Akko Old City is extremely small and almost wholly pedestrianised so the only way to navigate the labyrinthine alleys is by foot. From the New City and bus station, taxis can drop you at the visitors' centre (approximately 10NIS).

TOURIST INFORMATION

🗹 **Akko Old City Visitors' Centre**
1 Weizmann St; ✆9956706; ℮ visitorc@

bezeqint.net; www.akko.org.il; ⊕ 08.30–19.00
Sun–Thu & Sat, 08.30–17.00 Fri. This very

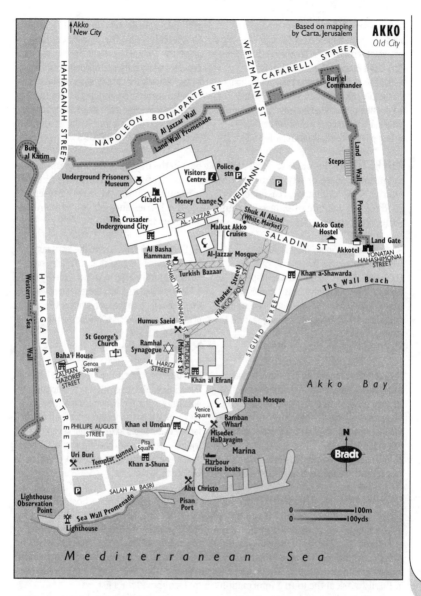

well-run centre is located on the right as you enter the Citadel (through the visitors' car park). They sell combination tickets to all of Akko's sites, can arrange tour guides, book hotels & arrange full-day excursions to attractions in the area. This should be your first port of call in the Old City. They also show an hourly film about Akko between 09.30 and 15.30 in a variety of languages.

WHERE TO STAY

Akkotel (16 rooms) Saladdin St; 9877100; e info@akkotel.com; www.akkotel.com. Beautiful boutique hotel located in the Old City. The 250-year-old building exudes Akko charm & rooms come with AC, TV, Wi-Fi, minibar, plush beds & sofas. A roof terrace café provides wonderful views of the ancient buildings below & there is a Mediterranean restaurant serving freshly caught fish. **$$$$**

🏠 **Zipi's Place** (20 beds) 10 Bilu St; 9915220; e zipi503@walla.com. Not far from the Old City (20mins' walk) is this cosy, family-run guesthouse. Facilities inc laundry, communal kitchen, Wi-Fi & there is a choice of dormitory beds or private rooms. *Dorms 100NIS.* **$$$**

🏠 **Akko Gate Hostel** (10 rooms) 14 Saladin St; 9910410; f 9815530; e walid.akko.gate@gmail.com; www.akkogate.com. Traditionally decorated family-run hostel offering an excellent budget option in the Old City. Rooms on the newly extended side of the building are a bit more spacious & modern. A nice little coffee shop is located on site offering drinks & b/fast & there is internet access & Wi-Fi throughout. *Dorms 70NIS.* **$$**

✖️ **WHERE TO EAT** Fish and seafood play a big part in the menus of the more upmarket restaurants, while hearty, traditional Middle Eastern food dominates the cheaper eateries. Plastic-chaired, reasonably priced restaurants along **Al-Jazzar Street** are good for a quick bite of *shawarma*, hummus, French fries and salads and there are some fabulous bakeries, sweet cakes, spices and nuts in the **souk**.

✖️ **Abu Christo** South Sea Promenade; 9910065; www.abu-christo.co.il; ⏲ 12.00–23.00 daily. Well-established & well-respected fish & meat restaurant that boasts the best view in the Old City. The menu inc plenty of elegantly prepared Greek- & Arabic-style salads, seafood & steaks. **$$$$**

✖️ **Uri Buri** HaHaganah St; 9552212; ⏲ 12.00–00.00 daily; www.uriburi.co.il. Often considered one of the best fish & seafood restaurants in the country. Although the fruits of the deep sea will burn a deep hole in your pocket, it is money well spent – the food is fabulous. Informal, classy atmosphere & a great location next to the lighthouse. **$$$$$**

✖️ **Misedet HaDayagim (The Fisherman's Restaurant)** Harbour entrance; 9911985;

⏲ 12.00–19.00 daily. Rustic little restaurant serving incredibly fresh fish at incredible prices. Head to the fish market next door, choose your fish & then head back into the restaurant where they'll cook it up on the spot. A buffet selection of salads & a drink costs 60NIS inc the fish. Simply wonderful. **$$$**

✖️ **Humus Saeid** Market St; 9913945; www.humus-saeid.com; ⏲ 06.00 Sun–Fri until the food runs out, usually around 14.30. Queues down the street attest to the incredible popularity of this tiny hummus bar. Known across the country, this is normally the first port of call for any visitor to old Akko. But don't expect a leisurely meal, as you'll have the eyes of the next customer in line boring into the back of your neck willing you to hurry up. **$**

ENTERTAINMENT AND NIGHTLIFE In July, the Crusader Hall plays host to concerts performed by the renowned **Haifa Symphony Orchestra**, the echoing hall providing the perfect accompanying acoustics and a unique setting. Around the Jewish holiday of Sukkot (the Harvest Festival which falls around October) is the **Acco Festival of Alternative Israeli Theatre** (*www.accofestival.co.il*) consisting of theatre performances by national theatre groups. These are mainly in Hebrew but there are some productions in English. Ask at the tourist information centre (see above) for a list.

OTHER PRACTICALITIES
Emergencies
Police Weizmann St; 9876736/056 273261

Money
$ **Bank Hapoalim** 6/8 Ben Ami St; 03 6532407; ⏲ 08.30–13.15 Sun & Tue/Wed, 08.30–13.00 & 16.00–18.30 Mon & Thu. Located in the New City.

$ **Money Change** Corner Weizmann & Al-Jazzar Sts; 9915097; ⏲ 09.30–18.30 daily. Changes euros & US dollars & has an ATM outside.

Post

✉ **Old City post office** 13 Al-Jazzar St; ☎9910171; ⊕ 08.00–12.30 & 15.30–18.00 Sun/ Mon & Wed/Thu, 08.00–13.00 Tue, 08.00–12.30 Fri.

✉ **Central post office** 11 Ha'atzma'ut St; ☎9910023; ⊕ 08.00–18.00 Sun & Thu, 08.00–12.30 & 15.30–18.00 Mon & Tue, 08.00–13.30 Wed, 08.00–12.00 Fri. Located in the New City.

Medical

✚ **Mizra Hospital** ☎04 9959595. Located north of the New City.

WHAT TO SEE

Underground Crusader City (☎ 9956706; ⊕ 08.30–18.00 Sun–Thu & Sat, 08.30–17.00 Fri (closes 1hr earlier in winter); admission adult/child combination tickets from 25/22NIS) Today resting under the foundations of al-Jazzar's Citadel, this was the headquarters of the Knights Hospitaller during the crusades. Excavated in the 1950s to reveal a maze of rooms, the subterranean city is a fascinating place to explore. A vast hall, believed to be a refectory, leads to what was once a secret tunnel that emerged 350m away in Akko's harbour. The tunnel has only partially been excavated and now leads to the Bosta, a large room used by the knights as a refuge for pilgrims. The crypt of St John, displaying a poignant and telling fleur-de-lis that dates the room to Louis VII's era, was once used as the knights' banqueting hall.

The Citadel Looming over the submerged Crusader City below, the Ottoman Citadel has been engraved in history books mainly through its role as a high-security prison during the British Mandate. It was in this supposedly impenetrable fortress that members of Jewish Zionist underground organisations were held and several executed. On 4 May 1947, it became the scene of one of the most famous prison escapes in history, when members of the Irgun militant Zionist group broke through its defences in an attempt to free the prisoners. While few escaped alive, it was seen as a major failure on the part of the British and marked a significant blow to their control. Today the Citadel holds a wealth of sights, most notably the **Underground Prisoner's Museum** (☎ 9918264/5/6; ⊕ 09.00–17.00 Sun–Thu, 09.00–13.00 Fri; admission adult/child 8/4NIS). The prison has been left in its original daunting and oppressive state and huge, high ceilings and thick walls make it easy to imagine the horror of being locked up here. The Gallows Room contains the noose from which the nine Jewish resistance fighters were hanged, and photographs and documents commemorating the prisoners who were kept here, including the first prisoner and Israeli hero Z Jabotinsky, are on display. In addition, the **prison cell of Baha'u'llah**, the Baha'i faith's founder, can be visited. He was imprisoned by the Ottoman government and spent the best part of his adult life within the walls. Outside is the **enchanted garden**, a replica of the one believed to have existed during the Crusader era.

Al-Jazzar Mosque (☎ 991303; ⊕ 08.00–18.00 Sat–Thu, 08.00–11.00 & 13.00–18.00 Fri (closes 1hr earlier in winter); admission 6NIS) The beautiful, green-domed Al-Jazzar Mosque is hard to miss. Built on the site of Akko's Crusader cathedral, it is not only the largest of the city's four mosques, but the third-largest mosque in the country. The submerged cathedral was later flooded and served as a reservoir which is today accessible from a door at the end of the compound (signposted). Many of the building materials, notably the ornate Roman columns in the courtyard, were taken from the ancient coastal city of Caesarea (see page 173) while inside the mosque is said to be housed a strand of hair from the Prophet Muhammad's beard. The entrance to the courtyard is up a flight of stone steps and through a small gate located on the lively Al-Jazzar Street just behind the Citadel. Visitors are welcome outside prayer times, provided they dress appropriately and respect Muslim religious traditions. A small, simple domed building on the right of the entrance contains the sarcophagi of Ahmed al-Jazzar and his successor Suleiman Pasha.

Al Basha Hammam (Municipal Museum)

The *hammam* was built in the 1780s by al-Jazzar as part of his vast mosque complex, and was modelled on Roman bathhouse styles. There are three rooms: one a dressing room, one functioning like that of a Roman tepidarium (warm room) and the last a hot steam room. The baths (⟍ 9551088; ⊕ *winter 08.30–17.00 Sat–Thu, 08.30–14.00 Fri; summer 08.30–18.00 Sat–Thu, 08.30–17.00 Fri; admission adult/child 25/21NIS; can be inc in combination tickets*) served as more than a place of religious purification, forming an important social centre where meetings were conducted and people came to relax. Colourful lighting, intricate ceramic tiling and marble statues combine with trickling water sounds and the **Story of the Last Bath Attendant** (a rather soapy bath attendant who regales lively tales of the history of Akko) making it an enjoyable and unique museum experience. The entrance to the baths is along Al-Jazzar Street opposite the Citadel a little way up from the Al-Jazzar Mosque.

Khan el Umdan

Translating as 'Pillar's Inn', the first glimpse of Akko's most impressive ancient merchants' inn will reveal why it was named thus. Built in the late 18th century, the khan was built on a series of large granite columns and acted as storeroom and hotel for merchants arriving at Akko's thriving port. The tiny entrance to this vast courtyard is easily missed. Look for the minaret of the Sinan Basha Mosque on the harbour's edge and the entrance is opposite. The khan is open to visitors all day and is certainly worth ferreting out. At the time of writing it was undergoing renovations and was closed to the public but could still be glimpsed through the gates.

The city walls

The sturdy, pentagon-shaped wall that today surrounds Akko was built in 1750 by Daher el-Omar upon the remains of the Crusader structures, and later fortified by al-Jazzar. When completed it encircled Akko on both land and sea perimeters. From the Weizmann Street entrance, steps on the left lead up on to the **Land Wall Promenade** and on to the **Land Gate**. The **Burj el Commander**, located on the northeast corner of the wall, was the tower said to have defeated Napoleon in 1799 and offers a fabulous view southwest over the rambling buildings of the Old City. The **Sea Wall Promenade** is accessed by steps located a few metres along from Abu Christo Restaurant in the south of the Old City and leads to the **Lighthouse Observation Point**. To see the walls from an invader's viewpoint, countless boats do tours leaving throughout the day. **Malkat Akko Cruises** (*Leopold the Second St;* ⟍ *9913890;* f *9913889; www.malkatakko.co.il; admission adult/child 20/15NIS*) operate boat tours around the walls (40mins) as well as to Haifa and Rosh Hanikra. Boats leave from the marina hourly throughout summer and tickets can be bought at the dock.

Templars Tunnel

(⊕ *winter 08.30–17.30 daily, summer 09.30–18.30 Sat–Thu, 09.30–17.30 Fri; admission adult/child 10/7NIS*) The tunnel, which was opened to the public in 1999, was built in the 12th century by the Knights Templar and leads from the port in the east to their long-since destroyed and submerged fortress in the southwest of the Old City. The arched tunnels are well lit and not especially narrow making this little-known attraction a worthwhile detour. There are two entrances to the tunnel: one through the rather dilapidated **Khan e-Shuna** opposite the Khan el-Umdan, and the second near the lighthouse car park.

Market Street (Benjamin Metudela Street) (⊕ *until 17.00 daily*) Running from north to south, Market Street is noisy, busy and crowded. It is also, however, one of the most fascinating parts of the present-day Old City, where stalls selling sweet pastries, dried fruit, fish, spices and household items squeeze together, the sights, sounds and smells accentuated in the narrow tunnel-like maze. At the end of the street and up a small lane on the right is the **Ramhal Synagogue** (⊕ *09.30–18.00 Sun–Thu & Sat, 09.30–15.00 Fri*), named after the Italian sage Rabbi Moshe Haim Luzatto (the Ramhal), who is best known for his moral guide *Mesilat Yesharim*.

AROUND AKKO

SHRINE OF BAHA'U'LLAH (*gardens:* ✎ *8313131; www.ganbahai.org.il;* ⊕ *09.00–17.00 daily; shrine:* ⊕ *09.00–12.00 Sun–Fri; admission free; modest dress*) The Shrine of Baha'u'llah is the holiest site for members of the Baha'i faith, topping even the vast Shrine of Bab, Haifa's most recognisable landmark. This is the final resting place of Baha'u'llah, founder of the Baha'i faith and the principal pilgrimage site for members of the religion. Following his death on 29 May 1892, Baha'u'llah was interred in the ornate shrine erected next to the **Mansion of Bahji**, where he spent his final days. It is in the direction of the shrine (*qibla*), that worshippers face when reciting daily prayers. The shrine is surrounded by immaculately kept, manicured gardens where not a blade of grass can be found out of place. There are free guided tours every day except Wednesday.

GHETTO FIGHTERS' HOUSE (BEIT LOHAMEI HAGETA'OT) (*Kibbutz Lohamei HaGeta'ot:* ✎ *9958080;* ⊕ *09.00–16.00 Sun–Thu, 09.00–13.00 Fri; Yad LaYeled: 10.00–17.00 Sun–Thu; admission adult/child 20/10NIS*) The vast museum complex was established by a group of Holocaust survivors who aimed to tell the story of the Jewish people throughout the 20th century and in particular remember those who died and suffered in the Holocaust. It focuses on Jewish resistance throughout World War II, exhibitions including 'The Warsaw Ghetto Fights Back' and 'Ghettos and Deportations'. The moving Yad LaYeled (Children's Museum) focuses on the children of the Holocaust, and is a combination of informative displays, symbolic objects and audio-visual presentations.

Getting there Both the above sights are located along route 4 between Akko and Nahariya. The Shrine of Baha'u'llah North Gate entrance is approximately 2km from Akko, located within walking distance from the Bustan Hagalil bus stop. Take the side road on the left a few metres from the bus stop in the direction of Akko from where the entrance is a further 450m. The Ghetto Fighters' House is in Kibbutz Lohamei HaGeta'ot. Bus 271 from Haifa to Nahariya stops opposite the museum regularly.

HAIFA *Telephone code 04*

Cascading down the slopes of Mount Carmel towards the sandy beaches of the Mediterranean, Israel's third-largest city is often overlooked as a tourist destination. Yet the city has a lot going for it, and is a great place to spend a few days.

Haifa is probably best known for its harmonious interaction among its different faiths, where Jews, Muslims, Druze, Christians and Baha'is exist contentedly alongside one another. The vast, landscaped gardens of the Shrine of Bab, the centre of the Baha'i faith, form the unexpected centrepiece of the city while its thriving port is the largest in the country. Prosperous industries, a large hilltop university, countless religious and historic sights, neighbourhoods old and new, a fascinating collection of museums and a lively restaurant and bar scene, make Haifa a firm favourite amongst Israelis and a pleasant contrast to Jerusalem and Tel Aviv.

HISTORY Finds discovered across the city date from the Stone Age to the Ottoman period, while Roman and Greek finds attest to occupation, although by no means comparable to the thriving port city at Caesarea. While not mentioned in the Bible, Haifa appears in the Talmud as an established Jewish settlement, which during the Middle Ages grew into a shipping centre.

The Crusaders and the Carmelites

In 1099, Haifa was conquered by the Crusaders who slaughtered the Jewish residents almost in their entirety. During their occupation of the region, groups of religious hermits began to live in caves dotted across the Carmel area in honour of Elijah the Prophet. Over the next 100 years they formed the Carmelite order, which spread as far as Europe. While the order continued to thrive in Europe, the founders on Mount Carmel were exiled when, in 1265, the city fell to the Mamluk sultan Baibars. From 1750 until the beginning of World War I, Haifa remained under Turkish rule following its conquest and refortification by the Bedouin sheikh Dahar el-Omar. The Turks were ousted in 1799 by Napoleon, but this was short-lived following his poignant defeat at Akko.

The German Templars

In 1868, the German Templars established a colony in Haifa which today remains one of the city's most picturesque areas (see page 162). The German Templars have been credited with the rapid development of the small, insignificant town they founded. It was, however, at around the same time that the Baha'u'llah, founder of the Baha'i faith, arrived in Haifa, a factor contributing to its development boom at the time. The Templar Society was founded in Germany in 1861 as a result of the severe socio-economic conditions in southwest Germany, and was formed with the aspiration of promoting messianic ideas as a path to salvation. They purchased lands in Haifa and set up an agricultural community, constructing a beautiful, wide boulevard. The Templars' contribution to the development of Haifa was dramatic: they were the first to use horse-drawn carriages to transport goods and people to Akko; they built modern buildings; a road up to the Carmel; brought with them tools; and introduced new agricultural techniques.

The British Mandate

During the British Mandate the city renewed its development, with the construction of Jewish neighbourhoods, factories (including the oil refinery) and the Technion College. After World War II, the port at Haifa became the site of several notorious confrontations between the British, and Jews attempting to enter Palestine. The Haganah Zionist organisation operated fervently in the area, smuggling in immigrants and Holocaust survivors. The *Af-Al-Pi-Chen*, a ship used by the British in their blockades, today resides as a lasting reminder outside the Clandestine Immigration and Naval Museum (see page 163).

The 2006 Lebanon War

In July 2006, Israel once again hit international headlines when military conflict broke out following Hezbollah's firing of Katyusha rockets

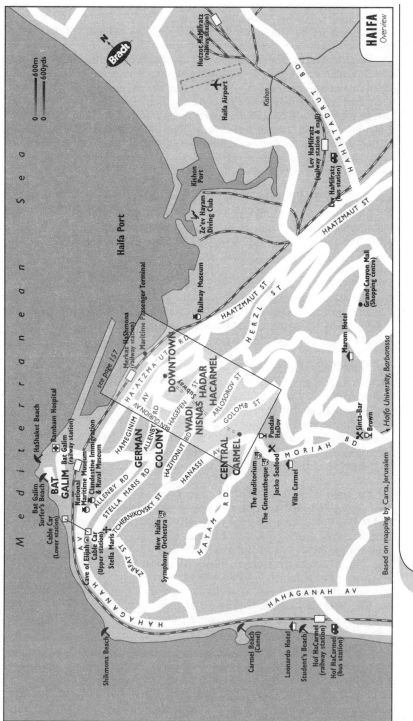

HAIFA
Overview

see page 157

Mediterranean Sea

Haifa Port

Mediterranean Coast HAIFA

5

Based on mapping by Carta, Jerusalem

153

at northern Israeli towns. The conflict, known as the 2006 Lebanon War, raged for over a month during which time the residents of Haifa and much of the north of the country spent most of their time beneath ground in bomb shelters and bunkers. The devastation caused by the conflict was massive on both sides and Israel lost 43 civilians and 120 soldiers in the month-long war. A UN ceasefire ended the shelling on 14 August when the residents of Haifa and northern Israel finally emerged from their shelters. Apart from the vast economic and social impact of the conflict, several events caused catastrophic environmental damage that impacted not just Israel but Lebanon, Turkey and Cyprus. The IDF bombing of the Jiyeh power station in Lebanon resulted in the largest-ever oil spill in the Mediterranean Sea while Hezbollah rockets caused numerous forest fires in northern Israel, destroying acres of forest that will take decades to recover.

GETTING THERE AND AWAY

By bus Buses from Nahariya, Akko and the Galilee terminate in the Lev HaMifratz bus station while buses coming from the south and Jerusalem stop at the Hof HaCarmel bus station (next to the Carmel train station). To Tel Aviv, express bus 910 (90mins/26.50NIS), and the slower 921 bus (3hrs/25NIS) depart every 20 minutes. Direct buses 940 and 960 leave every 30 minutes to Jerusalem (2hrs/45NIS), while bus 947 takes 45 minutes longer. To Nahariya, bus 271 leaves Lev HaMifratz station every 20 minutes (1hr/17.20NIS) and to Akko buses leave every ten minutes (50mins/13.50NIS). To Nazareth, bus 331 goes from Palmer Square and 339 departs from Lev HaMifratz several times a day while to Tiberias, bus 430 every 30 minutes (1hr 10mins/26.50NIS).

By train Haifa has five train stations: Hof HaCarmel, BatGalim, Merkaz HaShmona [157 B1], Lev HaMifratz and Hutzot HaMifratz. Lev HaMifratz in the eastern part of the city is useful for connecting to buses heading northwards and to the Galilee as it is adjacent to the bus station of the same name. Lev HaMifratz and Hof HaCarmel are the most convenient for trains to Tel Aviv, the latter being close to the Carmel bus station for buses to Jerusalem. Trains depart to Tel Aviv every 20mins (1hr/29.5NIS). From Hof HaCarmel and Lev HaMifratz trains head north to Nahariya hourly (50mins/19NIS) via Akko (35mins/15NIS).

By air Haifa Airport (✎ 8476100) ranks as Israel's third-busiest airport after Ben Gurion and Eilat and offers decently priced domestic flights to both cities. **Arkia** (✎ 03 6902222; www.arkia.co.il) offers flights only to and from Eilat for approximately 250NIS one-way. **Israir** (✎ 03 7955777; www.israirairlines.com) runs regular flights to both Tel Aviv and Eilat for between 180NIS and 375NIS one-way. Alternatively, **Golden Wings Air Tours** (Haifa Airport; ✎ 8476188; e goldenwg@netvision.net.il; www.canfeipaz.co.il) offers private-hire small planes to any landing strip in Israel, as well as several destinations abroad. A return flight for five people to Larnaka, Cyprus, for example, costs approximately 7,000NIS. Public transport to the airport is limited but bus 58 from Lev HaMifratz bus station runs hourly. **Monitax taxis** (✎ 8664343) also serve the airport and wait outside the terminal building.

By sea Haifa's port has become a popular addition to the cruises that ply the Mediterranean waters, where passengers hop on to Jerusalem-bound coaches for a day in the Holy City. Most of the major cruise lines now include Israel on their itineraries. Cruises to Turkey, the Greek Islands and Italy can be arranged through **Mano Tours** (*2 HaPalyam St;* ☎ *8606666;* ƒ *8667666; www.mano.co.il*) and leave from the rather nice **Maritime Passenger Terminal** [157 C1] (☎ *8518245; www.haifaport.co.il*).

ORIENTATION Haifa is divided into three distinct zones ranked one above another both in terms of geography and wealth. The **downtown area (Ir Ha-Tahitt)** with its Old City, harbour and coastal areas is the lowest zone; the central zone is made up of the **Hadar HaCarmel district**, the city's main shopping and commercial centre and home to some of the older neighbourhoods; and **Central Carmel** in the upper reaches of the city, which comprises the richest residential neighbourhoods and luxury hotels and restaurants. The **Universty of Haifa** occupies the highest point and furthest reaches of the city where buildings meet the sweeping greenery of the Carmel National Park.

Walking around the city is possible, but tough going. The steep slopes are linked by thousands of steps that make a nice downhill tour (see page 158) and a cable car operates from **Bat Galim** to just below the **Carmelite monastery**. The city is also home to Israel's only subway system, the **Carmelit underground railway**. The unmistakable gardens of the **Shrine of Bab** [157 A4] lead down to the **German Colony** at its base, where countless restaurants and cafés line the main **Ben Gurion Avenue**. The major downtown roads are **Ha'atzma'ut Street** and nearby **Jaffa Road**, both running along the coast, while the **Old City** is located one block back. Life in the Central Carmel district centres on **HaNassi Avenue** with its pricey restaurants and trendy bars. In between these, **Herzl Street** forms the hub of activity in the Hadar HaCarmel, an area in serious need of a makeover. While it is the busiest shopping district in the city, it doesn't have an awful lot else going for it. Cheap eateries and budget hotels often attract those on a tighter budget, while **Nordau Pedestrian Precinct** has become the Russian centre of the city, inhabited by scores of immigrants who have added their stamp on to the area.

GETTING AROUND Haifa's city centre cascades down Mount Carmel's northern slope, making for some interesting, but tiring, topography. Walking downhill is always an option but you'll soon run out of steam if you try and travel by foot. Thankfully Haifa has several good public transport options to combat foot fatigue, and it is also the only city in Israel where public transport runs on Shabbat (albeit limited services).

By bus Intra-city buses operate 05.00–23.30 Sunday–Thursday, 05.00–16.30 Friday, and a limited service runs 09.00–midnight Saturday. Fares within Haifa are usually 5NIS. For more information, call 8549131. The following bus routes run along most major streets and stop at the main attractions:

- **#3** From Hof HaCarmel bus station along Hayam Road and on to Arlosorov Street. From there it makes its way down HeHalutz Street, Bialik Street, on to Ma'ale Hashihrur Street and then down HaMeginim Boulevard.
- **#43** Begins at Hof HaCarmel bus station and runs along HaHaganah Boulevard on to Rothschild Boulevard, then on to HaMaginim Boulevard through the German Colony to HaHaganah Square. It then heads east on Shivat Ziyyon St.
- **#99 and #99a** Begin at Bat Galim bus station and run along Rothschild Boulevard and on to Stella Maris Road. From there they make their way to HaNassi Boulevard and along Moriah Boulevard before turning into Froyd Street and finishing at Hof HaCarmel bus station.
- **#24** Runs to the university on the fringes of the city. The route takes buses

along Pika Road, past the Grand Canyon Mall, Rupin Road, Ge'ula Street and Arlosorov. It then continues along Balfour Street and HeHalutz Street, on to HaMeginim and Rothschild boulevards and finishes at Bat Galim bus station.

- **#101** Starts in Lev HaMifratz bus station and runs along Ha'atzma'ut Street to Bat Galim bus station.

By underground The Carmelit underground railway (✆ *8376861; trains run 06.00–22.00 Sun–Thu, 06.00–15.00 Fri; fare 6.40NIS one-way, day ticket 15NIS*) is Israel's one and only underground metro system and is a great way of avoiding the steps of central Haifa. The line starts at Paris Square in the downtown area and finishes at the Gan Ha'em Park in the Carmel Centre. There are four stations in between: Golomb Street, Masada Street, Neviim and Solel Boneh.

By cable car The Haifa cable car (✆ *8335970; ⊕ summer 09.00–00.00 daily, winter 09.00–19.00 daily; fare one-way/return 16/22NIS*) consists of three little bubbles that zip up and down the steep slope between Bat Galim and the Stella Maris, and offers lovely views over the harbour.

TOURIST INFORMATION

ℹ Haifa Tourism Development Association [157 A3] 48 Ben Gurion Av; ✆ 8535606; e info@ tour-haifa.co.il; www.tour-haifa.co.il; ⊕ 09.00–17.00 Sun–Thu, 09.00–13.00 Fri, 10.00–15.00 Sat. They can organise museum tickets, guides & accommodation. They also have a great website.

Local tour operators Many of the nationwide tour operators arrange trips to and around the Haifa and Carmel region. For more information see page 36.

Egged Tours 4 Nordau St; ✆ 8623131; www.egged.co.il. Operate informative city bus tours that pass Haifa's most interesting sights. **Golden Wings Air Tours** Haifa Airport; ✆ 8476188; e goldenwg@netvision.net.il; www.canfeipaz.co.il. Arrange tours over the Haifa region. A 30min flight for up to 3 people costs 520NIS. **Society for Protection of Nature in Israel (SPNI)** 18 Hillel St; ✆ 8664135; e bela@spni. org.il; www.teva.org.il. Have good hiking maps & can arrange trips to the Carmel National Park.

Travel agencies

Issta Bei Hakranot Bldg, 20 Herzl St; ✆ 8682222; e admin@isstadirect.com; www.isstadirect.com; ⊕ 09.00–19.00 Sun–Tue & Thu. Can book budget air tickets. Several branches around town.

WHERE TO STAY

🏠 **The Colony Hotel** [157 A3] (40 rooms) 28 Ben Gurion Bd; ✆ 8513344; e info@ colony-hotel.co.il; www.colony-hotel.co.il. Located in a restored 100-year-old building in the picturesque German Colony at the base of the Baha'i Gardens, this boutique hotel exudes classical elegant charm. A wide range of in-room facilities exists, as well as a full b/fast, café, bar, spa room & sun roof. **$$$$**

🏠 **Dan Panorama Hotel** [157 A7] (267 rooms) 107 HaNassi Av; ✆ 8352222; e T.PanormamaHaifa@DanHotels.com; www.danhotels.com. Modern, contemporary décor, swish rooms & fabulous bird's-eye views over Haifa & the harbour. It is linked to the flashy Panorama Shopping Centre & has 2 restaurants, a café & bar, fitness centre & sauna. **$$$$**

🏠 **Leonardo** (197 rooms) 10 David Elazar St; ✆ 8508888; www.leonardo-hotels.com.

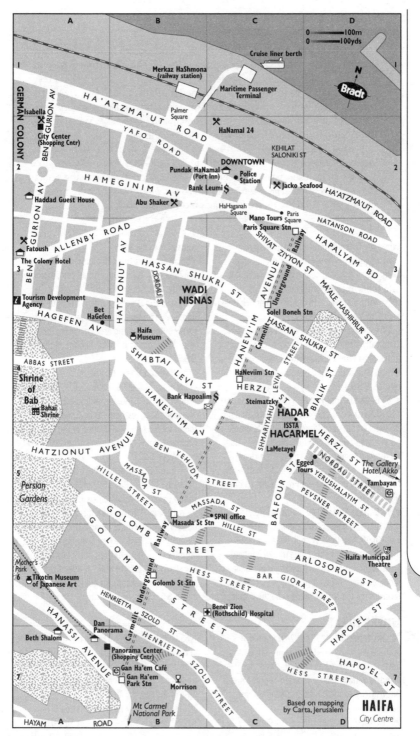

HAIFA
City Centre

157

While the hotel is irrefutably luxurious, its crowning glory is its seafront location. Large swimming pool, spa, health club, restaurant & café. Formerly Le Meridien Hotel. **$$$$**

🏠 **Villa Carmel** (16 rooms) 1 Heinrich Heine St, off 30 Moriah Bd; ☎8375777; e info@villacarmel.co.il; www.villacarmel.co.il. Classically elegant, newly renovated boutique hotel. Most rooms come with all mod-cons & jacuzzi bath & there is a restaurant & rooftop sun terrace. **$$$$**

🏠 **Beth Shalom Hotel** [157 A7] (30 rooms) 110 HaNassi Av; ☎8377481; www.beth-shalom. ch. Perched high on Mount Carmel, this simple hotel is well tended, comfortable & good value for money. Rooms are uninspiring but clean & airy & come with TV, AC & phone. A small, leafy courtyard is a welcome spot to rest after a day of sightseeing. **$$$**

🏠 **Gallery Hotel** (40 rooms) 61 Herzl St; ☎8616161; e gallery@hotelgallery.co.il; www.haifa.hotelgallery.co.il. Boutique hotel decked out in minimalist elegance in Bauhaus architectural style. Luxury packages available inc room, gourmet b/fast & massages. Full range of facilities inc spa centre, money change & guided

WHERE TO EAT

✗ **HaNamal 24** [157 C2] 24 Hanamal St; ☎8628899; ⏰ 12.00–00.00 Mon–Sat. Haifa's hottest new eatery has elegant, classic décor & a hugely varied menu composed of prime meats (inc ostrich), exotic & local fish & sumptuous pastas. **$$$$$**

✗ **Fatoush** [157 A3] 38 Ben Gurion Av;

tours of the city. **$$$**

🏠 **Marom Hotel** (48 rooms) 51 Palmach St; ☎8254355; e htlmarom@gmail.com; marom. yolasite.com. Set on the outskirts of the city amidst spacious green gardens the hotel offers good value for money. A gym, jacuzzi, spa & lovely outdoor seating areas make it a quiet & refreshing change from the hubbub of the city. **$$$**

🏠 **Haddad Guest House** [157 A2] (11 rooms) 26 Ben Gurion Av; ☎0772010618; e reservation@haddadguesthouse.com; www.haddadguesthouse.com. Simple, clean rooms with a fantastic location in the heart of the German Colony. Rooms have kitchenette, TV, AC & hairdryers. **$$**

🏠 **Pundak HaNamal (Port Inn)** [157 C2] (65 beds) 34 Jaffa Rd; ☎8524401; e port_inn@ yahoo.com; www.portinn.co.il. Big, bright, airy rooms & a port view make this a refreshing budget option. Comfy lounge area with cable TV, fully equipped kitchen & dining room, laundry facilities, internet, tourist information & a shady sun terrace make it one of the best budget choices. For dorm guests, b/fast is 25NIS extra. **$$**

☎8524930; ⏰ 09.00–01.00 daily. Great location in the German Colony with a lovely shady terrace. Arabic menu of big b/fasts, salads, hummus and traditional meals. Lovely décor & ambience at any time of the day. **$$$**

✗ **Isabella** [157 A2] 6 Ben Gurion Blvd; ☎8552201; ⏰ 10.00–midnight Sun–Thu,

10.00–02.00 Fri/Sat. Well-loved Italian restaurant with a great selection of fresh pasta & meats. $$$

✗ **Jacko Seafood** [157 C2] 12 Kehilat Saloniki St; ☏8102355; ⏰ 12.00–midnight daily. First branch of this 30-year-old chain of well-loved fish & seafood restaurants. Countless different fish, shellfish & seafood cooked any way you like it. There is another branch at 11 Moriah St. $$$

✗ **Sinta-Bar** 127 Moriah St; ☏8341170; ⏰ 12.00–00.30 Sun–Thu, 12.00–02.00 Fri & Sat. Elegant bistro bar specialising in meat, fish & seafood (although it's their juicy hamburgers that keep their regulars coming back). $$$

✗ **Abu Shaker** [157 B2] 29 HaMeginim St; ⏰ 06.00–18.30 daily. Tiny hummus joint that is super popular with locals. Squeeze on to one of the 7 tables & enjoy a filling meal of hummus, chips, salad & *mejadra*, a bowl of hot rice & lentils. $

✗ **Barbarossa** (see *Bars*, page 160)

ENTERTAINMENT AND NIGHTLIFE
The arts

🎭 **Haifa Municipal Theatre** [157 D6] 50 Pevsner St; ☏8600555; box office ☏8605000. Has regular performances, but few are in English.

🎭 **New Haifa Symphony Orchestra** 6 Eliahu Khakim St; ☏8599499; www.haifasymphony. co.il. One of the country's top orchestras with national & debut performances.

🎭 **The Auditorium** 138 HaNassi Av; ☏8353580. Seating up to 1,200 people, the auditorium plays host to concerts & events throughout the year. Buses 21, 22, 23, 28 & 37 stop outside, or take the Carmelit railway to Gan Ha'em station.

AN EATING OVERVIEW

DOWNTOWN With everything from **Turkish bakeries** to bureka **stalls**, it is one of the best places to get great, cheap food.

BAT GALIM The best place in the city if you're after the fruits of the sea. Fresh fish and seafood can be found in the many seafront restaurants.

GERMAN COLONY Elegant dining, trendy cafés and wonderful ice-cream parlours line the main Ben Gurion Avenue which provides a stunning night-time view of the illuminated Baha'i Shrine and Persian Gardens.

WADI NISNAS The souk that forms the core of the neighbourhood abounds with traditional Arabic fare at extremely low prices. Stalls serving falafel, hummus, *shawarma*, freshly baked pittas, sweet pastries and spices are squeezed into the hubbub of activity in the thriving market.

HADAR HACARMEL Offers a broad selection of restaurants, cafés, fast-food joints and bars at various prices. Masada and Hillel streets have recently become the new artistic centres of the area, and trendy cafés have sprung up in between art galleries and exhibits. Falafel stands can be found along Herzl and HaHalutz streets, while the Nordau pedestrian street has slightly pricier cafés.

CENTRAL CARMEL This area is renowned as being the *pièce de résistance* of eating out in Haifa. The best restaurants can be found alongside five-star hotels with views over the city and harbour.

🎬 **The Cinematheque** 142 HaNassi Av; 📞8353530/31; ⏱ 18.00–20.00 daily. The hub of all things cinematic. Twice-daily showings of non-mainstream films, cinema courses & a huge auditorium are on offer.

Bars

Bars Although not comparable with Tel Aviv's pumping nightlife scene, Haifa has come a long way in recent years and now offers plenty of decent and varied bars and pubs. The main cluster of bars is along Moriah Boulevard (which turns into HaNassi Street).

♀ **Barbarossa** 8 HaPika St; 📞8114010; www.barbarossa.co.il; ⏱ 18.00–late daily. Modern meat & seafood restaurant with a great bar atmosphere. They offer 9 types of beer, 110 types of whisky, some wonderful Italian appetisers & a mean hamburger. Attracts a slightly older crowd. $$$

♀ **Brown** 131 Moriah Bd; 📞8112391; ⏱ 19.00–05.00 daily. Leather-seated booths, wooden tables & cosy lighting make this a good choice for a relaxed beer & light meal. Music ranges from 1980s hits to Israeli & international rock.

♀ **Morrison** [157 B7] 111 Yefe Nof St; 📞8383828; ⏱ 20.00–late daily. Highly popular rock/pick-up bar that hosts Mon open mic nights, Tue live performances (starting at 22.00) & Wed student nights.

♀ **Pundak HaDov (The Bear)** 135 HaNassi Bd; 📞8381703; ⏱ 11.00–late Sun–Fri, 18.00–late Fri. Cosy pub with indoor & outdoor seating, an extensive cocktail menu, decent pub food & a mellow atmosphere. Often shows live sporting events (when the atmosphere is a little less mellow).

SHOPPING The awkward city layout is not conducive to window shopping and as such the city has become known for its numerous malls and shopping centres. The gargantuan **Grand Canyon Mall** (*Simcha Golan Way, Neve Sha'anan;* 📞*8121111;* ⏱ *10.00–22.00 Sun–Thu, 10.00–15.00 Fri, end of Shabbat–22.30 Sat*) is one of Israel's largest shopping centres with 150 shops, an indoor amusement park, countless food outlets and a spa. Although built in 1986 the **Panorama Center** [157 A7] (*109 HaNassi Av;* 📞 *8375011;* ⏱ *09.00–20.00 Sun–Thu*), located in the Carmel Centre, remains a firm favourite and has great variety of shops, cinemas and cafés. The **City Center** [157 A2] (*6 Ben Gurion Av;* 📞 *8530111;* ⏱ *10.00–20.00 Sat–Thu, 09.30–14.00 Fri*) is considerably smaller than the others but useful if you're in the German Colony area. It has more high-end shops. The **Talpiot Market** sells a lovely array of spices and fresh fruit and vegetables and is a nice alternative to the glitzy malls. **Herzl** and **Nordau streets** are your best bet for shopping streets.

Useful shops

LaMetayel [157 C5] 2 Kdoshei Yassi St; 📞0773334508; ⏱ 10.00–21.00 Sun–Thu, 10.00–15.00 Fri, 18.00–22.00 Sat. Good selection of camping supplies. Located in the National Congress Centre.

Steimatsky [157 C4] 16 Herzl St; 📞8665042; ⏱ 08.30–19.00 Sun–Thu, 08.30–14.00 Fri. Part of the international chain. Has a big selection of English books & newspapers.

OTHER PRACTICALITIES
Emergency

Ambulance 📞101
Fire 📞102

Police 28 Jaffa St; 📞100

Money ATMs are commonplace and you won't have to look far to find one. Likewise, change bureaux are located along all main roads. There are countless branches of Bank Hapoalim and Bank Leumi dotted around the city.

$ Bank Hapoalim [157 C4] 18 Hanevi'im St; \ 03 6532407; ⊕ 08.30–13.15 Sun & Tue/Wed, 08.30–13.00 & 16.00–18.30 Mon & Thu. Main branch. Changes money & travellers' cheques.

$ Bank Leumi [157 C2] 21 Jaffa St; \ 03 9544555; ⊕ 08.30–14.45 Sun–Thu, 08.30–12.00 Fri. Main branch.

Post

✉ **Central post office** [157 C4] 22a HaNevi'im St; \ 8304351; ⊕ 08.00–18.00 Sun–Thu, 08.00–12.00 Fri. Changes money & travellers' cheques. Other branches can be found at 19 HaPalyam Bd, 152 Jaffa Rd, 63 Herzl St & 7 Wedgewood Bd.

Medical

✚ **Benei Zion (Rothschild) Hospital** [157 C6] 47 Golomb St; \ 8359359

✚ **Rambam Hospital** Bat Galim; \ 8543111

✚ **Superpharm** 134 HaNassi Bd in Auditorium Haifa Mall; \ 8104844; ⊕ 08.30–10.30 Sun–Thu, 08.00–17.00 Fri, 08.00–23.00 Sat; also at 6 Ben Gurion Bd in City Centre Mall; \ 8507755; ⊕ 09.00–22.00 Sun–Thu, 09.00–16.00 Fri, 08.00–23.00 Sat

Internet

ℯ **Gan Ha'em Café** [157 B7] 122 HaNassi Av; \ 8384692; ⊕ 09.00–midnight Sat–Thu, 09.00–17.00 Fri. 25NIS/hr. Located at street level just outside the Gan Ha'em subway station.

ℯ **Tambayan** [157 D5] 31 Nordau St; \ 8669996; ⊕ 10.00–00.00 daily. 15NIS/hr.

WHAT TO SEE

Baha'i Shrine and Persian Gardens [157 A4] The immense golden dome of the Shrine of Bab (⊕ *09.00–12.00; admission free; modest dress*) and Persian gardens (\ *8313131; ⊕ 09.00–17.00 daily except 9 Jul & 2 May; admission & tour free*) dominate Haifa's skyline and are the world centre and one of the holiest sites of pilgrimage for members of the Baha'i faith. The structure was built in 1953 over the burial place of Said Ali Muhammad 'Bab', who is considered the founder of the faith. Tours around the gardens are given by Baha'i volunteers and while they must be booked in advance are free and informative (note there are no tours on Wed). The northern entrance is located just below Yefe Nof Street where grand marble steps stretch through immaculate gardens and past vibrant flowerbeds. From the Hadar bus station bus 23 stops at Yefe Nof Street. The Shrine of the Bab was, at the time of writing, under renovation due to be completed in 2012.

Cave of Elijah (*230 Allenby Rd;* \ *8527430; ⊕ 08.00–18.00 Sun–Thu (17.00 in winter), 08.00–13.00 Fri; admission free; modest dress*) According to tradition, Elijah the Prophet spent many years living in a cave nestled into the Carmel Mountain and many significant events in his life are said to have happened here; it was in this cave that he lived and meditated before defeating the Priests of Baal at Muhraka (see page 168); he took refuge here from King Ahab and his wife Jezebel; and he established his school here on his return from exile. It is also said to be the place where the Holy Family took shelter on their return from Egypt. Today the cave is worshipped by Jews, Christians, Druze and Muslims (who had a mosque here until 1948), who all venerate Elijah. Inside the cave is a small altar, illuminated by candles which can be bought for 2NIS from vendors at the base of the steps leading up to the cave. The steps and entrance are located on Allenby Road, 100m from the Maritime Museum but signposted in Hebrew only.

Stella Maris (*Mount Carmel;* \ *8337758;* ☉ *06.20–12.30 & 15.00–18.00 Mon–Sat; admission free; modest dress*) The 19th-century Carmelite monastery is located high on the slopes of Mount Carmel, offering fabulous views over the bay of Haifa and north towards Lebanon. Members of the 12th-century Carmelite order were exiled following the conquest by the Mamluk sultan Baibars, and didn't return until the 18th century when the monastery was commissioned. During Napoleon's unsuccessful attack on Akko, an earlier monastery on the grounds was used as a hospital for wounded French soldiers who were promptly slaughtered by the Turks upon Napoleon's retreat. In front of the monastery is a **monument** to the soldiers who died. The beautiful church that stands today is constructed of bright white marble, and the dome is adorned with paintings depicting stories from the Old Testament. The **cable car** makes its final stop opposite the monastery next to the **lighthouse**. The street opposite the Stella Maris hit the headlines in 2006 when it became the first place in Haifa to be hit by a Hezbollah Katyusha rocket.

German Colony The main street through the recently renovated colony is Ben Gurion Boulevard, which begins at the base of the Baha'i Shrine and runs south to HaMeginim Avenue. The 30m-wide boulevard is lined with stone houses, courtyards, large, leafy trees, trendy restaurants, outdoor cafés and ice-cream parlours, and is one of the undoubted highlights of any trip to Haifa. In the evening when the Persian Gardens are illuminated it makes for a lovely setting in which to sip on an iced coffee and enjoy the ambience.

University The university has claim to some of the prime real estate in the city, with fantastic views over both the harbour and city, and Carmel Mountain range. The 30th floor of the Eshkol Tower has been converted into an **observatory** and is unarguably the best viewpoint in the city. The **Hecht Museum** (\ *8257773; www.mushecht.haifa.ac.il;* ☉ *10.00–16.00 Sun/Mon & Wed/Thu, 10.00–16.00 Tue, 10.00–19.00 Fri, 10.00–14.00 Sat; admission free*) is located within the university grounds, and features, apart from archaeological collections, 19th- and 20th-century paintings and sculptures, including works by Monet, Pissarro and Van Gogh.

Wadi Nisnas The neighbourhood of Wadi Nisnas could serve as a model for peaceful co-existence. The area, located just below the Haifa Museum, is home to both Jews and Arabs who live harmoniously, and who actively try to demonstrate that religious preferences should be respected. Every year in December, the neighbourhood puts on the **Hag HaHagim** (Festival of all Festivals) in which Jews, Christians and Muslims take part in a celebration of Hanukka, Christmas and Ramadan. The **Bet HaGefen Jewish-Arab Centre** [157 A4] (*2 HaGefen St;* \ *8525252;* ☉ *08.00–13.00 & 16.00–20.00 Sun–Thu, 08.00–13.00 Fri, 10.00–13.00 Sat*) arranges Saturday tours of Wadi Nisnas in English, but it is best to call in advance. The neighbourhood is a fascinating place to visit, where churches, mosques and synagogues stand side by side, original buildings remain as testament to one of the city's oldest residential areas and colourful shops line the streets. **Horei Yohanan ha Kadosh Street** (between HaMeginim and Shivat Ziyyon streets), and the surrounding lanes and alleys, forms the centre of the neighbourhood and is a good place to start exploring.

Museums A combination ticket for many of Haifa's museums can be purchased at the museums' box offices for 45NIS for adults and 33NIS for children.

Haifa Museum [157 B4] (*26 Shabtai Levi St;* ✆ *8523255;* ⊕ *10.00–16.00 Sun–Wed, 16.00–19.00 Thu, 10.00–13.00 Fri, 10.00–15.00 Sat; admission adult/child 30/20NIS*) The museum incorporates the Museum of Modern Art and the Museum of Ancient Art and has departments dedicated to ethnography, folklore and Jewish ritual art. There are good archaeological exhibits of finds from Haifa and Caesarea and a collection of over 7,000 international and Israeli contemporary art pieces.

National Maritime Museum (*198 Allenby Av;* ✆ *8536622;* ⊕ *10.00–16.00 Sun–Thu, 10.00–13.00 Fri, 10.00–15.00 Sat; admission adult/child 30/20NIS*) The museum depicts the maritime history and development of shipbuilding in the region. Four floors of collections cover a whole spectrum of themes including maritime mythology, piracy, the Greeks and Romans, scientific instruments, naval ships and shipping over the past 5,000 years.

Tikotin Museum of Japanese Art [157 A6] (*89 HaNassi Av;* ✆ *8383554;* ⊕ *10.00–16.00 Sun–Thu, 10.00–13.00 Fri, 10.00–15.00 Sat; admission adult/child 30/20NIS*) The museum displays a unique collection of ancient and modern Japanese art.

Clandestine Immigration and Naval Museum (*204 Allenby Rd;* ✆ *8536249;* ⊕ *08.30–16.00 Sun–Thu; admission adult/child 10/5NIS*) The museum is easily identified by the large British blockade ship the *Af-Al-Pi-Chen* outside, which was at the centre of skirmishes between British officials and immigrants attempting to land in the country following World War II. The museum is devoted to Israeli naval history and the clandestine immigration, but pales in comparison with the National Maritime Museum.

Railway Museum (*1 Hativat Golani St;* ✆ *8564293; www.rail.co.il;* ⊕ *08.30–15.30 Sun–Thu; admission adult/child 20/15NIS*) The picturesque old train station dates to the Ottoman period, and has been restored complete with a steam train to make a pleasant museum complex. It also depicts Israel's long funicular history.

BEACHES AND ACTIVITIES Beaches in Haifa can be divided into two types: official, with bars, restaurants and the full set of facilities; and unofficial, which have none of these. The younger set tends to enjoy the unofficial beaches, where the wild sands and sea are facilities enough, while families often opt for the official beaches. The **Carmel Beach (Camel)** marks the beginning of the unofficial beaches, from which uninterrupted sand sweeps the length of the coast as far as Atlit naval base. Just south of the Carmel Beach is the ever-popular **Student's Beach**. Official beaches are located between Camel Beach and the Meridien Hotel and around Bat Galim. **Bat Galim Surfers' Beach** and **Shikmona Beach** are the most popular with surfers, windsurfers and kite surfers but often too rough for swimming. Opposite the Clandestine Museum is a **windsurfing centre** where equipment can be hired. The religious **HaShaket Beach** is one of the quietest in the city, with pond-like waters and plenty of shade. Men and women have separate swimming days except Saturdays when it is open to all (women: Sun, Tue, Thu; men: Mon, Wed, Fri). The **Ze'ev Hayam Diving Club** (*Kishon Port;* ✆ *8323911/8662005;* ⊕ *08.00–17.00 daily*) offers dive trips to sites in and around Haifa, where several wrecks have created reefs. **Harbour cruises** (*Kishon Port,* ✆ *8418765; cost adult/child 30/25NIS*) operate tours three times a day during Passover, Sukkot and summer school holidays. There

MEDITERRANEAN COAST
Gordon, Frishman and Bograshov beaches The city centre's most popular beaches are frequented by the complete cross-section of Tel Aviv's eclectic population. A wealth of amenities, cafés, restaurants, lifeguards and beach beds combined with the wide, golden sands make this the best city beach in the country.

Beit Yannai About 20 minutes north of Netanya is this wild, sweeping stretch of pristine coast which is the pride and joy of the residents who live in the cosy little moshavs nearby. With a definite neighbourhood feel, high rocky cliffs, scampering dogs, a rustic little café and miles of open sand, it exemplifies Israeli beach culture.

Achziv With the crumbling archaeological ruins of ancient Achziv (see page 144) forming the backdrop, this northern Mediterranean beach is a hidden paradise. Sheltered pools have been carved out of the rocky shoreline, their warm, shallow waters glimmering a vibrant turquoise under the summer sun.

Dor Beach Sheltered lagoons of shallow, turquoise waters make Dor Beach (see page 169) one of the most picturesque spots in which to take a dip (although during summer holidays it is hugely crowded).

SEA OF GALILEE
Ein Gev Resort Village Beach As the biblical waters of the Sea of Galilee lap against the green-grassed shores, an air of tranquillity and spirituality descends over the private resort village. In contrast to its more rambunctious neighbours along the coast, the Ein Gev Beach and those just to the south of it, characterise the air of mysticism that most hope to find.

DEAD SEA
Biankini and Siesta Beach At the northern end of the Dead Sea, where great hotels and the infringement of modernisation have yet to impinge on the untamed coast, the Biankini and Siesta Beach provides a mellow, exotic and authentic Dead Sea beach experience.

RED SEA
Coral Beach Reserve The aquatic, fish-laden tropical garden of Eilat's Coral Beach Reserve is the best-preserved stretch of Israel's Red Sea coast. Rainbow-coloured fish, swirling corals and the year-round warm, gentle waters make this one of the prettiest beaches in the country.

---

is a possibility of getting on group-booked cruises at other times of year but you need to call ahead. Bus 58 stops at the Kishon Port.

MOUNT CARMEL NATIONAL PARK *Telephone code 04*

Mount Carmel is a 23km-long limestone mountain ridge extending from Haifa in the north to the Galilee in the east and as far as the coastal Plain of Sharon in the south. Its rich, fertile soils have long been a draw for settlers, taking advantage of its lush greenery and thriving plant and animal species for as long as 200,000 years. The area is today under the umbrella of the Mount Carmel National Park (✆ *8231452; admission 33NIS per car, free on foot*) which is wholly dedicated to the preservation of this natural heritage and the indigenous habitat of the area.

The Carmel was designated a national park in 1971 and incorporates (among a whole host of picturesque and historically significant sites) the **Hai Bar Wildlife Reserve, Ein Hod** artists' village, **Muhraka Monastery** and **Carmel Caves**. You can easily spend days exploring the area and it is certainly a justifiable expenditure of your time, although the devastating forest fire in December 2010 destroyed a great portion of the park (see below, page 5).

The Mediterranean scrub forest, with its carob and rare kermes oak trees, provides for some wonderful walks, picnic and camping spots, cycling, jeep trips and nature spotting and is a strong favourite with weekending Israelis. Several streams flow through the mountains: Nahal Me'arot (which can be accessed through the Nahal Me'arot (Carmel Caves) Nature Reserve) and Nahal Galim.

HISTORY Sacred to Christians, Jews, Muslims and Baha'is alike, the Carmel region has seen its fair share of triumphs and defeats over the past 200,000 years. From the skeletal remains of a Neanderthal couple that were unearthed from one of the caves that dot the landscape, to World War I when the area's strategic prowess was drawn upon, a wealth of stories emerges. The 20th-century Battle of Meggido that took place on the head of the ridge saw British general Allenby lead his troops to victory, a battle considered a turning point in the war against the Ottoman Empire.

Even as early as Canaanite times the region was considered holy, and Baal of Canaan was worshipped from the hilltops. According to Jewish, Christian and Islamic belief, it was here that Elijah battled the prophets of Baal in a contest to determine the rightful ruler of the Kingdom of Israel and where, upon his victory, fire rained from the skies. The Assyrians conquered the area in 732BCE, restoring the worship of Baal of Canaan, who was associated by the Greeks with the god Zeus, and was known to the Romans as Deus Carmelus. The 12th-century Carmelites, a Catholic religious order, founded a monastery at the site of Elijah's victory which, during the crusades, was converted into a mosque, hence its present-day name Muhraka, meaning 'place of burning'. It was later restored (see page 168). In some Christian traditions it is celebrated that at this site Mary, mother of Jesus, gave the Scapular of Our Lady of Mount Carmel (a symbolic devotional cloth) to a British Carmelite.

GETTING THERE AND AROUND Buses from Haifa's city centre will drop you at the park's northern entrance near Haifa University (see page 162). The rest of the park runs parallel with the coast and can be entered from any point (see individual sites for more transport directions). Renting a car is by far the best way to get the most out of a trip to the Carmel National Park as public transport runs only along main arteries and does not delve into the heart of the park itself.

WHERE TO STAY The Carmel National Park covers a wide area and accommodation options are found scattered throughout the small settlements within it. Good choices for the quintessential picturesque Carmel experience are **Ein Hod** (see page 167), **Dor Beach** (page 169) and **Zichron Ya'akov** (see page 170). Campsites are also dotted throughout the park (*10NIS pp*). Ask at the national park information office for details of which ones have been opened following the fire.

Mediterranean Coast   MOUNT CARMEL NATIONAL PARK

5

THE MOUNT CARMEL FOREST FIRE

On 2 December 2010 a ferocious fire broke out on the Carmel Mountain just south of Haifa and spread quickly through the region, raging for four days. It is believed the fire started near the Druze town of Isfiya, but it is not fully clear why or how the fire began. Extremely dry conditions and little annual rainfall combined with flammable scrub and pine forests meant the fire moved quickly, decimating entire stretches of the beautiful mountain ridge and claiming 44 lives – making it the worst fire in Israeli history. Thirty-seven prison service cadets were trapped and killed in their minibus when the flames engulfed the area and several firefighters lost their lives.

The Israel fire and rescue services, along with the police, IDF soldiers and volunteer firefighters battled to control the blaze, but eventually Israel had to request international help. Firefighting teams, helicopters and planes from the US, Turkey, Greece, the Netherlands, Switzerland, Cyprus, Russia and the UK were dispatched and help from countless other countries was offered.

The damage wreaked by the fire is extensive. Entire villages have been destroyed, acres of land reduced to ashes, sensitive ecological areas have vanished and an estimated 1.5million trees burnt down. Some 17,000 people were evacuated in a mass operation, and villages such as Kibbutz Beit Oren, Ein Hod and Nir Etzion were severely affected.

WHERE TO EAT Druze villages dot the landscape and their hospitality (and food) is well renowned amongst Israelis. Small, makeshift stalls can be found in clearings by the side of the road, huddled between the trees for shade from the summer sun. They sell locally made olive oil in rudimentary bottles as well as freshly made *labane* balls, pitta and *zatar*; you haven't experienced the Carmel until you've sat on their small plastic stools and wolfed down a traditional Druze meal. Zichron Ya'akov and Ein Hod both have some high-quality restaurants as well as funky little cafés.

WHAT TO SEE

Nahal Me'arot (Carmel Caves) (*9841750; www.parks.org.il; 08.00–17.00 Sat–Thu, 08.00–15.00 Fri (closes 1hr earlier in winter); admission adult/child 20/9NIS*) The Nahal Me'arot Nature Reserve as it is officially known, sits amidst the lush vegetation of the Carmel Mountain range and centres on three large caves. The site has proved to be of crucial importance in prehistoric archaeological investigations, finds indicating that the caves were settled continuously for 200,000 years. This almost unprecedented discovery has highlighted three different prehistoric cultures and a great many artefacts, and has contributed greatly to the study of human evolution. The caves are only a ten-minute walk from the visitors' centre. The first of the three is the Oven Cave which displays a chronology of the long life of the area, while the smaller Carmel Cave has a reconstruction display of life during the Mousterian period (40,000–100,000 years ago). The last and most impressive Stream Cave is 70m long and provides visitors with an insight into prehistoric life with the aid of an audio-visual presentation and some resident bats flapping overhead.

A network of signposted trails leads from the centre of the reserve through the surrounding countryside and along the Carmel range. In spring and summer the area is awash with wild flowers whose scents fill the air, and it makes for some delightful and undemanding walks. Helpful and knowledgeable guides can take you on hikes or point you in the right direction, and maps are available in the visitors' centre.

On Saturdays at 10.00, 12.00 and 14.00 there are free guided tours from the park office.

Getting there Without your own transport it is difficult and involves a long walk. Bus 921 heading up and down route 4 between Haifa Merkazit Hof HaCarmel and Tel Aviv central bus station will stop at the Tzerufa junction every 30 minutes. From there walk about 1km north, cross the road and follow signs to the park (4km).

Ein Hod
The tiny artists' village of Ein Hod lies hidden in a sea of deep green, nestled against Carmel Mountain and surrounded by pine forests and olive groves. Whether you're an art lover or not, the picturesque beauty of this unique little village shouldn't be missed. With stunning views over the Mediterranean, visitors can spend from a few hours to several days immersing themselves in the creativity that emanates from every household. Painting, sculpting, ceramics, acting, stained-glass printing, photography and glass blowing are just some of the artistic techniques that visitors can observe, or partake in (workshops are designed for all levels).

Getting there Bus 921 runs between Tel Aviv and Haifa and is the closest to Ein Hod that you can get on public transport. Ask the driver to stop at the small village of Nir Etzion from where it is a 1km walk east.

Tourist information The **Ein Hod Information Centre** (☎ 9841126/054 811968; ein-hod.info) can book **guided tours** and help make reservations for accommodation and workshops. Ein Hod's very good website (www.ein-hod. israel.net) provides more information on classes and workshops, as well as contact information for booking bed and breakfast establishments.

Where to stay Bed and breakfast accommodation is plentiful, luxurious and pricey.

ArtRest (2 rooms) ☎9841560/050 6310047; e arma@netvision.net.il. Clearly designed by an artistic hand, these beautiful suites are reminiscent of a royal boudoir, oozing class & minimalist elegance. AC, TV & DVD, fully fitted kitchen, herb garden, private entrance, sea views & a huge mosaic bath. *150NIS less on w/days* **$$$. $$$$**

Batia and Claude (The Green Room) (1 room) ☎9841648/050 5319266; e batjan@research.haifa.ac.il. The cheapest of 3 rustic stone cottages. Simple & clean with a very pleasant garden, private entrance, AC, shower & TV. **$$$**

Yakir Ein Hod Country Accommodation (3 rooms) ☎9842656/050 5543982; e yakir_g@aquanet.co.il; www.yakireinhod.co.il. Fully equipped luxury rooms complete with private balcony with sea view & swimming pool. *100NIS less on w/days* **$$$. $$$$**

Where to eat There are three restaurants in the village: **Doña Rosa** (☎ 9543777; ⊕ 12.30–22.30 Mon–Sat; $$$) serving prime Argentinian meat dishes; **Abu Yaakov** (☎ 9843377; ⊕ 11.00–21.00 Mon–Sat; $) serving Middle Eastern salads, meats and hummus; and **Café Ein Hod** (☎ 054 4801985; ⊕ 08.30–19.00 Tue–Sun, until late Thu) providing a bohemian caffeine kick with a splash of secondhand arts and crafts blended in. Indian-style food and big breakfasts are also served. The **Art Bar** (☎ 9840071; ⊕ 10.00–15.00 Sun & Tue, 10.00–15.00 & 20.00–midnight Mon & Thu/ Fri) produces its own locally brewed beer, a perfect accompaniment for lounging under the shade of an ancient olive tree.

What to see

Janco Dada Museum ☎9842350;
www.jancodada.co.il; ⏰ 09.30–15.30 Sun–Thu,
09.30–14.00 Fri, 10.00–16.00 Sat. Celebrates
Marcel Janco, Ein Hod's founder & a member of
the Dada movement of modern art.
Artists' Gallery ☎9842548; ⏰ 10.00–17.00
Sun–Thu, 10.00–14.00 Fri, 11.00–16.00 Sat.

Exhibits one of the country's largest collections
of Israeli art.
Nisco Museum of Mechanical Music ☎052
4755313; ⏰ 10.00–17.00 daily; admission
adult/child 30/20NIS. Displaying antique music
boxes. There are guided tours every hr.

Isfiya and Daliat el Carmel
These once separate towns merged in 2003 to become what is now officially known as Carmel City (although they are still commonly known by their original names). Located about half an hour from Haifa, the first one you arrive at is Isfiya. The populations are predominantly Druze and the people's legendary hospitality draws locals and foreigners alike to bargain in the markets, eat in the traditional Middle Eastern restaurants, and experience the unique atmosphere of their secretive religion. Older men wear the traditional long gowns and headdresses, often sporting a large bushy moustache while the younger set has adopted a more modern style. In keeping with other Druze settlements square, Arabic-style houses characterise the architecture, the affluence and industriousness of its rural inhabitants clearly displayed. Unfortunately the big fire in 2010 (see page 5) destroyed much of the surrounding countryside here and with it the once lovely views over the green hills and terraced fields.

Historically it is possible that **Isfiya**, built on the ruins of an earlier Byzantine settlement, formed the centre of Crusader rule in the area, judging by extensive excavated finds. The 5th-century Jewish settlement of Husifah was excavated, which included a synagogue and mosaic floor bearing the inscription 'Peace be upon Israel', while copious amounts of gold coins dating to the Roman period demonstrate the town's extent at that time. The modern city of Isfiya was founded in the 18th century when residents prospered from a flourishing agricultural economy. Today the population of Isfiya alone is 9,000, 70% being Druze, the remainder Christian and Muslim.

Daliat el Carmel is the largest and most southerly of all Israel's Druze towns. The 13,000 Druze residents have traced their ancestry back to Aleppo (Halab) in Syria, which explains their strong accents and frequency of the surname Halabi. Today, Daliat el Carmel, whose name means 'Vine Branches of the Carmel', boasts a large central market selling handmade Druze crafts and products, and streets teeming with rudimentary, yet delectable local eateries. Markets are closed on Fridays.

Getting there Bus 37a leaves Haifa Bat Galim bus station several times a day (40mins/6.4NIS). *Sheruts* leave Haifa regularly between 06.00 and 18.00 and leave from the Hadar at the corner of Shemaryahu Levin and Herzl streets.

Muhraka
Just south of the Druze town of Daliat el Carmel, a winding mountain road leads through a dense oak and pine forest to Muhraka (☎ 052 8779686; ⏰ *daily Apr–Sep 08.00–12.30; Oct–Mar 14.30–17.00; admission 3NIS*), today the site of a Carmelite monastery. Tradition states that it was at this site that the Prophet Elijah battled the priests of Baal amidst fire that rained down from the heavens. Elijah then had the priests taken to Tel Kasis (the 'priests' mound' in Arabic) at the foot of Mount Carmel along the Kishon Stream, where they were slaughtered.

The Carmelite monastery that stands on the site today was constructed during the Crusades, and the four monks residing there today tend the quaint, peaceful

above   The peaceful lakeside site of Capernaum was once Jesus's Galilee base (E/DT) page 197

right   Nazareth of New Testament fame is today both a centre of Christian pilgrimage and Israel's largest Arab city (Z/DT) page 180

below   Tel Meggido, or Armageddon, certainly has a battle-weary past: this trading town was destroyed and rebuilt 25 times in its 4,400-year existence (SS) page 185

above left   The annual feast of Lag Ba'omer, celebrated at Meron, is a fascinating mixture of spirituality and partying, featuring bonfires and dancing (PI/A) page 216

above right   The Abuhav Synagogue in Tzfat, the world centre of Kabbalah, houses a Torah scroll that is the source of many traditions and legends (H/A) page 212

below   Israel's relatively recent success as a wine producer owes much to the award-winning Cabernet Sauvignon and Merlot of the Golan Heights Winery (RH/A) page 174

above right **The waterfalls at Banias are the most spectacular sight in Hermon National Park** (SS) page 244

right **Originally built by Saladin's nephew in an attempt to block the progress of the Sixth Crusade, the remains of Nimrod Fortress tower over the northern Golan landscape** (B/DT) page 243

below **The Hula Valley at the northern end of the Syrian-African Rift Valley is a crucial winter stopover for birds migrating south** (PZ) page 117

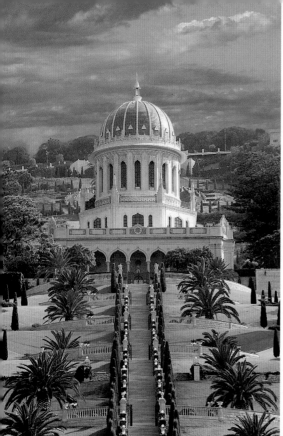

left   The massive dome of the Shrine of Bab, one of the most important sites of pilgrimage for members of the Baha'i faith, dominates the Haifa skyline (YS/DT) page 161

below   Only a few kilometres apart, the difference between Tel Aviv and Jaffa is striking: one is a hedonistic, determinedly modern metropolis, the other a tranquil port city steeped in Arabic culture (SS) page 109

above The ruined port town of Caesarea has a wealth of well preserved ruins, the legacy of phases of occupation by Phoenicians, Greeks, Romans, Crusaders and Mamluks (YB/DT) page 173

right The charming moshav of Zichron Ya'akov is Israel's longest-established wine producer (PI/A) page 170

below The stone houses and courtyards of Haifa's German Colony are now home to elegant restaurants and terraced cafés (SS) page 162

above left **A Bedouin woman and donkey in the Negev desert** (PZ) page 247

above right **Dromedary camel** (*Camelus dromedarius*) (IB/FLPA)

right **Eurasian griffon** (*Gyps fulvus*) (PZ)

far right **Goat on a desert cliff** (SA/DT)

below left **Common jackal** (*Canis aureus*) (YE/FLPA)

below right **Arabian leopard** (*Panthera pardus nimr*) (YE/FLPA)

above left **Yellow boxfish**
(*Ostracion cubicus*) (GK/DT)

left **Emperor angelfish**
(*Pomocanthus imperator*)
(AS/DT)

below Planted squarely in the middle
of Israel's 14km sliver of Red
Sea coast, Eilat's scores of
resort hotels are a draw with
partygoers and dedicated
scuba divers alike
(GK/DT) page 278

gardens. The view from the top of the monastery is unrivalled. It is possible, especially on clear days, to see right across the Galilee to the Jezreel Valley, Nazareth, Mount Tabor and even Mount Hermon. While of obvious biblical significance, the true magic of Muhraka lies in the picturesque landscape and staggering vista, a strong contender for the best in Israel.

The area around Muhraka provides for some fantastic walks, where the only other people you are likely to bump into are goat herders and their flocks. The Society for the Protection of Nature (see page 37) in Haifa sells good hiking maps of the Carmel range.

Getting there and away Bus 37a from downtown Haifa will take you to Daliat el Carmel where it is a half-hour walk to the site. By car follow signs from Daliat el Carmel and take a right when the forest road forks.

Atlit The **Atlit Detention Camp for Illegal Immigrants** (✆ 9841980; www.shimur. org; ⊕ 09.00–17.00 Sun–Thu, 09.00–13.00 Fri; admission adult/child 17/14NIS) was set up by British Mandate authorities in 1938 to house immigrants arriving in Palestine. The immigrants included refugees and Holocaust survivors from the Nazi regime as well as people escaping anti-Jewish persecution in Arab countries. The historic site, located on the original grounds of the camp, commemorates those who were kept here, and educates people of their plight. The emphasis is on personal stories, and a large archive has been commissioned to record individual tales. Stories of heroism, escape, and a battle for freedom are depicted through the restored barracks. The ship seen from the highway on the approach to the camp belongs to the site and was one of the 130 vessels used to transport the refugees to Israel. Guided tours can be arranged but you need to book in advance.

Nearby, perched at the end of Atlit's promontory, is an impressive UNESCO-listed **Crusader fortress**. Built in 1218, its main function was to control the coastal road with the aim of recovering Jerusalem. While the site has roots in prehistoric, Roman and medieval times, it was during the Crusader occupation of the area that the fortress and promontory were strongly fortified and these are the remains we see today. While not comparable to the great fortresses of Montfort (see page 219) and Belvoir (see page 200) its coastal location nonetheless makes it a nice place to explore if you're in the area.

Atlit is also home to some of the area's loveliest **beaches**. The beaches at the southern end of the small town can be easily accessed but the northern stretches are part of a naval base and thus out of bounds. It is, however, possible to walk all the way to Atlit from Haifa along the beach, a walk of 15km.

Getting there and away The easiest way to get to Atlit is by train from Haifa. Trains leave every 30 minutes (20mins/15NIS).

Dor Beach Dor Beach (admission 20–25NIS) is a strong contender for best Mediterranean beach in the country and, out of peak season, makes for an idyllic, tranquil holiday experience. Three sheltered bays have been carved out of the rock to form shallow natural pools, and still, turquoise waters and white sands complete the check list. The **Dor Holiday Village** (✆ 6399018/121; e tantura@bezeqint. net; www.dortantura.co.il) is located to the left of the beach as you enter the car park and provides unusual, igloo-shaped huts (**$$$–$$$$** depending on season) dotted like anthills amidst bright-green lawns only a few metres from the beach. A campsite (**$**) and more pricey bungalows (**$$$$**) are also on offer within the complex. The igloos and cottages have air conditioning, kitchenettes and cable television and can sleep two–five people. Two-person igloos have jacuzzi baths. Facilities include restaurants, a bar and watersports. Kayaks can be rented on the beach (30mins/20NIS).

Getting there and away There are no direct (or indirect) buses to the beach so it is highly recommended to hire your own car for this area. Bus 921 heading up and down route 4 between Haifa Merkazit Hof HaCarmel and Tel Aviv central bus station will stop at the Dor junction every half an hour from where it is a long 3km walk to the beach.

ZICHRON YA'AKOV *Telephone code 04*

Founded in 1882 by Romanian Jews during the first *aliyah*, Zichron Ya'akov has managed to come a long way without losing its quaint charm and old-worldly atmosphere. In the year following its founding the village came under the patronage of Baron Edmond de Rothschild (see opposite) who named it Zichron Ya'akov (Memory of Jacob) after his father. Rothschild had extensive vineyards planted, the country's first, which today are considered amongst the top wine producers in the country and recognised internationally. Winemaking soon became the primary economy within the moshav, and in the 1950s new immigrants to Israel flocked in great numbers to Zichron Ya'akov to settle.

Zichron Ya'akov boasts a proud pioneering history, and is Rothschild's final resting place; home of the renowned botanist and spy Aaron Aaronson. It is the centre of the secret Nili intelligence organisation.

In recent decades the town has developed a second crucial economy: tourism. Israelis flock to the beautiful leafy, cobbled lanes strewn with outdoor cafés, restaurants and art galleries; traditional gas lamps adorn the pavements and red shingle buildings and blossoming almond trees combine with the modern development to produce a truly unique Israeli town.

GETTING THERE AND AWAY Bus 872 between Tel Aviv and Zichron Ya'akov runs several times a day (1hr 45mins/26.50NIS) while bus 202 makes the journey to and from Haifa (30mins/15.40NIS).

GETTING AROUND Zichron Ya'akov is a small town and most of its interest lies in the single street that runs through its centre; Hameyasdim Street (also known as the Wine Road). Public transport is certainly not necessary to cover the small area and on foot it takes 10–15 minutes to walk from the cemetery and Founders Memorial at one end to the far end of Hamesyasdim Street.

TOURIST INFORMATION The tourist information centre can be found behind the Founders Monument (\ *6398892; www.zy1882.co.il;* ⊕ *08.30–13.00 Sun–Thu*). They have good free maps of the town.

⌂ WHERE TO STAY

⌂ **Hotel Beit Maimon** (25 rooms) 4 Tzahal St; \6290390; f 6396547; www.maimon. com. Lovely little hotel in a quiet street offering fabulous views of the sea; AC, breezy, modern rooms, a range of reasonably priced spa treatments & a heated jacuzzi. Lunch & dinner menus available (85NIS) with a good selection of local wines. *200NIS less on w/days* **$$$–$$$$**

Achouzat Zamarin (6 rooms)
16 Hameyasdim St; ✆6397404; e info@zamarin-spa.co.il; www.zamarin-spa.co.il. Elegant, intimate boutique hotel & spa in the heart of Zichron. The spa is open for day guests or can be

combined with overnight stays. Their packages inc massage treatments, the spa, overnight stay, b/fast & private jacuzzi for a couple for around 1,000NIS. **$$$**

✕ **WHERE TO EAT** Hameyasdim Street is lined with delightful cafés and restaurants, each one as quaint as the next. Come the weekend the pedestrian street and every seat lining it are packed full, but this rather adds to the carefree atmosphere in the town. Prices are predictably high so if you're on a tight budget then eat first and then splash out on a coffee whilst sitting on one of the leafy terraces.

✕ **Haneshika** 37 Hameyasdim St; ✆6390133; www.haneshika.com; ⏰ 09.00–22.00 Mon–Sat. Situated in the quaint back garden of one of Zichron's old stone houses, this is one of the most prestigious & pricey restaurants around.

The menu is changed regularly but can always be counted upon to be the best of the best. Book in advance especially on w/ends. **$$$$$**

✕ **Tishbi Coffee House** 33 Hameyasdim St; ✆6290280; ⏰ 09.00–23.30 Sun–Thu, 09.00–

BARON EDMOND DE ROTHSCHILD

Born into the powerful Rothschild banking family in 1845, Edmond was not interested in financial matters, preferring instead the more artistic side of life. He was an avid and prosperous art collector, with many notable works in his collections, including several Rembrandt pieces later donated to the Louvre Museum in Paris, his home city. But it is his successful endeavours to help the Jews fleeing the pogroms of eastern Europe, and to establish a haven for them in the Holy Land for which he is most widely and affectionately remembered in Israel.

His early offers of help soon grew into a desire to create a self-sufficient Jewish homeland and later, state. His financial support of settlements destined for monetary ruin awarded him the nickname 'Father of the Yishuv', but in the 1890s disagreements with Theodor Herzl and the Zionist organisation Hovevei Zion over the interpretation of 'political Zionism' resulted in the creation of 12 settlements under the Rothschild's Jewish Colonisation Association (ICA). In 1924, the Palestine Jewish Colonisation Association (PICA) was established, under the patronage of his son James Armand de Rothschild, who arrived in Palestine as a British soldier with General Allenby towards the end of World War I.

Rothschild was awarded honorary presidency of the Jewish Agency in 1929 and made countless visits to Palestine during his lifetime. Upon his death in Paris in 1934, he had purchased 500km² of land and funded the creation of almost 30 settlements at an estimated cost of US$50 million. He was interred in Paris until, in 1954, his and his wife's remains were transported to Israel. After a state funeral held by Israel's first prime minister David Ben-Gurion they were reburied in the Ramat Hanadiv Memorial Gardens near Zichron Ya'akov. His famous statement 'the struggle to put an end to the Wandering Jew, could not have as its result, the creation of the Wandering Arab', was perhaps a foresight and warning to future generations of the political turmoil that was to engulf this country and region from his early days to the present.

16.00 Fri. This is not only a great place to enjoy an Israeli b/fast or a meal of locally produced wine & cheese, but is also one of the oldest houses in Zichron. The coffee house is owned by the local winemaking Tishbi family. $ $

WHAT TO SEE

The Wine Road There is plenty to see in Zichron Ya'akov, most of which can be found by taking a very pleasant stroll along Hameyasdim Street (also referred to as the Wine Road) which is located in the heart of the small town. This was the pioneering colony's first street and has undergone heavy but meticulous reconstruction over recent years to return it to its former glory, with Rothschild's characteristic architectural features such as wooden window frames, tiled roofs, stone posts and traditional building façades having been fully restored. The Wine Road starts at the cemetery in the south end of town and finishes at the Carmel Winery in the north.

Cemetery Rothschild expressed a strong desire to be buried in the old cemetery in Zichron Ya'akov, a wish that was eventually fulfilled. It wasn't until 1954, 19 years after his passing, that the baron and his wife Adelheid were transported aboard a naval frigate from Paris and reinterred in the Ramat Hanadiv Memorial Cemetery in Zichron Ya'akov, which is located at the entrance to Hameyasdim Street (the Wine Road) opposite the Founders Memorial and tourist information office. They received a state funeral presided over by former prime minister David Ben-Gurion. Rothschild's simple yet impressive mausoleum can be found in the centre of the cemetery, while a stone-carved map showing the extent of his colonies can be found in the western part of the beautifully tended memorial gardens. The cemetery is part of a large nature reserve and is dotted with manicured gardens, fragrant blossoms and pools and fountains. The Samaria Observation Point is located between the Rose and Palm gardens and definitely worth the trip.

Founders Memorial This remarkable building is located next to the town's central bus station a little way up from the cemetery. Its construction is unique in that it has been designed to resemble an open scroll. A fascinating ceramic relief decorates the walls and depicts the story of Zichron's founding.

Aaronson House (*40 Hameyasdim St*) Zichron Ya'akov was home to the Nili group, an anti-Turkish spy ring that supplied the British with intelligence during World War I. The name Nili stands for Netzah Yisrael Lo Yishaker which translates as 'The eternal one of Israel will not be false'. Aaron Aaronson, an internationally reputed agronomist, and his sister Sarah were at the centre of the group's operations and spent several years living in the house that now acts as their memorial. Sarah Aaronson has become one of the country's most well-loved martyr heroines, a reputation strengthened by her refusal to divulge secret information upon her capture and brutal inquisition. She took her own life while in the captivity of the Turks. Aaron Aaronson was killed in a plane crash at the end of World War I. There is an impressive collection of photographs and documents on display depicting their heroic story.

Water tower Located on the right as you walk up Hameyasdim Street is the settlement's first water tower, built by Rothschild. Its outer façade has been designed to resemble that of an ornate ancient synagogue. A climb to the top offers a wonderful panoramic view over the green hills and valleys of the Carmel.

First Aliyah Museum (*2 Hanadiv St;* ✆ *6294777;* ☉ *09.00–14.00 Mon & Wed–Fri, 09.00–15.00 Tue; admission adult/child 15/10NIS*) Dedicated to the groups of pioneering families that arrived between 1882 and 1904, the museum illuminates their role in the founding of the State of Israel. The museum is housed in the 110-year-old council building built by Rothschild, at its time considered the most impressive in the country. Displays depict the history of the early settlers, its most precious relic being that of a short black-and-white film shot in 1913, which is believed to be the oldest film depicting Israel. Long believed lost, it was discovered in 1997 in a Paris film archive and shows, amongst others, Joseph Trumpeldor (see page 222).

Ohel Ya'akov Synagogue Named after Rothschild's father Jacob (Ya'akov) the synagogue was, at the time, the largest and most beautiful synagogue in all of the baron's colonies. It was founded in 1886 and has been carefully restored to its former elegance.

Carmel Winery (see box, *A bottle of Israel's finest*). A new centre for wine culture has opened alongside the wine cellars which, together with the plush bistro, is a real viticultural treat. There is also a small cinema, shop, tasting rooms and workshops, and tours can be arranged.

CAESAREA   Telephone code 04

Resting on the shores of the glittering Mediterranean Sea, Caesarea offers a wealth of attractions and luxury activities. The modern town is a sprawling series of wealthy, plush neighbourhoods, where large, mansion-like houses sit amidst green lawns and expensive cars line the driveways. Caesarea has been home to VIPs such as the ex-president Ezer Weizman. Yet the area is best known not for its well-to-do residents, but for the staggering ancient ruins that lie just south of it. The ruins at Caesarea are amongst some of the most valuable and fascinating in the world, where successive phases of occupation have left a treasure trove of archaeological remains, most notably the Crusader city and Roman theatre. Around the national park, Israel's finest golf course, several wide, sandy swimming beaches and a luxury spa make this a five-star stopover.

HISTORY The site at Caesarea was first settled in the 4th century BCE by the Phoenicians, who built a small harbour city named Straton's Tower. After Alexander the Great's conquest of the country in 332BCE, the city flourished under Greek rule. The Roman Conquest in 63BCE saw the city undergo a major phase of construction, and under Herod was renamed Caesarea, in honour of the Roman emperor. The Temple of Augustus, deep sea harbour, hippodrome, theatre, bathhouses, public buildings, wide roads, markets and state-of-the-art water supply all owe their origins to this time. It has been recorded that Roman procurators Pontius Pilate and Felix resided in Caesarea, and it was here the Apostle Paul was imprisoned and sent to Rome for trial. It was also the site of Paul's baptising of the Roman officer Cornelius. The Jewish uprising of 66CE was repressed by Vespasian who was later declared Emperor of the Roman Empire in Caesarea and the city became one of the most important in the eastern part of the Roman Empire, classified as 'Metropolis of the Province of Syria Palestina'. Following the Bar Kochba revolt, its leader Ben Akiva was tortured and died in the city in 135.

A BOTTLE OF ISRAEL'S FINEST

When asked to name a top wine-producing locale, most would utter the familiar names of France, Chile, Italy, Spain or California. But over recent years, Israel has managed to put itself on the prestigious wine map and now competes favourably with the giants of the wine world. Wine has been made in Israel since pre-biblical times; indeed Noah's first task after completing the Ark was to plant vines. Yet only in recent years has it been considered quality wine, a development owed mainly to the creation of the Golan Heights Winery which opened in 1983. From the outset the winery was a success, with its second wine, a 1984 Cabernet Sauvignon, winning the gold medal at the International Wine and Spirit Competition. Its Yarden series is considered its most reputable and prestigious, notably the Cabernet Sauvignon and Merlot. Today the country's largest winemaker is the Rothschild-founded Carmel Winery in Zichron Ya'akov (see page 170). It produces over 13 million bottles a year and has three main series: the Selected, the Vineyard and the prestigious Rothschild, which includes Merlot, Cabernet Sauvignon, Chardonnay and Emerald Rieslings. Much of the wine purchased in Israel and exported is kosher. While there are several rules that need to be abided by, there is no conflict of interest in the production of good wine and it remaining kosher. For example, grapes may not be used until their fourth year of growth, equipment must be kept kosher clean and only Sabbath-observant male Jews can take part in the wine-producing process.

TOURS Most of Israel's wineries offer tours, although you may need to book ahead. While the main attraction is the winemaking process and wine tasting, the wineries tend to be located within some of the country's most stunning landscapes and are lovely places to visit. For more information visit www.israelwines.co.il.

Carmel Zichron Ya'akov Wine Cellars Zichron Ya'akov; 04 6290977
Golan Heights Winery Katzrin, Golan; 04 6968420; www.golanwines.co.il (see page 233)
Galil Mountain Winery Kibbutz Yiron; 04 6868740; www.galilmountain.co.il
Tabor Winery Kfar Tabor, Lower Galilee; 04 6760444
Domaine du Castel Ramat Razi'el, between Tel Aviv & Jerusalem; 02 5342249
Hamasrek Winery (kosher) Beit Me'ir, near Jerusalem; 02 5701759
Yatir Winery Tel Arad, Judean Desert; 08 9959090
Sde Boker Winery Sde Boker, Judean Desert; 050 7579212
Neot Smadar Winery Neot Smadar, Negev Desert; 08 6358111

Caesarea prospered during the Byzantine Period until the Arab conquest of 637. The Crusaders captured the city during the First Crusade but it wasn't until 1251 that Louis VI fortified the city, constructing high walls and a deep moat. The fortifications were breached shortly afterwards however by the Mamluk sultan Baibars, who captured the town. The once-flourishing port had by this time completely silted over. The city fell into ruins and remained desolate until the 19th century when Bosnian refugees were settled on the land. It was later resettled in 1940 with the establishment of the nearby Kibbutz Sdot Yam but abandoned for a brief period during the 1948 Arab–Israeli War.

GETTING THERE AND AWAY There are no direct buses from Haifa or Tel Aviv. Get any number of regular buses heading north or southbound and get off at the Or Akiva junction 4km from Caesarea, where you can walk or hitch the final stretch. Trains leave to Binyamina from Tel Aviv and Haifa regularly which is 7km from Caesarea. Either find a taxi or hop on a bus going to Or Akiva where it is a 2km walk to Caesarea. If you're driving there be aware there is absolutely no continuity with the English spelling of Caesarea on road signs. It can range from Qesariya, to Kesariya, to Quesariyya, so try to be imaginative and keep an eye open.

🏠 WHERE TO STAY

🏠 **Dan Caesarea Hotel** (114 rooms) ☏ 1700 505080. Part of the luxury chain of Israeli hotels, the Dan Caesarea represents the country-manor member of the Dan family. Located on the fringe of the Caesarea golf course & its velvet lawns, the hotel prides itself on immaculate service & top-quality facilities. **$$$$$**

✗ WHERE TO EAT
Restaurants in the archaeological park tend to be a bit pricey but are generally of good quality. The **Crusaders Restaurant** (☏ 6361679; ⊕ 10.00–midnight daily; **$$$$**) serves a wide selection of meat, fresh seafood and fish while **Helena's** (☏ 6101018; ⊕ 12.00–23.00 daily; **$$$$**) specialises in Middle Eastern cuisine.

WHAT TO SEE
Caesarea Maritime National Park (☏ 6267080; e galic@caesarea.cc; www.caesarea.com; ⊕ Apr–Sep 08.00–18.00 Sun–Thu, 08.00–16.00 Fri; Oct–Mar 08.00–16.00 Sun–Thu, 08.00–15.00 Fri; admission adult/child 36/22NIS)

Theatre The theatre has become the symbol of Caesarea and has been fully restored to its former grandeur. Seating up to 4,000 people, it once again hosts concerts, operas and summer events and has been designed so that audiences have a view over the Mediterranean Sea behind. At some point after its original construction, the theatre was extended to form a quasi-amphitheatre, where it is likely gladiatorial battles would have taken place. It is located south of the Crusader city near the Herodian south wall.

Promontory Palace Jutting out into the sea, the high promontory located in the south of the Roman city was the site of King Herod's exquisite palace. The excavated complex, 110m by 60m in size, contained a large central saltwater pool and was surrounded by ornate porticoes. On display within the palace is a replica of a stone mentioning Pontius Pilate, the only physical evidence discovered bearing his name. The original is in the Israel Museum in Jerusalem.

Hippodrome A major feature of the Herodian town, it was here that great sporting events were played out and legendary gladiator games were hosted. The arena housed up to 15,000 spectators and was 250m long and 80m wide. It has yet to be excavated and is overgrown, but its shape and extent are still clear.

Bathhouses The excavated 4th-century bathhouses are a wonderful example of Roman architecture. A series of courtyards and rooms, many containing exquisite mosaics, made up the large bath complex that formed the core of Roman social life.

Byzantine Street Along the ancient shopping street are two headless statues, located near the entrance. Dated to the 2nd or 3rd centuries, one is made of white marble and the other from reddish, purple-coloured porphyry. It is believed the latter is the figure of an emperor, most likely Hadrian.

Crusader city   Entrance to the city is via the imposing East Gate. To the left of the gate are remains of houses while within the fortified area remnants of the ancient water supply and drainage system, the temple of Augustus and the still-standing Crusader cathedral can be found. The cathedral was dedicated to St Paul and built on the site of an earlier Byzantine church. Near the cathedral is the mosque built by Bosnian settlers in the 19th century.

Aqueduct   The aqueduct was commissioned by Herod to bring fresh water from Carmel Mountain 15km away and represents an incredible feat of ancient architectural engineering. The aqueduct was built on arches and the gradient precisely measured, allowing for a constant flow of water into the city. It was later extended by Hadrian and the Crusaders. Today part of the aqueduct is inside the national park and sections can be spotted along the entire coastal region to its source.

Underwater Archaeological Park (Caesarea Dive Club) (✎ 6265898; e *diving@post.com; www.caesarea-diving.com*) Most of what remains of the deep sea port today lies under the emerald waters of the Mediterranean Sea and has become an underwater park frequented by scuba-diving enthusiasts and archaeology buffs from around the world. Diving here is open to professionals and amateurs and a reputable dive centre operates informative and insightful expeditions to the ruins of the Roman and Crusader naval port, including several ancient shipwrecks.

BEACHES   The **Harbour Beach** (✎ *050 5385365; admission adult/child 25/20NIS*) is a lovely, well-kept beach that boasts shimmering green waters as its view and the ancient buildings of Caesarea as its backdrop. Parking, lifeguards, changing rooms, parasols and sunbeds are available. There is also a pleasant beach bar (complete with grill). The incredibly picturesque **Aqueduct Beach** just outside the national park is free and a lovely and tranquil place to go swimming. Facilities are limited, however, so families with small children are best advised to opt for the Harbour Beach.

OTHER CAESAREA ATTRACTIONS   Located within the boundaries of the national park (but not included in the entry price) are the Caesarea Experience, Caesarea's Stars and the Time Tower (*admission adult/child 40/35NIS inc park admission*) – three state-of-the-art, multi-media experiences aimed at illuminating Caesarea's tumultuous and fascinating past and the people who lived there.

Many people don't venture too far outside the archaeological park but there are several expensive and luxurious activities to partake in if your budget runs to it. The **Caesarea Golf Club** (✎ *6109602*) is Israel's one-and-only 18-hole golf course and is set within beautiful sea-view grounds complete with bird lake. It is located at the entrance to Caesarea in grounds donated by the Rothschild family. The nearby **Ralli Museum** (*Rothschild Bd;* ✎ *6261013;* ☺ *10.30–15.00 Mon–Sat; admission free*), housed in a vast mansion, displays a selection of modern and ancient paintings including a gallery devoted to Salvador Dalí. The **Caesar Spa** (✎ *6266669*) set within manicured grounds, takes pampering to a new dimension. For those with deep enough pockets this luxury complex offers everything one could need to relax and unwind; massages from mud to Thai, wraps, aromatic peeling, and face and body treatments.

Twenty minutes away from Tel Aviv's city centre is the town of Herzliya which, over recent years has become one of the major night-owl hotspots. In fact, all bars, restaurants and clubs centre on the expensive, oh-so-trendy area known as Herzliya Pituach, the strip running along the seafront to the left of the highway (the other part of town being purely residential). In contrast to Tel Aviv's Old Port area, Herzliya's marina is still very much active, being home to small, private yachts around which has appeared the **Arena Mall** (⊕ *10.00–22.00 Sun–Thu, 09.30–16.00 Fri, 11.00–23.00 Sat; cinema stays open later*), as well as dozens of cafés, restaurants and pubs. A wide, sandy beach 100m from the marina has a young, laid back atmosphere, with beach volleyball, a relaxed bar and plenty of towel space, while the strip 0.5km back from the seafront is packed with good restaurants, swanky bars and pubs and, come the small hours, pumping nightclubs.

GETTING THERE AND AWAY Buses 501 and 601 leave from Tel Aviv central bus station, and stop at the big junction by the highway (the 601 also stops at Arlozorov bus station). From there it is a ten-minute walk to central Herzliya Pituach but to get to the beach and marina you will need to find a taxi.

WHERE TO STAY

Dan Accadia Hotels (200 rooms) Herzliya Beach; ☏9597070; e accadia@danhotels.com; www.danhotels.com. Great beachfront setting & all the facilities & quality associated with the Dan chain & a 5-star resort hotel. *Rooms start at 2000NIS.* $$$$$

Shizen Spa Resort (40 rooms) Herzliya Beach; ☏9520825; www.shizenhotel.com. Oriental-themed boutique hotel where Zen, tranquillity & feng shui are the name of the game. A first-class spa, gourmet restaurants & artistic rooms with sea view. *Rooms start at 2000NIS.* $$$$$

WHERE TO EAT

✖ Segev 16 Shenkar St (corner of HaHoslim St); ☏9580410; ⊕ 12.00–16.00 & 19.00–23.00 Sun–Thu, 12.00–15.30 & 19.00–23.00 Fri, 13.00–17.00 & 19.30–23.00 Sat. It has been decorated to resemble the Neve Tzedek neighbourhood of Tel Aviv, giving it a cosy, friendly atmosphere. Cuisine is widely international & very varied. The 3-course business lunch (115NIS) is good value. $$$$$

✖ Tapeo 9 Shenkar St; ☏9546699; ⊕ 12.00–14.00 & 18.00–01.00 Sun–Thu, 18.00–01.00 Fri, 12.00–01.00 Sat. Huge Spanish restaurant where booking ahead at w/ends is a must. Despite the size it has a romantic, candlelit feel & serves garlicky, rich tapas at reasonable prices. $$$$

✖ Moses 14 Shenkar St; ☏9566628; ⊕ 12.00–04.00 daily. Part of a well-loved chain of American-themed restaurants serving big, juicy beef burgers & a huge selection of comfort foods. $$$

BARS

♀ Yam Bar Akadia Beach; ☏9597102; ⊕ 24hrs daily. Perched on the cliff edge above the beach with fantastic views & a gentle breeze, this is a relaxed watering hole attracting the chilled-out surfer types.

♀ Hattori Hanzo 1 Sapir St; ☏9514045; ⊕ 21.00–late daily. A 3-year veteran of raucous, pumping party nights, this bar-cum-nightclub is the ultimate 'pick-up' place.

♀ Murphy's Marina; ☏9569495; ⊕ 16.00–late Sun–Thu, 12.00–late Fri/Sat. Irish-style pub that's a bit softer around the edges than those in Tel Aviv. Live music on Tue & Wed & live sporting events on big screens. Big portions of nice bar food. Outdoor seating opposite the marina.

WHAT TO SEE AND DO

Marina and beach Herzliya Pituach is first and foremost a leisure town where a plethora of bars, cafés, restaurants and beachside activities converge. The marina is a pleasant place to spend an evening sipping drinks after a full day on the huge expanse of white sand. Sailing, surfing, scuba diving, beach volleyball and countless other active pursuits can all be arranged from the Acadia Beach.

Apollonia National Park (*Coastal plain north of Herzliya Pituach; www.parks. org.il;* ⊕ *08.00–17.00 daily (closes 1hr earlier in winter & on Fri); admission adult/ child 20/9NIS*) The site contains the recently excavated remains of a once-prosperous Crusader city and castle. It is easy to see why the Crusaders chose this spot – both defensively and aesthetically – and resting on a cliff overlooking the Mediterranean it makes for a pleasant afternoon exploring the ruins and piecing together the site. The entrance is located just outside Herzliya Pituach. Turn right on to Wingate Street when heading towards the town at the second set of traffic lights.

Herzliya Museum of Contemporary Art (*4 HaBanim St;* \ *9551011; www.herzliyamuseum.co.il;* ⊕ *10.00–14.00 Mon, Wed, Fri & Sat, 16.00–20.00 Tue & Thu; admission 10NIS*) Houses collections of Israeli and international contemporary art and focuses on works that offer an alternative angle to the political and social issues within the country. Exhibits change regularly.

Sidni Ali Mosque The mosque complex, which is today both a school and active mosque, in fact houses the shrine of the Mamluk chief for whom it was built and who died in battle on this hill – Ali ibn Alil. It is dated to the 13th century CE, the time of the great battles between the Mamluks and Crusaders.

6

Lower Galilee

Telephone code 04

The 1st-century historian Flavius Josephus once wrote of the Lower Galilee: 'One may call this place the ambition of nature.' Stretching from the sweeping, fertile plains of the Jezreel Valley (or simply 'HaEmek', 'The Valley') in the south to the natural border of the Jordan River in the east, and up to the more rugged terrains of the Upper Galilee, it is a land of true diversity. Agriculturally, the area has been the beating heart of the country for centuries, its fertile valleys seasonally blanketed with crops. The delicate microclimate of the region, coupled with its diverse geography account for its eclectic mix of produce. Almonds, citrus fruits and olive trees grow in the Beit She'an and Herod valleys, cotton and grain prosper in the warm fields of the Jezreel Valley while flowers and herbs blossom alongside the Jordan River. The Sea of Galilee's abundant fish stocks have long complemented agriculture in the vicinity of the sea, called thus through tradition rather than definition. Throughout the time of Jesus up until today a thriving fishing industry has prospered, forming the economy of many of today's kibbutzim that concentrate in the valleys. The country's pioneering kibbutz, Deganya Alef, is on the shores of the sea, and the area is now home to most of the country's kibbutz settlements. Nazareth, the heart of Arab life and culture in the region, together with the countless Arab villages that dot the landscape, denoted by their minarets and typical jumbled street planning, are home to one million of Israel's Arab residents, whose traditional way of life and close cultural ties flourish.

Historically, nowhere outside Jerusalem can compete with the Lower Galilee for drama, passion and religious tenor. The scene of legendary battles, it was on these soils that empires were won and lost. At the Battle of Hittin in 1187, the revered Arab leader Saladin defeated the Christian Crusader armies, a battle that marked the beginning of the conquest of Jerusalem and prompted the Third Crusade. Under the shadow of Mount Tabor, the prophet and heroine Deborah, alongside Barak, defeated the Canaanite captain Sisera, marking the first great Israelite victory since the days of Joshua, and the last battle they would ever have with the Canaanites. After this, during the Hasmonean period, the entire Galilee region was controlled by several empires and emerged as a Jewish stronghold, a claim that remained for five centuries after the demise of the Second Temple. The highly contested lands changed hands countless times throughout the succeeding centuries: Arabs, Crusaders, Mamluks and Ottomans all ruled at times throughout the Galilee's colourful past.

Sacred in the hearts of Christians and Jews the world over, the region is the destination for thousands of pilgrims. From the magnificent churches and picture-postcard cobbled alleys of Nazareth's Old City where Jesus's life began, to the sites of his numerous miracles that dot the shores of the Sea of Galilee, biblical stories abound. Tiberias, one of Judaism's four holy cities and often considered the capital

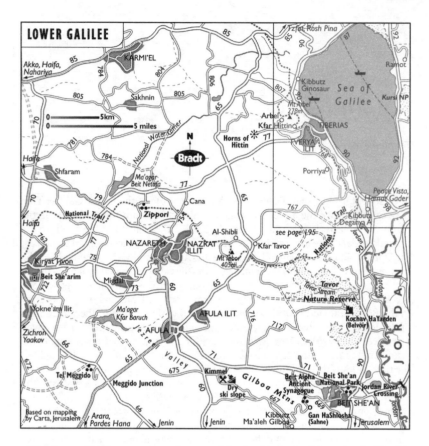

of the Lower Galilee, was once the seat of the Jewish Sanhedrin, school of Jewish learning, and home to Rabbi Judah HaNassi as he compiled the Talmud. Tiberias's party-going streets today belie the importance of the city in Judaism's history, the quiet tombs of some of the great philosophers and rabbis scattered around the city acting as reminders to this secular settlement.

One hour's drive from Jerusalem and Tel Aviv, it is easily accessible and thus regularly frequented by Israeli holidaymakers and day trippers, who escape the cities to unwind in the national parks, hot springs and lakeside beaches. Tour buses, laden with pilgrims and sightseers, trek through the valleys and hills, fuelling the region's ever-growing tourism economy. Be it by the rich history, spiritual allure or thriving flora and fauna that abound in the valleys and hills of the Lower Galilee, few could fail to be enchanted by the beauty and historic appeal of the region.

NAZARETH

Nazareth – Israel's largest Arab city – rests atop, between and around five round hills that form the end of the Galilee Mountains presiding over the Jezreel Valley below. Outside the country, it is probably most well known as being the childhood home of Jesus and a site for pilgrims over the last 2,000 years. Religious and historic sites centre on the Old City in the heart of Nazareth – or Natzrat as it is pronounced in Hebrew – where preconceived images of quaint cobbled stone alleys and bustling markets are fully realised. Outside the Old City, however, Nazareth is a hectic, modern and vibrant Arab city where the aromas of strong coffee, spices and sweets drift along the streets, where women sport traditional *jalabeya* coats, and where the loud chatter and the sounds of car horns dull only marginally at prayer times. With a population of 60,000 – 60% of whom are Muslim – there is an undeniable and refreshing feel of unity, where two major religions co-exist in relative success. Inconceivably to many other Arab Israelis, and certainly Palestinians living in the West Bank, the people of Nazareth are content with their situation, where Arab life and culture most certainly prevail. Modest dress is highly recommended – particularly for women – both in the Old City and outside.

HISTORY On account of its absence from both the Old Testament and Talmud it is likely Nazareth was a small and insignificant settlement during Jesus's time and it is likely that the city as it is known today flourished and grew alongside the spread of Christianity. Amongst the Christian sites in Israel and across the world, Nazareth holds its claim to being 'where it all began'. It was here that Jesus spent most of his early life and where the Bible states that Mary was told of the Annunciation by the Angel Gabriel.

From the Muslim Conquest of Palestine in 637CE throughout the First Crusade and long-lasting conflict, power changed hands regularly, which had a great impact on the religious balance of the population. In 1099, the Galilee was captured by the Crusader Tancred, and Nazareth was appointed as capital of the area. Following Saladin's victory at the Battle of Hittin in 1187, Muslim control was once more established in Nazareth where it lasted until it was once more returned to Christian hands, during part of the Sixth Crusade. In 1263, however, the Mamluk sultan Baibars had all Christian buildings destroyed and its people evicted, their absence lasting until 1620 when the Lebanese leader Fakhr-al Din II allowed their return. Throughout Ottoman rule Nazareth flourished, and it is well documented as a time of affluence for the city. Testament to this are the traditional two-storey mansions built during this period constructed at the base of the Nabi Sa'in cliff rising behind the city.

During the 1948 Arab–Israeli War, troops from the Arab Liberation Army entered Nazareth, but on 11 June the city surrendered to Israeli forces after signing a truce agreement to cease battling in exchange for assurances that no harm would come to the city's population. It is thanks to this that, while many other Arab towns in the area were forcibly evacuated, the Arab population was never evicted.

GETTING THERE AND AWAY Nazareth is fairly accessible by bus from most major cities. Buses and *sheruts* stop at several bus stops along Paulus VI Street, where the Egged information kiosk (*98 Paulus VI St*) is located. Make sure the bus is headed for Natzrat Ha-Atika and not Natzrat Illit, the nearby Jewish satellite town. Every day countless buses head to the nearby city of Afula, which serves closer, more rural areas. Bus 823 runs between Tel Aviv and Nazareth (3hrs/42NIS) five times daily, stopping in the Old City. Buses 331 and 339 leave Haifa (Palmer Square and Lev HaMifratz respectively) to the central bus station (35mins/17.20NIS). Bus 955 leaves Jerusalem at 16.00 and 18.00 (2hrs 25mins/48NIS) and for Jerusalem at 08.00 and 11.00. Bus 431 runs hourly between Tiberias and Nazareth (25mins/19NIS).

GETTING AROUND Nazareth suffers from dire congestion problems and weaving your way through the dusty, strangely organised roads is an arduous task. If you're arriving by car, it's recommended to park outside the Old City area and either walk or take a taxi into the centre. The worst of the traffic centres on Paulus VI Street,

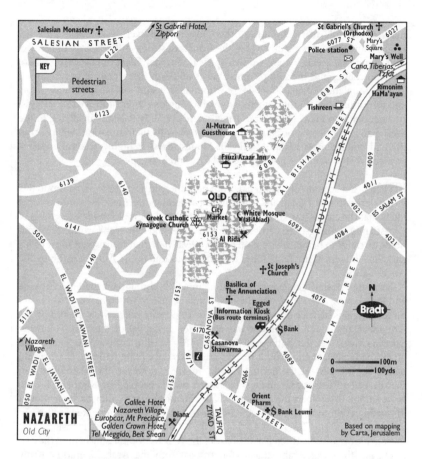

which during rush hour is bumper to bumper. Most of Nazareth's sights are within the Old City and within easy walking distance of each other. Cars can be hired from **Europcar** (*19 Paulus VI St;* ☎ *03 7918005;* ⊕ *08.00–18.00 Mon–Sat*).

TOURIST INFORMATION

ℹ️ Tourist information office 58 Casanova St; ☎ 6750555; e ronnye@tourism.gov.il; www. nazarethboard.org; ⊕ 08.30–17.00 Mon–Fri, 09.00–13.00 Sat. The main government tourist information branch is small & not particularly well equipped. Staff will provide free maps well designed for navigating the maze of alleys that make up the old market area (most of which are unnamed).

Local tour operators The tourist information office can supply contact details for local tour guides who charge approximately 450NIS for a two–three-hour tour. The **Fauzi Azar Inn** (see *Where to stay* below) offers a daily two-hour tour of the city (09.30 daily; 20NIS for guests, 35NIS for non-guests).

🏠 WHERE TO STAY

🏠 Golden Crown Hotel (240 rooms) Mount Precipice; ☎ 6508000; e res@goldencrown.co.il; www.goldencrown.co.il. Located on the southern entrance to the city near Mount Precipice offering beautiful views of the Jezreel Valley below, although a bit of a hike to the Old City. Large swimming pool, jacuzzi, gym, sauna, restaurants, shops … the list goes on. Rooms are clean & comfortable. **$$$$**

🏠 **Al Mutran Guesthouse** (11 rooms) 📞6020469; e info@al-mutran.com; http://mutran.aiforms.com. Charming, traditional decoration & a wide range of facilities & room options from 6-bed private, en-suite room, to dbl en suites, shared bathrooms & a dormitory are on offer in this Old City gem. **$$$**

🏠 **Fauzi Azar Inn** (14 rooms) 📞6020469/ 054 4322328; e info@fauziazarinn.com; www.fauziazarinn.com. By far the best mid-range option in town. Located in the true heart of the Old City & souk & housed in a 200-year-old Arabic courtyard house, it offers unparalleled comfort, character & ambience, as well as a variety of differently priced accommodation options. Internet available & organised tours of Nazareth & surrounding areas can be arranged. Rooms range from dbls to a 10-bed dorm (90NIS) and

there is free Wi-Fi throughout as well as a kitchen & buffet b/fast inc. **$$$**

🏠 **Rimonim HaMayaan (Mary's Well)** (226 rooms) Top end of Paulus VI St; 📞6500000; f 6500055; www.rimonim.com. In keeping with other members of the Rimonim chain, the hotel is nicely decorated, comfortable & equipped with absolutely everything (although it doesn't have the character of some of its counterparts). Perfectly situated in the midst of the hustle & bustle of the Old City next to Mary's Well Sq. **$$$**

🏠 **St Gabriel Hotel** (60 rooms) 2 Salesian St; 📞6572133; e nazsgh@yahoo.com; www.stgabrielhotel.com. Perched high on the hill behind the city with fabulous views, especially from the b/fast patio. Furnished in plush, Middle Eastern design, it once housed a congregation of Catholic nuns & its exterior has retained its ecclesiastical splendour. Often caters to big groups. **$$$**

✗ WHERE TO EAT

✗ **Al Rida** Al Bishara St; 📞6084404; ⏰ 13.00–02.00 Mon–Sat, 19.00–02.00 Sun. Situated in an old Arabic mansion house with an arched roof, heavy wooden furniture & a small garden, this is one of the nicest restaurants in Nazareth. The food combines Arabic style with contemporary flavours. The succulent meats are highly recommended, especially the lamb, while vegetable dishes such as stuffed mushrooms or artichokes are also excellent. The view of the Old City from the roof terrace is stunning. **$$$$**

✗ **Diana** 51 Paulus VI St; 📞6572919; ⏰ 11.00–midnight daily. Ask anyone in the country to recommend a restaurant in Nazareth & this is where you'll be sent. And justly so – it is simply terrific. Don't be put off by the unimpressive exterior or simple decoration,

the food is top-notch, freshly prepared Middle Eastern cuisine. Ordering the salad (*mezze*) will result in 22 different dishes being piled on your table – & that's just for starters. The kebabs are succulent & just mouth-watering. **$$$$**

🍵 **Tishreen** Hamaayan Sq; 📞6084666; ⏰ Mon–Sat 11.00–00.00, 18.00–00.00 Sun. Delightful Arabic coffee shop serving up creative, aromatic foods and sweet black coffee. Lovely ambience and ornate décor. **$$**

✗ **Casanova Shawarma** Casanova St; 📞6554027; ⏰ 07.00–19.00 daily. Without a doubt the best falafel in the city. Tiny, take-away stall halfway up Casanova St, it is unassuming & easily missed. Serving falafel (12NIS) with an array of varied, fresh salad accompaniments, *shawarma* (20NIS) & freshly squeezed orange juice (10NIS). **$**

OTHER PRACTICALITIES With the exception of Nazareth's three main hospitals, all major post offices, banks and the city's central police station are either inside (or within easy walking distance of) the Old City. The city keeps hours in accordance with Muslim and Christian holy days (Friday to Sunday).

Emergency

Ambulance 📞101
Fire 📞102

Police station 6077 St; 📞100 or 6574444. Located left off 6089 Street which heads northeast to Mary's Well Square from the souk. Next to the post office.

Money ATMs are commonplace outside banks, and found throughout the city. Paulus VI Street has many money-changing bureaux and branches of most major banks. The post office will also change money, cash travellers' cheques and has a Western Union service.

$ **Bank Hapoalim** Paulus VI St; \03 6532407; ⊕ 08.30–13.00 & 16.00–18.00 Mon & Thu, 08.30–13.15 Tue & Wed, 08.15–12.30 Fri

$ **Discount Bank** Paulus VI St; \6089120; ⊕ 08.30–13.00 & 16.00–18.30 Mon & Thu, 08.30–14.00 Tue & Wed, 08.30–12.30 Fri.

Post
Post office Moskovia Bldg, 219 St; \6554019; ⊕ 08.00–12.30 Sun, 08.00–18.00 Mon & Thu,

08.00–12.30 & 15.30–18.00 Tue & Fri, 08.00–13.00 Wed. Next to the police station.

Medical
French Hospital \650900
Holy Family Hospital \6508900
Nazareth Hospital \6571501–2

Orient Pharm 703 Iksal St; \6452258; ⊕ 08.30–21.00 Mon–Sat

WHAT TO SEE The Old City (El-Balda El-Qadima) provides the backdrop for most of the main religious and historic sites of interest.

Churches
Basilica of the Annunciation (*Casanova St;* ⊕ *08.00–18.00 Mon–Sat, 14.00–17.30 Sun & hols; admission free*) This is the most prominent and easily identifiable site in the Old City, and makes for a good starting and orientation point. The modern Catholic church stands 55m tall, the entrance of which is located up Casanova Street just off the main Paulus VI Street. Today's modern church – designed in the shape of the Madonna lily, a symbol of the Virgin Mary – was built in 1969 over the remains of earlier Byzantine and Crusader churches, and contains the **Cave (or Grotto) of the Annunciation** (⊕ *05.45–21.00*), where tradition states the Virgin Mary received news from Gabriel of Jesus's conception. Remains of the earlier churches are still visible in the lower stone cave. The unusual geometric design and grey stone walls dotted with stained-glass windows of the basilica, located up the spiral staircase on the right of the main entrance, are eerily impressive.

St Joseph's Church (⊕ *07.00–18.00 daily*) The church is located 50m from the northern exit of the basilica and is the early traditional site of Joseph's carpentry shop, and later the 'House of Joseph'. The current church was built in 1914 on the site of an earlier 12th-century one. In its heyday caves, granaries and wells – which today are located down the stone stairs from within the church – were used by early Nazarene inhabitants. It was later, when Christian pilgrims were appearing in greater numbers, that it turned into a site of worship.

Orthodox Church of St Gabriel (⊕ *08.00–17.00 Mon–Sat, 12.00–14.00 Sun; admission free*) This is another contender for the site where the Virgin Mary received news from Gabriel of Jesus's Annunciation. The church, the Orthodox equivalent to the Basilica of the Annunciation, was built over the spring said to be where Mary was fetching water at the time of Gabriel's appearance. The present church, built in 1750 along the south side of the chapel containing the spring, can be visited, although is often overcrowded with large groups of pilgrims. Descending from the small upper church downstairs into the lower chapel, a single, narrow aisle leads to the northern end where it is possible to look over an altar into the running spring.

Greek Catholic Synagogue Church From the top of the main souk street turn left and then take the next right. The small, stone entrance is easily missed. This is said to be the synagogue where Jesus preached to the people of Nazareth. It became a popular place of Christian worship after influxes of pilgrims, during which time the church was built. The building is extremely quaint and stands like an old grandfather clock, snuggled into the maze of souk streets.

Other sights

Mary's Well and Ancient Bathhouse (al-Sabil) The well and bathhouse are fed by the spring gushing through the Church of St Gabriel, and is a site whose importance in daily life and religious connotations is undeniable. Christian tradition states that it was here, whilst Mary was collecting water from the well, that Gabriel appeared to her and divulged news of the Annunciation. In the 1990s, beneath an adjacent souvenir shop, profoundly impressive remains of a bathhouse were discovered. Believed to be Roman, they would therefore have been built at around the time Jesus lived in Nazareth. Tours to the well-preserved remains can be organised through the **Cactus Gift Shop** (*Well Sq;* ✆ *6578539;* ⊕ *09.00–19.00 Mon–Sat; admission 120NIS for up to 4 people*)

Nazareth Souk As one of the largest markets in the country the souk is a well-trodden corner of the city, frequented by people from all over the Galilee. Its entrance is located at the top of Casanova Street where tight, winding cobbled lanes weave through a large part of the Old City, crammed to the hilt with stalls selling pretty much everything. A huge restoration project has seen the market returned to its original glory, where mansion houses, mosques, churches and squares compete for space.

The White Mosque (al-Abiad) The mosque was built between 1799 and 1808 to commemorate the end of the Ottoman governor al-Jazzar's heavy-handed rule. White was chosen to signify purity and the peaceful co-existence of religions in Nazareth. The mosque is located in the heart of the Old City and is easily identifiable by its colour and thin, elegant minaret.

Nazareth Village (✆ *6456042; www.nazarethvillage.com;* ⊕ *09.00–17.00 Mon–Sat; admission adult/child 50/22NIS*) The village is a reconstruction of Jewish Nazareth as it would have appeared during Jesus's time and provides a kitsch yet entertaining step back in time. Agricultural techniques, food presses, traditional costumes, food and even animals set this time capsule back 2,000 years.

AROUND NAZARETH

TEL MEGGIDO (ARMAGEDDON) (✆ *6590316; www.parks.org.il;* ⊕ *08.00–17.00 Sat–Thu, 08.00–16.00 Fri; admission adult/child 25/13NIS*) According to Christian tradition, Tel Meggido is the site where the battle for the world will take place and, judging by its tumultuous past, it seems a likely enough spot. Destroyed and rebuilt 25 times in its long existence, Meggido was a crucially important strategic site along the great trunk road leading trade caravans from Syria and Mesopotamia down to Egypt. Extensive excavations have revealed the remains of 20 phases of occupation through every period in Israel's history dating from 4000–400BCE, while its battle scars continue on into the 20th century and World War I. Perhaps rather poignantly, it was here that Israeli prime minister Levi Eshkol and Pope Paul VI chose to meet on the Pope's 1964 visit to Israel.

Meggido's location on the fertile plains of the Jezreel Valley would have given its rulers and occupants access to the Via Maris trade highway. It would have been here that the often miles-long camel caravans would have stopped off to trade in the city's abundant and flourishing marketplaces.

Today, the park provides but a mere glimpse into the city's prosperous and ever-changing past, and of the mighty battles that ensued here. Partial reconstructions of some of the major features of the park do help in putting together what can sometimes be, to the untrained eye, a mass of stones (tours can be arranged from the park office). A short but insightful video is screened at regular intervals in English or Hebrew at the request of the majority.

The Chariot City and tunnel remain the most impressive relics in the park. A 30m-long water system built during King Solomon's reign was constructed to enable the fortified city's occupants access to fresh water throughout times of conflict. Today, visitors can enter the tunnel by descending 183 steps, which are located at the southwest corner of the park. The tunnel leads outside the park boundaries, where a 600m walk will bring you back to the car park.

Getting there and away The park entrance is located approximately 2km from the Meggido junction on route 66. Bus 823 runs hourly between Nazareth (45mins/17.20NIS) and Tel Aviv (1hr 30mins/30.50NIS) and will stop at the Meggido junction if hailed. Buses 841, 830 and 835 running between Tel Aviv and Tiberias (1hr/26.50NIS) also stop there.

BEIT SHE'ARIM (*between Hashomrim & Hatishbi junctions;* \ *9831643; www.parks. org.il;* ⊕ *Apr–Sep 08.00–17.00; Oct–Mar 08.00—16.00 daily; admission adult/child 20/9NIS*) Extensive excavations that began in 1871 and have proceeded up until today, have revealed the ancient Jewish settlement of Beit She'arim and, more significantly to Jewish history, the underground cemetery built at its foot. The Sanhedrin – Jewish school of learning – was located here, and at its head was the much-revered Rabbi Yehuda HaNassi. After many years in Beit She'arim, Rabbi HaNassi relocated to the nearby city of Zippori, only to be returned posthumously in 220CE. Word of the rabbi's death spread the length and breadth of the Middle East and a fervent desire to be buried close to his grave became paramount to many. Beit She'arim hence became the holiest Jewish burial site throughout the Mishnaic and Talmudic periods.

The voluminous caves and countless graves shoehorned into every potential space that we see today are merely the tip of the iceberg of the possibly thousands who are buried in the surrounding hills. Large stone sarcophagi inscribed in Hebrew, Aramaic and Greek show Jewish symbols as well as secular images of figures and animals, and also families that derived from as far as southern Arabia and Syria. The catacombs are impressive and are certainly worth visiting. Cut out of the hillside, they contain dozens of sarcophagi, some caves being up to 30m deep and several metres high. Free tours, offered by volunteers from the nearby moshav, are certainly instrumental in making sense of the mounds of tombs and the intricate messages inscribed on them. Tours start at 10.00, 11.00 and 12.00 Sunday–Friday with an extra tour at 13.00 on Saturday.

Getting there and away The site is located off routes 75 and 722 between Hashomrim and Hatishbi junctions 20km southeast of Haifa. There is no direct transport to the park but bus 338 from Haifa Lev HaMifratz stops at nearby Kiryat Tivon from where it is a 2km walk to the entrance.

ZIPPORI (SEPPHORI) (✆ *6568272; www.parks.org.il;* ⊕ *08.00–17.00 Sat–Thu, 08.00–16.00 Fri; admission adult/child 25/13NIS)* Zippori was once a splendid city and a much-contested site throughout the Galilee region's dramatic past. Excavations that began in 1931 unearthed remains dating from the First Temple period, through the Roman conquest and Herod the Great's reign to the Byzantine period and beyond. Zippori was appointed capital of the Galilee region shortly after the Roman conquest in 63BCE and changed hands many times amidst fierce battles and revolts. It wasn't until the 3rd century CE that the Jews finally retook control of Zippori and it was during this time that textual and archaeological evidence points to the arrival of Rabbi Judah HaNassi and the Sanhedrin Jewish lawmakers. Rabbi Judah lived out his final 17 years here and it was during this time that, in c200CE, he drafted the Mishnah.

The Sanhedrin remained in Zippori until its relocation to Tiberias at the end of the 3rd century CE and the city's frequent appearance in the Talmud testifies to its significance in Jewish history. Zippori was razed to the ground by a violent earthquake in 363CE, shortly after the beginning of the Byzantine period and rapid spread of Christianity. The city was rebuilt and flourished as a Christian city – the population of which was still predominantly Jewish – until the beginning of the Arab period. Throughout the Crusader period, Arab revolt of 1936–39 and 1948 Arab–Israeli War, Zippori was contested, battled over and conquered.

Today the excavated ruins are fairly scanty. To the untrained eye there is little to be gleaned from the piles of stones and masonry walls, with the exception of the rather impressive mosaic floors and Roman theatre. The remains are best appreciated through an arranged tour, which can be organised through the park office. A circuitous route through the park's antiquities offers panoramic views over the surrounding area and takes you past relics of street patterns, a marketplace, bathhouses, Jewish and Christian ecclesiastical buildings and a Crusader fortress.

Getting there and away Bus 343 between Nazareth (10mins/6.40NIS) and Akko (1hr 30mins/26.50NIS) stops every 1½ hours at the Zippori Junction from where you will have a 4km walk to the entrance of the park. To reach the site by car from Nazareth head north out of the city on route 79 and turn right after 4km towards Moshav Zippori. Upon entering the moshav follow signs to the antiquities park.

CANA Today 8,500 people – 83% of whom are Muslim, 17% Christian – call Cana home. The small town is located approximately 8km north of Nazareth, and is a likely candidate for the biblical site of the same name, where Jesus performed his first miracle of turning water into wine. Jewish tradition also believes this to be the site of the tomb of the sage Rabbi Shimon ben Gamliel.

The town itself is characterised by several churches commemorating the miracle located on Churches Street, running through central Cana. The **Franciscan Wedding Church** (⊕ *08.00–12.00 & 14.00–18.00 Mon–Sat; admission free)*, was established in 1883, and is the traditional site of the home where Jesus performed his miracle. Next door, in the **Greek Orthodox Church of St George** visitors are shown an ancient-looking glass jar, purportedly – under Orthodox belief – one of the ten water containers involved in the miracle.

Further along Churches Street is the **Nathanael Chapel**. It was built towards the end of the 19th century in honour of Nathanael, later to become St Bartholomew, one of Jesus's most vocal opponents who later ended up being one of his disciples.

The ruins of the ancient village of Cana rest atop a nearby hill, which is only accessible by foot or 4x4. It is a demanding walk, but those who undertake the challenge will be rewarded by panoramic views of the southern Galilee region.

Getting there and away Bus 431 between Tiberias and Nazareth passes the town and will stop on request. From Nazareth, Nesiot buses 29 and 30 depart every 20 minutes. To reach Cana by car head north on route 754 for approximately 8km. The turning to the town is signposted on the right.

TIBERIAS

Tiberias is the hub of eastern Galilean life and often considered the capital of the region. Named in honour of the Roman emperor Tiberias, the city has seen its share of proverbial ups and downs. In more recent times, an extensive clean-up operation has been under way to create a Tiberias – pronounced Tverya in Hebrew – that offers more than tacky seaside attractions, shabby hotels and littered beaches. The project has seen some success and, while Jewish and Christian pilgrims never halted their yearly processions to the city, visitors now seem to want to stick around a little longer. While beaches in the near vicinity of urban areas are still overcrowded and littered in peak summer months, international restaurants, outdoor cafés and an improved standard of accommodation have gradually appeared. Tiberias has long been a top holiday spot with Israeli teenagers in search of a party atmosphere, and hence the school summer holiday months are the city's busiest. Yet pilgrims and partygoers have always seemed to co-exist in relative harmony in this city, where beer and the Bible are the main attractions for two very different kinds of visitors.

HISTORY Tiberias was founded in c20CE by Herod Antipas, son of Herod the Great, and the city was soon forcibly populated by reluctant Jews. Over time Tiberias became one of the country's four Holy Cities and was the seat of the Sanhedrin and centre of Jewish learning for many years after the Roman destruction of the Temple of Jerusalem. It was here that the Mishnah, which later grew into the Talmud – dictating Jewish civil and religious laws – was believed to have been compiled between the 3rd and 5th centuries CE.

The Jewish community continued to thrive throughout Byzantine and Arab rule, until the Middle Ages when wars and earthquakes ravaged the city and it fell into rapid decline. Throughout the crusades it was the central city of the Principality of Galilee in the Kingdom of Jerusalem until, in 1187 during the Battle of Hittin on the outskirts of Tiberias, Saladin defeated the Crusaders and the city was all but abandoned. It was at this time that the present-day city was established, just north of its ancestor.

In the 16th century, Suleiman the Magnificent returned Tiberias to the Jews until, in the 18th century, the Arab sheikh Daher el-Omar nominated Tiberias as capital of Galilean territory (which lasted until his assassination in 1775). The city prospered thanks to its abundance of fertile agricultural lands and mild climate and today continues to play a pivotal role in Galilean life and Israeli tourism.

GETTING THERE AND AWAY The central bus station [189 A5] is located down a small side road off HaYarden Street just past HaShiloah Street. Buses 961, 962 and 963 depart to and from Jerusalem hourly (2hrs45mins/48NIS) and buses 830, 835 and 841 every 20 minutes to and from Tel Aviv (2hrs 45mins/48NIS) with the 841 continuing to Kiryat Shmona (1hr/29NIS). Bus 430 departs every 20 minutes to Haifa

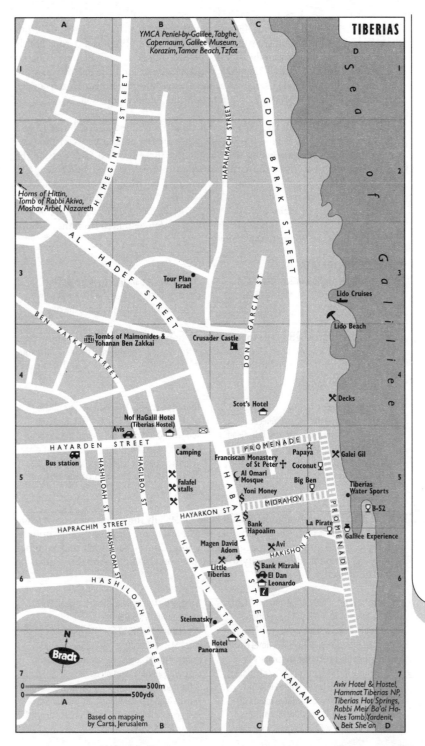

TIBERIAS

Sea

of

Galilee

YMCA Peniel-by-Galilee, Tabghe,
Capernaum, Galilee Museum,
Korazim, Tamar Beach, Tzfat

Horns of Hittin,
Tomb of Rabbi Akiva,
Moshav Arbel, Nazareth

HAMEGINIM STREET

HAPALMACH STREET

GDUD BARAK STREET

DONA GARCIA ST

AL - HADEF STREET

BEN ZAKKAI STREET

Tour Plan
Israel

Lido Cruises

Lido Beach

Tombs of Maimonides &
Yohanan Ben Zakkai

Crusader Castle

Decks

Scot's Hotel

Nof HaGalil Hotel
(Tiberias Hostel)

Avis

HAYARDEN STREET

Bus station

Camping

PROMENADE

Franciscan Monastery
of St Peter

Papaya

Galei Gil

Coconut

HASHILOAH ST

HAGILBOA ST

Falafel
stalls

Al Omari
Mosque

Big Ben

Tiberias
Water Sports

HABANIM

Yoni Money

B-52

MIDRAHOV

HAYARKON ST

HAPRACHIM STREET

Bank
Hapoalim

La Pirate

HASHILOAH STREET

Magen David
Adom

Avi

HAKISHON ST

PROMENADE

Galilee Experience

Little
Tiberias

Bank Mizrahi

El Dan

HAGALIL STREET

Leonardo

Steimatsky

Hotel
Panorama

N

Bradt

0   500m
0   500yds

KAPLAN BD

Aviv Hotel & Hostel,
Hammat Tiberias NP,
Tiberias Hot Springs,
Rabbi Meir Ba'al Ho-
Nes Tomb, Yardenit,
Beit She'an

Based on mapping
by Carta, Jerusalem

189

(1hr 15mins/26.50NIS) and bus 450 has regular services to Tzfat (1hr/22NIS). Bus 28 shuttles regularly to and from Beit Shean (40mins/24NIS). Bus 431 runs hourly between Tiberias and Nazareth (25mins/19NIS). Buses 15 and 19 leave Tiberias at 12.00, 13.25, 16.00 and 18.35 going anti-clockwise around the Sea of Galilee to Katzrin (1hr30mins/29NIS) stopping at the Tzemach junction near Deganya Alef, Lavnun Beach, Kursi junction, Ramot junction and Yehudiya junction.

GETTING AROUND With the exception of those mentioned above, buses to and from sites and beaches around the Sea of Galilee are few and far between and taxis can be exorbitant if you're using them regularly. There is a taxi rank outside the Leonardo Hotel next to the tourist information centre. The most convenient and economical means of getting around is by renting a car from one of the agencies in the city. **El Dan** (*HaBanim St;* `6722831;` ⊕ *08.00–17.00 Sun–Thu, 08.00–13.00 Fri*) and **Avis** [189 C6] (*2 Ha'amakim St;* `6722766;` ⊕ *08.00–17.00 Sun–Thu, 08.00–14.00 Fri*) rent cars from 150NIS per day. Bicycles can be rented from the **HaGalil Hotel** [189 B5] (see *Where to stay* below).

TOURIST INFORMATION
ℹ️ Tourist information office [189 C6] 9 HaBanim St; `6725666;` ⊕ 08.00–16.00 Sun–Thu, 08.00–19.00 Fri. Located in the small archaeological park directly in front of the Leonardo Hotel. Certainly worth a visit before embarking on excursions around the city.

LOCAL TOUR OPERATORS The tourist information office has a wealth of knowledge on local tour guides and they also organise a two-hour free walking tour of Tiberias. Tours leave from the tourist information office at 09.00 on Sundays and Mondays and 18.00 on Thursdays.

Lido Cruises Lido Beach; `6721538.` Operate 30min cruises around the Sea of Galilee. Schedules change from day to day so call ahead to find out sailing times. During the summer months there are regular sailings so it is possible to just show up at the dock.

Tour Plan Israel 18 Golani St; `6716850;` e info@tourplanisrael.com; ⊕ 08.00–18.00 Sun–Thu. Offers day tours around the Sea of Galilee (departs 08.30 Tues; $119), to the Golan Heights and Upper Galilee (departs 08.30 Wed; $119) and to Tzfat, Meron and Peki'in (departs 08.30 Thu; $119).

⌂ WHERE TO STAY Accommodation has been drastically improved over recent years and now there is a good range of higher-end hotels, some good mid-range options and some much improved budget choices too. Come the Jewish and summer holidays all are booked to capacity so if you plan on visiting around those times be sure to book well in advance.

⌂ Scot's Hotel [189 C4] (69 rooms) 1 Gdud Barak St; `6710710;` f 6710711; e scottie@ netvision.net.il; www.scotshotels.co.il. The Scot's Hotel is the jewel in Tiberias's hotel crown. Built as a hospital by Scottish missionary Dr David Torrance in 1894, the castle-like building today acts as a 5-star hotel. While all rooms are faultless, the so-called 'antique rooms' are especially charming (& considerably pricier). Manicured lawns, a swimming pool, lake views & a gourmet restaurant clinch the deal. Prices based on HB. **$$$$$**

⌂ Leonardo [189 C6] (198 rooms) Gdud Barak St; `6700800;` e reservations.leotib@ leonardo-hotels.com; www.leonardo-hotels. com. With a prime location on the seafront right in the midst of the bars & restaurants. In keeping with its high standard rooms are pleasant & well equipped & there is a pool, private beach & restaurant. **$$$$**

🏠 **YMCA Peniel-by-Galilee** (13 rooms)
Route 90 north; ☏ 6720685; www.ymca-galilee.co.il. Just 5km up the coast from Tiberias is this secluded YMCA hostel. Nestled amidst palm trees & shady gardens, the 1920s stone building exudes Middle Eastern charm. Located on the shore of the Sea of Galilee it has private beach access & hot spring pool as well as a Middle Eastern terrace restaurant. Rooms are simple but with views like these you won't be looking at them anyway. All northbound buses stop directly outside. **$$$**

🏠 **Aviv Hotel & Hostel** (90 beds)
2 Hanoter St; ☏ 6712272; e avivhotel@walla.com; ilh.hostels-israel.com. Located a short walk from the centre & offering a selection of clean, fresh rooms ranging from dorms to dbl & twin rooms. Facilities inc Wi-Fi, laundry & tour bookings. Dorm bed (60NIS). **$$**

🏠 **Hotel Panorama** [189 C7] (37 rooms)
HaGalil St; ☏ 6724811. Not the most charismatic hotel in the city, & in need of a lick of paint but offers decently priced dbl rooms, nice sea views & good central access. **$$**

🏠 **Nof HaGalil Hotel** [189 B5] (Tiberias Hostel) (18 rooms) Rabin Sq; ☏ 6792611; e m11111@012.net.il. Don't judge a book by its cover springs to mind here as the outside of the building is shabby & ramshackle but inside is a hostelling treat. Both the 4-bed dorm rooms & private rooms come complete with shower, AC, TV & fridge & the hostel is friendly & clean & offers bike rental, travel information, internet access (10NIS/30mins) & a bar & lounge area. Dorms 85NIS. **$$**

🍴 **WHERE TO EAT** Tiberias's restaurants have improved over recent years, but are still not on the same level as those in most other cities. Most places serve up a pleasant grilled St Peter's fish, the Sea of Galilee's local produce, or grilled meat and salad, which are fine once or twice. The pedestrianised HaKishon Street is lined with cafés, restaurants and late-night bars and is a good place to soak up the summer resort atmosphere. For light bites there are falafel stalls, bakeries and pizzerias dotted around the main streets, especially along north HaGalil Street.

🍴 **Scot's Hotel Restaurant** [189 C4] 1 Gdud Barak St; ☏ 6710710; www.scotshotel.co.il. Enjoying a sunset dinner on the terrace of the regal Scot's Hotel Restaurant is a true Tiberias treat, with views over the fragrant gardens & still waters of the Sea of Galilee. The menu changes regularly to incorporate seasonal specialities but expect fresh, home-grown vegetables & herbs, St Peter's fish & a selection of speciality cheeses. To top it off, the wine cellar is first rate & offers some local boutique bottles. 3-course meal **$$$$$**

🍴 **Decks** [189 D4] Gdud Barak St; ☏ 6721538; ⏱ 19.00–late Sun–Thu, end of Shabbat–late Sat. Kosher. Picturesque location on a wooden deck jutting out into the lake, this restaurant specialises in expertly prepared meats & fish grilled over wood renowned for its aromatic properties. The lamb, duck & local fish are highly recommended. **$$$$**

🍴 **Galei Gil** [189 D5] Promenade; ☏ 6720699; ⏱ 11.00–24.00 daily. With perfect views over the lake & a menu chocked full of grilled meats, locally caught fish & salads, this is a great place to while away an evening. **$$$$**

🍴 **Little Tiberias** [189 C6] HaKishon St; ☏ 6792806; ⏱ 12.00–24.00 daily. Cosy, home-style cooking in the middle of the busy pedestrian thoroughfare. Wide selection of meats & seafood & some cheaper pasta dishes if the budget doesn't quite run to the seafood platter. **$$$$**

🍴 **Avi Restaurant** [189 C6] Hakison; ☏ 6724384; ⏱ 12.00–24.00 Sun–Thu, end of Shabbat–24.00 Sat. Simple décor, but hearty, well-priced Middle Eastern meals & a pleasant location on the pedestrian walkway. **$$$**

ENTERTAINMENT AND NIGHTLIFE Tiberias's nightlife centres on the pedestrianised HaKishon Street leading down to the seafront. Throughout the busy summer months, this is where people congregate to chatter noisily amidst the pumping bar sounds, street vendors and abundance of late-night restaurants.

♀ **Big Ben** [189 D5] Midrahov; ✆6722248; ⏱ 12.00–late daily. An old Tiberias favourite, Big Ben pulls in the crowds with decently priced beer, a chilled-out atmosphere & plenty of live televised sporting events. Standard pub food fills a hole even if it's not particularly exotic. $$

☆ **Papaya** [189 D5] Promenade; ✆054 1241200; ⏱ 17.00–late daily. Although it has a great lakeside location, this isn't what most people come here for. Cocktails, karaoke, frenetic dancing & an open-air, Hawaiian tropics feel attract hordes of partygoers in summer.

Other popular bars to check out in the area include **La Pirate** [189 D6] where Midrahov and the promenade meet, **Coconut** [189 D5] next to Papaya on the promenade and **B-52** [189 D5] next to the Galilee Experience jetty.

SHOPPING
Camping [189 B5] Corner of HaGalil & HaYarden sts; ✆6723972; ⏱ 10.00–13.00 & 16.00–19.00 Sun–Thu, 10.00–13.00 Fri. Well-stocked camping & hiking equipment shop.
Steimatsky [189 C6] HaGalil Shopping Centre, HaGalil St; ✆6791288; ⏱ 08.00–19.30 Sun–Thu, 08.00–14.00 Fri. Good selection of English books, magazines & newspapers.
Galilee Experience Gift Shop [189 D6] (see Galilee Experience below). Has a big selection of souvenirs.

OTHER PRACTICALITIES Tiberias is a small and easily navigable city, with an even smaller and more easily navigable centre, which radiates out from the seafront promenade. Parallel to the sea is HaBanim Street where most services and facilities are located.

Emergency
Fire ✆102 or 6791222
Police station ✆100 or 6792444

Money
$ **Bank Hapoalim** [189 C5] 3 HaBanim St; ✆03 6532407; ⏱ 08.30–13.15 Sun & Tue/Wed, 08.30–13.00 & 16.00–18.30 Mon & Thu
$ **Mizrakhi Bank** [189 C6] Corner of HaKishon & HaBanim sts; ⏱ 09.00–13.30 Sun–Thu, 16.00–18.00 Mon–Wed, 08.30–12.00 Fri

$ **Yoni Money Currency Exchange** [189 C5] 2 HaBanim St; ✆6720017; ⏱ 08.30–19.00 Sun–Thu

Post
✉ **Post office** [189 B5] Corner of HaBanim & HaYarden sts; ✆6790066; ⏱ 08.00–18.00 Sun & Thu, 08.00–12.30 & 15.30–18.00 Mon & Tue, 08.00–13.30 Wed, 08.00–12.00 Fri. Changes travellers' cheques.

Medical
✚ **Magen David Adom (1st Aid)** [189 C6] 1 HaKishon St; ✆6790101/111
✚ **Porriya Hospital** 7km from Tiberias centre. Bus 39 from the central bus station stops outside.

✚ **Superpharm** 42 HaYarden St; ✆6676663; ⏱ 08.00–22.30 Sun–Thu, 08.00–20.00 Fri, 10.00–23.00 Sat

WHAT TO SEE
Tombs As the seat of the Sanhedrin and home to numerous Talmudic scholars over the years, Tiberias's hills are scattered with the tombs of influential men who had a profound impact on Judaism throughout the 2nd and 3rd centuries. Modest dress is

required to enter all and *yarmulkes* for men can be obtained at the entrances. About 300m from the northern end of HaGalil Street are several tombs including that of **Maimonides** [189 A4] (also known as Rambam). Born in Spain in 1135, he fled his country from persecution and travelled to Cairo where he worked as Saladin's personal physician. During this time he rose to rabbi and leader of the Jews in Egypt and made significant contributions to the Mishnah. After his death in 1204 his body was transported to Tiberias. There is very little to see at the tomb except the 14 pillars encircling it, which represent the 14 sections of the Mishnah Torah. Plans to improve the site are under consideration in an attempt to raise Maimonides's tomb to the status that other tombs enjoy. One such tomb belongs to **Rabbi Meir Ba'al Ha-Nes**, whose grandiose shrine is on the hill behind the city. Tradition has it that illnesses can be cured in the hot springs adjacent to the tomb. Near the tomb of Maimonides rests the **tomb of Yohanan Ben Zakkai** [189 A4] who was responsible for the relocation of the seat of the Sanhedrin from Jerusalem following its destruction in 70CE. The story of his escape from the capital hidden within a coffin, only to emerge in front of Roman general Vespasian, is legendary. Upon announcing to Vespasian that he was now the Caesar following the death of the Roman leader, he was granted one wish: he chose to found the Jewish learning centre, which was to become the Sanhedrin. In the areas now swallowed up by the modern city's sprawl is the **tomb of Rabbi Ben Akiva**, located just off the main road near the police station. Ben Akiva, one of the rabbis who is credited in the Talmud as being amongst those who carried Rabbi Yohanan Ben Zakkai out of Jerusalem, believed Bar Kochba to be the Messiah and was finally executed after his rising in 135CE .

Other sights

Crusader castle [189 C4] The dilapidated remains of the 12th-century castle are on the northern edge of the Old Town and worth a visit if only for the views over the lake. The castle, the remains of which are still visible today, was rebuilt in the local black basalt stone in 1738 by Daher el-Omar.

Franciscan Monastery of St Peter [189 C5] The apse of the monastery was designed in the form of a ship's bow, representing Peter's fishing boat. It was built towards the end of the 19th century over remains of the Crusader castle. It is located southeast from the Crusader castle towards the promenade.

Horns of Hittin To put ancient Tiberias into perspective, the somewhat exerting hike of approximately one hour to the top of the hill allows for views over the entire Galilee region and beyond into present-day Jordan. It was here that Saladin defeated the Crusaders in 1187, signalling the beginning of the end for the Crusader Kingdom in the Holy Land. It is also an important Druze gathering site. The trail starts at the main road leading west out of the city or can be reached by bus 42.

Tiberias Hot Springs (*Eliezer Kaplan Bd;* ✆ *6728580; www.chameytveria.co.il;* ⊕ *08.00–20.00 Sun/Mon & Wed, 08.00–22.00 Tue & Thu, 08.00–16.00 Fri, 08.30– 16.00 Sat*) Seventeen different springs emerge here and a whole menu of treatments and massages is offered. There are indoor and outdoor mineral pools, several restaurants and a fitness centre. Opposite the complex is the **Hammat Tiberias National Park** (✆ *6725287; www.parks.org.il;* ⊕ *Apr–Sep 08.00–17.00; Oct–Mar 08.00–16.00 daily; admission adult/child 13/7NIS*) which pays homage to the 17 natural springs that played a crucial part in the development of Tiberias. Throughout the Roman period thousands of people came to bathe in the therapeutic waters that flowed from the ground, and a large synagogue was built on the site indicating that it played a central role in the proceedings of the Sanhedrin. Within the ruins is an ornate mosaic, the oldest in Israel.

The Midrahov [189 C5] This is the place (a pedestrian walkway) where it all happens. Tourists can choose to relax in one of the countless bars, cafés or restaurants, soak up the sun, sea and spirituality of the lake or partake in one of the various activities. Boat trips can sometimes be organised from the dock although there is no set timetable for their departure. The tourist information office will be able to tell you what's what with respect to boat-trip departures on specific days. For those of us not able to walk on water, self-drive motorboats can be rented (30mins/120NIS) from **Tiberias Water Sports** (*Midrahov dock;* ✆ *052 2692664*). Banana boats, water skiing and a range of other watersports are available from the offices on the dock throughout summer.

The Galilee Experience [189 D6] (✆ *6723620;* ⊕ *09.00–23.00 Sun–Thu, 09.00– 15.00 Fri; www.thegalileeexperience.com; admission adult/child 25/20NIS*) Located on the second floor of the marina building, it has regular showings of a 38-minute movie depicting 4,000 years of Galilean history. There is also an impressively stocked gift shop and café.

BEACHES Tiberias's beaches leave a lot to be desired and people looking for the quintessential Sea of Galilee swimming experience are better off heading to the beaches further along the coast or on the eastern shore (see below). If you decide to opt for a beach closer to home then the **Gai Beach** belonging to the **Gai Beach Resort Spa Hotel** is your best option. The **Gai Beach Water Park** (✆ *6700713; Passover–Oct 09.30–17.00 daily; admission 60NIS*) is a big hit with kids and has an assortment of slides and pools as well as beach access. Hotel guests get free entry.

THE SEA OF GALILEE (LAKE KINNERET)

While Tiberias itself is not an unpleasant place to spend a couple of days, most visitors use it as a jumping-off point to the sights around the Sea of Galilee. Steeped in New Testament history, the sea was the site of many of Jesus's miracles, with small churches dotting the shoreline commemorating these events. For hundreds of years Christian pilgrims have made their way to the gently lapping shores of the Sea of Galilee (known in Hebrew as 'the Kinneret') to soak up the abounding tranquillity, gaze down at ancient lands and walk in Jesus's footsteps. Today is no different, and despite the scores of tour buses that make regular stops along the sea, it has managed to avoid a mass-produced, over-touristy feel. This, however, doesn't apply to the Sea of Galilee's beaches which are extremely popular with young Israeli teenagers. The following sights have been arranged in a clockwise direction starting from Tiberias, and recommended accommodation has been included under each site where appropriate. Beach campsites (see below) are good budget options, especially on weekdays and out of the school holiday season.

GETTING THERE AND AWAY Buses 15 and 19 makes an anti-clockwise circuit of the Sea of Galilee stopping at the Ohalo junction for Yardenit, the Tzemach junction for Kibbutz Deganya Alef, Ein Gev Beach, Lavnun Beach and the Kursi junction before continuing to the Golan Heights. Buses 59, 63, 450, 841 and

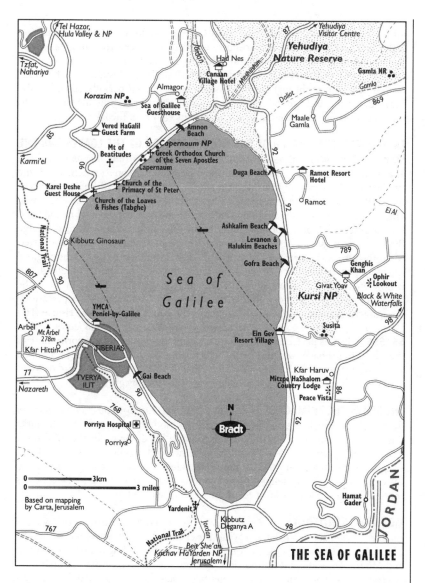

THE SEA OF GALILEE

963 head north hourly, stopping at Ginosaur junction (for the Galilee Museum) and Kfar Nahum junction. Buses 841 and 963 continue on to Korazim junction (2km from national park). There are no buses to sites along the north shore so get off northbound buses at the Kfar Nahum junction and take a delightful walk eastwards to Tabghe (2km), the Church of the Multiplication, Mount of Beatitudes, Capernaum and Amnon Beach.

THE GALILEE MUSEUM AT GINOSAUR (*Kibbutz Ginosaur;* ✎ *6727700; www. jesusboatmuseum.com;* ⊕ *08.00–17.00 Sun–Thu, 08.00–14.00 Fri, 08.00–16.00 Sat; admission adult/child 20/15NIS*) Also known as the Yigal Alon Centre in memory of the founding member of the nearby Kibbutz Ginosaur (and later deputy prime

minister), the Galilee Museum comprises several sections. The most interesting is the ancient Galilee boat, a 1st-century wooden ship excavated from the nearby shores. An audio-visual presentation depicts the arduous task of raising and preserving the 8.2m-long ship, often dubbed the Jesus Boat. Upstairs are exhibitions on Galilean culture throughout the Mishnah and Talmud periods, as well as the Yigal Alon remembrance room offering a more personal peek into his life. Head to the roof of the five-storey building for a fabulous view over the lake.

TABGHE AND THE CHURCH OF THE MULTIPLICATION OF THE LOAVES AND THE FISHES (08.30–17.00 Mon–Sat, 10.00–17.00 Sun; admission free; modest dress)
The church's rather long-winded title does in fact sum it up pretty nicely. This is the site believed to be where Jesus performed one of his most well-known miracles: the Multiplication of the Loaves and Fishes and the Feeding of the Five Thousand. The church, located in the minute village of Tabghe, was consecrated in 1982 and is a far descendant of the original, built in the 4th century CE. Remains of a large Byzantine monastery, devastated during the Arab Conquest, were discovered when the area was excavated in the 1980s. After restoration to its Byzantine glory (including sections of the original figurative mosaic, the church's highlight) it is now one of the top spots along the sea's pilgrimage route. Tradition has it the block of limestone under the altar is 'the table of the lord', where Jesus performed the miracle. Located just south of Tabghe is the **Karei Deshe Guest House (HI)** (65 rooms; 6720601; e kdeshe@iyha.org.il; www.iyha.org.il; 100NIS less on w/days **$$–$$$**) which is perfectly located for exploring the sites along the north shore of the lake. Rooms have two, four or six beds (dorms **$**), air conditioning, television and en-suite bathroom. Kosher breakfast is included; sprawling lawns lead down to private beach access; often fully booked long in advance by groups.

CHURCH OF THE PRIMACY OF ST PETER (08.00–12.00 & 14.00–17.00; admission free; modest dress)
Just along from Tabghe, the modest Franciscan church marks the site where, tradition has it, Jesus appeared to his disciples for the third time, and where he confirmed the Apostle Peter. The black basalt chapel is small and simple and pales in contrast to its more elaborate ecclesiastical counterparts along the coast. Aside from its religious connotations there isn't an awful lot here, but its tranquillity and beachside location make it a worthwhile stop.

MOUNT OF BEATITUDES (08.00–12.00 & 14.40–17.00; admission free; 5NIS per car to enter car park; modest dress)
While the exact location of Jesus's Sermon on the Mount is a much-contested topic, with potential sites including the Horns of Hittin and Mount Arbel, Mount Eremos just up from the Church of the Multiplication has been the site of commemoration and pilgrimage for the past 1,600 years. With funding from Italy, more specifically from Benito Mussolini, whose name plaque was later removed from the doorstep, a beautiful Catholic church was built in 1938. The church oozes numerical symbolism, its octagonal shape representing the eight virtues. Within the church hangs Pope Paul VI's cloak, a memento of his visit to Israel in 1964. Despite the regular stream of tour buses clogging the car park, the church and its shaded, serene gardens remain a quiet and tranquil place of worship.

From the car park, offering a fabulous view southwards over the ancient biblical lands and Sea of Galilee, a somewhat Herculean but worthwhile walk is possible. A steep path leads downhill towards the lake, likely part of the great trunk road coming from Damascus. Rain makes the path extremely slippery so you will need sturdy walking shoes.

CAPERNAUM A little confusingly, there are two sites along the lakeside that go by the name Capernaum. In fact, the 5km stretch of coast that begins at Tabghe is classified under the umbrella title **Capernaum National Park**. The park's headquarters (⏲ *08.00–16.00 Sat–Thu, 08.00–15.00 Fri; admission free*) form the northern boundary from where there is a beautiful view across the lake towards the Golan Heights. Privately hired boats leave the dock at irregular intervals but if there is space and if you talk nicely to the captain he might let you hop on board. Boats normally head towards Ein Gev Beach on the eastern shore. Alternatively, you can take one of several truly serene and picturesque walks along a stretch of lake that remains today as it did hundreds of years ago. The opulent, red-domed **Greek Orthodox Church of the Seven Apostles** (⏲ *08.00–12.00; admission free; modest dress*) can be accessed by the path leading west from the car park. A little further south of the church is the archaeological site of **Capernaum** (⏲ *08.00–17.00 daily; admission 3NIS; modest dress*), best known through the New Testament as the centre of Jesus's Galilean activities after his departure from Nazareth. Today a church stands over an earlier Byzantine one, erected over the spot believed to be the birthplace of St Peter. A little north of this are the remains of a once grand, white limestone synagogue, possibly dating to the 3rd century CE.

Just off the Sea of Galilee in the little village of Almagor is the **Sea of Galilee Guesthouse** (*Moshav Almagor;* ☎ *6930063;* e *seaofgalileegh@gmail.com; dorm 100NIS;* **$$$**), which is a great budget- and mid-range option in the area. Cosy, homely double rooms have television, air conditioning, kitchenette and a small table and chairs, while dormitories are spacious, clean and comfortable. Camping is also permitted in the spacious grounds.

KORAZIM NATIONAL PARK About 5km north of the lake between the villages of Korazim (also spelt Corazim and Chorazim) and Almagor lie some impressive archaeological remains (☎ *6934982; www.parks.org.il;* ⏲ *Apr–Sep 08.00–17.00; Oct–Mar 08.00–16.00 daily; admission adult/child 20/9NIS*) sadly often overlooked by many visitors to the region. The ruins are spread over a broad area and include residential buildings, streets, ritual baths, olive presses (some of which have been reconstructed) and the site's *pièce de résistance*, a large, highly ornate synagogue. The city is recorded from the Second Temple period and is mentioned in the Mishnah and Talmud as a flourishing agricultural hub. Korazim also appears in the New Testament in conjunction with Capernaum and Bethsaida as the three cities condemned by Jesus for their lack of belief in his preachings.

Just off the Korazim junction is the lovely **Vered HaGalil Guest Farm** (*route 90 north;* ☎ *6935785;* e *vered@veredhagalil.co.il; www.veredhagalil.com; up to half off-season midweek.* **$$$$**), which offers country wood cabins and suites complete with jacuzzi and a lovely deck perfect for morning coffee. A delightful rustic yet elegant **restaurant** (⏲ *08.00–22.00 Sun–Wed, 08.00–23.00 Thu–Sat.* **$$$$$**) serves sumptuous grilled meats and fish on a wisteria-covered terrace. The farm offers guided horseriding treks, ATV tours, a café and spa, which are open to non-guests as well.

BEACHES The pebbly beaches around the Sea of Galilee have long been a top destination for holidaying families and groups of teenagers who come all summer long to pitch their tents, light up a barbecue and soak in the mild waters of the lake. While pollution and plummeting water levels are two of the problems facing the lake, thankfully the one that aggrieved the Israelis most – the illegal privatisation of the beaches – has been resolved. Now almost all beaches are once again public, with a fixed entry rate of 57NIS. Unfortunately it has also meant that swimming is prohibited at almost all the beaches, as there are no longer lifeguards on duty. While almost all the beaches provide access for the set fee, there are still charges for camping. As a general rule, the beaches on the eastern shore are considerably better than the dirty, litter-strewn ones around Tiberias.

Amnon Beach (☉ *Apr–Sep; admission free*) Lovely beach located along the quieter northern strip of the sea that is one of the few privately owned beaches left. Despite the fact that swimming is not permitted, there are windsurfing rentals and toilet and shower facilities. **Camping** is possible (120NIS per car). The Kinneret Trail passes through the beach and from here a path leads to Capernaum (2km) and the Jordan Estuary (2km).

Duga Beach (*55NIS per car/free on foot*) Perfect for some quiet Sea of Galilee reflection. Swimming is prohibited and there aren't any grassy areas but the beach is not crowded, is clean and undeveloped.

Ashalim Beach (*55NIS per car/free on foot*) Despite its huge popularity and crowded car park, the beach is probably the wildest of all the Sea of Galilee beaches. A path leads through sand dunes down to the shore (no swimming) where kite surfers by their dozens fly through the sky and whizz across the waves. There are plenty of picnic spots but very few facilities.

Levanon (Lavnun) & Halukim beaches (⊙ *6732044; 55NIS per car/free on foot*) Located right next to each other, these beaches are popular with big groups of raucous teenagers in summer holidays, but lovely and quiet the rest of the time. Facilities include a small pebbly swimming beach with lifeguard, watersports, grass area for **camping** (included in the entry price), toilet and shower facilities and a snack-food kiosk.

Gofra Beach (*Admission 70NIS per car/free on foot*) Family-oriented beach where sound systems are prohibited. Swimming is also prohibited but the area is clean and has bathroom facilities.

Ein Gev Beach If your budget stretches to a night at the **Ein Gev Holiday Resort Village** ((*184 rooms*) ⊙*6659800;* e *resort@eingev.org.il; www.eingev.com.* **$$$$**), this is probably the Sea of Galilee's most beautiful, albeit private, beach. The four-star complex is set with green lawns and eucalyptus trees on the edge of the lake, and spacious rooms come with all the trimmings. Just south of the resort village are several kilometres of shady beaches, which are particularly pleasant midweek when there are fewer sun seekers (admission 14NIS pp).

YARDENIT (⊙ *6759111;* e *yardenit@kinneret.org.il; www.yardenit.com;* ☉ *08.00–18.00 Sat–Thu, 08.00–16.00 Fri (closes 1hr earlier in winter); admission free*) Just south of the lake, Yardenit is the traditional Christian baptismal site on the Jordan River. The strikingly green, fish-laden waters trickle through the northern valleys only to end up in the over-developed site of Yardenit. While the site has an obvious religious and spiritual draw for many, baptism by bulk seems a more apt description than peaceful confirmation. The site has, however, opened up the surrounding areas, so it is possible – and recommended – to get away from the crowds, gift shops and food outlets and walk along the banks of the river for some getting to one with nature, history and quiet reflection. While the site may be a little on the touristy

Mount Arbel's silhouette is one of the most unmistakable landmarks in the southern Galilee region. Its flat summit and drastically sloping edge is the result of a violent earthquake that shattered it into the two separate mountains we see today. A lookout at its peak proffers views over the Galilee region towards the Golan Heights, but even for seasoned hikers, getting to the top is difficult (but possible). The trail starts in the Valley of Doves at 206m below sea level and ascends directly up the sheer face of the cliff for 384m. Steps and handrails have been erected by the Israel Nature and National Parks Authority, which does ease things somewhat. Vertigo sufferers however would be best advised to drive up through Moshav Arbel and walk the short distance to the summit. Many believe that the graves of some of Jacob's children – whose 12 sons comprised the Tribes of Israel – are located here, in the caves that dot the cliff face. The caves – also used as shelter by Jews throughout the Roman and Greek periods – were again inhabited in the 17th century by the Druze. The scanty ruins of an ancient Jewish settlement include what little is left of a 4th-century synagogue dug into the cliff.

In the nearby moshav Arbel the excellent **Arbel Guesthouse** (6794919; e sara52@012.net.il; www.4shavit.com. **$$**) is a great choice just outside the hubbub of Tiberias in the beautiful Galilee countryside. It is a lovingly run family place that has a real community feel. There are five apartments that can comfortably house between two and eight people and each has kitchenette, en-suite, air conditioning and television. There is also a small swimming pool and lovely gardens.

side, a visit during a service, where up to 1,000 pilgrims clothed in white robes stand knee-deep in the river, is anything but touristy, and is a moving experience whether you're a believer or not. Call in advance for baptismal bookings.

KIBBUTZ DEGANYA ALEF Often referred to as the 'mother of kibbutzim', this is Israel's founding collective farm settlement, located to the east of Yardenit. It was established in 1910 during the Ottoman rule by 12 Jews from surrounding areas.

In 2006, the kibbutz decided to go 'private', relinquishing their long-standing collective system and opting for the increasingly popular style of living that allows people to seek jobs and own property. The small **Deganya Alef Museum and Courtyard** (6608410/053 749102 (for guided tours); ⊕ 09.00–12.00 Sun–Thu; admission free), built inside what was the original dining room, depicts the life and times of this small but nationally renowned kibbutz (ask for an English transcript of the information boards at reception). A destroyed Syrian tank remains in the grounds serving as a reminder of the 1948 Arab–Israeli War.

Several eminent Zionist names crop up in Deganya's past, many of whom are interred in the cemetery. Amongst these are the national poet Rachel, A D Gordon (an early Zionist figure) and General Moshe Dayan (general, politician and the kibbutz's second-born child). Albert Einstein and his wife also paid Deganya a visit.

AROUND TIBERIAS AND THE SEA OF GALILEE

KOCHAV HAYARDEN NATIONAL PARK (BELVOIR) (*Yissahar Ridge, 15km north of Beit She'an;* 6581766; www.parks.org.il; ⊕ 08.00–17.00 Sat–Thu, 08.00–16.00

Fri (closes 1hr earlier in winter); admission adult/child 20/9NIS) It is immediately apparent when climbing the steep, winding road of the Yissahar Ridge up to the Kochav HaYarden Crusader castle why such a site was chosen. With breathtaking views over the Jordan Valley, it offered strategic and defence capabilities that surpassed anywhere else in the region and thus became one of the most important fortresses in the country. Today, the heavily moated castle has been fully excavated, the only such example from the Crusader period in Israel.

Though it was inhabited for a mere 21 years (1168–89), other residents have called Kochav HaYarden their home for a lot longer. Egyptian vultures, indigenous to the area, have lived in the Galilee and Golan regions for centuries. Problems of farmers illegally poisoning calf carcases against predators, however, has led to severe decreases in their numbers. A sanctuary, erected 30m left of the castle, has given home and hope to several crippled birds. In 2007, a rare birth was celebrated, the baby chick destined for the wild when strong enough.

Getting there and away Getting there without a car is not easy. The steep 6km uphill walk from the main road is not for the faint-hearted and hitchhiking from the bottom is more realistic. Bus 28 from Tiberias to Beit She'an will drop you off on the main road at the small junction. By car from Tiberias head south on route 90 for approximately 12km and turn right at the Kochav HaYarden junction. Follow the road 6km up the ridge turning left at the T-junction at the top.

MOUNT TABOR, AL-SHIBLI AND KFAR TAVOR Mount Tabor is the most easily recognisable feature in the Jezreel Valley landscape. Almost completely symmetrical, the 405m-high domed mountain affords staggering views of the valley and surrounding areas. The mountain holds importance in both Christian and Jewish biblical history, although the scores of pilgrims who make the regular trip are predominantly Christian. While hotly contested, the **Church of the Transfiguration** (⊕ *08.00–12.00 & 14.00–17.00 Sun–Fri; admission free; modest dress*), holding pride of place on the summit, is the site many believe to be where Jesus was recognised as the Son of God. Jewish tradition places the battle between Deborah and Barak and Sisera on the slopes of the mountain. Cars and buses are no longer permitted up the road so the options are by foot or bicycle – both quite exerting. Walkers can ascend using the 4,300 steps built in the 4th century CE for pilgrims.

Ascend Mount Tabor through the Bedouin village of **Al-Shibli**, a dusty, rather nondescript place whose friendly residents are descended from a nomadic tribe who made Mount Tabor their permanent home. While many have adopted a 21st-century lifestyle, **Tabor's Tent** (\ *6766195;* ⊕ *daily 09.00–midnight. $$$*) provides a glimpse into this fascinating culture with demonstrations on making pitta, black coffee and herbal medicines. Simple, reasonably priced meals are served under the tent's canopy and it is possible to spend a communal night sleeping on the cushions and mats.

Catering to the abundance of hiking and cycling trails in this area is one of the most popular hostels in the country, located in the pleasant village of **Kfar Tavor** 2km north of the turn-off to Mount Tabor on route 65. The **HooHa Cyclist's House** (*(7 rooms) 7 Ha'charuvim St; Kfar Tavor;* \ *777080542; www. hooha.co.il; (200NIS less midweek); dorms 150NIS. $$$*) is fully geared towards those arriving on two wheels or two feet and offers a huge pool, bicycle storage, repairs and rental, cycling guides, free internet and spa and massage services. There is also a big garden, fully equipped kitchen and library. It is exceptionally popular so book ahead.

Getting there and away The village of Kfar Tavor is located just north of the turn-off to Mount Tabor on route 65 between Afula and the Golani Junction. By car from Nazareth or Tiberias make your way to the Golani junction on route 77 turning south onto route 65. Continue south to the Kfar Tavor junction. The mountain road will be signposted on the right. The road north of Shibli is steep, narrow and badly paved but traversable with caution. Buses 835, 962, 841 and 442 run regularly between Afula (for Nazareth) and Tiberias, stopping in Kfar Tavor at the base of the mountain. Non-express buses 841 and 442 will drop you at the Kfar Tavor junction for walking (or hitching) up the mountain, or at the following Gazit junction for the short walk to Shibli.

BEIT SHE'AN NATIONAL PARK (\ *6587189; www.parks.org.il;* ⊕ *08.00–17.00 Sun–Thu, 08.00–16.00 Fri, 08.00–17.00 Sat (closes 1hr earlier in winter); admission adult/child 25/13NIS)* Beit She'an was put on the ancient map owing to its strategic importance along the great north–south trade route, with the area's abundant fertile lands an added incentive for residents, who first settled in the 5th century BCE. Today the town of Beit She'an is a rather unappealing place. A small, unprosperous settlement, it seems to escape being forgotten only through the extremely impressive national archaeological park situated on its fringes.

The remains are awe-inspiring. Beit She'an's timeline spans 4,500 years, the decades following the Roman conquest truly its glory days when it became one of ten cities that formed the Decapolis, a federated alliance, and the only one west of the Jordan River. It flourished through Hadrian's reign and, after the Bar Kochba revolt, under Antonius Pius and Marcus Aurelius. Rapid and extravagant development saw the construction of statues, governmental buildings and after the adoption of Christianity, the amphitheatre, bathhouses and fountains, which remain Beit She'an's most striking features. The enormous amphitheatre is in fact but a fraction of its original size and is today honoured by live summertime concerts held within it. The new **She'an Nights** *(every ½hr after sunset Mon, Wed, Thu, Sat; adult/child 40/30NIS)* evening light show walks visitors through the site, illuminating features with displays on the natural canvas of the hill behind. In daylight hours a trip up the hill's steep steps affords a fabulous view over the ruins. Visit the national park's website to book tickets.

In the middle of the park, a single standing pillar, the only erect structure unearthed, acts as a poignant reminder of the fateful fall of a once-magnificent city when it was ravaged by a violent earthquake in 749CE.

In the town itself is the **Beit She'an Guesthouse (HI)** (*62 rooms; 126 Menachem Begin Bd;* \ *6060760;* e *beitshean@iyha.org.il; www.iyha.org.il.* **$$$**). Housed in a vast,

---

THE BIG ONE

Both seismologists and the Bible warn that Israel, sitting precariously on the fault line that stretches the length of the Syrian-African Rift Valley, is due for 'the big one', an earthquake to beat all others. Throughout history, violent earthquakes have devastated great cities and buildings the length and breadth of the country, many of which were never rebuilt. Beit She'an, Capernaum, Tzfat Old City and Jerusalem's Church of the Holy Sepulchre are but some of the casualties of Mother Nature's power. While Israel feels the effects of dozens of tremors and small quakes every year there is no need to panic yet – we could still be eons away from the devastating quake that experts believe is ultimately inevitable.

modern building, it even boasts its own swimming pool. Catering to large groups, it does have a rather mass-produced feel but is exceptionally clean. Single or double rooms have air conditioning, shower and television and kosher breakfast is included.

Getting there and away Buses heading to and from Jerusalem and Tiberias will pass through Beit She'an. Be sure to ask the driver if he stops there, as express services often don't. Buses 948, 961 and 966 depart hourly to and from Jerusalem (2hrs/45NIS). Buses 829 and 843 to and from Tel Aviv leave once a day at 14.30 and 14.00 respectively. From Tiberias bus 28 departs every 45 minutes (2hrs 20mins/45NIS). There are no direct buses from Nazareth or Haifa but buses 411 and 412 leave Afula every 15 minutes, where you can connect to both.

GAN HASHLOSHA (SACHNE) NATIONAL PARK (6586219; www.parks.org.il; ⊕ Apr–Sep 08.00–17.00; Oct–Mar 08.00–16.00 daily; admission adult/child 36/22NIS) Most Israelis would vote Gan HaShlosha one of the most beautiful national parks in the country, and rightly so. The crystal-clear spring waters weave through the park's numerous pools and waterfalls, framed by well-kept lawns and vegetation. The surprisingly impressive, albeit small **Museum of Regional and Mediterranean Archaeology** (6586352; ⊕ 10.00–14.00 Sun–Thu & Sat), barbecue areas, changing rooms, lifeguards and children's play areas have unfortunately meant that the park is also one of the most visited sites in the country, especially in the peak summer months and weekends. Needless to say, it is a different kettle of fish on weekdays and out of the school holiday season, and the constant 27°C waters mean swimming is possible any time of the year (although only one pool is full in the winter months). Early risers will most certainly be rewarded with solitude and tranquillity. An exact replica of the Tel Amal tower and stockade settlement that once stood on this spot is also worth a visit. The lovely little **Muse on the Water** (6588097; ⊕ 12.00–23.00 Sat–Thu, 10.00–16.00 Fri; kosher; $$$) is a vegetarian restaurant serving an array of quiches, salads, pasta and fish. They also have a book exchange. Inside the adjacent and extremely pretty **Kibbutz Nir David** are plenty of **zimmer** bed and breakfasts that make a nice choice for a couple of days' stay.

Getting there and away The park is located next to Kibbutz Nir David on route 669 next to the petrol station. Buses 411 and 412 from Afula to Beit She'an stop every 20 minutes outside the kibbutz.

GAN GAROO AUSTRALIAN ZOO (Adjacent to Kibbutz Nir David; 6488060; ⊕ 09.00–20.00 Sun–Thu, 09.00–15.00 Fri, 09.00–17.00 Sat (closes 1hr earlier in winter); admission 35NIS; combination ticket with Gan HaShlosha adult/child 50/40NIS) This relatively small but well-kept animal park was made possible by contributions from the Australian embassy in Israel and has now joined the ranks of only seven other zoological parks outside Australia to house koala bears. The nearby Kibbutz Nir David grows eucalyptus plants especially for their distinguished guests. Children and animal lovers enjoy the relative freedom given to the Aussie animals, which include free-hopping kangaroos, kookaburras and flying foxes. The park is recognised by the Australian Wildlife Protection Authority and offers a small education centre (albeit mostly in Hebrew).

Getting there and away The park is adjacent to Kibbutz Nir David on route 669 just outside the entrance to Gan HaShlosha next to the petrol station. Buses 411 and 412 from Afula to Beit She'an stop outside the kibbutz every 20 minutes.

The 500m-high Mount Gilboa ridge stretches for 18km across the southeastern part of the Jezreel Valley just south of Beit She'an. Every spring Israelis make their way up the mountain to see the blossoming of the famed purple Gilboa iris and hike in its abounding beauty. Mount Gilboa was the site where King Saul, the first king of Israel, and his sons died fighting the Philistines, a tragic event in Jewish history. The well-paved Gilboa scenic route (route 667), which runs the entire length of the ridge, offers magnificent views in all directions, as well as countless opportunities for hiking, picnicking and cycling. From here it is possible to see the ancient city of Beit She'an, the hill of Moreh where the Philistines assembled to fight King Saul, Mount Tabor and the Jordan Valley. While the mild year-round weather means visiting at any time is possible, the clearest views are during spring when the whole mountain is alive with blossom. At the eastern end of the Gilboa range is the **Gilboa Herb Farm** (\ *6531093;* ☺ *12.00–22.30 Mon–Sat; $$$*), a rustic farm building perched atop the mountain. The farm specialises in the growing (and exporting) of fresh herbs, which their delightful restaurant takes delicious advantage of. Housed in a charmingly simple wood building (if the weather is nice be sure to sit outside) it serves rustic French, Italian and Middle Eastern-style foods. Also on the eastern end of the mountain is the new **Kimmel Restaurant** (\ *057 944104; 12.00–late daily; $$$$$*), which offers excellent views over the valley below amidst a rustically elegant setting. Just outside is the newly constructed **dry ski slope** that is a rather unusual addition to the mountain but one that is becomingly increasingly popular with weekending Israelis.

BEIT ALPHA ANCIENT SYNAGOGUE (*Kibbutz Hefzibah;* \ *6532004; www.parks.org.il;* ☺ *08.00–17.00 Sat–Thu, 08.00–16.00 Fri; admission adult/child 20/9NIS*) Although under the care of the Israel Nature and National Parks Protection Authority, Beit Alpha can't really be described as a park. The site itself houses the ruins of an ancient synagogue dating to the 6th century CE. Its crowning glory and *raison d'être* is the elaborate and well-preserved mosaic floor, which can be viewed from raised platforms encircling it. Lights accentuate the significant features of the mosaic throughout a 15-minute video presentation detailing the history of the area and synagogues within Israel. It is a little pricey for the short time it takes to visit the park, but those with a national park combination ticket should definitely make the short detour.

Getting there and away The park is located next to the Kibbutz Beit Alpha on route 669. Buses 411 and 412 from Afula to Beit She'an stop every 20 minutes outside the kibbutz.

7

Upper Galilee

Telephone code 04

The landscape of the Upper Galilee provides the biggest surprise to visitors to Israel, who arrive expecting the barrenness of the Negev Desert, the cobbled lanes of Jerusalem's Old City and the white-sand beaches of coastal Tel Aviv. It is difficult to decide where the magic of the Upper Galilee region lies: in its tranquil, rural lifestyle perhaps, or in its abounding natural beauty, with roaring rivers, dense green forests and winding valleys. Yet perhaps its mystical (Note: this word is used a lot when describing Tzfat due to its centre as a place of Kabbalah worship) atmosphere arises from the Holy Jewish city of Tzfat, from its long-abandoned Crusader fortresses or its impressive archaeological ruins, the ghosts of the past retelling their stories through the remains of once-great sites.

With a landscape reminiscent of the verdant valleys of western Europe, the Upper Galilee is perfectly suited to a plethora of activities that you wouldn't necessarily associate with Israel, and plenty that you would. From kayaking down the bubbling Jordan River to inhaling the mysticism that abounds in Tzfat Old City's cobbled alleys, from witnessing the great bird migrations as they rest in the lush Hula Valley on their way south to getting swept up in the passionate celebration of Lag Ba'Omer at the tomb of Rabbi Shimon bar Yohai, this region is steeped in rural charm. Tiny villages dot the countryside, their family-run guesthouses a far cry from the chain hotels of the Mediterranean coast. A mesh of cultures and religions cohabit a land that has seen its fair share of turmoil, its long border with Lebanon acting as a launch pad for Hezbollah rockets throughout a number of wars and battles. Yet as you watch the sun set over the majestic Montfort Castle or listen to the breeze gently whistling through the leaves of Rosh Pina's enigmatic little artists' quarter it is difficult to imagine it in any way other than simply enchanting.

TZFAT

Through all of its countless names and spellings, from Tsfat, Safed, Safad, Tzefat, Zfat, Zefat to Zephath, there is but one name that stands out as the perfect fit: 'The Mystical City'. Perched high on the green, wooded slopes of the Upper Galilee mountains, Tzfat's clean, fresh air seems to whisper the secrets of the past, where Jewish mysticism abounds and whose spirit is still so clearly present. Cobbled stone alleyways, small cottages dotted with blue doors and windows and an abundance of ancient synagogues form the Old City, where today artists show off their talents in open studios.

Tzfat is regarded as one of Judaism's four Holy Cities (along with Jerusalem, Tiberias and Hebron) and was home to some of the religion's true greats. Scholars, spiritual leaders and religious philosophers gathered in the 16th century and together they gave Tzfat its proud status as a world centre for Jewish mysticism,

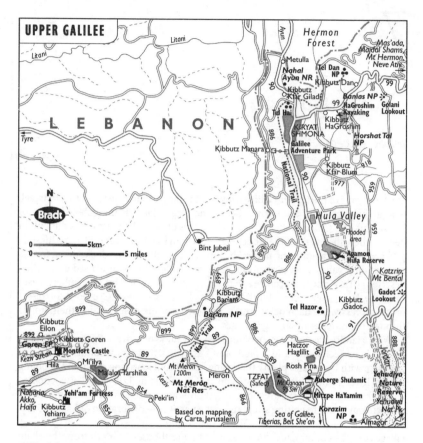

UPPER GALILEE

Litani

Litani

L E B A N O N

Tyre

N

Bradt

0 ——— 5km
0 ——————— 5 miles

Bint Jubeil

Ayun

Hermon Forest

Mas'ada, Majdal Shams, Mt Hermon, Neve Ativ

Metulla
Nahal Ayun NR
Kibbutz Dan
Tel Dan NP
Kibbutz Kfar Giladi
Banias NP
99 HaGroshim
Golani Lookout
Kibbutz Kayaking
Tel Hai
Kibbutz HaGroshim
KIRYAT SHMONA
Horshat Tal NP
Galilee Adventure Park
Kibbutz Manara
Kibbutz Kfar Blum
977

Hula Valley
Flooded area
Agamon Hula Reserve
Katzrin, Mt Bental
Gadot Lookout
Kibbutz Gadot
Tel Hazor
Kibbutz Bar'am
Bar'am NP
Hatzor Haglilit
Rosh Pina
Kibbutz Eilon
899
Goren P
Kibbutz Goren
Keziv Stream
Montfort Castle
Hila
Mi'ilya
Nat Trail
Yehudiya Nature Reserve
Yehudiya Nat Pk
Ma'alot-Tarshiha
Mt Meron 1200m
Meron
TZFAT (Safed)
Mt Canaan 955m
Auberge Shulamit
Naharia, Akko, Haifa
Yehi'am Fortress
Peki'in
Mt Meron Nat Res
Mitzpe HaYamim
Korazim NP
Almagor
Kibbutz Yehiam
Based on mapping by Carta, Jerusalem
Sea of Galilee
Tiberias, Beit She'an

Kabbalah. Today they rest atop the mountain in the ancient cemetery, whose views befit their status as the 'righteous ones'. With the swift rise in Kabbalah's popularity across the world, the quiet little town of Tzfat has suddenly found itself the centre of a budding spiritual tourism industry. Followers flock to study in the multitudinous centres of learning, where the substantial Hasidic Orthodox presence lends an air of antiquity, as though time has stood still. But somehow Tzfat's charm and sacred atmosphere have not been weakened (within the Old City at least), and it is an alluring and enchanting place to explore.

HISTORY Although legend has it that Tzfat was founded by one of Noah's sons after the Flood, the first textual mention is in the Roman period. The city is not mentioned in the Bible and didn't make its mark as one of Judaism's holiest centres until the 16th century. A large Crusader citadel fell to the Muslim conqueror Saladin in the 12th century and in 1266 the Mamluk leader Baibars made Tzfat one of his administrative centres, killing or dispelling much of the population in the process. In 1492, the same year that Columbus set sail for the Americas, Spanish Jews fled to Palestine escaping persecution. Top Jewish scholars and rabbis congregated, and Tzfat was transformed into a centre for Jewish mysticism, Kabbalah. Rabbi Isaac Luria, Kabbalah's principal proponent, was a key figure in its creation, along with many other notable sages and Kabbalists. Groups came from many parts of Europe and north Africa and by 1550 a Jewish population of 10,000 was thriving.

WHAT IS KABBALAH? Kabbalah is an aspect of Jewish mysticism that relates to a set of esoteric beliefs and practices that supplement the traditional Jewish interpretations of the Bible. It deals with the nature of divinity, the creation and the origin and the fate of the soul.

WHAT DOES KABBALAH MEAN? 'Kabbalah' literally means 'receiving', and is often used synonymously with the word 'tradition'.

WHERE AND WHEN DID KABBALAH ORIGINATE? While many Orthodox Jews date Kabbalah back to a system of interpretations of the scriptures handed down orally from Abraham, the system of Kabbalah seems to have been given its organised form in 11th-century Spain and arrived in Israel when Jews were expelled from the country. It centres on the Zohar, the principal source of Kabbalah.

WHAT EXACTLY IS THE ZOHAR? The Zohar is the principal book of Kabbalah written in the 13th century by Moses de Léon, a Spanish Kabbalist, but attributed to 2nd-century rabbi Shimon bar Yohai. It provides a commentary on the first five books of the Torah and a cosmic-symbolic interpretation of Judaism based on the view of God as the dynamic flow of force through ten *sefirot* (planes or realms). These *sefirot* are symbols for everything in the world of creation.

WHO PRACTISES KABBALAH? Traditional Kabbalists are generally Hassidic Orthodox Jewish men, many aspects of this mystical practice are meaningless outside the realms of Judaism. What are often referred to as Hermetic Kabbalists range from Jews who prefer this form to the traditional practice, as well as non-Jews.

WHAT EXACTLY IS HERMETIC KABBALAH? Hermetic Kabbalah is a variant on traditional Kabbalah and dates back several hundred years. It is an esoteric, mystical tradition that draws on influences such as traditional Kabbalah, astrology, tarot, alchemy, pagan religions, Gnosticism, Freemasonry and tantra. It is usually spelt 'Qabbalah' to distinguish it from the traditional form. It has become increasingly popular over recent years because of celebrities such as Madonna and Demi Moore promoting its attributes.

HOW CAN I STUDY KABBALAH? This depends on which form of Kabbalah you wish to learn. Traditional Kabbalah is considerably more complicated, a long-standing belief being that when a student is ready, a teacher will appear. However, there are workshops, centres and meetings you can attend (see *Tzfat*, page 205). A good grasp of Hebrew is essential for this and only male Jews may study it (although some women have been allowed). For those wishing to learn more about Hermetic Qabbalah, the internationally known Kabbalah Centre (*www.kabbalah.com*) has branches all over the world (the Los Angeles branch being where celebrity followers convene). Within Israel there are branches in Tel Aviv, Jerusalem and Haifa that offer classes, meetings and information.

Upper Galilee TZFAT 7

Throughout the 18th and 19th centuries Jewish residents suffered plagues, repeated Druze attacks and a severe earthquake that killed 5,000 people. Influxes of Russian Jews and Perushim (disciples of Rabbi Elijah ben Solomon Zalman) did little to maintain the dwindling population.

Amidst the 1929 Arab riots, Tzfat's Jewish quarter was attacked. Many fled and by 1948 the Jewish population numbered just 2,000. Upon the British withdrawal, the Palestinian residents attacked, a move that was successfully countered by divisions of the Palmach (a precursor to the IDF) and resulted in the fleeing of most of the Arab population. Amongst the Arab refugees was the family of Palestinian Authority prime minister Mahmoud Abbas.

GETTING THERE AND AWAY There is one direct bus a day to and from Tel Aviv leaving Tel Aviv's central bus station at 17.00 (3hrs 30mins/59NIS) and Tzfat at 05.20 and 08.15. It is also possible to change in Netanya, Herzliya or Megiddo junction for more regular routes. From Haifa Lev HaMifratz bus 361 runs every 30 minutes (1hr 50mins/40NIS) and to Tiberias bus 450 runs hourly (1hr/22NIS). Bus 982 runs between Jerusalem's central bus station (3hrs 35mins/45NIS) and Tzfat seven times daily, and buses 511 and 501 run hourly between Kiryat Shmona (45min/24.50NIS) and will stop at sights along route 90.

GETTING AROUND All of Tzfat's sights of interest are contained inside the Old City which is easily navigable by foot (and mostly pedestrianised, so you don't have a lot of choice). If you need to get to the hospital in the south of the city, take bus 6 or 7 from the central bus station. Alternatively there are several taxi companies operating in the city, **Moniot HaMavrik** (✆ *6974222*) and **Moniot Ilan Mazuz** (✆ *052 2692082*), for instance.

ORIENTATION Outside the Old City, with its quaint architecture and charming environment, Tzfat is rather ordinary and there isn't much to see. The main commercial area is Jerusalem (Yerushalayim) Street, which separates the artists' quarter to the south and Old Town and ancient synagogues to the north. Accommodation is cheaper in the New City, but if your pocket permits, staying close to the Old City is certainly worth the extra expense. Facilities, hotels and eateries concentrate in the east, which also has some of the best views.

TOURIST INFORMATION AND TOURS

ℹ Israel Extreme ✆ 052 6478474; e info@israelextreme.com; www.israelextreme.com. Tzfat-based tour agency specialising in walking tours around the Old City as well as customised adventure excursions to the Upper & Lower Galilee & the Golan Heights.

ℹ Kabbalah Tour International Centre for Tzfat Kabbalah; 17 Alkebetz St; ✆ 6821771; e office@tzfat-kabbalah.org; www.kabbalahtour.com. Kabbalah Tour packages inc master classes, workshops, excursions, lectures & performances. Activities & packages range from 1½hr workshops (500NIS) to 5-day all-inc deals. Works together with the International Centre for Tzfat Kabbalah.

ℹ Tzfat Tourist Information Centre 17 Alkebetz St; ✆ 6924427; ⊕ 08.00–16.00 Sun–Thu. Well-stocked centre that can offer information on attractions & courses. They show a 10min video depicting the history of the city. They also offer internet for 5NIS/15mins.

ℹ Richard Woolf ✆ 6935377/505 894647; e woolfr@netvision.net.il; www.israwebs.com/woolf. A well-known, highly reputable & extremely knowledgeable local tour guide, Richard can tailor trips to your preference & time constraints.

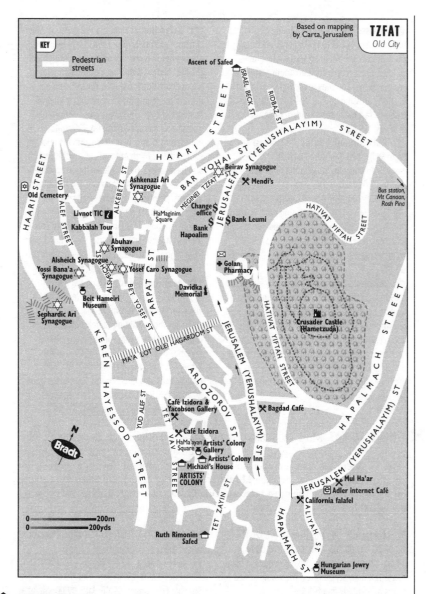

🏠 **WHERE TO STAY** Tzfat has a good variety of accommodation to suit tastes and budgets – from the luxury spa hotels on Mount Canaan to mid-range and budget guesthouses. Within the Old City there are lots of rooms to be rented and it is worth visiting the tourist information centre (or check their website) for contact details of these.

🏠 **Villa Galilee** (21 rooms) 106 Mount Canaan; ☎ 6999563; e info@Villa-galilee.com; www.villa-galilee.com. Luxury boutique spa hotel perched on top of Mount Canaan. Antique elegance has been twinned with excellent facilities & the intimate ambience of a small hotel. There is an unpretentious gourmet French restaurant, a choice of spectacular views from the rooms, a swimming pool & beautiful spa. **$$$$**

🏠 **Artists' Colony Inn** (4 rooms) 9 Simtat Yud Zayin St; ☎6041101; e benay@artcol.co.il; www.artcol.co.il. Set in an idyllic Tzfat stone building these rooms are a luxurious taste of the mysticism that abounds in the Old City. Jacuzzis, AC, fluffy dressing gowns, Wi-Fi, & a huge rustic kosher b/fast make this the ideal romantic getaway. **$$$$**

🏠 **Ruth Rimonim Safed** (82 rooms) Tet Zayin St; ☎6920456/1800 766766; www.rimonim.com. Built on the ruins of a 17th-century Turkish khan, the elegant hotel is one of the most picturesque & well positioned in the city. Luxurious outdoor swimming pool, health club & spa set within spacious grounds with breathtaking views of the Galilee. *US$70–100 extra per night in Jul/Aug, Jewish hols & w/ends.* **$$$$**

🏠 **Michael's House** (3 rooms) 55 Tet Vav St; ☎6970470/052 6334532. Located along the steps leading up to the artists' quarter is this delightful guesthouse. 3 large, comfortable rooms have been created within the 150-year-old cottage, each on a different level of the higgledy-piggledy building. The wooden penthouse apt sleeps 2, the Rose Courtyard sleeps 4 & the family unit can sleep up to 6. **$$–$$$**

🏠 **Safed Inn** (18 rooms) 191 Bialik St, Mount Canaan; ☎6971007/057 7498133; e leahbb@actcom.net.il; www.safedinn.com. Undoubtedly the best budget & mid-range option in Tzfat (& possibly the Upper Galilee). The building has been in the family for 75 years, but it opened its doors in 2008. This charming, comfortable guesthouse has everything from 'dormitories' (which only have 2 beds & en-suite facilities) to standard dbls (with AC) and deluxe dbls (which also have jacuzzi bath). All are fantastic value for money, especially when you add the lovely gardens, helpful, hospitable family owners, 24hr free internet room, Wi-Fi, 5NIS washing & drying machines, BBQ, table tennis, 10NIS for sauna & hot-tub use & bicycle rental. Bus 3 goes from central Tzfat or call for a pick-up. *Dorm bed 100NIS; 100NIS more for deluxe.* **$$–$$$**

🏠 **Ascent of Safed** (31 rooms) 2 Ari St; ☎6921364; e ascent@ascentofsafed.com; www.ascentofsafed.com. This large hostel caters for those wanting to delve more deeply into Kabbalah & partake in the many classes & workshops they organise. Trips, excursions & tours can also be arranged. Only married couples may stay in dbl rooms. Single-sex dorms 60NIS/195NIS on Shabbat. *All beds & rooms half price w/days; 545NIS on Shabbat.* **$–$$$**

✖ **WHERE TO EAT** Most of Tzfat's restaurants are kosher and abide by Shabbat hours. While many do serve meat, there is an abundance of vegetarian and fish eateries. There are also several nice bakeries dotted around town that provide for an affordable and tasty snack, and numerous kosher falafel and shawarma stands on Jerusalem Street, the most famous being **California** where 15NIS will get you a big falafel & a drink.

✖ **Mul Hahar** 70 Jerusalem St; ☎6920404; 🕐 08.00–01.00 Sun–Thu, 08.00–16.00 Fri, 19.00–01.00 Sat. Kosher. Mixed menu that leans towards Italian-style dishes. The whole grilled fish is particularly good. **$$$$**

✖ **Gan Eden** Mount Canaan; ☎6972434; 🕐 09.00–23.00 Sun–Thu, 09.00–14.00 Fri. Cosy, romantic Italian-style vegetarian & fish restaurant whose views from Mount Canaan are as exceptional as their food. The couple's b/fast, pasta selection & desserts are recommended. **$$$**

✖ **Bagdad Café** 61 Jerusalem St; ☎6923332; 🕐 08.00–10.00 Sun–Thu. Something of a Tzfat institution is this little café that has been around for decades. Toasted sandwiches, fruit shakes,

salads, desserts & falafel are on offer at decent prices. **$$**

✖ **Café Izidora** 22 Tet Vav St; ☎050 8861564; 🕐 winter 09.00–17.00 Sun–Thu, 09.00–Shabbat Fri; summer 09.00–late, 09.00–Shabbat Fri. Belonging to the artist who has the Yakobson Gallery next door this has a wonderful shady little courtyard in which to sit & enjoy light vegetarian dishes such as quiches, bagels, salads & b/fast platters. **$$**

✖ **Maximilian Artist's Café** HaMaayan Sq; ☎0777882887; 🕐 summer 08.00–00.00 Sun–Thu, 08.00–Shabbat Fri; winter 08.00–21.00 Sun–Thu, 08.00–Shabbat Fri. Kosher. Delightful little vegetarian café in the square serving a selection of pasta, Israeli cheeses, salads, fresh fruit juices & cakes. $$

Mendi's 29 Jerusalem St; 0774108002; 12.00–22.00 Sun–Thu, 09.30–3hrs before Shabbat Fri. Kosher. Traditional European Jewish dishes such as chunt, slow-cooked meats & hearty soups are served in this comfortable eatery. It is hugely popular with the yeshiva crowd, and offers Shabbat meals to be ordered in advance. Excellent value. $$

ENTERTAINMENT AND NIGHTLIFE Having a pumping night out in Tzfat is a distinct impossibility, unless of course you have arrived during the Klezmer Festival (early August) in which case concerts go on until the small hours. The alternative to an early bed is a night-time walk around the Old City, which is an extremely pleasant way to while away a few hours.

OTHER PRACTICALITIES

Emergencies

Ambulance 101
Police Station 100 HaGalil St; 6978444
Fire 102

Money

$ **Bank Hapoalim** 72 Jerusalem St; 03 6532407; 08.30–13.15 Sun & Tue/Wed, 08.30–13.00 & 16.00–18.30 Mon & Thu

$ **Bank Leumi** 35 Jerusalem St; 6994311; 08.30–14.00 Sun & Tue/Wed, 08.30–13.00 & 16.00–18.15 Mon & Thu

$ **Change office** Jerusalem St; 6822777; 08.30–13.30 Sun–Fri, 16.00–19.00 Sun/Mon & Wed/Thu. Located across the street from Bank Leumi.

Post

Post office 37 Jerusalem St; 6920115; 08.00–18.00 Sun & Thu, 08.00–12.30 & 15.30–18.00 Mon/Tue, 08.00–13.30 Wed. The main branch is on HaPalmach St.

Medical

Rivka Zieff Hospital Ofer Intersection; 6828811

Golan Pharmacy 50 Jerusalem St; 6920472; 08.30–19.00 Sun–Thu, 08.30–14.00 Fri

Internet

Adler Internet Café 88 Jerusalem St; 052 3447766; 10.30–02.00 Sun–Thu, 10.30–16.30 Fri, end of Shabbat–late Sat. 15NIS/hr. Sells cold drinks & snacks & offers free tourist information.

WHAT TO SEE

Synagogues

Yosef Caro Synagogue (*Beit Yosef St*) Named after the great scholar and Kabbalah follower Josef Caro, who is renowned for his authorship of the Shulchan Aruch (The Set Table), the basis of Jewish law. Upon expulsion from Spain he settled in Tzfat in 1536, serving as the city's chief rabbi and head of the rabbinic court.

Yossi Bana'a Synagogue (*Yud Aleph St*) Housing the tomb of Yossi Bana'a in a small chamber at the far end of the building, the synagogue dates to the end of the 15th century and was built by Jewish exiles from Spain. Yossi Bana'a, a 3rd-century Talmudic sage, was often referred to as the 'White Zaddik' after his famed miracle where he turned black chickens white on Yom Kippur. Inside the synagogue, an ancient Torah is housed in the Holy Ark, which is removed once a year on the eve of Bag La'omer for the pilgrimage to Meron (see page 216).

Ashkenazi Ari Synagogue (*Guri Ha'ari St*) According to tradition this is the site of one of Tzfat's many miracles where, during the 1948 Arab–Israeli War, people crowded inside seeking shelter. Direct attacks on the synagogue caused much damage, but not a single member of the congregation was injured. It was founded by Spanish exiles in the 16th century and associated with Rabbi Isaac Luri (known as Ari), the revered Kabbalah master. While named after its ties with the Ashkenazi community, it is frequented by the whole spectrum of Jewish worshippers.

Sephardic Ari Synagogue (*Ha'ari Rd*) Built in 1522 by north African Jews, this is the city's oldest synagogue. At the time of writing it was under renovation and was open a few hours a day for Torah lessons only. Throughout the 1948 Arab–Israeli War, the synagogue held an important defensive spot on the border between the Jewish and Arab quarters of the city, and was badly damaged during the conflict.

Abuhav Synagogue (*Alsheich St*) Aesthetically Abuhav Synagogue would probably take first prize, with its large, distinctive white-domed roof, whitewashed walls, blue window frames and elegant interior. Believed to be named after the 15th-century rabbi Yitzhak Abuhav, who is remembered as one of Spain's great sages, he became head of a yeshiva in Toledo where he studied philosophy and Kabbalah before moving to Tzfat. The Torah scroll, kept inside the ornate Ark, is not only the oldest scroll in the city, but is also the centre of numerous traditions and legends. It is taken out three times a year: on Yom Kippur, Shavuot and Rosh Hashanah.

Alsheich Synagogue (*Alsheich St*) This small synagogue, named after Rabbeinu Moshe Ben Haim Alsheich, is built in the style of 16th-century Sephardic synagogues. Tradition has it that during the severe earthquakes of 1759 and 1837 that ravaged the area, the synagogue remained totally undamaged, and this has become a legend handed down through the decades. A large blue door (with a number 10 on the doorpost) marks this rather modest synagogue, whose unkempt exterior somehow adds to its appeal. Note that this synagogue doesn't have a women's section.

Beirav Synagogue (*Meginei Tzfat St;* ✆ *6921849; www.beirav.org; services throughout the Sabbath & religious holidays, closed at other times*) Popular with visitors from all over the world thanks to its lively, traditional musical services, it was given a facelift a few years ago when English-speaking members of the Tzfat community renewed activity in the run-down 19th-century building.

Museums
Beit Hameiri Museum (*Keren HaYessod St;* e *yaniv@hameiri-cheese.co.il; www.hameiri-cheese.co.il; guided tours 12.00 Fri; admission adult/child 20/15NIS*) Situated in a beautiful stone building, Israel's first dairy has been maintained for over 160 years. Today, the family-run dairy offers weekly tours, presentations on cheese and dairy production with some gourmet cheese tasting to finish. It's an interesting detour off the religion trail, and offers the opportunity to buy some traditional Tzfat specialities.

Hungarian Jewry Museum (*Haazmaut Sq; [tel/fax:] 6923880/1; www.hjm.org.il;* ✆ *09.00–13.00 Sun–Fri; admission free*) Opened in 1986, the museum is still lovingly maintained by two of its original founders. It depicts Jewish life throughout Hungary, Transylvania, Slovakia, Carpathian Russia, Bachka, Banat and Burgenland through a collection of letters, books and personal possessions.

General Exhibition Artists' Colony (*HaMaayan Sq;* ✆ *6920087;* e *artistcolony@ netvision.net.il; www.artistcolony.co.il;* ✆ *10.00–18.00 Sun–Thu, 10.00–14.00 Fri & Sat*) Large gallery showcasing paintings and sculptures by renowned Israeli artists. Located in the square opposite the Market Mosque, which is identified by its minaret.

Rozenfeld Doll Museum (*Kikar Sadeh, Eshtam Bldg;* ✆ *6972041;* ✆ *10.00–18.00 daily.* Following the 1994 terrorist attack on the Tel Aviv Dizengoff Centre in which her daughter Alla died, Mila Rozenfeld started this museum in memory of the victims. It houses beautifully detailed porcelain dolls in various historical and ethnographic costumes.

Other sights
Artists' colony At the heart of the Old City just off Jerusalem Street, amidst a maze of cobbled lanes and ancient stone buildings, is Tzfat's artists' quarter. It was established in 1949 in the previously Arab part of town, following a need to centralise art within the newly formed country. It created a focal point for artists and attracted big names in the art world, both those from within Israel, and Europe's Holocaust survivors. Today about 60 artists have workshops and galleries here, ranging from paintings to ceramics to sculptures to photography, most in keeping with the underlying theme that abounds in Tzfat: Kabbalah. An amble around the area is one of the city's highlights, where amenable artists show off their works and engage in lively chatter and debate with anyone who wishes to join in. For more information about the galleries visit www.artists.co.il/safed/safed_e.html.

Old cemetery According to religious tradition, it is in the ancient cemetery at Tzfat that some of the holiest *tzaddikim* (righteous people) rest. The custom of praying at their gravesides is age-old in Judaism, and the cemetery here is comparable only to that of the Mount of Olives in Jerusalem. The beauty of the cemetery adds to its unquestionable air of peace and spirituality, the unusual blue tombstones and burial caves dotted with brightly coloured flowers resting quietly and majestically upon the hill. Whether you're a believer or not, a mellow stroll around the cemetery to meet some of Judaism's most revered followers is the perfect way to truly feel the Tzfat vibe. In the middle of the cemetery and often crowded with worshippers rests one of the five most important *tzaddik*, **Rabbi Isaac Luria, R'Yitzchak ben Shlomo** (or 'The Holy Arizal'), the great 16th-century Kabbalah master.

Clarinet and Klezmer in the Galilee (*www.clarinet-klezmer.com*) Normally held in July, this is a week of nightly classical, jazz and klezmer performances held in a variety of venues around town. Some of the world's leading clarinettists join forces to produce this week-long festival which culminates in the Gala Final Concert. People come from far and wide to appreciate the festival, especially at the weekend, so if you are planning to stay during this time, you will need to book accommodation ahead.

Crusader castle (*Hametzuda*) On the top of the hill at the centre of Tzfat stands the scanty remains of a Crusader castle built in 1140CE to control the thoroughfare to Damascus. The castle was built on the site of an ancient citadel, the result of the 66CE Jewish revolt against the Romans. It is a bit of a hike but the views from the top of Israel's highest city and the pleasant park setting are worth the effort.

The Davidka Memorial Located just beyond Jerusalem Street is an old and rather crass cannon, which is by tradition said to have driven the last of the Arabs out of the city in the 1948 Arab–Israeli War. The handmade weapon was rather ineffectual with regards to actual firepower but made an almighty blast that had the same end result.

ROSH PINA

According to Jewish Kabbalah tradition, it is in Rosh Pina that the Messiah will appear, and one can certainly see why. Cottages built from local stone perch high on the slopes of Mount Canaan amidst tree-lined cobbled stone lanes. A labyrinth of artists' workshops peeks out from behind spring blossoms, while gourmet restaurants lay beneath shady leaves. Even the internationally renowned Kabbalah follower Madonna was seen house hunting here, hoping to be one more of the lucky population of 2,400 that call this beautiful little town home. Yet the town is not just a pretty face, holding an honourable place in Jewish history when in 1883 it became the first Jewish settlement in Palestine to come under the patronage of the Baron Edmond de Rothschild (see page 171).

Rosh Pina has, with the obvious exception of the large and out-of-place shopping centre at its foot (in fact there are two shopping centres, the smaller and older **Galil Shopping Centre** and the new **Chan Rosh Pina Mall**), preserved its rural heritage, and restored early pioneer houses and a synagogue commissioned by Rothschild can be visited. It was also within this tiny settlement that the first Jew to be hanged by the British Mandate authorities, Shlomo Ben Yosef, is buried. There isn't an awful lot to do here, but that's kind of the idea. Wander through the small lanes of the Old Town, appreciate the beauty of the place, peruse the artists' workshops and sip a cool drink in one of the beautiful cafés and you'll feel it was a job well done.

Over recent years Rosh Pina has adopted a luxury tourism market, so accommodation is pricey but fantastic. Most accommodation is in luxury zimmers and there are plenty to choose from. Guesthouses further from the old part of town are slightly cheaper and lampposts are weighed down with signs advertising zimmers of all shapes and sizes. For all amenities and practicalities, the shopping centre is the place to go.

GETTING THERE AND AROUND Buses 511 and 522 leave every 30 minutes between Rosh Pina and Tzfat (5mins/13NIS) continuing to Kiryat Shmona. Rosh Pina is tiny, albeit positioned on a rather steep slope, so walking is your only option if you haven't rented a car.

TOURIST INFORMATION
ℹ Tourist information Ground floor of Galil Shopping Centre; ☎6801465; www.zhr.org.il; ⏰ 08.00–16.00 Sun–Thu. Small & not easy to find so ask around. Not a particularly big English selection.

WHERE TO STAY

Mitzpe HaYamim (83 rooms) Old Rosh Pina to Tzfat rd; 6994555; e sales@mitzpe-hayamim.com; www.mitzpe-hayamim.com. This is one of the most well-known & highly respected hotels & spa resorts in the country & deservedly so. Sprawling landscaped gardens, orchards & a fully operating organic farm envelop the luxury top-of-the-range hotel & spa facilities, whose ethos is to connect its guests to the magic of nature. Designed by Bauhaus architect Yehezkel Rozenberg & commissioned by German homeopath, physician & vegetarian Dr Yaros, this resort is the culmination of decades of fine tuning. Needless to say, you will need to have an accumulation of US$50 bills in your pocket to fully appreciate it. *Rooms start at 2,000NIS.* **$$$$$**

Ha Mei'ri Mansion (9 rooms) HaHalutzim St; 6938707; www.hrp.co.il. Identifiable by its 2 unusual palm trees standing sentry outside, this castle-like zimmer holds pride of place as the very last house at the top of HaHalutzim St. Large, beautifully maintained rooms are like something out of a medieval fairy tale. Sun terrace with views over the valley below. *150NIS less on w/days.* **$$$$$**

Pina Barosh (7 rooms) 8 HaHalutzim St; 6937028/6936582; e mail@pinabarosh.com; www.pinabarosh.com. Exceptionally attractive restaurant & zimmer with spectacular views. Stone cottage swathed in brightly coloured flowers & plants. Bright, airy rooms decorated with elegance & imagination. They also offer a wine bar & tours of nearby wineries. *250NIS less on w/days.* **$$$$$**

Auberge Shulamit (4 rooms) Old Rosh Pina to Tzfat rd; 6931494; f 6931495; e shulamit@shulamit.co.il; www.shulamit.co.il. Wonderful views over the surrounding countryside. Classy & elegant, French-style, family-run hotel. Beautifully decorated, luxury rooms are set within a stone lodge that once housed the Israeli–Syrian armistice conference of the 1940s. B/fast terrace & evening restaurant with wonderful vista. Communal rooftop jacuzzi. In-room massages available. *300NIS less on w/days.* **$$$$**

WHERE TO EAT
For budget-style eating there are several inexpensive restaurants, fast-food joints, cafés and a sushi bar in and around both the Galil and Chan shopping malls. A busy **falafel kiosk** is located opposite the mall car park, which is your best budget option.

Muscat Restaurant Old Rosh Pina to Tzfat rd; 6994555; e info@mitzpe-hayamim.com; www.mitzpe-hayamim.com; 13.00–midnight daily. Part of the ultra-deluxe Mitzpe HaYamim (see *Where to stay* above). A unique blend of the most freshly grown produce one could ever hope to find. Using only organic products grown or raised in the resort's farm, & wineries as well as quality meats & fish cooked on open grills. **$$$$$**

Auberge Shulamit Restaurant Old Rosh Pina to Tzfat rd; 6931494; e shulamit@shulamit.co.il; www.shulamit.co.il; 08.30–12.00 & 13.00–22.00 daily. Fine cuisine specialising in home-smoked fish & meats & terrific views of the Golan Mountains. Delicate

hors d'oeuvres & a mouth-watering dessert tray. Pasta or soup of the day makes a good cheaper-end option. **$$$$**

Rafa's House Artists' quarter; 6936192; 12.30–23.30 daily. Picturesque location. Selection of claypot dishes & prime steaks. Cool, shaded outdoor area or elegant grotto-style interior. **$$$$**

Shiri Bistro 8 HaHalutzim St; 6937028; www.pinabarosh.com; 08.30–late daily. French-style cuisine served in a covered patio area surrounded by an abundance of plants & flowers & offering stunning views. Delicate yet unpretentious meals with southern Mediterranean gourmet influence. Adjacent to Pina Barosh (see above). **$$$**

ENTERTAINMENT AND NIGHTLIFE

Blues Brothers Pub Erus St; 6935336; www.villa-tehila.co.il; 21.00–late Thu–Sat.

Attached to the delightful Villa Tehilla Guest House (**$$$$**; *(w/days & winter)*–**$$$$$**), this little

The small moshav of Meron might for the greater part of the year appear to be a quiet and relatively insignificant village, but once a year the entire area fills with pilgrims, here to celebrate the festival of Lag Ba'omer. The moshav and mountain are revered as the site of the final resting place of Shimon bar Yohai, a 1st-century rabbi who is attributed by many to having written the Zohar, the principal script in Jewish mysticism (Kabbalah) and his grave attracts tens of thousands of Jewish pilgrims every year. It was his request to his students that they should celebrate the anniversary of his death (which fell on Lag Ba'omer) with dancing, singing and feasting.

Lag Ba'omer is celebrated on the 33rd day of the Omer, which falls on the 18th day of Iyar on the Jewish calendar (usually in May on the Gregorian calendar). Its origins lay with Rabbi Akiva of whom Rabbi Shimon bar Yohai was a dedicated disciple. According to the Talmud, 24,000 of Rabbi Akiva's students were struck down by a divine plague, punishment for not displaying respect to one another. Lag Ba'omer is today celebrated as the day the plague ended, and of the day upon which it is believed Rabbi Shimon bar Yohai passed.

The festival at Meron is a fascinating mixture of spirituality, celebration, feasting and partying, a religious Woodstock of sorts. The annual pilgrimage centres on bar Yohai's large, domed tomb, where a huge bonfire belches out heat and smoke and male Orthodox members dance fervently around it. Women and children dance and sing traditional songs in the courtyard below. Dozens of sheep and cattle are slaughtered in ritualistic kosher manner, and tents and caravans sprawl across the surrounding countryside, a combination of Hassidic and Sephardim families, many of whom attend with their three-year-old sons. For it is on Lag Ba'omer at Meron that hundreds of toddlers receive their first *upsherin*, Jewish first haircut. The ceremony is a time of great happiness and pride as parents watch as their sons have *peyot* (temple curls) shaped.

Whilst doubtless a happy and celebratory event, it is a sacred and important part of Orthodox belief and sightseers must ensure they adhere to customs. Visiting the impressive tombs of Rabbi Shimon bar Yohai and other early rabbinical figures such as Rabbi Hillel and Rabbi Shammai is, at any time, worthwhile. A little further up the mountain from the tombs is one of the oldest synagogues in the Galilee, whose east wall is carved out of the steep rock cliff.

watering hole is one of the most pleasant options in town. A leafy beer garden & conservatory make an apt setting for a few relaxing drinks, while the cave-like interior is retro & friendly.

OTHER PRACTICALITIES There are two **shopping** centres at the base of Rosh Pina. The smaller and older Galil Shopping Centre houses most practicalities and several cheap eateries, while the new Chan Rosh Pina Shopping Centre has a selection of high street shops and more places to eat.

Police station ☎ 100. Located just outside the Galil Shopping Centre.

$ Bank Hapoalim Galil Shopping Centre; ☎ 03 6532407; ⊕ 08.30–13.00 & 16.00–18.30 Mon & Thu, 08.30–13.15 Tue & Wed, 08.15–12.30 Fri

✚ Newpharm pharmacy Galil Shopping Centre; ☎ 6860645; ⊕ 09.00–22.00 Sun–Thu. Look out for a red sign (in Hebrew only).

WHAT TO SEE

Artists' galleries Explore the maze of workshops at the top of the hill upon which Rosh Pina sits and watch the artists as they create leatherwork, ceramics, jewellery, pottery, paintings and anything else that takes their fancy. A wonderfully bohemian and almost spiritual atmosphere abounds, where artists happily show off their work and engage in enthusiastic chatter.

Baron Garden Flowers and plants imported from France in 1886 and planted under the care of Baron Rothschild still flourish in the small garden whose design is said to have been based on the gardens at Versailles.

Ancient cemetery Located opposite the artists' quarter, the cemetery rests on the hill, untouched for decades. Here rest the remains of Rosh Pina's founding members, mainly Jewish immigrants from Romania who settled here with the aid of Baron Rothschild. A small path leads to the cemetery from behind the iron gate.

MOUNT MERON At 1,200m above sea level, Mount Meron (Har Meron) was Israel's highest mountain until the 1967 Six Day War, which saw the Golan Heights and Mount Hermon brought under Israeli rule. The mountain is heavily forested, and dense, green wooded slopes hide caves and sink holes, a prime habitat for countless species of rare plants and animals. It is the third contender for the site of Jesus's Transfiguration (along with Mount Hermon and Mount Tabor, both of which are visible from the summit), and offers staggering views across the Sea of Galilee. Access to the mountain road is through the village of Meron and is a pleasant drive to the summit, which is a nature reserve. Several nice trails offer undemanding walks and wonderfully fresh air.

Getting there Buses 361 and 367 from Tzfat to Meron leave every 30 minutes (10mins/11.30NIS). To go up the mountain you will need to have your own vehicle or be prepared for an exerting but beautiful hike.

AROUND TZFAT AND ROSH PINA

TEL HAZOR (✆ 6937290; *www.parks.org.il;* ☉ *08.00–17.00 Sat–Thu (1hr earlier in winter), 08.00–15.00 Fri; admission adult/child 20/9NIS)* Covering 1km², Tel Hazor is the largest biblical site in Israel whose population, at its height, reached an estimated 40,000, four-times that of David and Solomon's Jerusalem. Extensive excavations have revealed 22 phases of occupation spanning 2,700 years, stretching from the early Bronze Age to the Hellenistic period. Hazor comprises two main sections: the acropolis and the fortified enclosure. Its location along the great Via Maris trade route was surely a key factor in its abounding success, and it is the only Canaanite site mentioned in the royal documents of Mari (located in modern-day Syria) which attest to its importance in trading tin. In its prime, Hazor covered an area twice the size of Meggido (see page 185). Biblically, Hazor didn't pale in importance. It is written that the King of Hazor, Jabin, headed a coalition of Canaanite cities against the encroaching Israelites, led by Joshua. Hazor is described as having been the 'head of all those kingdoms' (Joshua 11:1–5, 10). When the Canaanites were defeated, Joshua had Hazor razed to the ground.

Israelite Hazor's rebuilding is attributed to Solomon, who fortified the city in order to control movement along the Via Maris. In the 9th century BCE, presumably under the rule of King Ahab, the city was developed. It was during this time that the massive water system, a major feature of this national park today, was built. Ruins from many of the significant phases of Hazor are visible in the park (a trip to the small archaeological museum in Kibbutz Ayelet Hashahar is recommended before delving into the archaeological ruins). Fortifications from the Canaanite period, a large casement wall and gate believed to be from King Solomon's time, and a late Canaanite altar shed some light on the tumultuous past of this great city.

GETTING THERE AND AWAY The national park is located along route 90 between Kiryat Shmona (15mins) and Rosh Pina (15mins), 4km from the Mahana'im junction. Most buses heading to Kiryat Shmona or south will stop there although some express buses coming from Tel Aviv or Haifa don't, so be sure to ask the driver before boarding.

BAR'AM NATIONAL PARK ✎ *6989301; www.parks.org.il;* ⊕ *08.00–17.00 Sat–Thu (1hr earlier in winter), 08.00–15.00 Fri; admission adult/child 13/7NIS)* A Jewish village in Mishnaic and Talmudic times, Bar'am is now the site of one of the most beautiful ancient synagogues in the country. Many believe the village was built in this remote location because of the legend that Queen Esther was buried here. A biblical figure, Esther rose to be Queen of Persia and is famed as having saved the kingdom's Jewish population from persecution. Today, the lively and joyous Festival of Purim is celebrated in her memory, with the Megillah (Scroll of Esther) read in Bar'am.

That the village was affluent is indicated by the presence of two synagogues, only one of which remains today. An inscription discovered at the smaller synagogue reads 'Peace in this place and all of Israel' and is now housed in Paris's Louvre Museum. The larger of the two synagogues is the *raison d'être* of the national park, its majestic façade, large basalt blocks, sculptures and its three gates facing Jerusalem unarguably impressive.

Following the Arab conquest, Christian Arab villagers of the Maronite Church chose to leave the synagogues standing, building their own church – located next to the synagogue – which is today the spiritual centre of the Maronite faith. In 1948, the village was abandoned after the residents were evacuated by the IDF owing to its proximity to the Lebanese border.

The rare kermes oak forest of the **Bar'am Oaks Nature Reserve**, located near the archaeological site, makes a nice conclusion to a visit.

Getting there and away Bus 43 leaves Tzfat at 06.45, 12.35 and 17.00 (35mins/13.70NIS) and stops in Kibbutz Bar'am from where it is a short walk to the park entrance. Bus 522 leaving Haifa Lev HaMifratz at 15.20 also stops in the kibbutz (1hr 45mins/40NIS).

PEKI'IN The small, charming village of Peki'in, with its predominantly Druze population, is rather unexpectedly one of the most notable sites in Judaism. It claims to be the only place that Jews have lived in continuously for 2,000 years, and evidence of their historic presence can be seen in the form of Jewish symbols embedded in stone houses dotting the village. As the originally large Jewish population dwindled, Jews began to adopt the language and customs of their Arab neighbours, all along retaining their religious beliefs. A restored synagogue dating to the Roman period is located in the centre of the village and is cared for by a member of the Zenati family, whose ancestors were some of the founding Jewish members of Peki'in. The synagogue contains a fragment of an ancient Torah scroll and stone carvings believed to have been brought by refugees escaping the Roman destruction of Jerusalem.

Peki'in is also the site where it is believed Rabbi Shimon bar Yohai and his son Rabbi Eliezer hid in a cave to escape persecution by the Romans during the Bar-Kochba rebellion. It was during their 13 years in hiding that they compiled the Zohar, the foremost book of Kabbalah. According to the village tourist department, Peki'in, with its population of 4,200, receives 60,000 visitors a year, many of whom come to light candles and slip prayer papers into the cracks of the cave.

Besides its obvious historic and religious draw, the village is beautiful in its own right, perched high on the hill overlooking the Bet Kerem Valley below, its ancient stone houses clinging to the slopes. Olive groves and fruit trees fill the surrounding fields, a testament to its rural, agricultural roots, where Druze, Christians and Jews have lived harmoniously for thousands of years.

Getting there and away Bus 44 to and from Nahariya passes the town every two–three hours (35mins/13.70NIS).

Where to stay and eat There are countless small Druze restaurants in Peki'in serving traditional, hearty meals ($). Pitta, hummus, labane cheese, olives, grilled meats and salads are all extremely well priced, one of the most characteristic traits of Druze hospitality and customs. Locally produced olive oils and marinated olives are sold in plastic bottles, and make for an authentic souvenir.

Peki'in Guest House HI (50 rooms) \02 5945677; e pkiin@iyha.org.il. Geared towards large groups, it is housed in a vast complex & is a good budget option, if not the most visually pleasing choice in town. Kosher b/fast inc & internet & small cinema available. Ask at reception for guided tours or Druze homestay options. Located on the outskirts of the village. *Dorm 137NIS.* **$$$**

MONTFORT CASTLE, NAHAL KEZIV AND GOREN PARK As the sun sets over the Nahal Keziv Valley and the dense pine forests that engulf it, Montfort Castle (⊕ *in daylight hrs; admission free*), rising high on a jagged ridge, remains the last thing illuminated, as though left alone on a grand stage. The area here is laden with fantastic hiking opportunities, the Keziv Stream winding its way through the deep valley providing for some Herculean but immensely rewarding walks.

The castle was built by French Crusaders during the late 12th century, but was later bought by the German Teutonic Knights. Following conflicts with the Knights Templar and Knights Hospitaller in Akko, the Teutonic Knights moved to this location, declaring it their Holy Land headquarters. With papal funding, they fortified the castle, turning it into a grand fortress and the largest in the Upper Galilee. The keep that stands in the centre is probably the most indicative of the full extent and magnificence of the structure. In 1271, the Teutonic Knights surrendered

ZIMMER IN THE GALILEE

The whole of the Galilee, upper and lower, is blanketed with zimmer accommodation (see page 53). It is possible to simply drive through the small moshavim and kibbutzim and look for signs outside to get good last minute deals. Alternatively, websites such as www.zimmeril.com and www.zimmer. co.il have comprehensive, region-by-region listings.

to the Mamluk sultan Baibars in exchange for free passage and escaped with their treasury and archives, thus ending the short and turbulent life of Montfort Castle.

Because of its precipitous location the castle can only be reached by a fairly arduous uphill trek. A 1km trail leads from the Hila lookout at the end of Me'ilia village through road. To avoid the walk, **Goren Forest Park**, with its great picnicking opportunities and population of rather confident jackals, has a lookout terrace. It is located across the valley from the castle. A path can begin or end a lovely hike down into the Keziv Valley and up to the castle, and it offers fabulous views of both, especially at sunset. It is possible to camp unofficially in the park although the ground can be rather rough

An alternative way to approach the castle is to embark on a truly wonderful trek along the Keziv Stream and valley. A 6km circular walk following the black-marked trail starting in Hila leads you through vast pine forests reminiscent of the remote wildernesses of Canada and Scandinavia.

Getting there and away Goren Park is located between Kibbutz Eilon and Moshav Goren on route 899. From Nahariya, bus 27 stops at Kibbutz Eilon and the Goren junction four times a day (09.05, 12.30, 15.10, 17.15). Only bus 28 returns and leaves from the junction on route 899 five times a day (08.35, 12.35, 15.35, 18.05, 20.20). Alternatively there are countless buses leaving every 30 minutes to Ma'a lot Tarshiha from Nahariya where you can hitch to Hila.

🏠 Where to stay

🏠 **Eilon Traveler's Hotel** (28 rooms) Kibbutz Eilon; ☏ 9958568; e ghazivbb@ netvision.net.il; www.travelhotels.co.il. Excellent location for exploring the rural countryside of the region, & a relaxed & affordable place to base yourself. Rooms have kitchenette & AC & are simple but comfortable. It is a big favourite with families as there are plenty of outdoor areas & self-catering facilities. **$$$**

YEHIAM FORTRESS (☏ 9856004; www.parks.org.il; ⊕ 08.00–17.00 Sat–Thu, 08.00–15.00 Fri; admission adult/child 13/7NIS) The massive fortress is situated within the boundary of Kibbutz Yehiam and holds a tender place in the hearts of all who live there. While the strong walls and imposing buttresses were built centuries ago, the fortress's defensive stature was used in more recent times when, during the 1948 Arab–Israeli War, residents sought refuge and protection from the surrounding conflict.

The exact date of construction is unknown but at some point in its life it, like the nearby Montfort Castle, it was sold to the Teutonic Knights upon their departure from Akko. In 1265, it was conquered by the Mamluk sultan Baibars in his rampage through the region. Much of the fortress was destroyed and remained derelict until the Bedouin sheikh Zahir al-Amr returned it to its former glory in the 1760s, constructing the great square defences we see today.

While there is an interesting movie presentation within the national park, the most rousing and worthwhile reason to visit (besides the impressive remains themselves) is the fabulous view of the green peaks and valleys of the Galilee offered from the top.

A **campsite** (inc park admission: adult/child 40/30NIS) has a bathroom block, barbecue area and shade.

Getting there and away From Nahariya take route 89 heading towards Tzfat and turn on to route 8833 at the Ga'aton junction. From Nahariya, buses 39 and 42 go to and from Kibbutz Yehiam several times a day.

KIRYAT SHMONA

With a population of approximately 22,000, Kiryat Shmona is the largest city in the Upper Galilee. Sitting amidst the stunning landscape of the region, with its verdant valleys, fresh mountain peaks and its proud religious and Zionist history, it is most certainly the ugly duckling of the area. And Kiryat Shmona is showing no signs of flourishing into a beautiful swan any time soon. The city centre is dilapidated and run-down, seemingly forgotten about in the midst of the tourism boom seen in recent years in the surrounding settlements. While it claims to be the centre of tourism for the region, there really is very little of interest for visitors, and it is highly recommended to stay in one of the countryside zimmers or national park campsites nearby. Large manufacturing plants scar the area directly around the city, their bright lights and incessant noise humming throughout the night. The city is a major transport hub however, and there are buses to and from the otherwise relatively inaccessible northern Golan region. In fairness, the suburbs are marginally better, some parts even passing as quaint, but overall time would best be spent in other areas.

HISTORY The city was founded in 1949 on the site of a ruined Bedouin village whose residents fled after Tzfat was captured by Israeli forces in the 1948 Arab–Israeli War. It was initially used as a camp for immigrants involved in agriculture in the region but has slowly developed over the years into a large, if not particularly appealing, city. The city is named in honour of Joseph Trumpeldor and his seven comrades (*shmona* translates as eight) who died in 1920 defending **Tel Hai** (see box, pages 222–3). The city regularly makes international headline news as it is a popular target for Hezbollah and PLO rockets, launched from behind the nearby Lebanese border. Throughout countless skirmishes, residents have found themselves packing their bags and temporarily relocating south or spending days or weeks in underground bunkers.

GETTING THERE AND AWAY Kiryat Shmona is the transport hub of the region and can be reached from all major cities across the country. It also has good connections with the more inaccessible parts of the northern Golan and Upper Galilee. Bus routes 841 and 963 run regularly to and from Tiberias (1hr 30mins/29NIS) stopping at Rosh Pina and the Hula Valley, the 963 continuing to Jerusalem (4hrs/63NIS). Direct routes 842 and 845 leave hourly to Tel Aviv (3hrs 50mins/61NIS). Route 500 leaves every 45 minutes to Akko (1hr 30mins/40NIS) and Haifa Lev HaMifratz (2hrs/48NIS). Bus 58 leaves at 13.00 and stops at Shear Yashuv (15mins/9.80NIS), Neve Ativ (20mins/19NIS), Majdal Shams (25mins/20NIS), Masade (30mins/23NIS), Merom Golan (50mins/29NIS), Katzrin (1hr 30mins/37NIS) and Gadot (1hr 45mins/40NIS).

GETTING AROUND The bus station is centrally located and within easy walking distance of shops. If you are planning on hanging around in the city then inter-city buses, *sheruts* and taxis all run from outside the main bus terminal.

🚗 **Eldan Car Rental** Tel Hai St; ✆6903186; ⏱ 08.00–17.00 Sun–Thu, 08.00–13.00 Fri. Cars from 170NIS per day.

🚗 **Sixt** Kiryat Shmona South Industrial Area; ✆6941631; ⏱ 08.00–17.00 Sun–Thu, 08.00–12.00 Fri. Cars from 175NIS per day.

TOURIST INFORMATION
ℹ️ **Tourist information centre** 70 Tel Hai Bd; ⏱ 08.00–17.00 Sun–Thu, 08.00–13.00 Fri

⌂ **WHERE TO STAY AND EAT** Kiryat Shmona has no major hotels and very few eating options. You are strongly advised to take advantage of the beautiful countryside lodging and restaurants on the doorstep of this unsightly city, notably Kibbutz Manara, Shear Yashuv, Horshat Tal and Kibbutz HaGroshim (see pages 223–6).

⌂ **Manara Guest House** (51 rooms)
℡ 6908198, e tayarot@manara.co.il; www.
manara.co.il. Simply decorated but well equipped & roomy. Facilities inc TV, AC, refrigerator, microwave & en-suite bathroom with bath & separate shower. Guests can use the swimming pool (in summer) & the price inc b/fast in the kibbutz cafeteria. **$$$**

✕ **Nehalim** Gan Hatzafon; ℡ 6904875;
⏱ 12.00–23.00 daily. This is an extremely pleasant restaurant specialising in meat & fish dishes with a selection of creative sauces. Located on a delightful spot near the convergence of the Banias, Hatzbani and Dan rivers, 2.5km east of the Hametzudot junction on the right (look out for the petrol station). **$$$$$**

OTHER PRACTICALITIES There is a small shopping centre opposite the bus station that has all the standard high-street chain stores and is your best bet for getting provisions.

A ONE-ARMED FREEDOM FIGHTER – THE STORY OF TEL HAI

Straddling the border with Lebanon, the site of **Tel Hai** (℡ 6951331; ⏱ 08.00–16.00 Sun–Thu, 10.00–17.00 Fri; adult/child 18/15NIS) has long since come to represent Zionist heroism, and has become a pilgrimage for scores of Jewish tourists and Israeli schoolchildren. The lands upon which Tel Hai, a modest farming settlement, was built, were originally purchased in 1893 by the wealthy Jewish French baron, Edmond de Rothschild (see page 171). In 1918, members of the Galilee Farmers Union settled here and it became one of only four Jewish settlements in the Galilee. The 1916 Sykes–Picot agreement called for the division of large areas of the Middle East, where the Galilee would have been split in half. The secret agreement left the British, French and Arabs in dispute about the future of the area, and although the British conceded to allow the Upper Galilee to be under French control, the Arabs were strongly opposed. A retaliation on 1 March 1920 saw the community of Tel Hai attacked. As the story goes, a group of Arab soldiers demanded to search the premises, believing the Jews to be harbouring French soldiers. The Jewish farmers signalled for reinforcements from nearby Kfar Giladi, who arrived shortly after led by the one-armed Russian Zionist and founder of the Zionist Mule Corps (a British army battalion formed of Jewish volunteers), Joseph Trumpeldor. A raging conflict ensued and Trumpeldor and his seven comrades were killed. Remaining defenders burnt down the courtyard buildings and abandoned Tel Hai. Later the same year, members of Kibbutz Kfar Giladi returned and rebuilt the farm, a move that resulted in Tel Hai (along with Metulla and Kfar Giladi) being included in the British Mandate over Palestine and therefore, later, in the State of Israel.

The story of Tel Hai is one that has come to represent Jewish determination and today acts as a poignant symbol of heroism, self-defence and sacrifice told throughout Israeli households. Trumpeldor and his seven soldiers have left a long legacy, notably the city of Kiryat Shmona (City of Eight), which was named in their memory. Claimed to be Trumpeldor's last words, the phrase 'Never mind, it is good to die for our country' became legendary in Israel, although many award the origin of these words to the ancient Latin phrase *Dulce et decorum est pro patria mori* (It is sweet and honourable to die for one's country). Every year, the battle at Tel Hai

$ **Bank Hapoalim** Tzahal Sq; 03 6532407;
🕐 08.30–13.15 Sun & Tue/Wed, 08.30–13.00 &
16.00–18.30 Mon & Thu

WHAT TO SEE

Shehumit Hill Offers a bird's-eye view of both Kiryat Shmona and the nearby Hula Valley.

The Golden Park Traversed by the Ein Zahav Stream, this is a rather pleasant escape from the drabness of the city centre. Green lawns, a small wood, an Ottoman-period flour mill and a small, quaint mosque, today housing the **Kiryat Shmona History Museum** (*26 Hayarden St;* 6940135; 🕐 *08.00–12.00 Sun–Thu*) are all features of the park.

Manara Cliff and kibbutz These days Manara is most well known for its cable-car system leading down Israel's highest cliff (888m). Zimmer have been created

and the death of Joseph Trumpeldor are honoured in a memorial held on the 11th day of Adar in the Jewish calendar.

The fort that stands today provides visitors with an insight into the historical background of the site, and a monument commemorating the eight heroes stands in the form of a stone lion erected near their graves. Audio-visual presentations in a host of languages are available and a collection of tools from the time is on display.

On the opposite side of the road is the **Bet Ha'Shomer Museum** (6941565; 🕐 *08.00–15.30 Sun–Thu, 08.00–12.00 Fri; admission adult/child 20/15NIS*) at Kibbutz Kfar Giladi. Often referred to as the precursor to the IDF, Ha'Shomer (meaning 'Watchman'), was a group of 108 men and women selected to protect Jewish settlements in the country. Until its formation in 1907, settlement protection was outsourced to Circassian and Arab guards. Ha'Shomer was successful in its protection of Jewish interests, to the antagonism of the Arab population. Many, mainly Russians, were exiled by the Ottoman government, yet the group survived until 1920 when it was succeeded by the Haganah, a more organised military organisation. The museum here displays early 20th-century clothing, buildings, photos, weapons and an audio-visual presentation. Batia Lichansky, sister-in-law of Yitzhak Ben Zvi, one of the primary members, also has a sculpture display in one of the rooms.

GETTING THERE AND AWAY Tel Hai is located on route 90 just south of Kiryat Shmona. Head through the city and follow signs to the site and the nearby kibbutz of Kfar Giladi. Bus 21 from Kiryat Shmona runs to and from Metulla every two hours and will drop you off at the kibbutz (15mins/11.30NIS).

WHERE TO STAY

🏠 **Tel-Hai Guest House (HI)** (83 rooms) Kibbutz Tel Hai, opposite side of the junction to Kibbutz Kfar Giladi; 6940043; e tel-hai@iyha.org.il, www.iyha.org.il. In keeping with the Hostelling International reputation for exceptionally clean yet uninspiring rooms this hostel provides a good, cheap option in the area. Private rooms, & dorms (137NIS), have AC & TV & the price inc kosher b/fast. **$$$**

by the residents, and the stunning views offered by being perched high on a cliff edge are one of its key assets (especially if you look beyond Kiryat Shmona at its foot towards the lush greenery of the Hula Valley). The **Galilee Adventure Park** (\ 6905830; f 6905833; www.cliff.co.il; ⊕ 09.30–16.30 daily; admission w/day/w/end 59/69NIS) is a little kitsch and clearly aimed mainly towards the younger (or more fearless) set, but the 1,940m-long cable car is a novel way of getting up the cliff to the kibbutz. A 1,200m-long mountain slide that snakes its way back down the cliff hit the headlines during the 2006 Lebanon War when Hezbollah rockets destroyed a significant section.

Rappelling, a zip line, a trampoline bungee dome and climbing wall give thrill-seekers a choice of extreme activities. For those less disposed to throw themselves off cliffs, a one-hour guided hike can be arranged providing an explanation of the area, land and surrounding sites. Alternatively, the kibbutz's apple orchards are open to summer fruit pickers as is the well-maintained (but often crowded) swimming pool. Price packages can be purchased together with nearby Kibbutz Kfar Blum activities (see page 226).

The entrance to the Manara Cliff cable car is along route 90 just south Kiryat Shmona. Buses heading to and from Kiryat Shmona will drop you at the cable-car entrance. To drive to the kibbutz, follow route 90 north and turn left at the Tel Hai turn-off. After 3km, turn left and follow the signs to Manara.

METULLA

Metulla is a small, rural town located at the end of the north–south highway 90, straddling the border with Lebanon. Founded in 1896 as one of Baron Edmond de Rothschild's purchases, the land on which it stands originally belonged to a Druze landowner. Until the 1980s and the construction of the Canada Centre (a vast sporting complex, see opposite) the local economy depended on agriculture, namely fruit, wine and cattle. Today, the Canada Centre and the town's surrounding natural and historic attractions have created a prosperous tourist economy, although agriculture still plays a pivotal role. Several waterfalls gush through the orchard-lined valleys on their route from the snow-capped peaks of Mount Hermon to the Hula Valley, visible to the south. The Ayun River, which enters Israel from Lebanon, has carved out a small canyon on its way to the lower lands around the Jordan Valley. The town oozes tranquillity and an appreciation of the nature that surrounds it. The lovely little main street is lined with white limestone houses, restaurants and galleries, and accommodation, mainly zimmer cabins and bed and breakfast, is plentiful. Because of its proximity to the Lebanese border, the town does bustle with soldiers, particularly during times of high alert. But for the most part it is a quiet, peaceful, rural farming community.

GETTING THERE AND AWAY Buses 20 and 21 leave every two hours between Kiryat Shmona and Metulla (15mins/11.30NIS).

🏠 **WHERE TO STAY**

🏠 **Beit Shalom Estate** (13 rooms)
28 HaRishonim St; \ 6940767; e miriam@ beitshalom.co.il; www.beitshalom.co.il. Refined elegance & antique glamour exude at the luxury Beit Shalom Estate. Exquisitely decorated with no 2 rooms alike, the family-run guesthouse offers a small spa, gourmet restaurant & a real personal touch. *Suites cost up to 1,200NIS per night & w/day prices are up to 200NIS cheaper* **$$$**.
$$$$

WHERE TO EAT

✗ Beit Shalom Restaurant 28 HaRishonim St; ✆6997177; ◷ 10.00–midnight daily. Rustic country-style dishes with a taste of the Mediterranean. Housed in a 19th-century stone mansion, this is the place to treat yourself. Mains inc lamb kebab on green tahini & chicken liver in plum sauce as well as more simple pasta dishes. $$$

WHAT TO SEE AND DO

Canada Centre (*1 HaRishonim St;* ✆*6950370; www.canada-centre.co.il;* ◷ *10.00–20.00 Mon–Sat* (*ice skating & spa 10.00–16.00 Mon–Thu, 10.00–18.00 Fri*)) In rather distinct contrast to the sleepy little town in which it sits, this huge complex is a hub of sport, exercise and leisure facilities. It features the country's largest ice-skating rink, sizeable indoor and outdoor swimming pools, squash courts, table tennis rooms, a fitness centre, bowling alley and basketball court. There is also a shooting range, and a health club offering treatment packages.

Nahal Ayun Nature Reserve (✆*6951519;* ◷ *08.00–17.00 Sat–Thu, 08.00–15.00 Fri (1 hr earlier in winter); admission adult/child 25/13NIS*) Located on the edge of Metulla is the beautiful Ayun Nature Reserve. As the Ayun Stream sweeps across the border from Lebanon it flows through a canyon, creating in turn four waterfalls. The rest of the year however sees a raging flow, providing for some lovely hiking opportunities.

One entrance to the reserve is located in Metulla's upper car park (signposted), and is the beginning of the longer of two trails (1hr 30mins). For a lovely hike follow the path downstream, passing all the falls as you go. The *pièce de résistance* of the reserve is the 30m-high Tanur Waterfall, the last of the four. It gushes over the steep canyon shelf, spraying the wild flowers, oleander and honeysuckle with a fine mist of ice-cold water. Note that if you can't arrange for transport to pick you up at the lower car park, there is a rather hefty walk back upstream to the upper one.

The shorter trail through the reserve forms a circular route, beginning and ending in the lower car park. It incorporates the Tanur Waterfall and a birdwatching post (30mins).

To get to the Tanur Waterfall and lower car park, turn right approximately 1km before Metulla. For the Ayun and Cascade Falls (and upper car park) take the road near the border fence in the north of the town.

AROUND KIRYAT SHMONA AND METULLA

TEL DAN NATIONAL PARK (✆*6951579; www.parks.org.il;* ◷ *08.00–17.00 Sat–Thu, 08.00–15.00 Fri; admission adult/child 25/13NIS*) Kill two birds with one proverbial stone at Tel Dan Nature Reserve, combining nature and archaeology. The River Dan is the most crucial source of the Jordan River, fed by meltwater from the Hermon Mountains. Countless streams converge in the park's grounds as they pour into the river on their way to the Jordan Valley. Vegetation and wildlife thrive in the abundance of water and the mild climate, forming a shady forest in which to explore. Four trails lead through the park's grounds, providing access to its different attractions. Follow the course of the river through the sometimes 20m-tall Syrian ash trees (1hour 15mins) or head to the remains of the ancient biblical city of Dan (45mins), which according to the Book of Judges was captured from the Caananites by the Tribe of Dan. It has been associated with Jeroboam, a biblical figure who was the first king of the northern tribe of Israel. Hilltop reconstructions of an arched Canaanite gate and Israelite-period city gateway are good accompaniments to the remains.

GETTING THERE AND AWAY Buses 36 and 55 (58 returning) run between Kiryat Shmona and the northern Golan Heights stop at Kibbutz Dan (1km from the park entrance) several times daily (16mins/9.80NIS) as well as Shear Yashuv and Horshat Tal (15mins/9.80NIS) along the way.

⌂ Where to stay

⚐ Horshat Tal Campsite `6942360`; www.parks.org.il; ⊕ 24hrs, last admission 22.30 (closed in winter); admission (campsite & national park) adult/child 60/50NIS. The Horshat Tal National Park is pleasant, but not really much to write home about. The adjacent campsite, however, provides a fantastic choice of cheap accommodation and is located approximately 2km from Tel Dan National Park on route 99. Pitch your tent next to the gushing streams flowing through manicured lawns or rent one of the bungalows or cabins. Clean showers & toilets & plenty of space under the shade of the oak trees (unless it's a summer w/end in which case it's peg to peg). A night in the campsite grants you access to the park for an early-bird swim in the frosty waters of the natural pools. Bungalows 350NIS up to 4 people (100NIS more on w/ends), cabins 450NIS up to 4 people (200NIS more on w/ends), wooden cabins 700NIS up to 4 people (300NIS more on w/ends).

⌂ She'ar Yashuv The quaint She'ar Yashuv holiday village sits in a prime location, equidistant from the sites of the northern Golan Heights & those in the Upper Galilee. The village is small but chock-full of dainty wooden zimmers as well as a clinic, small gym, grocery store, restaurant & horseriding centre. There is also access to the Banias River from within the village. A map on the right as you enter the village will direct you to the 26 family-run zimmers & other amenities.

✗ Where to eat

✗ Dag Al Hadan North of Kibbutz HaGoshrim; `6950225`; www.dagaldan.co.il; ⊕ 12.00–midnight daily. Kosher. Situated on the confluence of the Hatzbani & Dan rivers, this delightful open-air fish restaurant dishes up a fabulous selection of fresh- & saltwater fish, as well offering a lovely riverside location. The local trout is highly recommended. There's a 10% discount for guests taking part in **kayaking & rafting** (`6950225`) activities in the kibbutz. There is also a well-equipped **campsite** (50NIS pp). **$$$$**

What to do

HaGoshrim Kayaks (`6816034`; *www.Kayak.co.il*) This is a popular kayaking centre on the Jordan River, offering 'extreme' routes and for the more faint-hearted and families a gentler route (70NIS). There is a campsite, children's paddling pool, bike rental and ATV tours also on offer – but be warned, this place is shoulder-to-shoulder during school summer holidays.

KFAR BLUM

Founded in 1943, Kibbutz Kfar Blum was named after the Jewish socialist and former French president Leon Blum. From its founding until the present day it has survived on an economy formed primarily of agriculture, although of late, tourism seems to have snuck in and taken over, and now the kibbutz offers an array of family activities in the shape of **Kfar Blum Kayaks** (`6902616`; *www.kayaks.co.il*). They offer two-person kayaks or six-person rafts on trips down the Jordan and Hatzbani rivers. A one hour 15 minute circular route costs 79NIS per person while a two hour 30 minute 'adrenalin' trip is 112NIS per person. Children's activities, bicycle tours and a rope park complete with zip line and climbing wall are all offered for around 79NIS per person. It is highly recommended to visit midweek and out of school holidays, as come weekends it is overrun with excitable children and raucous families.

In summer, the week-long **Voice of Music Festival**, also referred to as the Kfar Blum Festival, marks the centre of all activity in and around the kibbutz. Up to 15,000 music-lovers attend the fantastic mix of classical compositions and modern experimental pieces each year.

GETTING THERE AND AWAY Buses 30 and 32 depart Kiryat Shmona (8mins/ 9.80NIS) at 11.00, 11.40, 14.00 & 15.50 returning at 06.30, 15.15 and 18.35. By car turn east at Gomeh junction off route 90 and follow the road for 4km before turning left to the kibbutz.

WHERE TO STAY AND EAT

Pastoral Hotel Kfar Blu (125 rooms) 6836611; e pastoral@kbm.org.il; www.kfarblum-hotel.com. Luxury hotel & spa decorated in a Mediterranean-style elegance. Bright & airy rooms overlook the kibbutz's olive orchards & outdoor swimming pool. Suites have jacuzzi baths & separate living rooms. Tennis courts, a gym, sports facilities & restaurant are open to hotel guests. *Rooms up to 400NIS less off-season* $$$. $$$$$

Kfar Blum Kayaks Camping Located in the grounds of the kayaking centre (see below) next to the Jordan River. Hot showers, a cooking area, picnic tables & a kiosk are 50NIS pp.

AGAMON HULA VALLEY BIRDWATCHING RESERVE

6817137; www.agamon-hula.co.il; 09.00–1hr before dusk Sun–Thu, 06.30–1hr before dusk Fri/Sat; admission 52NIS (inc shuttle)) South of Kiryat Shmona, HaGoshrim and Tel Dan National Park, the Hula Valley sits tucked into the northern part of the Syrian-African Rift Valley, south of Kiryat Shmona, HaGoshrim and Tel Dan National Park, and is one of the most crucial winter stopovers for the 360 species of migratory birds who drop in on their way south. Between the months of October and March, an estimated 500 million birds jostle for space in the skies and waters of the Hula Valley, a large proportion of which is today utilised for agriculture. Up until 1950, when most of the area was drained, the Hula Valley was one of the largest wetland areas in the Middle East. Following environmental objections to the drainage, a small swampland was created in 1963 and claimed the honour of being Israel's first nature reserve. Today the area is undoubtedly the single most important wetland in the country for waterbirds and is graced with the presence of 20 globally threatened species, including the imperial eagle, spotted eagle and marbled duck.

Lake Agamon sits at the centre of the Agamon Hula Reserve and is the stage for spotting countless species of wildfowl, including hundreds of thousands of cranes. Other wildlife is in abundance too, with water buffalo, once indigenous to the area, having been reintroduced.

A large array of eco-friendly transport methods is on offer to get out into the heart of the park, ranging from bicycles (52NIS), tandems (125NIS), four-man bicycles (175NIS), golf carts (190NIS) or the safari wagon (52NIS pp). There are two flat and fairly undemanding routes (6km and 10.5km) following a circular route around the lake. A small introduction video is presented at the entrance, which can be played in English on request.

Getting there and away All Kiryat Shmona-bound buses will stop along route 90 from which it is a hefty 3km walk to the park entrance. Follow directions through agricultural buildings to the large car park. There is a nature reserve run by the Israel Nature and National Parks Protection Authority a little further south along the valley which can be easily mistaken for the birdwatching centre, so look out for signs.

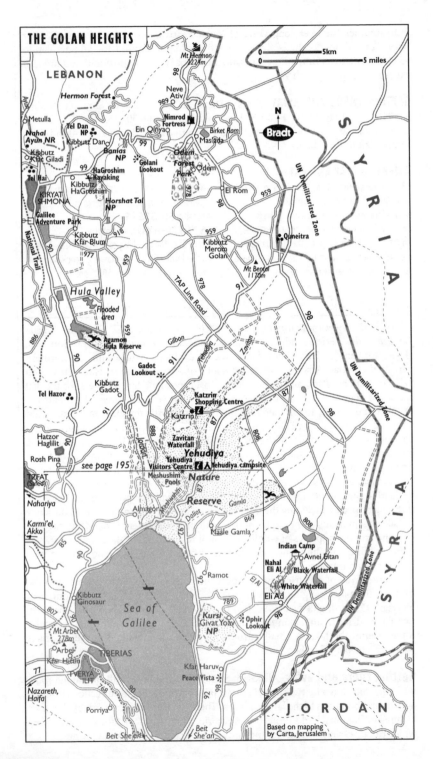

THE GOLAN HEIGHTS

LEBANON

Mt Hermon 2224m

Neve Ativ

Hermon Forest

Metulla

Nahal Ayun NR

Kibbutz Kfar Giladi

Tel Dan NP

Kibbutz Dan

Ein Qinya

Nimrod Fortress

Birket Ram

Masada

Banias NP

Kibbutz Dan

Golani Lookout

Odem Forest Park

Odem

El Rom

Tel Hai

HaGroshim Kayaking

KIRYAT SHMONA

Kibbutz HaGroshim

Horshat Tal NP

Galilee Adventure Park

Kibbutz Kfar Blum

Kibbutz Merom Golan

Mt Bental 1170m

Quneitra

UN Demilitarized Zone

S Y R I A

Hula Valley

Flooded area

TAP Line Road

Agamon Hula Reserve

Gilbon

Gadot Lookout

Kibbutz Gadot

Tel Hazor

Katzrin Shopping Centre

Katzrin

Hatzor Haglilit

Rosh Pina

Jordan

Zavitan Waterfall

Yehudiya

Yehudiya Visitors Centre

Yehudiya campsite

TZFAT (Safed)

see page 195

Meshushim Pools

Nature

Nahariya

Almagor

Daliot

Reserve

Gamla

Karmi'el, Akko

Maale Gamla

Indian Camp

Avnei Eitan

National Trail

Kibbutz Ginosaur

Sea of Galilee

Ramot

Nahal Eli Al

Black Waterfall

White Waterfall

Eli Ad

Mt Arbel 278m

Arbel

Kfar Hittin

Kursi Givat Yoav NP

Ophir Lookout

TIBERIAS

TVERYA ILIT

Nazareth, Haifa

Porriya

Kfar Haruv

Peace Vista

Beit She'ar

Beit She'an

J O R D A N

Based on mapping by Carta, Jerusalem

0 — 5km
0 — 5 miles

Bradt

N

228

8

The Golan Heights

Telephone code 04

Please note that the region known as the Golan Heights is, according to UN classification, an Israeli-occupied area of land. Israel's annexation of the Golan Heights in 1981 was not recognised by the UN and as such remains a disputed zone. For the purposes of this guidebook and the ease of use to travellers, however, it has been included under the title of Israel. The area has no borders or checkpoints, posing few or no problems for visitors to the area.

Conjuring images of war-torn lands, ferocious battles and heavy rocket fire, the Golan Heights is often overlooked by foreign visitors to Israel, its tumultuous existence and remote location acting as deterrents to most. Yet it is Israel's most misunderstood region, and in fact exudes a peace, harmony and beauty that few other places can claim. Culturally and geologically it stands apart from its neighbouring Galilee, its rugged, untamed landscape sparsely inhabited by Druze and Jewish communities. Roaring rivers, jagged mountain peaks, deep canyons and gushing waterfalls have found their place in the wild 55km stretch of land that forms Israel's northern- and easternmost frontiers.

Life in the Golan has for years relied on agriculture, vineyards, orchards and, most significantly, cattle rearing. In recent years, however, tourism has started to creep in and now rural pursuits are being offered to those in search of solitude, nature and an escape from all things urban.

Beginning at the Sea of Galilee, the southern Golan plateau offers a tranquil environment, where rolling hills dotted with cattle and grazing horses spill into the lake below. Inhabited by Jewish communities, the southern region is characterised by its rich archaeological remains and stunning natural scenery. In contrast is the rugged northern region of the Golan Heights, the towering Mount Hermon range sitting at its northernmost point overlooking Syria and Lebanon. A few Druze communities farm the lower slopes where imposing Roman castles and grand Crusader forts guard the ancient highways.

Oak forests, blossoming wild flowers and alpine meadows combine to form an impressive and unexpected landscape and an environment that supports the country's most varied wildlife species. As a meeting point for fauna arriving from the cold steppes of Asia and Europe and the desert lands of the Syrian-African Rift Valley its variety is immense. Gazelles, hyenas, wild boars, foxes, wolves and hundreds of species of birds including the Bonelli's eagle and Egyptian vultures roam over the lands.

The population of the Golan Heights is approximately 39,000, over half of whom are Druze. Inhabiting the four Druze settlements of Majdal Shams, Masada, Buqata and Ein Qinya they are famed for their hospitality, loyalty and traditional food. The 16,500 Jews who live here are spread across more than 30 tiny villages, their luxury guesthouses, rustic restaurants and laid back lifestyle well known across the country.

HISTORY

ANCIENT–19TH CENTURY The mélange of historic, archaeological and modern battle sites that are scattered across the Golan Heights are testament to its colourful and turbulent past. Although archaeological evidence dates the Golan's habitation as far back as the late Stone Age, permanent settlement didn't arrive until much later. It acted as a buffer zone between the warring Israelites and Arameans, and it was during this time that the city of Golan was founded as an Israelite refuge. The Golan Heights, along with the rest of the region, came under the control of Alexander the Great in 332BCE and in the years following his death was heavily settled, the empire coming to an end when the Golan was conquered by the Romans. During the booming years that followed, cities such as Banias, Gamla, Hippos, Gadera, Seleucia and Sogane became centres of Greco-Roman culture, flourishing until the Jewish revolt against iron-fisted Roman rule. With the coming of the Byzantine Empire came also Christianity and the Golan prospered, new towns, churches and synagogues emerging in great numbers.

After the defeat of the Byzantine Empire in 636BCE the Golan, and all of Syria, fell into the hands of Muslim Arabs. Over time, the centre of power migrated further east to cities such as Damascus and Baghdad, and the Golan was once again wandered by few other than nomadic Bedouin tribes. That is until Crusader rule in the Holy Land when the Golan found itself once again a buffer zone, this time between Christian and Muslim forces, each fortifying this no-man's-land with huge castles and forts. Throughout the Golan's long Ottoman rule the region was all but forgotten, inhabited mainly by Bedouins and, in the 19th century, Druze communities who migrated from Lebanon and Syria.

MODERN HISTORY The end of World War I and the signing of the Sykes–Picot Agreement saw the Golan come under French control. The establishment of Syria in 1946 signalled the end of the French mandate, and upon the British departure from Palestine in 1948 (and Israel's subsequent declaration of independence) the Syrians invaded the Golan Heights. They heavily fortified the entire region, converting it into a launch post for attacks against Israel. Bunkers, camps and military towns appeared, the bullet-ridden remnants of which still dot the landscape in the northern highlands.

Years of skirmishes between the Syrians and Israelis over the important water supply in the area culminated in the Six Day and Yom Kippur wars which saw Israel capture and later defend the Golan Heights. During the wars most of the Druze inhabitants fled the area, those who remained cut off from their neighbours on the

---

HITCHHIKING THE ISRAELI WAY

Hitchhiking is standard practice in Israel and you are unlikely to see a bus stop without a small gaggle of youngsters and soldiers pointing at the floor. In contrast to most countries where a smile and a thumbs up is your best hope of getting a free lift from a stranger, in Israel the technique is to look aloof and carefree whilst casually pointing at the ground with one index finger. While it needs to be said that hitchhiking always comes with certain risks, they are minimal in Israel, and you needn't worry about giving it a go. Indeed, in some of the more remote parts of the country, it may be your only option.

other side of the border. By the end, Israeli troops were stationed only 35km from Damascus, which eventually resulted in the signing of a disengagement agreement whereby Israel returned 100km^2 of land to Syria. Military forces on both sides were regulated, leaving a minimal number of troops and a UN observer force installed along the border.

In 1981, the Israeli government made the decision to incorporate the Golan Heights under Israeli law and jurisdiction, a highly controversial move that is to this day not recognised by the UN and much of the international community. Syria has always demanded the return of the pre-Six Day War lands, a factor which, combined with Israel's requirement for the disarmament of the Syrian-backed Hezbollah, stands in the way of any sort of negotiations and peace talks between the two countries. While war is unfortunately never off the table, there have been no battles between the two countries in over 40 years.

ORIENTATION

Travelling in the Golan Heights is somewhat different from other areas of the country and it is a good idea to orientate yourself with the region and what it has to offer before embarking on a trip. Firstly, the region has an extremely limited – if not obsolete – public transport network. Where possible, buses have been included, but the ideal – and sometimes only – way to travel is to rent a car from nearby Galilean towns such as Tiberias or Nazareth. As in other parts of Israel, hitchhiking is possible, but the sparse communities and lack of traffic on the often near-deserted roads mean you may be waiting around for a long time.

Katzrin is the largest urban centre in the region, and a preliminary glance will tell you that it is not exactly large. For basic services though, it is a good bet (there is also a small shopping centre just outside **Givat Yo'av**, which has a selection of services and a decent supermarket). Otherwise, the tiny but hospitable and beautiful moshavim, kibbutzim and Druze villages that house the rest of the Golan's population provide rural-style accommodation, rustic home cooking and activity centres such as horseriding, bicycle rental and jeep tours. **Ramot** is a good base for these activities in the south and **Merom Golan** or **Neve Ativ** are lovely options in the north. Accommodation in the Golan is expensive; there's no two ways about it. In summer, **campsites** are a good budget option, but the emergence of a couple of well-equipped hostels in the southern part of the area is a godsend to the thrifty traveller. In the north, **zimmers** will be your only option in winter months when it's too cold to camp. If your budget stretches to it then you're in for a real treat as the Golan's zimmers are some of the most luxurious in the country. While these can be extremely pricey in peak season and at weekends, weekdays are more reasonable. Several are listed in this section, but it is possible (and recommended) to drive through any of the dozens of moshavim or kibbutzim and look for vacancy signs outside. In peak seasons it is certainly advisable to book ahead.

Although rugged and sparsely populated, the Golan Heights is a small region. It is easily navigable, although roads closer to the Syrian border (which is separated by the UN Demilitarized Zone) are sometimes unpaved. Owing to its altitude, most notably in the mountainous zones of the northern Golan, temperatures can plummet and a substantial blanket of snow covers the slopes of Mount Hermon throughout the winter months. Warm clothing is essential, even in the summer months, where the air at the peak of Mount Hermon can still be fairly brisk.

Unexploded landmines, unstable, dangerous relics left from the Yom Kippur and Six Day wars, are scattered across the Golan Heights, both in fields and along the sides of roads. Warning signs are everywhere and barbed-wire fences surround 'no entry' zones but beware, especially when hiking. Always stick to marked trails and heed all warnings. The IDF do extensive training up in the rugged terrain of the northern Golan Heights so be on alert or you might find yourself staring down the barrel of a tank gun. It is important to adhere to 'no entry' signs for both **landmine zones** and **army training areas**. For more information call 04 6977224, but if in doubt, don't enter.

KATZRIN

Katzrin (or Kisrin, Qasrin and Qazrin as various road signs spell it) is the only semi-major settlement in the entire Golan Heights region, and is often referred to – rather generously – as the capital. There is no real need to stay in the town, but if you are in search of a post office, supermarket, bank, police station or medical centre then it is the obvious choice. There are of course such facilities dotted around the Golan Heights' many moshavim, but Katzrin's concentration of services, centred on its nearby shopping centre, make it the most convenient. While the town itself is not unattractive, there isn't an awful lot to do. So if you do choose to stopover then expect an early night.

GETTING THERE AND AWAY There is one bus a day to and from Tel Aviv (3hrs 50mins/51NIS) leaving at 16.00 (12.15 on Fri) and returning at 04.50 (07.45 on Fri). Bus 966 leaves Jerusalem twice a day at 08.45 and 17.15 (12.15 Fri) (4hrs/59NIS) and returns at 06.00 and 13.00 (07.00 only on Fri). Bus 55 leaves Katzrin at 11.30 (1hr 50mins/37NIS) to Kiryat Shmona, stopping at Merom Golan, El Rom, Masade, Majdal Shams, Neve Ativ and Hagroshim/Horshat Tal along the way. Bus 58 leaves Kiryat Shmona at 16.40 to Katzrin, and the 55 leaves at 13.30 and makes the same stops. To Tiberias, buses 15 and 19 leave at 05.50, 06.50 and 14.00 (06.00 & 07.00 Fri, 16.16 & 19.30 Sat) (1hr 20mins/29NIS) taking a clockwise route around the Sea of Galilee. Heading from Tiberias to Katzrin buses 15 and 19 leave at 12.00, 13.30, 16.00 and 18.35 (12.00 & 13.00 Fri, 22.45 Sat).

TOURIST INFORMATION A new and rather oddly placed **shopping centre** has been built on the outskirts of the town, about 2km from the centre, which contains most of Katzrin's facilities. The industrial centre is located directly behind the shopping centre. The **Golan Heights Tourist Information Centre** (*Katzrin Shopping Centre;* ✎ *04 6962885;* e *tour@golan.org.il;* ◷ *08.30–16.30 Sun–Thu, 08.30–13.00 Fri*) is located in the shopping centre, although tourist information signs still incorrectly direct you into town. It is small and the staff unenthusiastic but there are lots of leaflets to pick up.

⌂ **WHERE TO STAY, EAT AND DRINK** Sleeping options are limited to small bed and breakfasts of which the tourist information centre can provide an updated list. The Golan's magic, however, most certainly isn't in Katzrin and you are well advised to seek refuge in the beautiful rural accommodation in nearby villages. For budget eats there are several fast-food outlets and a supermarket in the shopping mall.

🏠 **SPNI Golan Field School** (34 rooms) Zavitan Rd; ✆6961234; e rafim@spni.org.il. Has 6-bed rooms that can be rented for 330NIS including b/fast (beds cannot be reserved individually as with dorms). Often full with school groups so best to call ahead.

OTHER PRACTICALITIES

$ Bank Leumi Katzrin Shopping Centre; ✆03 9544555; ⊕ 08.30–13.00 & 16.00–18.15 Mon & Thu, 08.30–14.30 Tue/Wed, 08.30–12.30 Fri. Has an ATM.

➕ **Emek Pharm** Katzrin Shopping Centre; ✆6962578; ⊕ 08.30–19.00 Sun–Thu, 08.30–13.00 Fri

🍷 **Golan Brewery** Katzrin Shopping Centre; ✆6961311; www.beergolan.co.il; ⊕ 11.00–late daily. Offering a cloudy glass of locally brewed ice-cold beer, its location in the shopping centre is rather soulless, but the beer (& lack of alternatives) makes it a pleasant choice.

Mayaan Laundry Katzrin Industrial Park; ✆6964422; ⊕ 08.00–17.00 Sun–Thu, 08.00–13.00 Fri. Located just past the Golan Heights Winery (see below).

WHAT TO SEE

Golan Archaeological Museum (*Katzrin;* ✆*6961350; www.museum.golan.org.il;* ⊕ *09.00–16.00 Sun–Thu, 09.00–15.30 Fri, 10.30–13.30 Sat; admission adult/child 26/18NIS (with entry to Katzrin Ancient Village)*) The museum is located in the town itself, next to the small commercial centre, and houses finds from prehistory through to Talmudic times. A reconstruction Chacolithic house is one of the museum's top attractions.

Katzrin Ancient Village (*Katzrin Rd East;* ✆ *962412; www.parkqazrin.org.il;* ⊕ *09.00–16.00 Sun–Thu, 09.00–14.00 Fri, 10.00–16.00 Sat; admission adult/child 24/16NIS (with entry to the Golan Archaeological Museum)*) Located next to the shopping centre about 2km from town is a large-scale reconstruction of a Talmudic village and synagogue. The village was built here to commemorate the ancient village discovered and excavated nearby, whose synagogue was undoubtedly its crowning glory. After a violent earthquake in 746ce, the flourishing town was abandoned and remained deserted until the Mamluk period when it was resettled and a mosque erected inside the synagogue. Reconstruction wine and olive presses, traditional houses, a spring and the synagogue have been built to create an entertaining and informative experience.

Golan Magic (*Katzrin Shopping Centre;* ✆ *6963625; www.magic-golan.co.il;* ⊕ *09.00–17.00 Sun–Thu, 09.00–16.00 Fri, 09.00–17.00 Sat; admission adult/child 25/18NIS*) This 180° show features the history and geography of the Golan Heights and incorporates smells, sights and sounds. It is an entertaining sensory experience and probably the least energetic activity you can do in the Golan region.

Golan Heights Winery (*Katzrin Industrial Park;* ✆ *6968435;* e *dudi@golanwines. co.il; www.golanwines.co.il;* ⊕ *08.00–17.00 Sun, 08.30–18.30 Mon–Thu, 08.30–13.00 Fri.*) Call ahead to make reservations for a visit. (See box, *A bottle of Israel's finest,* page 174.)

AROUND KATZRIN

YEHUDIYA FOREST NATURE RESERVE (*Route 87;* ✆ *6962817; www.parks.org.il;* ⊕ *Apr–Sep 08.00–17.00; Oct–Mar 08.00–16.00 (1hr earlier in winter); admission adult/child 20/9NIS*) The Yehudiya reserve spreads like an outstretched hand across the southern Golan, and is characterised by its five rivers, verdant vegetation, gushing waterfalls, clear pools and steep canyons. The park's 66km² are home to wild boar, jackals, red foxes, Syrian hyrax and porcupines who live amidst the huge variety of tree and plant species. It is also one of the best spots in the region to spy the Bonelli's eagle and Egyptian vulture that are often seen soaring in the skies above. Flowing through the 'fingers' of the park are the Meshoshim, Zavitan, Yehudiya, Gamla and Daliyot rivers that emerge from deep, rock-cut canyons into the Beit Zaida Valley just north of the Sea of Galilee.

There are innumerable hiking trails in and around the park and the information centre can offer a wealth of advice and recommendations. Trails range from mild, family-oriented walking paths to extremely challenging routes that involve rappelling or swimming, so be sure to choose carefully before setting off. The Gamla Nature Reserve, once one of the top sites in the area both for its archaeological ruins and as a nesting site for the vultures, was ravaged by a fire in 2010. The beautiful landscape was charred and the vultures wisely chose other areas in which to nest.

The well-equipped **Yehudiya Campsite** (✆ *6962817; admission adult/child 40/30NIS*) is located next to the information centre midway between the Katzrin road and the Yehudiya junction on route 87.

Getting there and away The park entrance is located 5km south of Katzrin on route 87. Bus 15 runs between Tiberias and Katzrin and will stop outside the park

HIKING IN THE YEHUDIYA FOREST NATURE RESERVE

MESHUSHIM POOLS The hexagonal pools in the west of the park are among the most famous features in the region, and a dip in the clear waters is an undoubted highlight. Surrounded by eight-sided columns the pools are a geological marvel, formed when mineral-rich molten rock slowly cooled. There are several ways to approach the pools, the shortest and easiest being the 1½-hour hike from the Meshushim car park. To reach the car park follow route 888 north from the Beit Zaida junction and turn left just after the village of Had Nes. The trail leads down the canyon, across the river bridge to the pools on the other side. For a longer and considerably tougher hike start at the Yehudiya car park on route 87 and follow the trail westwards to the pools (4hrs). Note that this isn't a circular route so you will need to arrange for transport to pick you up at the end.

UPPER YEHUDIYA CANYON Beginning at either the Yehudiya Campsite or car park on route 87 the trail leads to the ancient village of Yehudiya from where it continues along the top of the canyon before descending steeply to the stream below. At one of the falls, the trail leads across a deep pool so it is important to note that you will need to swim across with all your belongings or turn back at this point. The trail then continues down the canyon where you can either carry on for a further 2km (through some more pools and waterfalls) or follow the green route, which will bring you back out at the ancient village of Yehudiya. The circular route takes approximately four hours.

UPPER ZAVITAN CANYON A long but moderately challenging hike leads from kilometre 6.5 on the Katzrin road to the Yehudiya car park (5hrs). The trail follows the Black Gorge southwards, passing the Zavitan Hexagon Pools and Zavitan Waterfall along the way.

entrance. From Tiberias buses leave at 12.00, 13.30, 16.00 and 18.35 (12.00 & 13.00 Fri, 22.45 Sat) (40mins/20NIS) and from Katzrin 05.50, 06.50 and 14.00 (06.00 & 07.00 Fri, 16.16 & 19.30 Sat) (25mins/13.50NIS)

GAMLA NATURE RESERVE (\ *6822282; www.parks.org.il;* ⊕ *Apr–Sep 08.00–17.00; Oct–Mar 08.00–16.00; admission adult/child 25/13NIS)* The dramatic landscape of the Gamla Nature Reserve once provided an apt home for both the wildlife and ancient history that was within its boundaries. The steep sides of the ridge were home to Israel's largest flock of griffon vultures, that made their nests on the steep inclines above the ravines. Unfortunately a ferocious fire in May 2010 ravaged the area and now a charred scrubland poses little appeal to visitors and indeed the vultures who, in late 2010, did not nest in the area. National park authorities hope that Gamla will return to its original beauty as quickly as possible, but this may take several years.

The park is also home to some fine archaeological remains which play a key role in the Golan's history. The ancient city of Gamla was the capital of Jewish Golan from 87BCE–68CE, and it was here that one of the heroic stories of the Jewish revolt unfolded. Led by Josephus Flavius, Commander of the Galilee, the fortified city of Gamla was the setting for mighty battles between the Jewish army and Vespasian's Roman troops, battles that ultimately resulted in Roman victory. Thousands of Gamla's residents were slaughtered, while others chose to leap from the cliffs rather than surrender. Extensive excavations have revealed impressive and substantial remains, including a 2nd-century synagogue, Byzantine church, an aqueduct, ritual bathhouse and several public buildings.

Getting there and away Follow the Sea of Galilee road until you reach the Gamla junction and then follow route 869 to the Daliot junction. After 2km turn north where a signposted dirt road leads to the park. Buses 15 and 19 leave Tiberias (45mins/19NIS) to Katzrin at 12.00, 13.30, 16.00 and 18.35 (12.00 & 13.00 Fri, 22.45 Sat), and will stop outside the park. From Katzrin the bus leaves at 05.50, 06.50 and 14.00 (06.00 & 07.00 Fri, 16.16 & 19.30 Sat) to Tiberias.

RAMOT

The tiny moshav of Ramot has developed as a hub of Golan tourism and, if your budget allows, is a beautiful, quaint little place to base yourself for exploring the area. Almost without exception every house has created luxury zimmer accommodation, each competing with its neighbour for novelty, quality and, unfortunately, high prices. Ramot is not a cheap place to stay and those on a budget are limited to camping (see below). During peak times the moshav can get booked up so it is certainly worth making reservations during this time. There is a comprehensive list of zimmers at www.zimmeril.com.

Ramot is perfectly located for exploring the landscape of the lower Golan, with its undulating green hills and views of the Sea of Galilee. Horseriding, jeep tours, cycling and hiking can all be arranged from within the moshav and the weather in the lower lands is generally milder than the highlands of the northern stretches of the Golan Heights. There are several excellent restaurants in the village plus two simple supermarkets.

GETTING THERE AND AWAY Public transport is limited to buses 15 (13.25, 16.00, 18.35) and 22 (12.40 and 16.45) from Tiberias. Going in the other direction buses leave Ramot for Tiberias at 06.40, 07.20, 13.30 and 18.15 (40mins/20NIS).

CRASH OUT OR SPLASH OUT IN THE SOUTHERN GOLAN HEIGHTS

Apart from the accommodation recommended in the villages and towns covered in this chapter, there are some other great spots that are worth considering, especially if you're looking for something a bit special, or are travelling on a tight budget.

CRASH OUT

⌂ **Genghis Khan** Givat Yo'av; ☎ 052 3715687; www.gkhan.co.il. The best budget option in the southern Golan Heights. Yurt tents, each with their own shower & toilet are set amidst green lawns with picnic tables & BBQ area. There are excellent views over the Golan hills. **$**

⌂ **The Indian Camp (Mapalim)** Avnei Eitan; ☎ 6762151; e indiantipi@hotmail.com; www.tipi.co.il. Budget-priced tepees are a big favourite with Israeli families. Budget options consist of huge tents with matting for bedding down for a communal night's sleep (they also have less rudimentary private tents $$$). 95NIS pp (min 4 people). **$**

⌂ **Yehudiya Campsite** Yehudiya National Park; ☎ 6962817; adult/child 40/30NIS (see page 234). **$**

SPLASH OUT

⌂ **Cnaan Village** (5 rooms) Had Nes; ☎ 6822128; e spa@cnaan-village.co.il; www. cnaan-village.co.il. Luxury, intimate spa village in the heart of the lower Golan Heights. The 5 exquisite, romantic suites each reflect a different emotion & inc king-size beds, jacuzzis & private terraces with stunning views. The spa boasts a beautiful indoor swimming pool & a range of massages & treatments. *300NIS less on w/days* **$$$$–$$$$$**

⌂ **Mitzpe HaShalom Country Lodge** (27 rooms) Kfar Haruv; ☎ 6761767; f 6761771; www.mitzpe-hashalom.co.il. Located next to the Peace Vista (see page 240) & set within manicured grounds. While the service is homely & accommodating (they even deliver b/fast hampers to your door), here it is all about the location. The utterly spectacular views of the Sea of Galilee will take your breath away. Cabins have kitchenette, jacuzzi, AC & living room. They also offer a unique holistic experience involving calming cave pools, music & wine. *200NIS less on w/days* **$$$–$$$$**

⌂ **Zimmers** The whole of the Golan Heights kibbutzim & moshavim are awash with luxury, romantic zimmers, whose rustic yet elegant cabins all sport jacuzzi baths, elegant décor & pretty surroundings. There are literally hundreds & while on w/ends they are extremely expensive, during the week you can get some good last-minute deals. It is also worth noting that most zimmers have a 2-night minimum stay on w/ends. For a complete list visit www.zimmeril.com.

TOURIST INFORMATION/TOUR OPERATORS Ramot is so tiny that most establishments don't use street names. As you enter the village myriad signs will point you to the right hotel, or just ask for directions.

Orchan Ramot ☎ 6732317/050 5209146; e alef1@netvision.net.il; www.orchanramot.co.il. Offer guided jeep tours in the surrounding countryside. 2hr tours cost 550NIS per jeep inc drinks & snacks. The well-equipped ranch also has a tidy campsite (or you can sleep on mattresses in the barn), & newly built bathroom block & kitchen (100NIS/night). Located at the far end of town.

Ofan Na'im Bicycle Rental ☎ 6732524. Bicycles, helmets & maps are provided which will lead you on several self-guided tours around the area. Prices range from 50NIS for a 2hr tour to 60NIS for a longer journey down to the Sea of Galilee from where you will be picked up. **Ramot Horse Ranch** North Ramot; ☎ 6737944/057 7364751; e justuri@hotmail.

com; www.ramotranch.com. Extremely well-equipped & well-managed horseriding centre located 3km north of Ramot (signposted). Owners Justine & Uri Peleg offer guided treks ranging from a few hours to a few days. At the time of writing plans were under way to build accommodation for riders, so it is worth enquiring beforehand.

🏠 WHERE TO STAY

🏠 **Golan Rooms** (10 rooms) ☎6731814/052 3393277; e golanrms@ramot-bb.co.il. Stunningly located guest rooms with sweeping views over the Sea of Galilee. Rooms are bright & fresh & have kitchenettes. Large swimming pool, jacuzzi, sauna & restaurant available. B/fast inc. *300–500NIS less off-season.* $$$–$$$$$

🏠 **Barak Guest Rooms** (8 rooms) ☎6732525/050 2850225. Lovely wood cabins complete with jacuzzi bath, TV, kitchenette, AC & private veranda. *200NIS less w/days.* $$$–$$$$

🏠 **Ramot Resort Hotel** (109 rooms) Entrance to Ramot; ☎6732636; e nramot@bezeqint.net; www.ramot-nofesh.co.il. This accommodation offers the best value for money in the area with a plush hotel & cabins overlooking the Sea of Galilee. Facilities inc in-room massages, a spa, gym & swimming pool. Cabins have jacuzzi baths, huge-screen TVs & patios while rooms offer breezy balconies. The reception can arrange tours, guides & activities. $$$

🏠 **Orchan Ramot** (see above, page 236)

✖ WHERE TO EAT

✖ **Betty and Nachi's Bistro** ☎6732889; www.nachi.co.il; ◷ 18.00–23.00 Sun/Mon & Wed–Fri. Set meal inc dozens of small, unique dishes allowing you to sample all the delights of their cooking. Choices inc chicken hearts stuffed with almonds, baked Camembert wedge wrapped in lamb cheese dough, lamb ossobuco & beef on a bed of rice. Set meal $$$$$

✖ **Italkiya b'Ramot (Italian in Ramot)** ☎057 9443778; ◷ 17.00–22.30 Mon–Thu, 09.00–22.30 Fri & Sat). Hearty Italian pasta & pizzas, with traditional ingredients imported from Italy. $$

AROUND RAMOT

KURSI NATIONAL PARK (☎ 6731983; www.parks.org.il; ◷ Apr–Sep 08.00–17.00, Oct–Mar 08.00–16.00; admission adult/child 12/6NIS) During construction of a road in 1976, workers stumbled across what was to be later identified as the largest Byzantine monastery in Israel. Measuring 123m by 145m the church contains large and highly ornate mosaics depicting animals and plants. During the Talmudic and Mishnaic periods, Kursi was a Jewish fishing village, and has long been believed to be the Christian site where Jesus performed his miracle of healing a man possessed by demons. Mark 5: 1–20 tells of Jesus casting the evil spirits from the man into a nearby herd of swine, who then ran down the hill and drowned in the Sea of Galilee. Just south of the monastery and church a small chapel was discovered with an apse covering a cave, considered in Christian tradition to be the place where the miracle occurred. Although the monastery and church suffered vandalism and damage by the Persians in 614CE they were rebuilt, only to be ravaged by an earthquake in the 8th century.

Getting there The Kursi junction is located on route 92, which runs along the east side of the Sea of Galilee. Buses leave from Tiberias (30mins/15.40NIS) every two hours and will stop at the junction on request.

HAMAT GADER (☎ 6659964; www.hamat-gader.com; ◷ 08.30–17.00 Sat–Sun, 08.30–22.00 Mon–Fri, admission w/day 77NIS, w/end 87NIS) The hot, mineral-rich waters of the Hamat Gader spa draw thousands of visitors every year in search of a revitalising, youth-enhancing experience. The wafts of sulphur as you enter the park grounds are as unexpected as its alligator park, the largest in the Middle East. Parrot shows, baboons and two rather ominous-looking pythons are some of the inmates of the animal park, located on the opposite side of the park to the spa facilities. Hamat Gader's popularity is certainly not new founded. As early as the 2nd century, people were bathing in the spring's hot waters, and the site was frequented through to its abandonment in the 9th century. While the development of the park has seemed to focus on entertainment rather than history, a few structures are worth exploring. A synagogue, built during the Roman–Byzantine period represents the Jewish sages who mention the baths in the Talmud, while the scale of the beautiful Roman bathhouses are testament to its significance in society at the time. The crowds on weekends and holidays – especially in winter, when people look for respite from the cold in the 30°C waters – can unfortunately add grey hairs rather than invigorate the spirit, so it is highly recommended to visit off-season or on weekdays. Pools have been created with, for better or worse, a variety of features including fountains and jacuzzi beds. The spa's luxury **hotel village** (↘ 6655555; e spa-villagehotel@hamat-gader.com; www.spavillage.co.il. **$$$$$**) offers cabins, complete with mineral jacuzzi, as well as an extensive range of massages, classes and therapies. The price includes bed and breakfast, a meal in the on-site kosher Thai restaurant **Siam**, massages and the spa facilities. The hotel is for over 16s only and bookings must be for a minimum of two nights at weekends.

Getting there and away A daily bus (24) leaves Tiberias at 09.15 and returns from Hamat Gader at 14.10 (30mins/15.40NIS). By car heading north from Jerusalem or south from Tiberias along route 90, turn on to route 98 following the Jordanian border fence. The site is signposted from the main road.

MOUNT BENTAL AND KIBBUTZ MEROM GOLAN

The slopes of the 1,170m Mount Bental played a key role in the 1973 Yom Kippur War that saw Israel take control of the Golan Heights. Today the summit has been turned into a memorial site for one of the war's bloodiest battles that played out in what has been coined the Valley of Tears, the deserted town of Quneitra, sitting in its midst in the stretch of land now patrolled by the UN Disengagement Observer

Force (UNDOF). Rather ironically, the view that stretches over the bloodied lands of the Valley of Tears and beyond (Damascus is but 60km away) is one of the region's most stunning, and a must on any visit. An abandoned Israeli bunker has been left as a monument to the 160 Israeli tanks that held off Syria's 1,500-strong force, a win that saw a turning point for Israel in the battle for the Golan Heights. The mountain's facilities are run by **Kibbutz Merom Golan** at its base, the first kibbutz established in this region following the 1967 Six Day War and a lovely place to base yourself for some rural pursuits and Golan relaxation. Guest cabins, reputable horseriding stables, jeep and quad bike tours and an excellent restaurant are all located within the tiny moshav, giving it a relaxed, cosy resort-like feel.

GETTING THERE AND AROUND There are two buses to and from Merom Golan daily. Bus 55 leaves at 12.15 (1hr/29NIS) to Kiryat Shmona, stopping at Masade, Majdal Shams, Neve Ativ and Horshat Tal along the way. Bus 58 leaves at 17.30 to Katzrin (45mins/17.20NIS) and continues to Gadot. For bicycle rental and repairs call Laurie (✆ *054 2247489*).

TOURIST INFORMATION/TOUR OPERATORS The **Merom Golan Tourism Office** (✆ *6960267; www.meromgolantourism.co.il*) is located near the ranch and can arrange bookings for all the activities and accommodation on offer in the kibbutz.

Merom Golan Quad Bike ✆6960483/052 8695832; e tractoronim_mg@walla.com; www.tractoronim.co.il. Can arrange professional quad-biking & TomCar trips across the surrounding countryside, ranging from 1 to 3 hrs. A driving licence is required to be able to drive quad bikes.
Jeep Point ✆6963232; e perry_s@merom-golan.org.il; www.jeepoint.co.il. Authentic jeep tours around the Golan Heights where stops for strong coffee & BBQs allow you to get at one with nature.
Merom Golan Cattleman Ranch ✆6960267. Offering day treks around Mount Bental, which leave from the exceptionally well-tended stables & meander through the leafy kibbutz out into the fields.

🏠 **WHERE TO STAY** The kibbutz is a good choice for somewhere to stay, with several eating options and plenty of tourist facilities. Jeep and ATV tours, horseriding treks, a swimming pool and weekend bar make this the ideal place to base yourself for a couple of days. The **tourism office** (see above) can point you in the right direction.

🏠 **Merom Golan Hotel** (52 rooms) ✆6960267; e tour_mg@merom-golan.org.il; www.meromgolantourism.co.il. The hotel has 32 very pleasant guest rooms & 20 luxury wood cabins set within the rustic, quiet grounds of the kibbutz. Both the stone-built rooms & enormous cabins have the full range of amenities, the cabins offering an extra veranda & eating area. **$$$**

✖ **WHERE TO EAT** The kibbutz has a kosher dining room that serves simple meals either to the table or in buffet style.

✖ **HaBokrim Restaurant** ✆6960267; ⏱ 12.00–late Sun–Thu, 12.00–Shabbat Fri, varies on Sat so call ahead. Kosher. The name, which translates as 'the cowboy', gives a pretty good idea of the kind of meals served in this comfortable, ranch-style restaurant. Yes, this is meat heaven. Steak, prime rib & lots of potatoes. There is a huge buffet at w/ends. **$$$$**
☕ **Coffee Anan** ✆6820664; ⏱ 09.00–sunset daily. The tongue-in-cheek name not only translates as 'in the clouds', but is also a reference to the former UN secretary-general who classified the Golan Heights as military-occupied & thus belonging to Syria, not Israel. The café serves an assortment of cakes & vegetarian sandwiches, quiches, pasta & salads. **$$**

The controversial little stretch of land that forms the Golan Heights bears the scars of its violent and bloody past, where long-forgotten, unexploded landmines lay in their hundreds, bullet-ridden buildings stand abandoned and memorial sites dot the landscape. Yet today there is something peaceful about this beautiful and wild terrain, something that draws visitors in search of rural escape and nature. To help understand the Golan's history a stop at some of its most stunning lookouts offers more than a view over the landscape. On the following sites, fierce battles unravelled that shaped this hotly contested little region of the Middle East into what it is today.

PEACE VISTA North along route 98 the Peace Vista (Mitzpe HaShalom) is signposted on the left just before the small moshav of Kfar Haruv. The view looks north and west across the shimmering waters of the Sea of Galilee edged by the green plantations of the kibbutzim that dot its shores.

OPHIR LOOKOUT Heading north along route 98 from the Peace Vista, turn left on to route 789 at the Kursi junction. Signposted on the left just after Givat Yoav an unpaved road follows an olive grove until reaching the car park. At 350m above the level of the Sea of Galilee the view, enjoyed from the shade of the ancient olive trees, is wonderful. A three-hour hike to the ancient ruins of the Jewish settlement of **Bnei Yehuda** can be started from the car park. Blue markers lead the way down the winding path to Kibbutz Ein Gev on the eastern shore of the lake. Getting back to the car park can be problematic, so it is best to either hitch up and leave the car in the kibbutz or arrange to be met at the bottom.

BENTAL LOOKOUT (VALLEY OF TEARS) (see *Mount Bental*, page 238)

GOLANI LOOKOUT The site is a memorial to the fallen troops of the Golani Brigade in the Tel Fahr battle of the Six Day War. A 650m trail takes visitors past the abandoned Syrian outpost to the lookout point over the Hula Valley. Along the trail memorial plaques tell the story of the battle that resulted in the capture of the Syrian stronghold.

GADOT LOOKOUT Perched on the natural boundary that separates the uplands of the Golan from the valleys of the Upper Galilee, the lookout provides a view not of aesthetic beauty but of historical drama and political consequence. This site marks the spot where the pre-1967 Syrian border stood. As you stand at the lookout, there is a clear and poignant divide between the rocky, once-Syrian lands and the green valleys of Israel behind it. The no-man's-land that you see is in fact the remnants of the Syrian front line of defence during the Six Day War, and today thousands of unstable mines remain. The area is heavily fenced off and warning signs are aplenty, so be sure not to venture off any paths. Scattered eucalyptus trees grow on the vista, obviously non-native to the region and mark the site of submerged Syrian bunkers, purportedly planted on the suggestion of the legendary Israeli spy Eli Cohen who used the trees as targets for Israel's air force planes.

AROUND MOUNT BENTAL AND MEROM GOLAN

Odem Forest and El Rom This is what remains of the once huge forest that covered this part of the Golan Heights. Route 978 goes straight through the middle of the forest and there are plenty of lay-bys where you can park and have a wander. In little clearings on the side of the road Druze families sell freshly made flat breads and labane cheese ($) as well as homemade olive oil and fresh honey.

On the other side of the forest along route 98 is the little kibbutz of **El Rom** in which you will find **Camping El Rom** (✎ 6838092; *www.camping-elrom.co.il*). The campsite is set amidst shady pine trees with a toilet and shower block, picnic benches, campfire and tatty sofas available. It is located on the outskirts of the quiet, pretty village.

MOUNT HERMON

Often referred to by Israelis as 'the eyes of the nation', Mount Hermon's strategic location for the military, as it 'peers over the neighbour's walls' into Syria and Lebanon, is a crucial component in the country's early warning system. As it is heavily patrolled by IDF forces, it is difficult to forget the ever-present animosity that Israel and Syria hold towards each other over this land. But while the military presence is unarguably strong, Mount Hermon's size, rising to 2,224m, and sheer beauty, easily overshadow any thoughts of conflict. Israel's highest point, Mount Hermon is significantly cooler than anywhere else in the country, which together with its volcanic basalt rocks and pine forests produces a uniquely alpine quality. Summer snowmelts and an abundance of springs feed the rivers that roar their way down to the valleys, its plentiful and influential water source one of the factors fuelling the region's border disputes. The peak can be snow-capped year round, and a drive up the winding forested road to the summit bestows panoramic views and a temperature drop of up to 15°C (even in the height of summer) that will quite literally take your breath away. Even throughout the stifling hot summers of the lower Golan plains and shores of the Sea of Galilee, the fresh breezes that blow off the mountain demand warmer attire.

Mount Hermon has been a sacred landmark in Hittite, Palestinian and Roman times and stood as the northwestern margin of the Israelite conquest under Moses and Joshua. According to the Gospels, it was the site where Jesus revealed to his disciples his purpose to construct his Church and go to Jerusalem to be resurrected, and is another contender for the site of Jesus's Transfiguration.

The throngs of visitors who today make their way to the summit up the steep, snaking mountain pass are not thinking of Mount Hermon's ancestral ghosts or political tensions but are instead heading in the direction of Israel's only **ski resort** (✎ 6981333; *www.skihermon.co.il*; *admission adult/child 49/44NIS* (*daily ski pass 245NIS; ski rental 150/135NIS*)). A vast car park 2km below the summit is serviced by shuttle buses, ferrying budding alpinists to and from the resort's range of ski trails and slopes. While not exactly on a par with the Swiss Alps, a ski school, sled riding, cross-country trails, restaurants and emergency Magen David centre have been incorporated to make it an enjoyable experience and a great diversion off the history trail. Out of ski season entry is 10NIS (lift 43/38NIS).

GETTING THERE AND AWAY There is no public transport up the mountain so you will need your own transport to get to the summit and ski resort. Route 98 leads past Majdal Shams to the single road at the base of the mountain, from where it is a windy route up to the summit.

ELI COHEN – A LEGENDARY SPY

In the years following the Six Day War, stories of great bravery and self-sacrifice emerged to a nation reeling in its aftermath. Among these, one man's name stood out, a name that has become legendary in households across the country and whose heroism is unparalleled in Israeli minds: Eli Cohen. An Egyptian-born Jew, Cohen was recruited by Mossad in 1960 after making *aliyah* and serving out his army conscription. He adopted a false Syrian identity under the alias Kamel Amin Tsa'abet, and spent a year in Buenos Aires establishing his cover as a wealthy businessman before moving to Damascus. Over the next few years he managed to infiltrate Syrian ruling circles, gaining the confidence of military and government officials and sending classified information back to Mossad. Information gathered by Cohen on Syrian air force pilots was allegedly used to deter fighter pilots from attacking Tel Aviv in 1967. Upon threat to their families, the fighter pilots dropped their bombs into the Mediterranean Sea, reporting back to Damascus that the targets had been hit. In 1965, one of Cohen's radio transmissions to Israel was intercepted and he was sentenced to death, despite protests from several world leaders and Pope Paul VI. He was publicly hanged in Damascus and until this day his remains have never been returned to his family in Israel. Four decades on, negotiations for Eli Cohen's remains continue to be a breaking point in peace talks between Israel and Syria. According to many, at the time of his death Eli Cohen was third in line to the presidency of Syria.

WHERE TO STAY AND EAT

Neve Ativ Located 2km from Majdal Shams and 10km from Mount Hermon, the tiny moshav of Neve Ativ has embraced the tourism trade and not only runs the Hermon Ski Resort but is also home to countless zimmers, guest rooms and the luxury Rimonim Hermon Hotel. The **Neve Ativ Tourism Office** (↖ *6981333*) can help arrange rafting, trekking, horseriding, cycling, skiing and jeep tours in the area.

Rimonim Hermon Hotel (44 rooms) ↖ 6985888; www.rimonim.com. Swiss Alp-style wooden cabins, complete with sloping red roofs are nestled amongst pine trees & have great heating for those freezing winter nights. It also has a spa centre, heated swimming pool & restaurant. W/day prices are 200NIS cheaper per night. **$$$$**

Nimrod The minute moshav of Nimrod (barely more than six families live here) has managed to get itself firmly established on the Golan tourist trail thanks to the acclaimed restaurant **The Witch's Cauldron and the Milkman** (↖ *6870049*; ⊕ *10.00–late daily*. *$$$$*). From miles around big, witch-shaped signs cast their spell of intrigue, directing motorists to the large rustic cabin in the hilltop village overlooking the Birkat Ram pool. The restaurant developed out of a roaring trade in the owner's homemade goat's cheese and now includes a whole variety of dishes. Winter warmers made from the fruits of the Golan are the general theme with hearty casseroles, creative meat dishes, robust pastries and fresh salads.

Within the moshav are several luxury zimmers, including the **Chalet Nimrod Castle** (↖ *6984218/052 2697718*), a delightful eco-lodge. The passionate owners left the urban life behind and have created an oasis in the northern Golan. They have an organic garden, rustic-style dining room and winery whose profits go to charity, as well as beautiful double cabins, each unique (**$$$$**), a campsite (**$**) and occasional dormitory beds when the luxury cabins aren't full (**$**).

There are no direct buses to Nimrod and it is a 5km walk from Neve Ativ so your own transport is necessary. Watch out for signs to the Witch's Cauldron and the Milkman Restaurant on routes 98 and 989 that lead to the turn-off for the moshav.

AROUND MOUNT HERMON

MAJDAL SHAMS AND MASADA Of Israel's 104,000 Druze residents, 18,000 live within a small area in the northern Golan Heights, distributed among four main towns: Majdal Shams, Masada, Ein Qinya and Buqata. With 8,000 residents, Majdal Shams is considered the centre of the Druze community in the Golan, with Masada, a short distance south of it, a close second.

While the towns themselves are rather higgledy-piggledy, their small, simple restaurants are one of the Golan's true highlights. What these small eateries lack in finesse and elegance (and they certainly do) they make up for in quality, traditional dishes cooked with an expertise you cannot find elsewhere. Hummus, salads, freshly baked pitta, olives plucked straight from the surrounding groves, vegetables and meats followed by sticky *baklava* and strong coffee combine to form a simple, yet oh-so-memorable meal prepared from the fields of Mount Hermon. The unassuming, rudimentary **Nidal Restaurant** (Route 98, *Masada;* ✆ *6981066;* ⏱ *07.30–23.00 daily.* **$$**) offers hospitality like no other and serves hot, fresh pitta, hummus and chips as well as grilled meat dishes and salads.

While one wouldn't call Majdal Shams and Masada beautiful, it is clear from the outset that they, along with most other Druze towns, are comparatively affluent. Modern houses are under constant construction and new cars vie for space on the dusty roads alongside the timeless horse and cart. The towns are a constant buzz of agricultural fervour: tractors chug through from the fields, a shepherd on a mobile phone urges his bleating goats through the town centre while young boys in Nike shirts trot their horses out to pasture.

Finding somewhere to stay in Majdal Shams and Masada isn't difficult, but prices do seem decidedly overinflated for what you get. A simple room in the middle of the town generally costs the same as plusher zimmer cabins in nearby villages such as Nimrod or Neve Ativ.

Getting there Bus 55 leaves Kiryat Shmona at 13.30 (30mins/23NIS) and bus 58 leaves at 16.40. In reverse only bus 55 returns to Kiryat Shmona (12.40). Bus 58 leaves to Katzrin at 17.10 (1hr/23NIS) stopping at Masade and Merom Golan and continuing to Gadot.

NIMROD FORTRESS (✆ *6949277; www.parks.org.il;* ⏱ *08.00–17.00 daily; admission adult/child 20/9NIS (combined ticket with the Hermon National Park 31/15NIS))* One

> ## BIRKAT RAM
>
> Located just above Masada, at the base of Mount Hermon, is the volcanic crater pool of Birkat Ram (which translates as the 'ram pool'). According to Talmudic text, the pool opened up during the Great Flood of Noah, never to close again thereafter. The Talmud speaks of only three such places, the other two being the springs in Hamat Gader and Tiberias.

Following the 1967 Six Day War that left much of the Golan Heights under Israeli control, the unsuspecting Druze village of Majdal Shams found itself quite literally torn apart. The new border meant that many families were suddenly living in separate countries and completely isolated from one another. To date, Syria and Israel have no means of communication, neither telephone nor mail. The borders are completely closed and all ties between local people severed. As a desperate measure to catch a glimpse of their loved ones, relatives started to gather on a 1,110m-high hill within Syrian-controlled land to shout affections and wave. This hill has become known as the Shouting Hill, and provided the backdrop for the acclaimed Israeli film *The Syrian Bride*. Rising above a narrow, heavily IDF-patrolled valley beginning a few metres from Majdal Shams, it is but a distance of 3km that seems like hundreds, for all know that it is the closest they will ever again get to each other. Today, megaphones and binoculars aid communication, but the air is filled with sadness, weddings, funerals and family occasions shared at a distance that seems nowhere near to ever being closed. A trip to the edge of the village to witness this display of stoicism and family loyalty is certainly a humbling experience and a shocking reminder of the state of affairs within the Middle East.

of the most striking sights in the northern Golan landscape is the Nimrod Fortress. Sitting high on the slopes of Mount Hermon above the deep valley and ancient road that once connected Damascus and the Galilee, it is an eerily imposing sight.

The early phase of the fortress was built in 1228 by Al-Aziz Uthman, Saladin's nephew, as an attempt to block the march of the Sixth Crusade heading to Damascus from Akko. The fortress was later aggrandised after its capture by the Mamluk sultan Baibars to include the striking towers we see today. Inscriptions, including the carving of a cheetah, Baibars's symbol, are evidence of its ruler at the time. Not long after the Muslim conquest of Akko in the 13th century and subsequent demise of Crusader rule, Nimrod fell into disrepair. Once more brought into commission after the Ottoman Turks conquered the country, it was used as a luxury prison for exiled Ottoman aristocrats from Palestine.

It is possible to spend a few hours exploring the restored sections of the fortress. Of particular interest are the 'secret corridor', large stone brick halls, central keep and towers.

Getting there and away Bus 55 leaves Neve Ativ to Kiryat Shmona at 12.45 (35mins/19NIS) and will stop at the entrance to the fortress.

HERMON NATIONAL PARK (BANIAS) (6950272; *www.parks.org.il*; 08.00–17.00 Sat–Thu, 08.00–16.00 Fri; admission adult/child 25/13NIS (combined ticket with Nimrod Fortress 31/15NIS)) The Hermon National Park, which is commonly referred to as Banias, sits on the western border with the Upper Galilee and is famed for both its impressive waterfall and dramatic history. The park has two entrances located a few kilometres from each other. Heading from Kiryat Shmona, the first entrance offers an easy ten-minute walk down to the waterfall, while the second entrance a little further along route 99 provides access to the archaeological ruins and springs. Three designated routes of differing length and ardour can be taken, but only one, approximately 90 minutes in length, will lead you from the waterfall to the ruins and springs and vice versa. Be sure not to venture off the designated trail that follows the stream, as the park sits amidst several mined areas. Note that this longer route is not circular so make sure you have enough energy to get yourself back again.

The Hermon Stream is fed by waters descending from Mount Hermon, with a series of waterfalls created as the waters cascade down the steep gradients towards the Hula Valley. The largest of these waterfalls is located here at Banias and is the *pièce de résistance* of the park. The torrent is most impressive throughout the April and May snowmelt (although it flows year round), so be prepared to get a bit wet.

The archaeological park displays phases of the once-prosperous city's history. Scanty remnants of Greek culture, brought to the region following Alexander the Great's conquest, can be seen, whilst the extravagant Palace of Agrippa is a lasting legacy of the Agrippa II settlement here. Crusader remains and a steady stream of pilgrims hold testimony to the importance of the site in Christianity. According to tradition, it was here that Jesus gave Peter the 'keys to heaven' and performed the miracle of healing the bleeding woman. The Crusaders viewed Banias as a strategic point between their stronghold in Palestine and the surrounding Muslim regions, and it was strongly defended. Throughout the Crusades, power over Banias changed regularly until eventually Saladin reigned victorious, and remains of these mighty battles are left as testament across the landscape.

Getting there and away Bus 55 leaves Kiryat Shmona once a day at 13.30 and bus 58 at 16.40 and both will drop you at the springs and archaeological site. From northern Golan only bus 55 will pass the park entrances back to Kiryat Shmona at around 13.00.

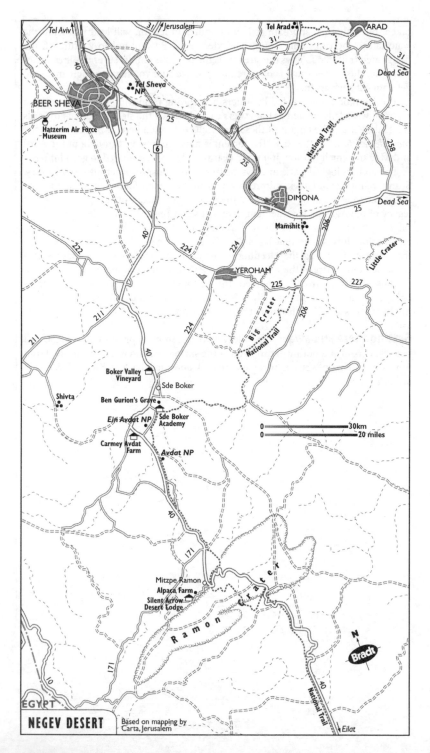

NEGEV DESERT

Based on mapping by
Carta, Jerusalem

9

The Negev Desert

Telephone code 08

In his book *The Innocents Abroad,* Mark Twain described the Negev Desert as 'a desolation that not even imagination can grace with the pomp of life and action', an observation that 150 years on remains rather apt. The vast Negev Desert occupies half of Israel, and is characterised by the geological phenomenon that is the Ramon Crater, as well as its remarkable landscapes, waterfalls, caves, archaeological sites and rich history. The path of the ancient Nabatean Spice Route once wove its way through the peaks and troughs of the desert mountains, prosperous cities appearing along the way; Abraham built his well in the present-day city of Beer Sheva; and Israel's first prime minister settled and died in the remote Kibbutz Sde Boker.

Beer Sheva marks the gateway to the region but is little more than a through route to the wonders of the desert below. Mitzpe Ramon's isolated location teetering on the edge of the crater has made it the capital of highland tourism, where nature, active pursuits and ecotourism prevail.

Tourism in the desert is still in its infancy and if you plan on visiting under your own steam – a highly rewarding and recommended experience – then be prepared for the harsh desert elements. While the region is big, this isn't the Sahara and you're never too far from some sort of civilisation, but stick to marked roads, as the IDF do extensive training in the region, and make sure you have plenty of water, petrol and sunscreen. Picnics are recommended, as eating options are almost non-existent and it would be a shame to waste the amazing landscape sitting indoors anyway. Beer Sheva is virtually your last port of call for buying provisions, although Mitzpe Ramon does have some basic facilities and a small supermarket. Public transport is extremely limited and independent travellers often have to resort to hitchhiking. Renting a car is undoubtedly the best option to get the most out of your trip and avoid standing in the sweltering desert heat on the side of a dusty road waiting for sporadic buses to pass.

BEER SHEVA

Often referred to as 'the capital of the Negev', Beer Sheva is (with the exception of Eilat), Israel's southernmost city. It sits on the fringes of the desert and acts as a gateway for those delving into the rural depths of the Negev Desert. The city is unsurprisingly rather dusty, run-down and sprawling, new neighbourhoods clearly defined by their white, modern apartment blocks and out-of-place greenery. Yet culturally, Beer Sheva is quite a treat. While there is no real need to hang around for too long, it lays claim to an interesting history and ethnographic make-up, acting as a trade centre for surrounding Bedouin settlements. A weekly market is held by these communities and it is undoubtedly worth timing your visit to coincide with one. Today Beer Sheva is Israel's sixth-largest city and manages to maintain a certain allure through its highly reputable Ben Gurion University. The university campus forms the hub of modern life, where bars and nightlife attract the younger set. The run-down old Turkish town (Old City) forms the heart of the ancient city where character, not beauty, is the main charm. In all, Beer Sheva can be quite a surprise and not nearly as drab and unappealing as it may appear at first sight.

HISTORY The Old Testament phrase 'from Dan to Beer Sheva' indicates that the city marked the southern limit of Palestine, and is associated with Abraham, Isaac, Jacob and Elijah. When in 1902 the Ottomans chose Beer Sheva as their administrative centre for the Negev it was but an abandoned site, frequented only by Bedouin groups using the area's water sources. Buildings were erected along with police and train stations and train lines were opened to Ashkelon, Gaza and Damascus.

The city played an important role during the British Mandate period under which it continued to develop, and was at the time home to around 4,000 Muslim Arabs. During the 1936–39 Arab riots, many Jews fled the city, not returning until after the 1948 Arab–Israeli War. Because of the predominantly Arab population, Beer Sheva was given to the Arabs in the 1947 UN Partition Plan of Palestine, only to be taken by Israel the following year. Upon the Israeli conquest, the city was all but abandoned by its Arab inhabitants.

GETTING THERE AND AWAY Beer Sheva acts as the gateway to the south and there are subsequently good bus and rail links with the rest of the country.

By bus To and from Tel Aviv's central bus station bus 370 makes the journey every 20 minutes (90mins/16.50NIS); likewise buses 470 and 446 from Jerusalem (2hrs/32.50NIS). There are regular buses linking Beer Sheva with Arad (45mins/17.20NIS) from where you can connect to the Dead Sea (bus 385 goes all the way to Ein Bokek and Ein Gedi). To reach Eilat express buses 394 and 397 make the journey every two hours (4hrs/63NIS). Buses 60 and 392 hurtle between Mitzpe Ramon and Beer Sheva (1hr 25mins/29NIS) every 20 minutes with bus 60 stopping at every stop along the way including Sde Boker.

By train The train links Beer Sheva with the rest of the country through Tel Aviv. Trains depart every hour (1hr 20mins/29NIS).

GETTING AROUND Bus 7 starts at the central bus and train stations, heads down to the market, on to the Old City and then heads north along Yitzhak Rager Boulevard towards the Soroka Hospital and university. Bus 31 from the central station will drop you directly outside the Hatzerim Air Force Museum (10 mins).

By car Car rental is a good option in Beer Sheva and allows for easy exploration of the surrounding landscape, including the air force base (10-minute drive).

Car rental companies
Avis 2 Amal St; ☎6271777; ⊕ 08.00–18.00 Sun–Thu, 08.00–14.00 Fri

Sixt 1 Pinhas HaHozev St; ☎6282589; ⊕ 08.00–17.00 Sun–Thu, 08.00–12.00 Fri

TOURIST INFORMATION
Tourist information office 1 Hevron St; ☎6463600/6463810; ⊕ 08.30–16.00 Sun–Thu. Located at Abraham's Well. English-speaking staff will help with bus routes, tours of the city & can provide maps. At the time of writing the information centre & well area was undergoing a huge renovation.

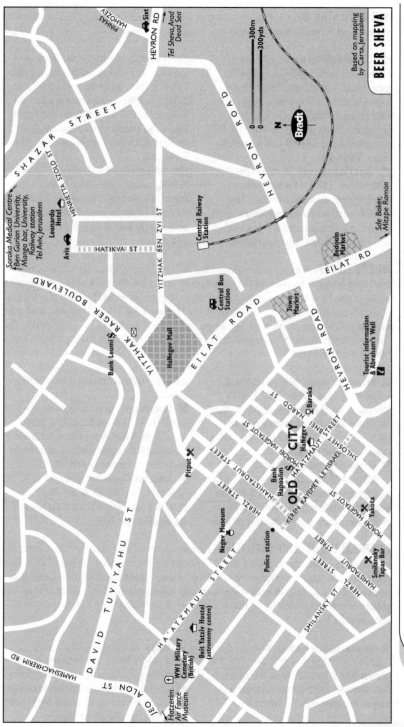

BEER SHEVA

Based on mapping
by Carta, Jerusalem

WHERE TO STAY

Beer Sheva is somewhat lacking in hotels as most visitors tend to merely stop in on their way south.

Leonardo Hotel Negev (244 rooms) 4 Henrietta Szold St; 6405444; f 6405445; www.leonardo-hotels.com. Previously the Golden Tulip, this is Beer Sheva's plushest hotel option. Centrally located it offers comfortable rooms with kitchenette as well as a swimming pool, health club & business centre. $$$$$

Beit Yatziv Hostel (95 rooms) 79 Ha'Atzmaut St; 6277444; e beit_yatziv@ silverbyte.com; www.beityatziv.co.il. This hostel & guesthouse is the best budget option in town and offers basic private rooms with AC, TV & kosher b/fast, luxury private rooms

(50NIS more) & dormitory beds. Rooms are spacious, clean & decorated in a modern style & there is also a swimming pool & big buffet dining room. The science centre in which the rooms are located is linked to the Ilan Ramon Center – an astronomical observatory in the desert to which they can organise trips. *Dorms 120NIS.* $$

HaNegev Hotel (22 rooms) 26 Ha'Atzmaut St; 6277026; e liei5@ actcom.co.il. The hotel is in need of a lick of paint but rooms are simple, comfortable & cheap. Good location in the heart of the Old City. Dbls have AC & TV. $$

WHERE TO EAT

While not renowned for its fine dining, Beer Sheva does have a few good options. In the Old City, Smilansky Street has the bulk of the restaurants while in the New City you're best heading to the area around the central train and bus stations, around the university or to the HaNegev Mall. The Thursday **Bedouin market** offers the chance to try some traditional Bedouin cooking while the covered **Town Market** has a wonderful selection of shwarma, *burekas*, falafel and freshly baked breads.

Yakota 27 Mordei HaGeta'ot (corner 18 Anilevich St); 08 6232689; 12.00–0.00 Sun–Thu, 11.00–Shabbat Fri, end Shabbat–00.00 Sat. Kosher. Moroccan restaurant serving all the favourites inc slow-cooked tagine, aromatic salads & succulent meats. $$$$

Pitput 122 Herzl St; 6289888; 08.30–02.00 daily. Italian-style cuisine with an emphasis on meat & fish. They also do some wonderful big b/fasts. In the evening it's also a great place to enjoy a beer. A changing exhibition

inside displays work from artists from the Negev Desert. $$$$

Sami Vesusu Town Market, shops 170–180; 6652135; 11.00–20.30 Sun–Thu, 10.30–15.30 Fri. Much-loved & raved about Romanian meat stand in the market. Kebabs & all manner of meaty delights from the freshest cuts. $$$

Smilansky Tapas Bar 23 Smilansky St; 6654854; 17.00–02.00 Sun–Thu, 12.00–02.00 Fri & Sat. Considered one of the best bars outside of Tel Aviv. $$$

ENTERTAINMENT AND NIGHTLIFE

Thanks to the large number of university students there are many places where you can go out and let your hair down. Big, raucous party nights are frequent but there is also a good selection of quieter, more relaxed places to just sit and enjoy a drink. Alternatively, the HaNegev Mall has plenty of cafés in which to sit and while away the evening over a cappuccino and a slice of cake.

☆ **Baraka** 70 Shloshet Bnei Harod St; 6287111; 22.30–late daily. One of the most popular clubs in town, it is loud, flashy & fun. Each night sees a different theme ranging from karaoke to student nights to live music.

Manga 85 Yitzhak Rager Bd; 6499951; 18.00–late daily. Located near the teachers' centre, Manga is the quintessential student pick-up bar: loud, crowded & cheap, but it has a nice covered garden area, comfy sofas & decent sushi.

Pitput (see *Where to eat* above)

SHOPPING

Bedouin Market (*Eilat Road;* ☉ *Thu*) The market officially opened in 1905, although the area had long been a meeting place for the groups of Bedouins who would come to buy, sell and swap pretty much everything. Today it has become slightly more contemporary, with cheap clothes, shoes and home-ware stalls (a lot of it from China) standing alongside authentic Bedouin craft stalls and livestock. It is a fantastic place to buy traditional Bedouin keepsakes such as glassware, jewellery and precious stones, as well as mats, carpets and cushions. It is also a great place to get exceptionally cheap Bedouin food.

OTHER PRACTICALITIES
Emergency
Ambulance ☏101
Fire ☏102
Police 30 Herzl St; ☏100 or 6462744

Money
$ **Bank Hapoalim** 40 Ha'Atzmaut St; ☏03 6532407; ☉ 08.30–13.15 Sun & Tue/Wed, 08.30–13.00 & 16.00–18.30 Mon & Thu, 08.15–12.30 Fri

$ **Bank Leumi** 11 Yitzhak Rager Bd; ☏6239222; ☉ 08.30–14.30 Tue/Wed, 08.30–13.00 & 16.30–18.15 Mon & Thu, 08.30–12.30 Fri

Post
✉ **Post office** Corner of Yitzhak Rager Bd; ☏6295835; ☉ 08.00–18.00 Sun–Tue & Thu, 08.00–13.30 Wed, 08.00–12.00 Fri. Has Western Union & offers commission-free cash & travellers' cheque exchange & phone. Located opposite the mall just along from Bank Leumi.

Medical
✚ **Soroka Medical Centre** Yitzhak Rager Bd; ☏6400111

✚ **Superpharm** HaNegev Mall; ☏6281371 & 70 HaMeshachrerim St; ☏6424313; ☉ 08.00–23.00 Sun–Thu, 08.00–17.00 Fri, 17.00–23.30 Sat

WHAT TO SEE

Abraham's Well (*1 Hevron St;* ☏ *6234613; admission 5NIS*) Within the small archaeological site is the stone well believed to have been dug by Abraham. It is recorded in the Bible that at the beginning of 2000BCE, Abraham and Isaac arrived in Beer Sheva where they dug wells and formed alliances with Abimelech, the King of the Philistines. The well itself has been dated to at least the 12th century BCE. At the time of writing the site was undergoing a major renovation to include a movie about the area and small museum.

Old City The Old City dates to the end of the 19th century and owes its origins to the Turks who designed and constructed it based on a grid pattern. While it has undoubted charm, don't expect the quaint cobbled alleys of Jerusalem, Akko or Nazareth's Old City counterparts. The area is run-down and badly maintained, and the local government has done little to restore some of the more impressive Ottoman buildings. Smilansky Street has been partially remodelled and has some restored buildings that provide a glimpse of what the area would have once looked like. Today it forms the centre of the Old City and is home to several good restaurants and cheap shops.

Negev Museum (*60 Ha'Atzmaut St;* ✆ *6993535;* ◷ *08.30–15.30 Sun–Mon &* *Wed–Thu, 08.30–14.00 & 16.00–18.00 Tue, 10.00–14.00 Sat; admission adult/child 12/10NIS*) The small museum is housed in a stone Ottoman building dating from 1906 and displays a range of changing exhibitions including contemporary and early Israeli art. The building first acted as Beer Sheva's city hall until 1953 when it was converted into a museum.

Town market (*Corner of Hevron and Eilat roads*) The covered market is a fascinating hubbub of activity and certainly worth a visit, if only for the food stalls and bakeries. Wandering around the stalls laden with meats, cheeses, vegetables and a whole host of home wares is a great insight into real city life.

British World War I Military Cemetery (*Ha'Atzamaut St*) A little further up from the Negev Museum is Israel's largest British, Australian and New Zealand military cemetery. Beneath the rows of white tombstones lie soldiers who died in battles against the Turks during World War I.

Air Force Museum (*Kibbutz Hatzerim;* ✆ *9906853; www.iaf-museum.org.il;* ◷ *08.00–17.00 Sun–Thu, 08.00–13.00 Fri; admission adult/child 30/20NIS*) The museum is located 6km west of Beer Sheva, just past Kibbutz Hatzerim adjacent to the IDF's southern air force base. With the roaring drone of fighter jets above, visitors can walk around the large outdoor museum and get up close and personal with air force jets and helicopters from the IDF's past. Guided tours in English can be arranged at the entrance and there is a rather nice audio-visual presentation displayed inside a Boeing plane. Bus 31 from the central bus station stops outside.

Tel Beer Sheva National Park (✆ *6467286; www.parks.org.il;* ◷ *Apr–Sep 08.00–17.00; Oct–Mar 08.00–16.00; admission adult/child 13/7NIS*) East of the city, near the Bedouin settlement of Tel Sheva, is the national park at the centre of which sit the excavated remains of a fortified city dating from the Israelite period. The city was built atop a *tel* (mound composed of the remains of successive settlements) and much of the ancient city has been restored, which adds a certain humanity and understanding to a visit. Of particular interest are the well, city streets, storehouses, public buildings and private homes, the city wall and gates, and the reservoir.

SDE BOKER

The small isolated kibbutz of Sde Boker resting high in the Negev Mountains is famed across the country as being the last home, and final resting place, of Israel's first prime minister David Ben-Gurion and his wife Paula. Ben-Gurion's Zionist vision for the desert lands that occupy half of the country was to cultivate and settle, claiming that 'the future of Israel lies in the desert'. In honour of Ben-Gurion's love for this remote region and his passion for creating more land in which Jews from around the world could settle he – and later his wife – were interred on a nearby cliff, adjacent to the *midrasha* (research academy) that was founded from his inspiration. Today the kibbutz and surrounding farms act as a good base for exploring the surrounding Negev, most notably the **Ein Avdat** and **Avdat national parks**, and while facilities are fairly limited Sde Boker does offer a small supermarket and a few guesthouses and hostels.

GETTING THERE AND AROUND Buses 60 and 392 run along route 40 between Beer Sheva and Mitzpe Ramon (1hr 25mins/29NIS) several times a day, stopping outside the kibbutz entrance (40mins/24.50NIS), which is located 3km north of the entrance to the research academy (see *Sde Boker Academy*, below), memorial park and Ein Avdat National Park access road, where the bus will make another stop on request.

TOURIST INFORMATION

i Sde Boker Tourist Information Centre
✆ 6554418; ☺ 08.00–16.00 daily. Located in the entrance to the research academy.

⌂ WHERE TO STAY AND EAT

⌂ **Boker Valley Vineyard** (4 rooms)
✆ 052 6822930; e hilda@kms.org.il; www.hnbw.net. The family-run winery located 8km north of Kibbutz Sde Boker is rustic Negev at its best. Their luxurious wood cabin is a rural retreat with all the comforts of home. There are family & dbl cabins as well as a khan tent for dormitory-style accommodation for groups. *200NIS less on w/days* **$$$. $$$$**

⌂ **Carmey Avdat Farm** (6 rooms)
✆ 6535177; e carmey-avdat@bezeqint.net; www.carmey-avdat.co.il. Run by the Izrael family who followed their dream into the desert & established a vineyard on the ancient Nabatean spice route, their luxury cabins take advantage of the natural resources & beauty of the desert & offer peaceful landscape views, natural construction materials & not a TV in sight. Plunge pools & fruit orchards complete the oasis effect. B/fast inc. *150NIS less midweek* **$$$. $$$$**

⌂ **Ecological Hamburg Guesthouse**
(20 rooms) ✆ 6532016; www.boker.org.il. The guesthouse forms the higher-end option offered by the field school (reception is in the field school office). Comfortable, modern rooms have TV, AC, refrigerator & nice bathrooms. Often fully booked in summer months so best to reserve ahead. **$$$**

⌂ **Krivine's Guest House** (14 beds) ✆ 052 2712304; e guesthouse@krivines.com; www.krivines.com. Well-priced, bright, sunny private apts (for 2–10 people), a kitchen for guest use, Wi-Fi, a large shady garden and a hearty b/fast option make this an excellent choice in the region. *100NIS less on w/days* **$$. $$$**

⌂ **Sde Boker Field School Hostel**
(47 rooms) ✆ 6532016; e orders@boker.org.il; www.boker.org.il. 2 hostels attracting mainly school groups so dorms (**$**) are often fully booked. Rooms are clean & bright, with en-suite bathrooms, AC & b/fast. Discounted use of academy swimming pool. The field school can also organise jeep & camel tours & recommend hiking routes. **$$**

WHAT TO SEE

Ben-Gurion's home (*Kibbutz Sde Boker;* ✆ *6560320;* ☺ *08.30–16.00 Sun–Thu, 08.30–14.00 Fri, 09.00–15.00 Sat; admission adult/child 10/7NIS*) The hut in which Ben-Gurion and his wife lived until his death in 1973 stands untouched and is a fascinating insight into the humble home life of the country's first leader. The area around the hut has been converted into a small museum of sorts including displays of his famous statements, photographs of the early kibbutz and an archive of the more than 5,000 books that formed his personal library. The hut is located on the southern edge of the kibbutz.

Ben-Gurion Tomb Memorial Park In honour of his love for the desert, Ben-Gurion and his wife are buried on a cliff 3km south of the kibbutz. The tombs form a central space within a beautiful memorial park offering a staggering view of the sweeping Zin Valley. Picnic tables and public toilets make it a popular lunch spot along the route south.

Sde Boker Academy (✆ *6532016; www.boker.org.il;* ☺ *08.00–16.30 Sun–Thu, 08.00–12.00 Fri*) Adjacent to the Ben Gurion Tomb Memorial Park is the desert research centre. It opened in 1965 and has since established more than 12 scientific and educational institutions, including a national solar energy centre, school for environmental studies and institute for desert research. The **Desert Sculpture Museum** displays art created from desert materials and tours can be arranged by calling in advance.

Sde Boker Winery (*Kibbutz Sde Boker;* \ *050 7579212;* e *winery@ sde-boker.org.il; www.sde-boker.org.il/winery*) Wine tastings and tours can be arranged by contacting the winery in advance.

EN AVDAT NATIONAL PARK

(\ *6532016; www.parks.org.il;* ⊕ *Apr–Sep 08.00–17.00; Oct–Mar 08.00–16.00; admission adult/child 25/13NIS*) This highly picturesque national park is often overlooked, not receiving the fame (and subsequent crowds) of other desert oases like the Ein Gedi Nature Reserve on the shore of the Dead Sea. The park runs along both sides of the dramatic Zin Canyon through which trickles the Zin Stream. The park's geography is unique, characterised by pools, waterfalls and ice-cold springs while the abundance of water and vegetation has created an oasis for wildlife. A mild one–two-hour circuitous hike takes visitors along the river's edge to the palm-fringed **lower pools** and 15m-high **waterfall** which form the *pièce de résistance* of the park. A longer

THE NABATEAN SPICE ROUTE

When the Nabateans settled in the Negev in the 4th century BCE they took control of the transport of spices, incense, herbs, gems and medicines that were crossing from the Far East and Arabian Peninsula to Gaza Port. What has become known as the 'Spice Route' was the source of the Nabateans' famed affluence, and their will and passion to defend it are legendary. With the Roman conquest of Egypt came a struggle for control over the prosperous route, one that ended with the Romans creating alternate routes across the desert. The competition had its effect, however, and as the spice trade started to wane Nabatean inhabitants adopted farming, a practice in which they proved successful. In 105CE, however, the Roman emperor Trajan finally annexed the Nabatean kingdom and incorporated it into the Roman Provincia Arabia.

The route itself was paved around the 1st century BCE, linking the Nabatean capital of Petra in Jordan to Gaza's port. Along the route appeared great camps, stopovers for the mile-long camel caravans that transported their wealth across the desert. In 2005, UNESCO declared the route and the four great Nabatean cities of Avdat, Mamshit, Shivta and Haluza World Heritage Sites, compounding and protecting their historic importance and allowing visitors to follow in the footsteps of the ancient Nabateans.

AVDAT (See above.)

MAMSHIT (MEMPHIS) (\ *6556478; www.parks.org.il;* ⊕ *Apr–Sep 08.00–17.00; Oct–Mar 08.00–16.00; admission adult/child 20/9NIS*) The walled Nabatean city of Mamshit is the smallest yet best preserved of the Spice Route cities and the site of one of the biggest ancient treasures ever discovered in Israel, consisting of over 10,000 coins. Well-preserved and restored houses, streets, churches and two–three-hour hike incorporates the **upper pools, En Ma'arif spring, poplar grove** and **caves** where monks lived during the Byzantine period. The long trail begins in either the upper or lower car park and ends in the other meaning you will either have to walk back or arrange for transport to collect you at the other end. For those wishing to see both the upper and lower pools it is recommended to begin and end your visit from the upper car park accessed from route 40 approx 5km south of the entrance to the field school and Ben-Gurion Tombs. The lower car park entrance is along an access road beginning in the Ben-Gurion Tombs car park.

AVDAT NATIONAL PARK

(6551511; ⊕ *Apr–Sep 08.00–17.00; Oct–Mar 08.00–16.00 (closes 1hr earlier Fri); admission adult/child 25/13NIS*) When you're driving south along route 90, the ancient hilltop settlement of Avdat is unmistakable. Avdat once stood as one of the most important cities in the Negev, where great Nabatean caravans stopped on their long journeys across the desert's Spice Route (see below). The city was named after the Nabatean king Obodas III (Abdah in Arabic) who is believed to have been buried here. The king was revered as a deity and it was under him that the city's temple was built. In 106CE, the Romans annexed the Nabatean kingdom and the city moved into another phase of prosperity and prestige. The Romans incorporated Avdat and the Nabatean kingdom into their empire, Provincia Arabia, and created

defensive towers (one of which can be climbed for a great view over the site) provide a true insight into Nabatean culture. Mamshit's two churches, complete with highly ornate mosaics, are a particular highlight of the site and on some Jewish holidays the city's market street is recreated, providing a kitsch but enjoyable insight into Nabatean life. There are several good accommodation options within the site including a communal tent with mattresses (65/40NIS), five-person bungalows (450NIS) and five-person *tukuls* (thatched tents) (350NIS). In the summer months it is possible to live like the ancient Nabateans and camp in the city's ancient khan (caravanserai) (adult/child 50/40NIS).

SHIVTA (*www.parks.org.il; ⊕ 24hrs daily; admission free*) In the far west of the Negev stands the vast Nabatean city of Shivta whose remains have survived the tests of time beautifully thanks to the region's dramatically low humidity. Although the city started life as a Nabatean caravan stop, most of the remains date to the Byzantine period and include two ornate marble churches and a large baptismal font hewn from rock. A 700m trail leads north to a modern orchard which utilises ancient methods to grow desert fruits, no mean feat in one of the driest places in the country. At the Telalim junction along route 40 follow signs to Nitzana along route 211. The site is on the right after approximately 15km.

HALUTZA Excavated rather hastily, the Nabatean city of Halutza (or Elusa) in the west Negev Desert cannot compete with its Spice Route counterparts for impressively preserved relics. The site, which can be accessed only by 4x4, is covered with sand, only a few of its once-impressive buildings visible above ground. Two churches, a theatre and many inscriptions have been discovered, accurately dating the site and putting it firmly on the map as an integral part of the Spice Route.

a series of defence fortresses stretching across their empire's southern border. As the spice trade dried up Nabatean inhabitants adopted agriculture as their means of livelihood, in particular the production of wine. At the end of the 3rd century CE, a fortress was built on the eastern half of the acropolis hill, most likely to serve as a defence against threatening Arab tribes. The city reached its peak during the Byzantine period by which time Christianity had taken a firm hold. During this time the acropolis was rebuilt complete with churches, a monastery and citadel. Today, St Theodore's Church, with its Greek-inscribed marble tombstones inserted in the floor, is the most interesting Byzantine relic in Avdat. Early in the 7th century CE, the town was totally destroyed by an earthquake and was never reinhabited.

A visit to the park is crucial to the understanding of the fascinating and unique history of the Negev and in particular the Nabatean Spice Route. The remains themselves are incredibly impressive (in particular the churches and reconstructed Roman villa) and the view from the top of the hill unparalleled. The information centre is particularly good and has small displays of artefacts unearthed from the site and an audio-visual presentation detailing its history.

MITZPE RAMON

Few towns can attest to the kind of view that Mitzpe Ramon's residents wake up to on a daily basis. On the edge of the gargantuan Ramon Crater in the heart of the Negev Desert, Mitzpe Ramon is about as remote as it gets. Small though it is the town makes a good base for exploring the desert, and facilities have sprung up over recent years in the area's rural tourism boom. Compared with several other desert towns, Mitzpe Ramon is almost pretty, and certainly clean. Attempts have been made to liven the place up with small gardens and greenery adding a touch of colour to the otherwise brown landscape. Ibex and bicycle-mounted children cruise the quiet, dusty streets where traffic is minimal. Yet it isn't all roses as the town suffers from intensely hot summers, freezing winters, mass unemployment and a lack of entertainment. But those looking to partake in true desert adventures and ecotourism have a choice of places to stay at the end of the day. The town is so small which, compounded with the myriad signs pointing to all tourist attractions and hotels, means street names are rarely used in addresses and it is impossible to get lost.

GETTING THERE AND AWAY Bus 60 to and from Beer Sheva makes the journey every 20 minutes (1hr 25mins/29NIS) while express buses 392 and 382 only take 1hr and continue on to Eilat.

TOURIST INFORMATION On the precipice of the crater, the **visitors' centre** (\ 6588691/8; ⊕ 08.00–16.00 Sat–Thu, 08.00–15.00 Fri) offers plenty of local information, particularly about hiking and rappelling, as well as a good bilingual map of the town (2NIS), which considering its diminutive size might be a bit of an overkill. An audio-visual presentation depicting the unique history, geology, zoology and archaeology of the crater is shown at intervals inside the centre. At the time of writing it was undergoing a massive $12million renovation and was temporarily located in the Bio Ramon next door (see page 258).

Local tour operators
Guide Horizon \ 6595333; m 052 3690805; e guidmi@netvision.net.il; www.guidehorizon.com. Adrenalin-fuelled buggy tours ranging from half a day to 2 days that end with a sizzling BBQ & a soak in the attached spa (see Where to stay below).

Karkom Jeep Tours 📞052 8813112; www.negevjeep.co.il; e info@negevjeep.co.il. Specialists in jeep tours across the Negev & further afield to the Dead Sea, the Spice Route & into Jordan.

Negevland 📞1800 200870; e alengt@ bezeqint.net; www.negevland.co.il. All-round adventure masters, the list of activities is inexhaustible: inc jeep tours, mountain biking, rappelling, archery & paintballing. Experienced guides & quality equipment.

WHERE TO STAY A good variety of accommodation is represented in Mitzpe Ramon, ranging from the most basic communal tents to the luxurious Isrotel Ramon Inn. Family-run zimmers make up the wide choice of mid-range accommodation and the visitors' centre can supply you with a list. When choosing a zimmer or cabin it is worth checking out the kitchen facilities, as eating options are sparse. Nights in the desert camps can be a great way of being at one with nature but are a bit rough and ready. Be sure to take some warm clothes, even in summer. There are also several campsites in the crater itself. Pitch your own tent or sleep in a communal Bedouin one.

Alpaca Farm (5 rooms) 📞6588047/052 8977010; e alpaca4@gmail.com; www.alpaca.co.il. The bright, spacious cabins sleep 4–7 people & are great value for money & a unique experience in the desert. Guests can wander around the farm, get involved in daily tasks & help with the animals. Cabins have fully equipped kitchenettes, TVs & big verandas. It is also possible to sleep in a communal area on mats for 80NIS per night. *100NIS less on w/days*. Cabin **$$$**

Guide Horizon (8 rooms) 📞052 3690805/ 08 6595333; e guidmi@netvision.net.il; www.guidehorizon.com. Rustic wood cabin offering private rooms full of character. A funky spa, holistic centre, sauna & decks scattered with cushions are a perfect way to chill out after a rigorous day buggying (see *Local tour operators* above). **$$$**

Isrotel Ramon Inn Hotel (96 rooms/ apts) 1 Ein Akev St; 📞6588822; e info@ isrotel.co.il; www.isrotel.co.il. Offers the complete luxury package inc tours, spiritual workshops, spa, indoor swimming pool, desert activities, top-quality restaurant & of course, immaculate self-catering apts with staggering views. This is the desert à la carte. **$$$**

Adama Dance Inn (70 beds) 📞6595190; e info@adama.org.il; www.adama.org.il. Located in the Spice Quarter on the edge of town is this unusual inn. A dance space attracts those looking to express themselves & there are workshops & summer camps, while the delightful attached accommodation has been built in locally sourced, organic materials. 2- & 4-person mud houses plus several small, cosy 'tepee' rooms (for 2–5 people) are great value. **$$**

Silent Arrow Desert Lodge (50 beds) 📞052 6611561; e hetzbasheket@gmail.com; www.silentarrow.co.il. Go one with nature & the wild desert by sleeping in the private dome tents (120NIS pp), the communal tent (80NIS pp) or in your own tent in the campsite (80NIS pp), which has kitchen toilet & shower facilities. Desert activities can be arranged through the lodge. **$$**

WHERE TO EAT Food options are rather limited so most visitors opt for self-catering. The small but sufficient **Hyperneto Supermarket** (⊕ *08.00–20.00 Sun–Thu, 08.00–14.00 Fri*) in the main square sells fresh fruit and vegetables and there are some decent bakeries, notably **Cafeneto** (📞*6587777; ⊕ 08.00–23.00 daily*) near the cliff which also does good sandwiches.

Chez Eugene Spice Quarter; 📞6539595; www.mitzperamonhotel.co.il. Elegant gourmet restaurant that comes as a surprise amidst the rustic desert & Bedouin-style eateries. Chef Yair Feinberg combines Mediterranean cuisine with the fruits of the desert to create fusion meals using prime ingredients & a blend of flavours. It is attached to the luxury hotel of the same name (**$$$$$**). **$$$$**

✕ HaHavit Restaurant and Café
✆6588226; ⊕ 08.00–late Sun–Thu, 08.00–
16.00 Fri. Better on the inside than it appears on
the outside, it has simple pub food, ice creams,
snacks & drinks & what it lacks in culinary finesse
it makes up for in the view. $$

✕ HaKatzeh 2 Har Ardon St; ✆057 9441865;
⊕ 09.30–20.30 daily. Rustic home-cooking
where almost any meal will be accompanied by
rice & potatoes. Quiches & lighter bites are a good
lunch option. $$

OTHER PRACTICALITIES
Fire ✆102
Magen David Adom (first aid) ✆101
Police ✆100. The closest police station is in the
town of Dimona 67km away.
$ Bank Hapoalim 1 Ben Gurion Bd; ✆03
6532407; ⊕ 08.30–13.15 Sun & Tue/Wed,
08.30–13.00 & 16.00–18.30 Mon & Thu

✉ **Post office** 4 Tzichor St; ✆6588416;
⊕ 08.00–18.00 Sun & Thu, 08.00–12.30 &
15.30–18.00 Mon/Tue, 08.00–13.30 Wed,
08.00–12.00 Fri. Changes travellers' cheques &
offers Western Union.

WHAT TO SEE AND DO The word 'activity' certainly sums up the range of things
to do, as most of the unusual selection of tourist attractions involve breaking a
sweat. If it's horseriding, bone-shaking jeep tours, hiking, archery, riding a llama
or rappelling you're looking for, then you're in luck. The town has also discovered
the appeal of alternative therapies and massage centres, and apart from the Isrotel
Ramon Inn spa there are countless independent therapists who work from home
or a small clinic. The visitors' centre (see *Tourist information* above, page 256) can
provide you with a list and contact details. Therapies include massage, shiatsu,
fortune telling, Chinese medicine, acupuncture and reflexology.

Ramon Crater Nature Reserve At 45km long, 8km wide and 500m deep, the
Ramon Crater is a vast gash across the Negev Desert. The spectacularly impressive
crater holds claim to being the world's largest karst erosion cirque (often referred
to internationally by its Hebrew name *machtesh*), and was formed millions of years
ago as the ocean that once covered this part of the desert retreated northwards.
Around five million years ago, the Arava Rift Valley was formed causing great rivers
to divert their course, their powerful flows eroding the land and leaving in their
wake a great crater.

The entire crater and its surrounding mountains have been incorporated into
the nature reserve and it is one of the few places in the Negev where the IDF do not
train. This has resulted in a fantastically open and free area to explore both on foot
and by car. Hiking trails are exhaustive and the visitors' centre can sell you a book
detailing hiking opportunities, while countless organisations arrange jeep tours
around the main sites (see *Local tour operators* above, page 256).

Desert Archery Park (✆ 050 5344598; *www.desertarchery.co.il*) The unusual
activity that is desert archery is played somewhat like a game of golf, yet instead
of clubs you have bows and arrows and instead of a golf green, you have the vast
expanse of the Ramon Crater. Courses of between 1km and 4km accommodate
fitness levels and a half-hour archery training session is provided before setting off.

Bio Ramon (✆ 6588755; ⊕ 08.00–17.00 Sat–Thu, 08.00–16.00 Fri (closes 1hr
earlier in winter); admission adult/child 12/6NIS) Located near the visitors' centre
this small 'live museum' is generally aimed at children but can be fun for all ages
wanting to learn about the four-legged residents of the desert.

MAKHTESH PROMENADE A good place to start exploring the crater is from the HaGamal (Camel) Lookout, which is located south of the visitors' centre along the Makhtesh Promenade. While not particularly over-exerting, the trail isn't for the faint-hearted as it skims the edge of the cliff to a suspended platform providing panoramic views of the crater. From the lookout the trail continues on past a sculpture garden and takes approximately one hour.

THE PRISM From a little past the HaGamel Lookout a trail (4km/2hrs) leads down the sharp face of the crater to the Prism, a unique sandstone hill. The geological formation was created after the stones were baked in the roasting summer sun only to crystallise as they cooled, leaving prism-like shapes covering the hillside.

SAHARONIM STRONGHOLD This is one of the most beautiful spots in the crater, a fact that seems compounded by the groups of onager (wild ass) and ibex, which are often spotted at the natural spring here. From the Be'erot campground make your way by car to the Saharonim car park. From this point several trails fan out offering hikes of differing length and difficulty. The simplest (0.5km/1hr) incorporates the Nabatean stronghold at the top of the hill directly in front of the car park and then descends to Ein Saharonim (spring), which in winter flows with water. For a longer hike (5.5km/4hrs) continue on from Ein Saharonim across the Saharonim Ridge to the Wadi Gavanim campsite (crossing route 40). Continue in a clockwise direction along Nahal Gevanim ending back in the Saharonim car park.

Alpaca farm (↖ *6588047/052 8977010; www.alpaca.co.il;* ⊕ *summer 08.30–18.30 daily; winter 08.30–16.30 daily; admission 25NIS*) This lovingly run farm began with the arrival of 190 llamas and alpacas who entered Israel from South America aboard a jet plane. Today the farm raises its 400+ animals for their fine wool. Activities include touring the farm, feeding the animals, visiting the petting centre, horseriding into the desert, learning wool-making techniques and yoga classes. The farm is located a few kilometres out of town and is well signposted. There is no public transport so you will need to get there under your own steam.

10

The Dead Sea and the Judean Desert

Telephone code 08

The eerie name of the sea that marks the lowest point on earth couldn't in fact be more apt. Shark-a-phobes be reassured, for in the salty waters of the Dead Sea nothing can live, its extreme salinity meaning all forms of organism are unable to survive, both in the water and on the shores that surround it. Yet in contrast to this rather gloomy picture of a barren and lifeless region, the Dead Sea has had a colourful religious, cultural and geological life and is today one of the country's most alluring and popular places to visit.

Biblical history abounds along the shores of the sea, with names such as John the Baptist, King David, King Herod, Sodom, Gomorrah and Lot intricately connected with its history. With the discovery of the Dead Sea Scrolls at Qumran in 1947 the sea's religious significance became unparalleled. In recent years, the phenomenon that spurred King Herod to build his majestic spa on the cliff at Masada has been tapped and the sale of Dead Sea products for their therapeutic properties has become a worldwide trade, thrusting Israel into the tourist limelight.

GEOGRAPHY AND GEOLOGY

The Dead Sea is in fact a large, saline lake. Fed by the Jordan River that winds its way from the north forming the natural border between Jordan and Israel, the sea lays

SAFETY

While drowning in water in which you can barely swim let alone fully submerge yourself in may seem ridiculous, the fact that it is difficult to swim in often causes the most problems for bathers. While you're bobbing around enjoying the newspaper, winds can quickly push you out to sea where you won't stop until reaching Jordan. It is therefore imperative (and the law) to only swim in designated areas where there are lifeguards.

The anecdote 'salt is good for healing wounds' couldn't be more appropriate – or painful – as at the Dead Sea. While it is said to be effective in the treatment of skin problems, the extreme salinity means it can burn excruciatingly if you have any broken skin. If you think you're free of scrapes and scratches, fear not, the sea will find a tiny one you didn't even know existed. Needless to say, splashing or putting your eyes anywhere near the water is painful and dangerous.

Danger signs along the coast, which should be strictly adhered to, warn of sinkholes. The fragile coast is prone to suddenly and dramatically dropping away and leaving a gaping hole in the ground, a geological phenomenon not so impressive if you're standing on it at the time.

claim to being the lowest point on earth at 418m below sea level. Its inhospitable environment is due to the fact that the water comprises 30% salinity, up to nine times saltier than other seas and oceans (that's about 300g of salt per kilogram of water). Yet this isn't just your ordinary table salt (although it does become that after a trip through the salt works at the southern end of the Dead Sea); the sea is laden with highly concentrated mineral salts. These extremely high concentrations mean its density is a lot greater than that of fresh water and is the underlying cause of both the sea's famed buoyancy and its therapeutic properties.

GETTING THERE

Visiting the Dead Sea is relatively easy either under your own steam or as part of a coach tour. Nothing however can beat renting a car and cruising along the coast road at your own pace. Public transport to and from the Dead Sea and desert in general is limited but there are regular services from Jerusalem and Tel Aviv that will drop you at the major sites.

TOURS

Finding a tour going down to the Dead Sea, Masada and Qumran is about as easy as finding sand in the desert but is not always an enjoyable experience. Cramming in as much as possible, tours hurtle out of Jerusalem zooming round the sites and heading home again. If time is of the essence and this is your only option, ask at any hotel or hostel reception and they will book you on to a tour. Flat fees of around 100NIS normally get you on the bus and you then pay for entrance tickets separately.

PRACTICALITIES

The entire coast of the sea is 65km and can be divided into three main sections based on geography and tourist sites. The northern reaches are undoubtedly the most 'wild' where the coast is yet to see the infringement of great hotels and spa resorts and is home to the Qumran Caves where the Dead Sea Scrolls were discovered. The central section incorporates the Ein Gedi region and Masada archaeological site while the ultra-touristy Ein Bokek spa resort can be found at the sea's southern end. Ein Bokek is home to the **tourist information office** (see page 270), whose staff are extremely knowledgeable and helpful. They can supply you with a good map of the area and a list of rooms to let.

Accommodation, eating options and facilities are in short supply in the area so you're best advised to book ahead, especially in summer when getting a room anywhere is unlikely at the last minute, and stock up on provisions. If you can stand the heat then camping is also an option.

EIN GEDI

The western stretch of coast known as Ein Gedi is one of the most popular and most visited sections of the Dead Sea. Its proximity to Jerusalem (a mere one hour's drive) and the Masada archaeological site, its abundance of beach facilities, a beautiful valley oasis and a kibbutz spa make it a top spot along the route south. Unfortunately it has become a regular stop for busloads of children on school visits and groups of partying teenagers who pitch their tents and smoke up a *nargilah* at the beach's campsite.

Ein Gedi has a long and unique history and countless excavations in the area have unearthed evidence of settlement here for centuries. Throughout the Chacolithic, Persian and Hasmonean periods, settlers concentrated around the springs while biblical references tell us that David sought refuge here from King Saul. During the Bar Kochba revolt (132–135CE), Ein Gedi was an important rebel outpost and it continued to thrive throughout the Roman and Byzantine periods. The antiquities park in the nature reserve delves further into the rich history of the area.

GETTING THERE AND AROUND Buses 486 and 487 from Jerusalem make the journey several times a day (1hr 20mins/37NIS), while bus 421 from Tel Aviv's Arlozorov bus station does the journey only once a day at 08.40 (2hrs 30mins/59NIS), returning at 14.30. Bus 384 to and from Beer Sheva (2hrs 25mins/48NIS) and Arad (1hr 10mins/34NIS) makes the journey four times daily and will drop you at Masada or Ein Bokek along the way. Bus 444 passes four times daily in each direction to Eilat (4hrs/67NIS).

WHERE TO STAY

Ein Gedi Resort (148 rooms) ☎6594222; e eg@ein-gedi.org.il; www.ein-gedi.co.il. Nestled amongst the green lawns of the kibbutz, its clean, spacious rooms feature kitchenettes, AC, TV & are based on HB or FB (kosher). The price inc entry into the Ein Gedi Spa. **$$$$**

Ein Gedi Youth Hostel (HI) (51 rooms) ☎6584165; e eingedy@iyha.org.il; www.iyha. org.il. The fact that it is extremely hard to get a bed in the hostel attests to its popularity & value for money. Located a short walk from the entrance to the nature reserve it is exceptionally clean, offers dorms (**$**) & dbl rooms, AC & kosher b/fast. *Dorm 137NIS.* **$$$**

Ein Gedi campsite In front of Ein Gedi Beach. The desert is hot, so don't expect to get any sleep whatsoever if you pitch your tent at the campsite between May & Sep. Out of season it is much more pleasant but be warned: in winter

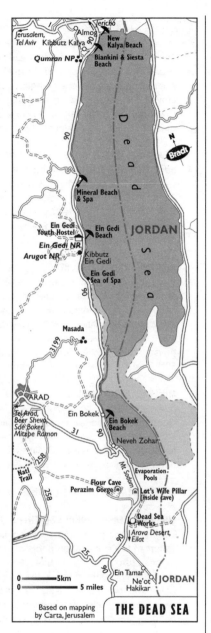

Based on mapping by Carta, Jerusalem

THE DEAD SEA

10

temperatures drop drastically as the sun goes down & you will need extremely warm attire & good sleeping bags. The campsite uses the beach facilities which are top-notch. Use of the beach is free, but there's a charge of 2NIS to use the toilet block.

DEAD SEA BEACHES

The incredible buoyancy of the Dead Sea makes for a fun and slightly surreal experience, bobbing up and down like a cork. Beaches have subsequently popped up along the coast ranging from free and crowded to expensive and crowded to private and crowded. In peak seasons finding a place to put your towel is unlikely but out of season (especially midweek) beaches are much quieter. The following beaches run from north to south:

NEW KALYA BEACH (☉ *summer 08.00–18.00; winter 08.00–17.00; admission adult/child 25/15NIS*) This stretch of coast marks the northernmost end of the Dead Sea and while it is a big favourite with Jerusalemites (a mere 25mins' drive from the capital) it is yet to establish itself on the foreigner trail. Named after the nearby Kibbutz Kalya, the beach is a relaxing place to enjoy the fruits of the Dead Sea – salt and mud. Facilities: a beach bar, towel rental and massages.

BIANKINI AND SIESTA BEACH (✆ *050 7616162/9400266; www.biankini.co.il; ☉ 08.00–20.00 daily; admission 30NIS*) This area has an atmosphere of unpretentious, laid back Moroccan charm, a range of facilities and a decent beach (although with rapidly decreasing water levels it is a longer walk to the actual water). Facilities: tented Moroccan restaurant (✆ 02 9944111; ☉ 08.30–19.30 daily; mains $$), a communal tent for dormitory-style sleeping ($), private cabins (✆ 02 9400266; f 02 9947303; $$$) and a campsite (✆ 02 9400266; 50NIS pp). For details of how to get there, see page 267.

MINERAL BEACH AND SPA (☉ *09.00–17.00 Sun–Thu, 09.00–18.00 Fri/Sat; admission 35NIS*) The unflashy, wide Mineral Beach, located 20km south of Qumran, has good sea access, especially for children, with plenty of shaded areas. The spa is simple but enjoyable and there are plenty of mud pools for slathering yourself in. Facilities: warm sulphur pool, spa with massage treatments, freshwater pool and cafeteria.

EIN GEDI BEACH (✆ *6594433; admission free*) (see page 263)

EIN BOKEK BEACH (HORDUS BEACH) (✆ *6594433; ☉ 08.00–17.00; admission free*). This free beach has several pros and unfortunately several cons. The shallow waters of the evaporation pools create white sandy beaches leading down to clear, turquoise waters that gently lap against the sheltered shore. On the downside, behind you is the sprawling and unsightly mass of gigantic hotels and tourist tack. It is also one of the sea's busiest beaches, especially in peak seasons. Facilities: a 24-hour restaurant (see page 270), showers and a plethora of shops, malls and eateries in the resort behind.

�груWHERE TO EAT Eating options in the Ein Gedi area are as sparse as fish in the Dead Sea. Your best bet is the **Pundak Ein Gedi** (✆ *6594761; ☉ 10.00–18.00 daily; mains $$*) a cafeteria-style restaurant near the petrol station. Meals are mediocre but fresh and the air conditioning means it's normally full. The **Ein Gedi Botanical Garden Restaurant** (☉ *07.00—09.30, 12.00—14.00 & 18.00—21.00 daily; $$$*) offers a big buffet with Israeli wines, salads and Mediterranean-style foods. Guests at the Ein Gedi Resort get breakfast and lunch and/or dinner so if you're staying a few days you might want to consider this option. There is also a restaurant in the resort **spa** (see above).

OTHER PRACTICALITIES There is a petrol station near the Ein Gedi campsite and beach, and a small supermarket in the kibbutz itself, but other than these, services are sparse.

WHAT TO SEE

Ein Gedi Beach Ein Gedi Beach is perhaps the most popular beach along the Dead Sea. The fact that it is free, however, is pretty much all it has going for it. The picnic area is crowded with barbecuing, music-playing families and entry to the water is hindered by sharp rocks and mud. Shower and toilet facilities, however, are top-notch and if you don't mind the noise the people-watching opportunities are great. A 24-hour beach snack bar and a petrol station are also on site.

Ein Gedi Nature Reserve (✎ *6584285;* ⊕ *Apr–Sep 08.00–17.00; Oct–Mar 08.00– 16.00; admission adult/child 25/13NIS*) The 25km² Ein Gedi Nature Reserve is a true tropical oasis, providing a lifeline for flora and fauna in an otherwise dry, barren expanse of desert landscape. Situated on the Syrian-African Rift Valley the reserve is fed year round by four springs: David, Arugot, Shulamit and Gedi. Marked trails of varying length and difficulty wind gently uphill, along (and sometimes through) rivers and streams, allowing for fantastic views over the Dead Sea and Jordan Mountains, wildlife spotting and spectacular waterfalls. The **David spring trek** can vary in length between 1.5km and 3km depending on the route chosen and detours to hidden waterfalls. Allow 90 minutes to three hours, which leaves time for a cooling-off swim in one of the waterfall pools. The longer, 4km **Arugot trek** is for the slightly more energetic and takes approximately four hours. The extra effort is rewarded by an impressive waterfall.

Historically the Ein Gedi Nature Reserve was an important area for growing unusual plants. Therapeutic and aromatic species were grown and dates, a highly sought-after commodity, could be grown successfully. To this day the oasis still boasts an impressive and fundamental array of plants and trees of east African origin. A large variety of mammals, birds and reptiles are also drawn to the natural oasis, the Nubian ibex and Syrian hyrax being the most noticeable and easily spotted residents. The local celebrities however are the small colony of leopards who live in the nearby hills, but these shy creatures are infrequently seen.

Just outside the reserve, the Ein Gedi antiquities park contains the remains of an ancient synagogue and gives a brief insight into the history of the area. Built during the Byzantine period by Jewish residents of the area, this ornate synagogue was an integral part of the flourishing community. After the Arab conquest, however, Ein Gedi was reduced to the small kibbutz settlement it is today. Kibbutz Ein Gedi is situated just above the reserve.

While the reserve and antiquities park are open year round, winter flooding of the David and Arugot rivers often results in the park's closure and hiking is prohibited. The best time to visit is spring or autumn when the summer heat relents and the park is less crowded.

Ein Gedi kibbutz and spas (✎ *6594221/726; www.ein-gedi.co.il;* e *eg@ein-gedi. org.il*) The beautiful, palm-fringed kibbutz has successfully cashed in on the rapidly growing international phenomenon of Dead Sea treatments. Its main economy today centres on tourism and while the flash hotels along the coast at Ein Bokek

Renowned worldwide for its purported therapeutic properties, the Dead Sea has become a honeypot for those in search of natural relief from a whole host of ailments. Spa resorts and health clinics along the coast have harnessed the region's climate, unique conditions and medicinal products to offer a series of specialist treatments: **climatotherapy**, which draws on climatic elements such as humidity, pressure and temperature; **balneotherapy**, a treatment that uses the thick, black Dead Sea mud; and **thalassotherapy**, which involves bathing in the unique waters of the sea. The following are considered the best Dead Sea spas:

DMZ Medical Spa Lot Spa Dead Sea Hotel, Ein Bokek; 6689200; www.dmz-medical-spa. com. Treats psoriasis, asthma, orthopaedic & cardiac rehabilitation, cystic fibrosis & skin diseases.

Dead Sea Clinic Central Solarium, Ein Bokek; 6520297; e: deadseaclinic@gmail.com; www.deadseaclinic.com. Offers over 100 different kinds of treatments specialising in respiratory diseases, joint problems, dermatological diseases & anti-stress.

Ein Gedi Spa (see page 266) Renowned for treating neurological metabolic disorders, traumatic ailments, allergies, bronchial asthma & rheumatic illnesses.

may have all the mod cons, Ein Gedi has years of experience and the added bonus of its pretty, leafy surroundings and a real family atmosphere. A small supermarket here is a good place to stock up on the basics if you are planning picnics or self-catering meals, but don't expect too much. The kibbutz runs both the on-site **Nature's Creation** spa (6594220) offering top-of-the-range holistic treatments including Ayurveda, massages, mud wraps, salt peeling and herbal saunas. Just along the coast the **Ein Gedi Sea of Spa** (6594813; ☺ summer 08.00–19.00; winter 08.00–17.00 Sat–Thu, closes 1hr earlier on Fri; w/day/w/end 90/100NIS), 4km south of Ein Gedi Kibbutz, has honed promotion of the internationally famed Dead Sea products to the maximum. The spa is a fantastic way to experience the sea's therapeutic properties with a huge array of facilities and treatments. Six thermo-mineral water pools, massages, mud baths and an outdoor freshwater pool will leave you feeling clean, young and healthy. A meal in the spa's restaurant, which serves a selection of meat dishes, salads and desserts, is included in the entry price.

AROUND EIN GEDI

QUMRAN NATIONAL PARK (02 9942235; www.parks.org.il; ☺ Apr–Sep 08.00–17.00; Oct–Mar 08.00–16.00 (1hr earlier on Fri); admission adult/child 20/9NIS) The isolated site of Qumran, perched on the cliffs at the northernmost end of the Dead Sea, was the scene of the discovery of perhaps the world's most significant biblical texts, the Dead Sea Scrolls. Today housed inside their very own display hall in Jerusalem's Israel Museum, the scrolls have been dated from between the 3rd century BCE to 68CE and are older than any other surviving biblical manuscripts by almost 1,000 years. Their discovery by a Bedouin shepherd in 1947 gave rise to almost a decade of intensive excavation, archaeologists and historians desperate to discover the authors and age of the thousands of fragments (totalling 800–900 scripts) that were found. It was during this time that they stumbled upon Qumran, a complex of structures located on a barren terrace between the caves and the Dead Sea.

While Qumran had been populated since as far back as the 8th century BCE it was its later inhabitants who put their hand to the scrolls. The Essenes were a sectarian community who lived in this remote region for 200 years, from the Hasmonean period through the Jewish revolt against the Romans. They were breakaways, rejecting the rest of the Jewish people, and appear to have lived a communal life of ritual purity. The scrolls themselves contain versions of the Old Testament as well as texts relating to their sectarian existence. One of the most hotly contested theories that arose from the discovery of the scrolls was that they may have been an early influence on Christianity. Parallels in belief and rules of conduct between the scrolls and the New Testament have sparked heated debate across the world.

The site itself is nowhere near as interesting as its history and the scrolls themselves but is worth a quick stop if you're in the area. The ritualistic and pure life led by the Essenes can be seen in the remains of assembly halls, ritual baths and scriptorium (writing room) as well as a kitchen, dining room and large water cistern.

Getting there and away All buses heading from Tel Aviv and Jerusalem towards Ein Gedi will drop you at the Kalya junction for access to the Biankini and Siesta Beach and Qumran junction for the archaeological park.

MASADA

(↘6584207/8; www.parks.org.il; ⊕ Apr–Sep 08.00–16.00; Oct–Mar 08.00–17.00 (1hr earlier on Fri); admission & cable car adult/child 49/26NIS, eastern side plus cable car 67/38NIS, snake route 25/13NIS) More than just one of the country's most-visited tourist destinations, the archaeological site of Masada represents Israeli patriotism at its proudest. Upon the protruding rock that towers some 400m above the western shore of the Dead Sea, IDF soldiers come to swear allegiance, repeating the mantra 'Masada shall not fall again'. For it was here, on the precipitous rock shelf, that the ancient fortress built by Herod the Great in the 1st century BCE became the 20th-century symbol of Jewish heroism. The fortress was captured by the Zealots, a Jewish sect, in 66CE in their revolt against Rome and became the last standing Jewish stronghold. After a long siege, the Romans finally stormed the fortress in 73, only to find that all 960 Zealots had committed suicide rather than surrender to their forces. Today, it is one of the most important stops on the Jewish pilgrimage route and in 2001 was awarded UNESCO World Heritage status. A new museum complex opened in 2007 now displays some of the most impressive artefacts excavated from the ruins as well as depicting the life, times and history of this fascinating site.

HISTORY Although finds date the origin of the site to the Chacolithic period 6,000 years ago, it wasn't until Herod got his hands on it that Masada really came into its own. Major fortifications between 37BCE and 31BCE included two beautiful, ornate palaces, heavy defensive walls, state-of-the-art aqueducts and water cisterns and a bathhouse complex. In 66CE, following Herod's death, the Jewish revolt against the Romans saw a group of rebels overcome the Roman garrison stationed at Masada. After the fall of Jerusalem in 70CE, the rebels were joined by Zealots and families fleeing the devastation, only to be stormed by the Romans three years later. They established camps at the base of the fortress and laid a complicated and arduous siege to it, one that would last many months.

GETTING THERE AND AWAY There are two ways to approach Masada: from route 90 that runs along the Dead Sea (5mins off the main road) or along route 3199 from Arad. The youth hostel, visitors' centre, cable cars and Snake Path are all accessed from the eastern Dead Sea entrance while visitors arriving for the sound and light show (see opposite) or wishing to ascend the Roman Ramp will need to approach from the direction of Arad. There isn't a through road from the western side to the Dead Sea so be aware that if you come from this direction you will need to take the very long route back to Arad and down past Ein Bokek (1hr drive) to reach the coast and hostel. Buses heading to Ein Gedi from Beer Sheva and Arad will stop at the junction on the way (see *Arad*, page 272) while buses coming from Jerusalem and Tel Aviv will continue on to the archaeological site from Ein Gedi (see *Ein Gedi*, page 262).

WHERE TO STAY

⌂ **Masada Guest House (HI)** (88 rooms) ✆9953222; e massada@iyha.org.il; www.iyha.org.il. Located just off the Dead Sea route 90 sits this huge, immaculate hostel offering more than just staggering views over the Dead Sea. Rooms have AC, TV & minibar & there is a swimming pool in summer. Internet access is available & guests receive a 25% discount off Masada cable-car tickets. Kosher b/fast inc & other meals can be ordered for 45NIS. *Single-sex dorms 142NIS.* **$$$**

WHAT TO SEE

The Snake Path The path provides the eastern entrance to the site but the walk uphill is steep and tiring, especially during the blistering summer heat. The alternative is to take the cable car, which leaves from near the car park and finishes at the top of the Snake Path. Both begin from the Dead Sea road.

The Roman Ramp The ramp that ascends to the fortress from the west side is a third option of entering and exiting the site. The ramp can be accessed only from the Arad road.

Palaces Many of the ancient structures and buildings have been restored, one of the most striking being the wall paintings inside the two Herodian palaces. The three-terraced Northern Palace acted as Herod's personal quarters, while the vast complex that comprised the Western Palace was home to servants, workshops and storehouses. Inside, it is possible to see the remains of Herod's throne room, arranged around a central courtyard. Just to the south of the Western Palace are the remains of Herod's swimming pool, another example of the luxurious lifestyle that he enjoyed at Masada.

Bathhouses Designed in a Romanesque style, the bathhouses have been well restored and show the intricate engineering that went into the creation of Herod's luxurious early spa. The bathhouses are located just south of the Northern Palace.

Roman villa With an architectural design reminiscent of the great villas of Rome, the wonderfully restored mansion is a perfect example of the level of luxury and grandeur afforded to those who resided here. After the Zealots took control of the fortress, many of the buildings were divided up to accommodate the substantial population.

Synagogue The incredible discovery of the Masada synagogue has led archaeologists and historians to believe that it may be the oldest Jewish house of prayer in the world. It is the only synagogue to be dated to the time of the Second Temple and contained fragments of scrolls from Ezekiel and Deuteronomy.

Roman camps There are a total of eight Roman camps that surround the lower reaches of the Masada cliff. It was here that Roman garrisons stationed themselves during their long and relentless siege of the fortress. Thanks to the arid climate and soil, the camps are considered the best-preserved Roman army camps ever discovered.

Byzantine church Southeast of the synagogue is another large building complex within which was discovered a 5th-century Byzantine church. A small portion of semi-restored mosaics can be seen at the rear of the building.

Storehouses On the right just through the East Gate are the semi-restored remains of 11 storehouses. Amphorae and jars containing remnants of wine, oil and flour were found in the larger rooms while it is believed valuables and weaponry may have been kept in the smaller ones.

Sound and light show (☎ *9959333; Mar–Oct 21.00 Tue & Thu; admission adult/child 45/35NIS*) Shown against the backdrop of the western side of the mountain (reached from the Arad road), this 40-minute show depicts the history of the site in an impressive light display. The audio is in Hebrew but there are earphones for English, French, German and Spanish visitors. Tickets must be booked in advance through the Arad visitors' centre (☎ *08 9954409*), which also organises transport there and back (see page 272).

Ahava Factory Store (☎ *6584319;* 🕘 *08.00–16.00 Sun–Fri, 08.00–17.00 Sat*) Peruse the shelves laden with Dead Sea products from Israel's biggest and most famous manufacturer. They make great souvenirs and cost half what you'd pay in Europe or the US.

EIN BOKEK

All good things have to come to an end and the natural, rugged beauty of the Dead Sea does so at the Ein Bokek hotel resort, about 12 miles south of Masada. This conglomeration of enormous chain hotels and their attached luxury spas, souvenir shops and food kiosks are an eyesore along the wild stretch of coastline. However, the hotels are expensive and specialist, attracting guests who come to relax and enjoy some pampering and relaxation, not to party all night. There is a definite touristy feel to the highly developed strip, but the very nice (if overcrowded), free **Hordus Beach** (🕘 *08.00–17.00*) can be found nestled amidst the towering buildings. And as a guest, there is no doubt that your Dead Sea therapeutic experience would be top-of-the-range, if decidedly mass-produced.

GETTING THERE AND AWAY There are four buses a day (348) to and from Arad (45mins) which continue to Ein Gedi, stopping at Masada along the way. By car follow route 90 that runs along the Dead Sea until just south of Ein Bokek, where you then turn on to route 31 which leads to Arad.

GETTING AROUND There are few roads and limited public transport in this region, so a car is a great way to get around. Route 90 runs from just outside Jerusalem all the way along the coast of the Dead Sea and continues southwards into the Arava Desert (see page 275). The **Hertz** car-rental office (☏ *6584530*; ⏲ *08.30–17.00 Sun–Thu, 08.30–14.00 Fri*) is located in the Solarium Spa building at the entrance to Ein Bokek.

TOURIST INFORMATION The well-equipped tourist information office (☏ *9975010*; e *tamar266@bezeqint.net*; ⏲ *summer 10.00–17.00, winter 09.00–16.00*) is located in the Solarium Spa building, and the friendly and knowledgeable staff can help with all manner of information, recommendations and desert and Dead Sea trivia.

WHERE TO STAY Four star is the lowest-ranked hotel you're likely to find at Ein Bokek and all pride themselves on quality, service and top-of-the-range facilities. All the major chains are represented, including Rimonim, Leonardo, Crowne Plaza and Fattal.

🏠 **Crowne Plaza Dead Sea** (304 rooms) ☏6591919; e ds_gmsec@hiil.co.il; www.ichotelsgroup.com. Luxury, compliments of the Crowne Plaza chain of international hotels. Rooms are wood floored & elegant & have all mod cons. Facilities inc the Asian fusion Sato Bistro ☏6591975; ⏲ 18.00–23.00 Sun–Thu; 90NIS), a state-of-the-art fitness & spa centre & indoor & outdoor pools. **$$$$$**

🏠 **Daniel Dead Sea Resort & Spa** (302 rooms) ☏6689999; www.tamareshotels.co.il. The hotel has a cosy & relaxed atmosphere & rooms all have views of the Dead Sea & a fresh & pleasant décor. Expansive swimming pools, a top-of-the-range spa & wealth of treatments complete the Dead Sea experience. HB & FB available. **$$$$$**

WHERE TO EAT For eating options, Ein Bokek is like an oasis of restaurants, cheap kiosks and supermarkets. Inside all the hotels are excellent fine dining options.

✗ **Taj Mahal** In the Tulip-Inn Hotel; ☏057 6506502; www.taj-mahal.co.il; ⏲ 12.00–sunrise daily. Bedouin-style tent with rich-coloured cushions & twinkling lanterns. Indulge in some bare-footed eating & drinking with a Middle Eastern grill & *nargilah* pipe. Live music & belly dancing on Fri. **$$$$**

✗ **On the Beach Restaurant** ☏6520231; ⏲ 24hrs daily. Offers standard sandwiches, grilled meats, pizza & pasta with views of the Dead Sea. **$$$**

OTHER PRACTICALITIES Ein Bokek has countless shops (particularly on the strip directly in front of Hordus Beach) selling the fruits of the Dead Sea. There is a supermarket, a pharmacy and hotel receptions can offer post and internet services. The small Sky Blue Mall has a money change office.

VALLEY OF SODOM

Spanning the southern portion of the Dead Sea is the area known as the Valley of Sodom, named thus for the belief that it was here that God unleashed his fury upon the city of Sodom for its 'sins'. Today, Mount Sodom marks the precise spot and is a must-stop on the tour route. The region is today characterised by the mountain and its range of walks, caves, gorges and powder-like chalky sand. At the base of the Dead Sea, just after the Salt Works and a 20-minute drive from Ein Bokek, are the moshavim of Neot HaKikar and Ein-Tamar which offer a more low-key desert experience, where nature and adventure prevail.

GETTING THERE AND AWAY There is no public transport to the moshavim so you will need to get there under your own steam. Coming from Ein Gedi and Ein Bokek on route 90 turn right just after the evaporation pools and follow the road for about 8km. If you reach the Arava junction you've gone too far.

PRACTICALITIES The moshavim have geared themselves up for visitors to the desert and southern Dead Sea region, and now offer accommodation options from camping to private rooms; family eateries, local tour guides, adventure activities, workshops, small supermarkets, a swimming pool and medical centre. Almost all of these facilities are located in Neot-HaKikar.

WHERE TO STAY Many of the families have created guesthouse accommodation and visitors have a choice of campsites, simple rooms and pleasant cabins. There are also opportunities to stay in desert Bedouin tents. Pick up a copy of the moshavim leaflet in the Ein Bokek tourist information office (see page 270) or visit www.ma-tamar.org.il for full listings.

Belfer's Dead Sea Cabins (3 rooms)
08 6555104; e michaelbelfer@gmail.com.
Split-level cabins are suitable for families & have kitchenette, large porch, outdoor BBQ facilities & free bicycles. Great location for exploring the desert. **$$$**

Cycle Inn (6 rooms) 6552828;
e esteeuzi@zahav.net.il; www.cycle-inn.co.il.
Family-run guesthouse offering a campsite & private rooms. It has a very communal, friendly atmosphere & is a good budget option for exploring the desert & Dead Sea region. **$$$**

WHERE TO EAT Home-cooking is the name of the game here and there are a handful of rustic meals to be had in the moshavim. **Yossi's Place** (052 8808111), **Mothers Secrets** (052 8991199) and **Pnina's** (6555107) offer baked goods, hummus, grilled meats and sandwiches but they must be ordered in advance.

WHAT TO SEE AND DO

Sodom Mountain and Lot's Wife Cave While there is no proof that this is in fact the biblical site of Sodom, it has been the traditional spot. The 11km by 3km mountain range consists almost wholly of salt and is, according to the Book of Genesis, the site of the two towns of Sodom and Gomorrah that were destroyed by God with a rain of fire and brimstone (sulphur) for their wickedness. Before the destruction ensued, God sent two angels to warn all good men to leave the evil towns. The angels found only one good man, Lot, whom they saved, along with his wife and daughters, warning them not to look back. When Lot's wife disobeyed the warning she was turned into a pillar of salt. Tour buses and signposts today point to a pillar above the entrance to a cave just off the main road as that of Lot's wife and it marks another quick stop along the pilgrimage route.

Nahal Perazim and the Flour Cave At 3km south of Lot's Wife Cave, a small turn-off on the right between kilometre markers 193 and 194 leads to the **Flour Cave**. So named because of the fine, white powdery chalk that covers everything it touches (including your hair, clothes and face), the cave is part of **Nahal Perazim**, a beautiful, narrow, dry gorge. A 15-minute walk through the gorge will bring you to the entrance of the pitch-black cave (torches are advisable) where it is but a short walk to the other end. White floury steps lead up and out of the 18,000–20,000-year-old cave where you can return to the car park along the path above the gorge. Alternatively, more seasoned hikers can follow a blue (then black) marked trail that leads from the exit of the Flour Cave up Mount Sodom.

Jeep tours Several outfits and private guides offer jeep tours out into the heart of the desert. These include **Masa Midbar** (✆ *052 2317371*), **Barry Hermon** (✆ *052 8491115*) and **Camel Lot** (✆ *052 8666062*). The last also offer camel and donkey treks.

Art galleries Within the two moshavim are several artists' galleries ranging from pottery and ceramic sculpting to metal arts and furniture to glass sculpting. Many offer workshops.

ARAD

The small, desert city of Arad is most well known for its ancient namesake, today located a few kilometres away at Tel Arad. Yet the city is rather pleasant, if not attractive, in its own right, and considerable efforts over recent years to improve its image have been successful. Its altitude and unique arid climate make it an ideal place for asthma sufferers, and plans to develop the city into a centre for medical treatments are under way. Public transport links with the Dead Sea (25km away), Jerusalem and Beer Sheva are good in desert terms and there is a modern, ethnically diverse feel to the place. The Artists' Quarter (Eshet Lot) in the industrial zone (see opposite) is worth a visit if you're in the area, and comprises works by local artists who aim to capture the beauty and ruggedness of the desert in their works.

GETTING THERE AND AWAY Bus 389 from Tel Aviv makes the journey four times daily (10.10, 12.50, 18.30 and 20.15) (2hrs/40NIS) returning at 06.00, 08.30, 14.15 and 17.00. To Ein Bokek on the Dead Sea there are four buses daily at 07.07, 10.15, 13.00 and 15.45 (45mins/24.50NIS), which continue to Ein Gedi, stopping at Masada along the way. There are several buses a day to and from Beer Sheva (1hr/17.20NIS) from where you can connect to Jerusalem, Eilat, Sde Boker and Mitzpe Ramon.

TOURIST INFORMATION AND PRACTICALITIES The **Arad Visitors' Centre** (✆ *9950190*; ⊕ *Apr–Sep 08.00–17.00; Oct–Mar 08.00–16.00 daily; admission adult/child 23/12NIS*) contains the **Museum of Biblical Arad**. They also arrange tickets and transport to Masada's sound and light show (see page 269). The centre is located in central Arad near the mall. They can also supply you with a list of guesthouses in the town.

⌂ **WHERE TO STAY AND EAT** There are a few small hotels, guesthouses and a selection of eateries and pubs in the town. Eateries range from simple pizzerias to international cuisine such as Chinese and pub/restaurants. While the cuisine is most certainly not on a par with Eilat or Tel Aviv there is something to suit every taste and pocket.

⌂ **Kfar Hanokdim** (35 rooms) ✆ 9950097; e kfar@kfarhanokdim.co.il; www.hanokdim. com. Set in the desert just outside of Arad is this authentic Bedouin experience. To get there take route route 3199 out of Arad and continue for 8km. It is signposted on the right. Choose to stay in the communal tent on colourful mattresses or in the private cabins, all made from locally sourced, organic materials. Be entertained by Bedouin hospitality, enjoy traditional cooking, or embark on a donkey or camel trek into the desert. Must be reserved in advance. Packages inc a trek & a night's accommodation: 250NIS pp (**$$**) (or 450NIS HB).

⌂ **Arad Guest House (HI)** (50 rooms) 4 Ha'atad St; ✆ 9957150; e arad@iyha.org. il; www.iyha.org.il. Clean, simple dorms with TV, AC, bunks & kosher b/fast. The reception is closed on Shabbat & you need to call ahead if you're arriving in the afternoon. Dorm rooms not available on w/ends. *Dorms 104NIS.* **$$$**

WHAT TO SEE

Tel Arad (⌕ *7762170; www.parks.org.il;* ◔ *Apr–Sep 08.00–17.00; Oct–Mar 08.00–16.00 (1hr earlier on Fri); admission adult/child 13/7NIS*) About 10km east of Arad on the road to Beer Sheva are the remains of not one but two ancient settlements. In the 2nd century BCE, a huge Canaanite city was built here, its 1km² area making it the largest excavated Canaanite settlement in the country. Some of the excavated remains of houses have been fully restored, their distinctive shape and layout having coined a new archaeological term 'Aradian house'. Further up the hill, an Israelite settlement dates to about 1000BCE during the reign of King Solomon, and came into being some 1,500 years after the abandonment of the Canaanite city. Referred to as a citadel fortress, it lasted throughout the reigns of the kings of Judah until its destruction between 597BCE and 577BCE, during which time Jerusalem was under siege from the Babylonians. Inside the fortress courtyard is an Israelite temple, a smaller version of King Solomon's Temple in Jerusalem.

Artists' Quarter (*Industrial Area*) Small artists' galleries display their works which reflect the beauty, barreness and ancient traditions of the desert. Tours can be arranged through the visitors' centre.

11

The Arava Desert

Telephone code 08

As the desert makes its way towards the vibrant city of Eilat, there appears to be a lull before the party storm. Civilisation gets sparser, the landscape more remote and facilities fewer and farther between. Yet the Arava Desert is in fact one of the most bewitching regions of Israel's south where Bedouin communities thrive, the Spice Route starts its long trek westwards and where the air is the freshest in the country. Kibbutzim dot the fringes of route 90, their isolated positions and organic farming practices producing an ideal getaway for those seeking the utmost in seclusion and nature. And nature is the name of the game in the southern Arava, the Yotvata Hai Bar Reserve (see page 275), Timna Park (see page 277) and International Birding and Research Centre (see page 286) providing a great insight into the desert's wilder strip of land.

GETTING THERE AND AROUND

This is one of the most inaccessible areas of the country and getting to sights/sites is difficult by public transport. Renting a car in Beer Sheva is by far the best way to get the most out of your time in this remote region. Route 40 from Beer Sheva passes Sde Boker and Mitzpe Ramon and joins with route 90 coming down from the Dead Sea and Jerusalem. Route 90 then continues all the way through the Arava Desert to Eilat. Bus 397 from Beer Sheva stops at the junctions to the kibbutzim and parks along the Arava Desert on its way to Eilat. There are seven buses daily in each direction.

TOURIST INFORMATION/TOUR OPERATORS

The small **Yotvata Visitors' Centre** (⊕ *08.00–15.00 Sat–Thu, 08.00–13.00 Fri*) is located directly outside the mall in Kibbutz Yotvata along route 90. The **Shaharut Camel Riders** (see below, page 278) organise camel treks in the wilds of the Arava Desert and there are countless tour operators in Eilat (see page 279) that can arrange 4x4 and birdwatching trips.

⌂ WHERE TO STAY

Sleeping (almost) under the stars, getting out into nature and learning to appreciate the fruits of the wild desert, is becoming hugely popular, and as a result eco-lodges and Bedouin-style khans (tents) have appeared throughout the Arava. Whether it's meditating, communal living, organic toilets or rustic, home-cooked meals over a campfire, the lodges offer them all. All also offer private rooms with air conditioning and hot water so you don't have to rough it. Most of the lodges also

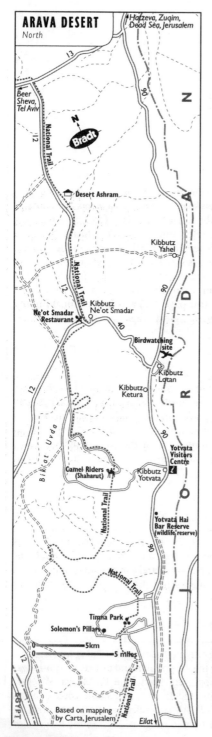

offer campsites if you have your own tent, and there are campsites too in the Timna Park, Yotvata Hai Bar Reserve and the **Ye'elim Desert Holiday Village** (📞 *6374362; check in from 10.00 Sun–Fri, 19.00–21.00 Sat*) at Kibbutz Yotvata. Some of the kibbutzim dotted along route 90 also offer nice, clean rooms and use of the swimming pool and dining room. For accommodation at Shaharut Camel Riders or the Kibbutz Lotan Guesthouse, see page278.

🏠 **Desert Ashram** (80 beds) Shittim; 📞6326508; e ashram@desertashram.co.il; www.desertashram.co.il. Located on the west side of the Arava Desert on the path of the Israel National Trail (see page 50) is this serene centre of meditation in the heart of the remote desert. Prices inc accommodation (in rooms or wooden huts with AC, in a dorm or the campsite) FB organic, vegetarian food & meditation sessions. *Dorm 90NIS. 320NIS less on w/days* **$$. $$$**

🏠 **Keren Kolot** (22 rooms) Kibbutz Ketura; 📞6356658; e kerenkolot@ketura.co.il; www.keren-kolot-israel.co.il. If you're not opposed to the smell of cow excrement (& you get used to it rather fast) then the spacious, comfortable rooms offered on the kibbutz are a good base for visiting the area. A communal pool (in summer), simple kosher dining room (25NIS extra), café & bicycle rental are extras as well as tours of the experimental orchards where exotic, hard-to-pronounce fruits are grown. *100NIS less on w/days.* **$$$**

🏠 **Negev Eco Lodge** (40 beds) Zuqim, north Arava south of Hatzeva; 📞052 6170028; e desert-days@arava.co.il; www.desert-days.co.il. This eco-lodge is constructed from sustainable desert materials & offers 7 rooms (sleep up to 6 people) each with an ecological toilet, hot water, coffee facilities & shared kitchen. A communal khan (tent) offers dormitory accommodation & there is a real community feel to the lodge where people can get close to nature. A pool, animal corner & desert tours are other attractions. *Dorms 90NIS. 100NIS less on w/days.* **$$$**

🏠 **Desert Routes Inn** (60 beds) Hatzeva, northern Arava just south of the Dead Sea; 📞6581829; e shvilimbamidbar@gmail.com. Enjoy the isolated peaceful atmosphere of the desert with the modern comforts of home. 11 self-contained apts have kitchenette, cable TV & AC, while a khan (tent) offers dormitory accommodation on mattresses. Internet, BBQ area & a community swimming pool. There is a small supermarket in the moshav as well as tour booking facilities. *Dorms 100NIS.* **$$**

✖ WHERE TO EAT

Dining options are sparse and often eating in the simple kibbutz dining rooms is the only choice. In moshav Hatseva there is the simple but good restaurant **Bar BaMidbar** (◊ *6581406*) while the **Yotvata Rest Stop** (◊ *6357363;* ⊕ *05.30–19.00 Sun–Thu, 05.30–18.00 Fri, 07.00–20.00 Sat; mains* **$$**) has a buffet-style canteen with OK mains and a really good selection of desserts (be sure to try some of the Choco chocolate milk for which the kibbutz is famous). The wonderful organic farm shop **Ne'ot Smadar** (◊ *6358111;* ⊕ *06.00–21.00 Sun–Thu, 06.00–15.00 Fri, 18.00–21.00 Sat; mains* **$$**) at the Ketura junction offers a lovely little menu of creative dishes which are delicious and oh-so-healthy while the **Shaharut Restaurant** (see *Camel Riders*, page 278) serves freshly baked Bedouin fare in a traditional atmosphere.

OTHER PRACTICALITIES

Between Beer Sheva in the Negev Desert and Eilat in the far south of the Arava there is a distinct lack of any kind of facilities. The tiny Kibbutz Yotvata has a small supermarket and petrol station and the kibbutzim dotted along route 90 offer minimal services.

WHAT TO SEE AND DO

TIMNA PARK (◊ *6316756; www.timna-park.co.il;* ⊕ *08.00–16.00 daily (Jul & Aug open until 13.00); admission adult/ child 44/39NIS)* The 90km² Timna Valley is home to some of the country's most impressive geological formations, a rich and powerful history and a never-ending array of hiking trails. Historically Timna stands alone as the earliest, most technologically advanced and productive centre in the ancient world. From the 14th to the 12th centuries BCE, the Egyptians operated a vast copper-mining enterprise here. While this was the site's most productive period, evidence has pointed to continued mining communities operating as far back as the late Neolithic period.

The vast U-shaped valley is surrounded by mountains that appear myriad colours over the course of a day, and with hiking trails radiating in every direction over and around them.

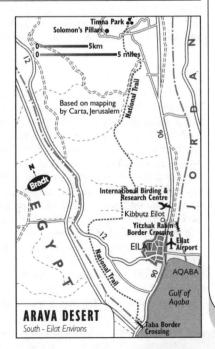

ARAVA DESERT
South - Eilat Environs

A car is a prerequisite for visiting the park as there is no public transport though most sites can be driven to. Nevertheless, there are ample opportunities to get away from the road and into the heart of the desert. A hiking map is supplied at the entrance detailing treks of between one and ten hours. Among the park's many attractions are the famous **Solomon's Pillars**, formed by years of erosion of the pink sandstone cliff face from which they protrude. Other notable sites include the rock-cut **Mushroom**, **Valley of Inscriptions** and the **ancient mines**. Camping is possible at the park's entrance but you will need to call ahead to reserve a spot (30NIS).

KIBBUTZ LOTAN (☎ 6356935; e *lotan-programs@lotan.ardom.co.il; www.kibbutzlotan.com*) The bohemian kibbutz of Lotan is ideal for hippies-at-heart or weekend hippies in search of some natural living. With the word 'eco' in front of all their activities guests are left in no doubt as to their ethos (and no, you won't be finding televisions inside any of their mud-coated guesthouses). At the kibbutz you can learn how to build your own eco-friendly house, enjoy a *watsu* (water shiatsu) massage in the spa centre, relax in the swimming pool or do a spot of birdwatching. Guesthouses (**$$$**) are pleasant but simple and there is also dorm accommodation (100NIS). The atmosphere on the kibbutz is lovely however, and you pay for the experience.

DESERT ASHRAM (see page 276) Spiritual and meditational haven in the depths of the desert offering a Work Meditation Programme (WOMP), festivals and workshops.

CAMEL RIDERS (*Shaharut;* ☎ 6373218; *www.camel-riders.com*) Camel caravan trips ranging from a few hours up to eight days (75–1,500NIS) are the quintessential desert experience, with roaring open fires, sleeping under the stars and a mighty sore rear end being part and parcel of the trip. They also organise jeep tours, have a restaurant and offer Bedouin-style half-board accommodation in a large communal tent (60NIS) or simple, private huts (**$**). If you're arriving by bus (397 between Beer Sheva and Eilat) call ahead to get picked up from the junction.

EILAT

For a touch of culture, history and Holy Land charm, don't come to Eilat. If, however, you're after some hedonistic, raucous and rather tacky seaside fun, then this is definitely the place. After driving through the serene, staggeringly beautiful landscape of the Negev and Arava deserts, Eilat comes as quite a shock. Perched on the tiny strip of Red Sea coast that Israel lays claim to, it is something of a Middle East Las Vegas (without the gambling). Row upon row of big chain hotels line the coast, the glittering Red Sea water swarms with all manner of sea craft and squealing sunseekers, and the pumping neon-lit pedestrian strip is crammed with restaurants, beach bars and shopping malls. A big favourite with boisterous Israeli teenagers enjoying their first trip away from the folks, Eilat can be rowdy and wild. Nevertheless, it has also managed to maintain a noisy family atmosphere, especially on the beaches further along the south coast. The 14km stretch of Israel's Red Sea coast means that day trips to Petra in Jordan and Egypt's Sinai coast are easily accessible, while day trips into the southern Arava Desert are welcome ways to escape the city.

Eilat enjoys almost 365 days a year of sunshine, a year-round water temperature of 21°C and a winter low of 20°C, making it the country's only beach resort that quite literally never stops. Summer temperatures can reach in excess of 40°C but because of its dry, desert atmosphere and lack of humidity, it remains rather pleasant and often more bearable than the intense, sticky humidity of the Mediterranean.

GETTING THERE AND AWAY

By bus The central bus station [280 B2] is located on HaTemarin St (\ 6365120) and can be a somewhat disorganised and busy place. Bus 394 from Tel Aviv's central bus station does the journey every 90 minutes (5hrs 20mins/75NIS) and goes through Beer Sheva, but gets booked up in summer by hordes of loud teenagers so reserve a seat in advance. From Jerusalem bus 444 departs Eilat at 07.00, 10.00, 14.00 and 17.00 (5hrs/75NIS) and heads along the Dead Sea, past Ein Gedi.

By air Most of the commercial flights to Eilat come from Haifa, Tel Aviv's Dov Hoz or Ben Gurion airports with Arkia, Israir or El Al airlines. **Arkia** (*Red Canyon Mall;* \ *6384888*) and **Israir** (*Shalom Centre;* \ *6340666*) offer flights to Tel Aviv for between 150NIS and 500NIS, or Haifa for about 450NIS, while El Al offer excellent prices of around 100–150NIS each way from Tel Aviv. The airport is smack bang in the centre of town and is a five-minute walk to the promenade or city centre

By land The Taba and Arava (Yitzhak Rabin) border crossings provide overland entry into Egypt's Sinai Peninsula and Jordan respectively (see page 42).

GETTING AROUND Eilat's city centre is small, so walking is the easiest way to get around. There are taxis everywhere and fares generally cost around 10NIS. Bus 15 from the town centre makes the 7km journey along the south coast to the Taba border regularly, stopping at the beaches, major hotels and underwater observatory along the way.

Car rental

🚗 **Avis** [280 B2] Shalom Centre, 2 Sderot HaTemarim Bd; \ 6373164/5; www.avis.co.il; ⏰ 08.00–17.00 Sun–Thu, 08.00–14.00 Fri. Minimum of 3 days' rental.
🚗 **Europcar** [280 B2] Shalom Centre (Store 1387); \ 7918014; f 6378937; www.europcar.com; ⏰ 08.00–18.00 Sun–Thu, 08.00–13.00 Fri

🚗 **Sixt** [280 B2] Shalom Centre (Store 1018); \ 6373511; f 6373512; www.sixt.com; ⏰ 08.00–17.00 Sun–Fri. Cars from 160NIS per day.

TOURIST INFORMATION The **Eilat Tourist Information Office** (*Bridge Hse, North Beach promenade;* \ *6309111;* e *eilatinfo@tourism.gov.il;* ⏰ *08.30–17.00 Sun–Thu, 08.00–13.00 Fri*) sells tickets for most of Eilat's attractions and can offer help and advice on booking accommodation, particularly about budget places, which can be difficult to find in peak seasons.

Tours

Land tours The **Red Sea Sports Centre** (see page 287) offers one of the best all-round packages of excursions to get you out into the wild desert lands. Jeep safari tours include destinations such as Petra in Jordan, Timna Park and the Red Canyon. **Holit Desert Tours** (*Chan Centre;* \ *052 8082020;* f *6331210; www.israelpetratours. com;* ⏰ *09.00–16.00 daily (for bookings 08.00–22.00)*) also has several well-priced tours to sights around southern Israel, Jordan and Sinai. They also arrange cycling tours, rappelling, camel and donkey trips, paintballing and archery in the area. **Desert Eco Tours** [280 A3] (*Zofit Centre;* \ *052 2765753/3382946;*

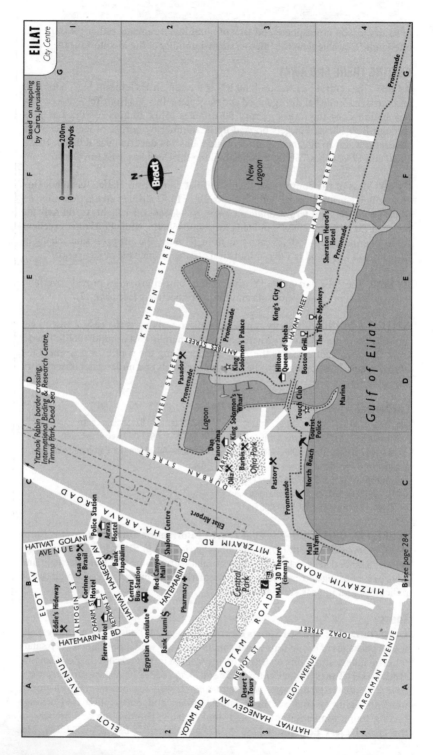

EILAT
City Centre

Based on mapping
by Carta, Jerusalem

Gulf of Eilat

New Lagoon

Lagoon

HA'YAM STREET
Sheraton Herod's Hotel
Promenade

King's City
Hilton
Queen of Sheba
HA'YAM STREET
Boston Grill
The Three Monkeys

KAMPEN STREET

Promenade
King Solomon's Palace
ANTIBES STREET
Pasador
KAMEN STREET

Dan Panorama
TARSHISH
King Solomon's Wharf
Barbis
Ofira Park
Olla
Pastory
Promenade
Touch Club
Tourist Police
Marina
North Beach

DURBAN STREET

Yitzhak Rabin border crossing,
International Birding & Research Centre,
Timna Park, Dead Sea

ROAD
HA'ARAVA

Police Station
Arava Hostel
HATIVAT GOLANI AVENUE
Casa do Brasil
Eddie's Hideway
ALMOGIN ST
OFARIM ST
Corinne Hostel
ELOT AV
Bank Hapoalim
Pierre Hotel
HATIVAT HANEGEV AV
RETAMIN ST
Central Bus Station
HATEMARIN BD
Egyptian Consulate
Bank Leumi
Shalom Centre
Red Canyon Mall
HATEMARIN
Pharmacy
Eilat Airport
MITZRAYIM RD
Central Park
IMAX 3D Theatre (cinema)
Desert Eco Tours
NEVIOT ST
YOTAM ROAD
MITZRAYIM ROAD
Mall HaYam
B see page 284

ELOT AVENUE
YOTAM RD
HATIVAT HANEGEV AV
TOPAZ STREET
ELOT AVENUE
ARGAMAN AVENUE

N

0   200m
0   200yds

280

f *6371598;* **e** *erez@desertecotours.com; www.desertecotours.com*) has an exhaustive list of tours going as far afield as Cairo or as close as Timna Park. Another great way to see the beautiful countryside around Eilat is to take a camel safari at the **Camel Ranch** (*Nachal Shlomo;* \ *6370022;* **e** *tal-p@actcom.co.il; www.camel-ranch.co.il*). A half-day tour (200NIS) departs both morning and afternoon. The ranch is well signposted from the south beach road. There is no public transport so you will need to take a taxi from the centre or walk from Coral Beach. The national **United Tours** (see page 37) also offers tours from Eilat to other parts of the country.

WHERE TO STAY From first appearances Eilat might look like a mass of hotels but on closer inspection you'll find that, um, indeed you were right. Big, small, cheap, expensive, classy, grubby – you name it, Eilat has it. Yet despite the number of places to stay, the city's continuing tourist boom means that you might have a hard time finding a room in the peak summer months. Budget accommodation isn't as well represented as the mid-range and certainly high-end establishments, and finding a decent, cheap hostel with vacancies is not always an easy task. Mangy mattresses and poky rooms are unfortunately commonplace in many hostels so be sure to see what you'll be getting before handing over any money. Because of the stiff competition amongst higher-end establishments however, prices are considerably lower than in Tel Aviv or Jerusalem and you get a lot more for your money. What might get you a simple room in a two- or three-star hotel elsewhere, might get you a four-star hotel in Eilat, especially midweek.

Hilton Queen of Sheba Hotel [280 3] 8 Antibes St; \ 6306666; **f** 6306677; www.hilton.com. The US$100 million spectacular that is the Hilton's first theme hotel, the Queen of Sheba has to be seen to be believed. Its jaw-dropping interior design focuses on Solomon & Sheba & the hotel & rooms are decorated in rich, regal colours & style. A spa, swimming pool, 6,500m² shopping mall & countless restaurants combine to form Eilat's most impressive hotel. **$$$$$**

Orchid Hotel and Resort (178 rooms) South Beach; \ 6360360; www.orchidhotel.co.il. Standing like a gleaming tropical oasis cascading down the desert hills, the Orchid is a spectacular swirl of palm-fringed pools, luxury oriental cabins & exotic greenery. Facilities inc a spa, health resort, gourmet & Thai (kosher) restaurants & access to the beautiful Migdalor Beach opposite. *Rooms start at 1,700NIS.* **$$$$$**

Sheraton Herod's Hotel [280 E4] (468 rooms) Ha'Yam St; \ 6380000; **f** 6380100; www.herods.co.il. Occupying prime beachfront land, the hotel is something of a tourist attraction in itself as passers-by stop to gawp. It oozes opulence & extravagance in every way

& is the ultimate in self-indulgence & glamour. The adjacent, adults-only Vitalis Spa is the icing on the cake for those in search of some 'me' time. *Off-season rooms up to 1,000NIS less (**$$$$$**).* **$$$$$**

Dan Panorama [280 C3] (277 rooms) North Beach; \ 03 5202552; **e** Reservations-T. PanoramaEilat@DanHotels.com; www.danhotels.com. Located right on the beach & offering a wealth of facilities inc a huge pool (heated in winter), spa, a selection of restaurants & bars & spacious, tasteful rooms. **$$$**

Prima Music (144 rooms) Almog Beach; \ 6388555; www.galahotels.com. This unpretentious, 4-star star hotel is a great family option & excellently located just opposite the Coral Beach Reserve to the south of the city. Rooms are spacious & bright (in varying musical themes), there is a big swimming pool, plenty of outdoors areas, free bicycle rental & on-site scuba diving centre. **$$$**

Arava Hostel [280 C1] (90 beds) 106 Almogim St; \ 6374687; **e** harava@bezeqint.net; www.a55.co.il. Founded in 1986 this hugely popular hostel has had plenty of years getting it right & now offers some of the best budget accommodation in town. Private rooms (for

2, 3 or 4 people) all have small en-suite bathrooms & AC or there is a dormitory option (50–80NIS). There is a snack bar, sun terrace, shared kitchen & BBQ area available for guest use. **$–$$**

🏠 **Corinne Hostel** [280 B1] (70 beds) 127/1 Retamim St; ✆6371472; e corinne_bz@yahoo.com; www.corinnehostel.com. Another well-established hostel offering good-quality budget accommodation in the city centre. It has all the features of a successful backpacker hostel, from a shared kitchen to communal areas to a TV area & tour bookings (to Petra). There are private rooms with TV, fridge & AC as well as zimmer accommodation in wooden huts (that slightly resemble garden sheds but are nice inside). *Dorms 80NIS.* **$–$$**

🏠 **Hotel Pierre** [280 B1] (34 rooms) 123 Retamim St; ✆08 6326601; e pierrehotel@bezeqint.net; www.eilat-guide.com/pierre. This simple little hotel offers pleasant rooms with TV, AC & minibar. There is a small 24hr bar & continental b/fast courtesy of the French management. Good budget option for those wanting to avoid a hostel & the signature hotel of several of the watersports shops inc the Dolphin Reef. **$**

🏠 **Siam Divers** (10 rooms) Coral Beach; ✆6323636; e info@deepdivers.co.il; www.siam.co.il. Attached to the highly reputable diving centre, this newly renovated hostel has one of the best budget locations in the city away from the hubbub of central Eilat. *Dorms 80NIS.* **$**

Camping Camping on the city's beaches is illegal and the law often enforced. That being said, just up from the Egyptian border, families pitch enormous tents and set up barbecue areas and settle in for the week. It has a fun atmosphere and soft white sand if you can find space. Alternatively the campsite at the **SPNI Field School** (✆08 6371127; *40NIS pp*) opposite the Coral Beach Reserve has clean amenities and is open year round.

✖ **WHERE TO EAT** Eilat's restaurant options range from the sublime to slime. The city has a restaurant on every inch of space that isn't occupied by a hotel, and most are of a very high standard. Unsurprisingly, fresh fish and seafood can be found on most menus and is highly recommended. For something a bit cheaper, there are plenty of fast-food chains and kiosks selling *burekas*, soggy pizza and hamburgers. For something quick and cheap there is **Domino's Pizza** along the promenade, a **Burger Ranch** in the Red Canyon Mall [280 B2], a branch of the popular **Giraffe Noodle Bar** (*Herod's promenade*; ✆6316583; **$$**) and **McDonald's** and **Burger King** everywhere.

✖ **Casa do Brasil** [280 B1] 3 Hativat Golani St; ✆6323032; www.casadobrasil.co.il; ⏲ 12.00–midnight daily. This is probably the best all-you-can-eat anywhere in the country. It is fantastic value for money as you get the choice of pretty much any kind of meat you can imagine grilled, rotisseried or fried as well as sides of salad, bread, pasta & pizza if you have space. All-you-can-eat lunch/dinner. **$$$$$**

✖ **Eddie's Hideaway** [280 B1] 68 Almogim St; ✆6371137; ⏲ 18.00–midnight Mon–Fri, 12.00–16.00 Sat. As you approach the building, head round the back to find the entrance. Once inside it is easy to see why this has become one of Eilat's favourite restaurants. The menu is eye-popping with treats such as Nairobi shrimp

cooked in spicy pineapple sauce or honey BBQ'd ribs gracing the pages. Comfortable, well priced & deliciously different. **$$$$**

✖ **Last Refuge** Coral Beach; ✆6373627; ⏲ 12.30–23.30 daily. Specialising in locally caught fish & seafood, this restaurant oozes nauticalia. While prices are a bit steep, you do get what you pay for in terms of quality & quantity as well as a pleasant ambience. You can sit outside on the deck if the weather isn't too stifling. **$$$$**

✖ **Olla** [280 C3] 17 Tarshish St, Bell Hotel; ✆6325566; www.olla-tapas.co.il; ⏲ 18.30–late Sun–Thu, 13.00–late Fri & Sat. Chic, elegant Spanish-style restaurant serving an interesting (if not very Spanish) selection of tapas (*25–35NIS* *each*) & wonderful, fresh fish & seafood mains. $$$$

✗ Pasador [280 D2] Americana Hotel, 10 Kaman St; ✆6378228; www.passador.co.il; ⏱ 12.30–00.00 daily. Square wooden booths are designed in a slightly oriental décor & the set menu offers great value. The 2-course lunch or dinner menu inc salads, carpaccio, ceviche or soup followed by dishes such as lamb kebab, chicken liver, pasta or steak. Fish is available for an extra charge. $$$$

✗ Pastory [280 C3] 7 Tarshish St; ✆6345111; ⏱ 13.00–23.00 daily. Popular Italian restaurant with a mouth-watering menu inc fresh gnocchi, fettuccini & tortellini, as well as steaks, gluten-free pasta & homemade ice cream. There is a big wine bar in the restaurant & a good wine selection. $$$

✗ Barbis [280 C3] 19 Tarshish St; ✆6342404; ⏱ 12.00–02.00 daily. Succulent, juicy burgers make this a huge local favourite. With red leather booths & imaginative toppings it is American diner food with a twist. $$

✗ Dolphin Reef Pub (see below) Certainly one of the most tropical & atmospheric-feeling places in the city; you can enjoy grilled meats, fresh fish, hamburgers, salads or lighter bar food snacks as the dolphins splash away in the background. The sandy floor, swinging music (often live) & thatched roof make it a great place to spend an evening. There is a 25NIS cover charge on live music nights. $$

✗ Duda Restaurant North Beach; ✆6330389; ⏱ 24hrs. Good cheap Israeli staples such as hummus, salads & chips. Located inside the Dahlia Hotel. $$

ENTERTAINMENT AND NIGHTLIFE Many of Eilat's nightlife spots can be found around the North Beach area and along the hotel promenade, although there are some lively beach bars further along the coast. It is the city's beach bars that often form the hub of night-time activity, the balmy weather, warm sand and relaxed atmosphere (and wild parties) attracting the younger set. The tourist information centre produces the weekly *Events in Eilat*, which is certainly worth picking up when you arrive.

Many of the larger hotels have discos and live music concerts, **Platinum** at the **King Solomon's Palace** [280 D3] being a big favourite with locals and visitors. The **Three Monkeys** [280 E4] (✆ 6368800; ⏱ 21.00–03.00 daily) has long been Eilat's flagship boogie bar and forms the centre of the North Beach nightlife. A sandy beachfront location, cheesy dance music, colourful cocktails and lots of beer have ensured its continued popularity. **Paddy's Irish Bar** (*New Tourist Centre bldg*; ✆ 6370921; ⏱ 12.00–04.00 daily) is a big fun place with loads of imported beers, while the huge **Unplugged Bar** (*New Tourist Centre*; ✆6334423; ⏱ 20.00–late daily) is divided into three different sections comprising a sports bar with big screens, a Bedouin-themed area complete with floor cushions and an area to play computer games and billiards. Located on the seafront it attracts a loud, young crowd and has a different DJ every night. The trendy **Touch Club** [280 D3] (✆ 6339088; ⏱ 23.00–late Wed–Fri) located inside the Spiral building in front of the marina is a huge space incorporating an indoor dance floor and bar and outside decking with tons of seating. **Penthouse** (*5 HaMelacha St*; ✆ 6339088; ⏱ 23.00–late daily) located in the industrial zone has national DJs and is popular with the local crowd; Admission is to over 21s (over 25s on Thursday). The outdoor seating area of the **Boston Grill** [280 D3] (✆ 6333007) along the promenade in front of the Royal Beach Hotel is another great place to sip a glass of chilled wine and people-watch. For something a little more tropical, the **Dolphin Reef** bar (see page 285) further south along the coast is another classic Eilat hangout.

For something a bit different there are evening cruises that offer an open bar, dancing and jacuzzis. **Lamie Tourism** (*Eilat Marina*; ✆6333560; cruise 21.30–23.30 Tues & Thu (bar ⏱ until 01.00)) and the **Red Sea Sports Club** both have regular outings in summer.

The Arava Desert   EILAT

11

283

SHOPPING Israelis love shopping and nowhere more so than in Eilat's glitzy malls where everything is minus the 16% VAT. Eilat has been granted exemption from value-added tax and has subsequently seen a rise in designer and brand-name shops. For foreigners, however, prices in airport duty-free shops are probably still lower. The **Mall HaYam** [280 B4] has the biggest concentration of fashion shops as well as countless cafés, restaurants and sunglasses stores. The **Red Canyon Shopping Centre** [280 B2] on the HaTemarin Boulevard boasts three cinemas, clothes and shoe shops, bookstores and most of the city's administrative offices including Arkia Airlines and the post office, while the nearby **Shalom Centre** has souvenir shops, more clothes and shoes and several car-rental agencies.

OTHER PRACTICALITIES
Emergency
Ambulance ☎101
Fire ☎102
Police station [280 B1] Hativat HaNegev Av; ☎100

Tourist police [280 D3] North Beach; ☎100; ⏱ 10.00–15.00 Sun–Wed, 10.00–18.00 Thu–Sat

Money
$ **Bank Hapoalim** [280 B1] 3 Hativat HaNegev St; ☎03 6532407; ⏱ 08.30–13.30 Sun & Tue/Wed, 08.30–12.45 & 16.00–18.30 Mon & Thu
$ **Bank Leumi** [280 B2] HaTemarin Bd; ☎03 9544555; ⏱ 08.30–13.45 Sun & Tue/Wed, 08.30–13.00 & 16.00–18.15 Mon & Thu
$ **Currency exchange** There are commission-free currency-exchange booths everywhere & most hotels offer money change (although the commission can often be a little on the steep side). There are countless ATMs, especially in the city centre & malls.

Post
✉ **Post office** Red Canyon Mall; ☎6372348; ⏱ 08.00–18.00 Sun–Tues & Thu, 08.00–13.30 Wed, 08.00–12.00 Fri. Changes money & travellers' cheques.

Medical
✚ **Yosef Tal Hospital** Yotam Rd; ☎6358011/ 6358025
✚ **Superpharm** 9 HaTemarin Blvd; ☎6383000; ⏱ 08.30–22.00 Sun–Thu, 08.00– 17.00 Fri, 10.30–23.00 Sat

Internet
▣ **Unplugged Bar** (see page 283) ⏱ midday–late daily. Offers fast internet for 25NIS per hour & a selection of drinks & snacks.

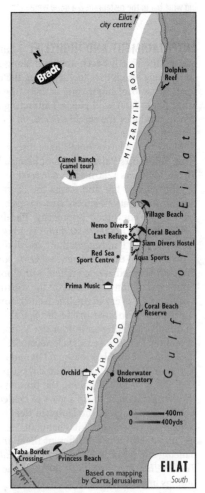

EILAT
South

Based on mapping by Carta, Jerusalem

WHAT TO SEE AND DO

Beaches With such a small claim on the Red Sea coast, pretty much the entire stretch of Israeli land has been developed for beach activities, with the exception of the distinctly unsightly commercial port. In the midst of the city centre is **North Beach**, which forms the hub of all things gaudy and noisy but is often a big hit for youngsters or those wanting to sip a cocktail in the sun. By far the more beautiful and relaxing beaches are found closer to the Egyptian border, namely the **Princess Beach**, which is the best place to swim, snorkel and chill out on the sand. Not far from the Princess Beach is the beautiful underwater garden reef of the **Coral Beach Reserve** (✆ *08 6376829; www.parks.org.il;* ⊕ *09.00–17.00; admission adult/ child 30/18NIS; mask & snorkel 16NIS*) which is a snorkeller's dream. Over 100 types of stony coral and 650 species of fish have been identified in the reserves, and marked buoy trails lead visitors past its highlights. Just north of the reserve are the free **Coral** and **Village beaches** which also offer pleasant snorkelling opportunities, shaded sun loungers and waiter-serviced bars. The Village Beach in particular is known for its young atmosphere and if you're slightly self-conscious about your physique then a day here won't help things much. The Coral Beach has a more wholesome, family atmosphere frequented by a whole mishmash of shapes and sizes. For a beach experience with a difference a day at the **Dolphin Reef** (see below) will let you share the waters of a family of bottlenosed dolphins.

Underwater Observatory Marine Park (✆ *08 6364200; www.coralworld.com;* ⊕ *08.30–17.00 Sat–Thu, 08.30–16.00 Fri; admission adult/child 99/89NIS, with oceanarium 76/58NIS*) The futuristic-looking white observatory is an Eilat landmark, jutting out into the reef along the coast. For non-divers and children, the observatory is a lovely way to see life beneath the waves with its 360º, 6m-deep observation deck. For a less natural experience there is a shark tank, aquariums and outdoor turtle and stingray pool, while the newly built **oceanarium** is an extremely enjoyable all-moving, all-shaking simulative movie theatre that takes delighted visitors on a tour of the deep blue seas. The Coral 2000 **semi-submarine** that has regular departures (35/29NIS) from the park is in fact no more than a fancy-looking glass-bottomed boat but is an enjoyable way to see the reef nonetheless.

Dolphin Reef (✆ *08 6300100; www.dolphinreef.co.il;* e *info@dolphinreef.co.il;* ⊕ *09.00–17.00 Sun–Thu, 09.00–16.30 Fri/Sat; admission adult/child 64/44NIS*) The special relationship between human and dolphin is nowhere more prevalent than at the Dolphin Reef, where a group of bottlenose dolphins, given the choice between human interaction or not, have chosen to stick around. Floating pontoons allow visitors to see the dolphins playing, feeding and interacting, while snorkelling (280NIS/½hr) or diving (320NIS/½hr) encounters provide a once-in-a-lifetime opportunity to get up close and personal. The small beach in the park is separated from the dolphins by a net allowing even swimmers to get close to the dolphins. Snorkelling and diving experiences should be booked up to two weeks in advance in peak seasons. There is no admission fee after 17.00 when the dolphin sessions finish for the day but the lively bar and café remain open until the small hours (see page 283).

IMAX 3D [280 B3] (*4 Yotam Rd;* ✆ *6361000;* e *marka@imaxeilat.co.il; www.imaxeilat.co.il;* ⊕ *11.00–midnight Sun–Thu, 11.00–Shabbat Fri, 21.00–01.00 Sat; admission 89NIS*) As you enter the city the vast 'Blue Pyramid' is unmistakable. Showing a selection of 3D movies ranging from dinosaurs to sea creatures to aliens, this is a fun-for-all-the-family activity.

King's City [280 E3] (*Opposite New Lagoon;* ✆ *6304444;* e *sales3@kingscity.co.il;* *www.kingscity.co.il;* ◷ *09.00–01.00 Sun–Thu, 09.00–Shabbat Fri, end of Shabbat–01.00 Sat; admission adult/child 118/95NIS*) This biblical theme park takes visitors (generally those under the age of 15) on a journey through time, using state-of-the-art technology and equipment. Travel from the Egyptian pharaohs to King Solomon past optical illusions, labyrinths, a water flume ride and into the biblical cave for a 3D movie.

International Birding and Research Centre (✆ *050 2112498;* e *ibrce@eilatcity. co.il; www.birdsofeilat.com*) While Eilat's tourism boom has soared over the past decade and people flock to its warm waters and party atmosphere, the city has long since been a holiday destination for visitors of the winged variety. Along with the Galilee's Hula Valley (see page 227), this region is one of the world's best birdwatching spots as they pass on their north–south migration routes from Europe and Africa. The Birding and Research Centre offers expertly guided birdwatching tours in 4x4 jeeps (150NIS/2hrs, 400NIS/full day) as well as the possibility of helping in the tagging and releasing of birds for research. The birdwatching park and centre are located just north of the city near the King Hussein border crossing to Jordan. Turn right at the Eilot junction (just after the kibbutz), from where it is signposted. The park includes both salty and freshwater pools fringed with different species of vegetation, and can be accessed by a variety of picturesque walking trails perfect for wildlife spotting. Binoculars can be rented at the centre for a small charge. In March of every year the **Eilat Spring Migration Festival** (*www.eilatbirdsfestival. com*) is held to coincide with one of the biggest fly-bys of migratory birds. Special all-inclusive flight, transfer, hotel and birding activity packages can be arranged through their website.

Activities

Scuba diving Eilat's crystal-clear waters that maintain a year-round temperature of 21°C have long been a magnet for scuba divers. Rapid and extreme over-development however has led to a serious decline in fish numbers and species, and today the area is rather disappointing for seasoned divers and pales in contrast to the great dive resorts along Egypt's Sinai coast. Nevertheless, its shallow, currentless waters are perfect for beginners and still certainly pretty enough to attract scores of divers from around the country.

Diving regulations in Israel are stringent. If you have forgotten your certification card or haven't dived in the last six months expect to be asked to complete a one-hour refresher course or be refused completely. Insurance (175NIS for one year) is a must-have and can be bought from any dive centre. Strict safety rules mean that all Eilat's dive centres now hold a high standard of equipment, tuition and facilities. Needless to say, this comes at a price and you can expect to pay double what you would pay in Egypt. Packages offered by some centres are the most economical option and normally include day trips to the more fish-laden waters of Aqaba, Jordan and Sinai. Diving live-aboards to Sinai and Egypt proper are an amazing experience if your budget runs to it.

Aqua Sports (*Coral Beach;* ✆ *6334404;* e *info@aqua-sport.com; www.aqua-sport. com*) Well-established centre offering the complete diving experience to both beginners and pros. Daily dive and snorkel trips to Sinai are one of their most popular excursions and they also offer live-aboard safaris to Egypt and PADI courses, with a good range of options for snorkellers.

Dolphin Reef (see page 285)

Manta Diving Centre (*Red Sea Sports Centre, Coral Beach;* `6370688; f 6370655; www.redseasports.co.il*) Part of the fantastic Red Sea Sports Centre, the diving club has probably the best choice of packages and dive excursions. Their three-day dive package (with/without equipment 620/365NIS) is great value for money as is the one-week package (1,200NIS without equipment) which includes a night dive, two days' diving in Aqaba with overnight accommodation and a cruise to Taba or Coral Island.

Nemo Divers (*052 3515808/08 6317616; e contact@nemodivers.co.il; www. nemodivers.co.il*) A small, friendly dive shop which offers a comprehensive range of facilities including PADI dive courses, introductory dives and an array of four- to nine-day live-aboard safaris to Sinai.

Siam Divers (*Coral Beach;* `6323636; e info@deepdivers.co.il; www.siam.co.il; 8 dives/with equipment 400/750NIS*) Specialising in technical diving, this big dive resort also caters for beginners and recreational divers. Activities offered include a range of diving courses, more safari live-aboards than you can shake a snorkel at, shore and boat dives and an underwater photography lab (the photographs are underwater, not the lab).

Watersports Eilat has managed to come up with more ways to get wet than Israelis have found to eat hummus, and these days the sea is abuzz with the sound of raucous splashing and the hum of motorboats. No-one does watersports better than the **Red Sea Sports Centre** (*Coral Beach, Ambassador Hotel;* `6333666; www.redseasports.co.il*) who operate most of their activities from Jetty C on the King Solomon's Wharf. Canoes, motorboats, waterskiing, parasailing and banana boat rides leave regularly and don't need to be booked in advance. Cruises to Coral Island (280NIS/1 day) and Taba (160NIS/half day) can be combined with parasailing and scuba diving.

Appendix 1

LANGUAGE

The Hebrew *alephbet* consists of 27 letters almost all of which are consonants, although there are several letters that can function as vowels. A series of dots and dashes that represent vowels are marked beneath words in children's books and the Bible but are generally omitted from other text. Hebrew words run from right to left and, as such, books, cards, magazines, etc will open in reverse to what is common in many other countries. Pronunciation is generally on the last syllable of the word. Some letters are known in Hebrew as *sofit* or final, and are used at the end of words. They have the same pronunciation but take a different form, for example ךhich is at ךhe end of words. The Hebrew words below have been spelt phonetically in the alphabet although it is important to note that 'ch' should be pronounced like a throaty 'h', not as in cheese or church.

א *aleph*	Is used either as a silent letter or to make an 'a' sound.	
ב *bet*	Can be pronounced as both 'b' or 'v'.	
ג *gimel*	Pronounced like the English 'g' as in goat.	
ד *dalet*	Pronounced like the English 'd' as in duck.	
ה *hey*	Pronounced like the English 'h' as in harp. Takes on a more 'ar' sound when used at the end of words.	
ו *vav*	Pronounced like the English 'v' as in volcano. Often used as the vowels 'o' as in octopus or 'u' as in tuna.	
ז *zayin*	Pronounced like the English 'z' as in zebra.	
ח *chet*	Pronounced like a throaty 'h' (there is no similar sound in the English language).	
ט *tet*	Pronounced like the English 't' as in tumble.	
י *yud*	Pronounced like the English 'y' as in yak. Can also be as 'i' as in igloo or 'ee' as in sweet.	
כ (ך) *kaf*	Pronounced like the English 'k' as in kettle.	
ל *lamed*	Pronounced like the English 'l' as in lemon.	
מ (ם) *mem*	Pronounced like the English 'm' as in mountain.	
נ (ן) *nun*	Pronounced like the English 'n' as in notebook.	
ס *samech*	Pronounced like the English 's' as in summer.	
ע *ayin*	Pronounced like a throaty 'i' or 'a' as in iron.	
פ (ף) *pey*	Can be pronounced as either 'p' or 'f'.	
צ (ץ) *tzadik*	Pronounced like 'tz' as in 'pssst' when trying to get someone's attention.	
ק *kof*	Pronounced like the English 'k' or 'c' as in coffee.	
ר *resh*	Pronounced like a throaty 'r' as in the French *raison d'être*.	
ש *sheen*	Can be pronounced as either 'sh' or 's'.	
ת *taf*	Pronounced like the English 't' as in tea.	

ESSENTIALS

Good morning	boker tov	בוקר טוב
Good evening	erev tov	ערב טוב
Goodnight	layla tov	לילה טוב
Hello/goodbye	shalom	שלום
My name is…	kor-eem li…	קוראים לי
What is your name?	eich kor-eem lecha (m)/lach (f)?	איך קוראים לך?
I am from…England/ America/Australia	ani me…anglia/ america/ostralia	אני מאנגליה/מאמריקה/מאוסטרליה
How are you?	ma shlomcha (m)/shlomech (f)	מה שלומך?
Pleased to meet you	naim lehakir otcha (m)/othach (f)	נעים להכיר אותך
Thank you	toda	תודה
Please	bevakasha	בבקשה
Don't mention it	al lo davar	על לא דבר
Cheers!	Lechaim!	לחיים
Yes	ken	כן
No	lo	לא
I don't understand	ani lo mevin (m)/mevina (f)	אני לא מבין/מבינה
Please would you speak more slowly	bevakasha daber (m)/ dabri (f) yoter le-at	בבקשה דבר/דברי יותר לאט
Do you understand?	ata mevin (m)/at mevina (f)?	אתה מבין/את מבינה

QUESTIONS

How?	eich?	איך?
What?	ma?	מה?
Where?	eifo?	איפה?
What is it?	ma ze?	מה זה?
Which?	eize?	איזה?
When?	matai?	מתי?
Why?	lama?	למה?
Who?	mi?	מי?
How much?	kama?	כמה?

NUMBERS

1	echad	אחד
2	shtaim	שתים
3	shalosh	שלוש
4	arba	ארבע
5	chamesh	חמש
6	shesh	שש
7	sheva	שבע
8	shmoneh	שמונה
9	teshah	תשע
10	eser	עשר
11	echad esreh	אחד עשרה
12	shteim esreh	שתים עשרה
13	shlosh esreh	שלוש עשרה
14	arba esreh	ארבע עשרה
15	chamesh esreh	חמש עשרה
16	shesh esreh	שש עשרה
17	shvah esreh	שבע עשרה
18	shmona esreh	שמונה עשרה
19	tsha esreh	תשע עשרה

20	esrim	עשרים
21	esrim ve echad	עשרים ואחד
30	shloshim	שלושים
40	arbaim	ארבעים
50	chamishim	חמישים
60	shishim	שישים
70	shivim	שבעים
80	shmonim	שמונים
90	tishim	תשעים
100	meah	מאה
1,000	elef	אלף

TIME

What time is it?	ma hasha'a?	מה השעה
It's…in the morning/at night	Hasha'a…baboker/balayla	השעה...בבוקר/בלילה
Today	hayom	היום
Tonight	halayla	הלילה
Tomorrow	machar	מחר
Yesterday	etmol	אתמול
Morning	boker	בוקר
Evening	erev	ערב

DAYS

Sunday	yom rishon	יום ראשון
Monday	yom sheni	יום שני
Tuesday	yom shlishi	יום שלישי
Wednesday	yom reviee	יום רביעי
Thursday	yom chamishi	יום חמישי
Friday	yom shishi	יום שישי
Saturday	yom shabbat	יום שבת

MONTHS

January	yanuar	ינואר
February	februar	פברואר
March	mertz	מרץ
April	april	אפריל
May	mai	מאי
June	yuni	יוני
July	yuli	יולי
August	ogust	אוגוסט
September	september	ספטמבר
October	october	אוקטובר
November	november	נובמבר
December	detzember	דצמבר

GETTING AROUND
Public transport

I'd like...	ani rotzeh (m)/rotzah (f)...	אני רוצה
...a one-way ticket	...cartis chad kivuni	כרטיס חד כיווני
...a return ticket	...cartis du kivuni	כרטיס דו כיווני
I want to go to...	ani rotzeh (m)/rotzah (f) lehagia le...	...אני רוצה להגיע ל
How much is it?	kama ze oleh?	כמה זה עולה?
What time does the...leave?	be eize sha'a ha...ozev?	באיזה שעה ה...עוזב?
The train has been delayed/cancelled	harakevet mitakevet/butlah	הרכבת מתעכבת/בוטלה
Platform	ratzif	רציף
Ticket office	misrad cartisim	משרד כרטיסים
Timetable	luach zmanim	לוח זמנים
From	meh	מ
To	el	אל
Bus station	tachanat otobus	תחנת אוטובוס
Train station	tachanat rakevet	תחנת רכבת
Airport	namal te'ufah	נמל תעופה
Port	namal	נמל
Bus	otobus	אוטובוס
Train	rakevet	רכבת
Plane	matoss	מטוס
Boat	oneeyah	אוניה
Ferry	ma'aboret	מעבורת
Car	mechonit	מכונית
4x4	arba al arba	ארבע על ארבע
Taxi	monit	מונית
Minibus	minibus	מיניבוס
Motorbike	ofanoa	אופנוע
Bicycle	ofnaim	אופניים
Arrival/departure	nichnasim/yotzim	נכנסים/יוצאים
Here	po	פה
There	sham	שם
Bon voyage!	derech tzlecha!	דרך צלחה!

Private transport

Is this the road to...?	zot haderech le...?	?...זאת הדרך ל
Where is the service station?	eifo hatachanat delek?	איפה התחנת דלק?
Please fill it up	bevakasha maleh ad hasof	בבקשה מלא עד הסוף
I'd like...litres	ani rotzeh (m)/rotzah (f)...litres	אני רוצה ...ליטר
Diesel	diesel	דיזל
Leaded petrol	ragil	רגיל
Unleaded petrol	netul oferet	נטול עופרת
I have broken down	nitkati	נתקעתי

Road signs

Give way	zchut kdima	זכות קדימה
Danger	sakanah	סכנה
Entry	knissah	כניסה
Detour	ma'akaf	מעקף
One way	chad sitri	חד סיטרי
Toll	mass	מס
No entry	ein knissah	אין כניסה
Exit	yetziah	יציאה

Directions

Where is it?	eifo?	איפה?
Go straight ahead	lech (m)/lechi (f) yashar	לך/לכי ישר
Turn left	pneh (m)/pni (f) smola	פנה/פני שמאלה
Turn right	pneh (m)/pni (f) yamina	פנה/פני ימינה
...at the traffic lights	...bah ramzor	...ברמזור
...at the roundabout	...bah kikkar	...בכיכר
North	tzafon	צפון
South	darom	דרום
East	mizrach	מזרח
West	ma'arav	מערב
Behind	meachor	מאחור
In front of	lifnei	לפני
Near	leyad	ליד
Opposite	mul	מול

Street signs

Entrance	knissah	כניסה
Exit	yetziah	יציאה
Open	patuach	פתוח
Closed	sagur	סגור
Toilets – men/women	sherutim – gvarim/nashim	שרותים גברים/נשים
Information	meidah	מידע

ACCOMMODATION

Where is a cheap/good hotel?	eifo yesh malon zol/tov?	איפה יש מלון זול/טוב?
Could you please write me the address?	bevakasha reshom li et haktovet?	בבקשה רשום לי את הכתובת?
Do you have any rooms available?	Yesh haderim pnuim?	יש חדרים פנויים?
I'd like...	ani rotzeh (m)/rotzah (f)...	...אני רוצה
...a single room	...cheder yachid	...חדר יחיד
...a double room	...cheder zugi	...חדר זוגי
...a room with two beds	...cheder im shtei mitot	חדר עם שתי מיטות
...a room with a bathroom	...cheder im miklachat vesherutim	חדר עם מקלחת ושרותים
...to share a dorm	...cheder meshutaf	...חדר משותף
How much is it per night/person?	kama ole lelayla/leadam?	כמה עולה ללילה/לאדם?
Is breakfast included?	haim kolol aruchat boker?	האם כולל ארוחת בוקר?
I am leaving today	ani ozev hayom	אני עוזב היום

FOOD

Do you have a table for...people?	yesh shulchan le...anashim?	?יש שולחן ל...אנשים
...a children's menu?	...tafrit yeladim?	?תפריט ילדים
I am a vegetarian	ani tzimchoni	אני צימחוני
Do you have any vegetarian dishes?	yesh manot tzimchoniot?	?יש מנות צימחוניות
Is this restaurant kosher?	ha'im hamisada ksherah?	?האם המסעדה כשרה
Please may I have...	bevakasha efshar lekabel...	בבקשה אפשר לקבל
...a fork/knife/spoon/the bill	...mazleg/sakin/kaf/cheshbon	...מזלג/סכין/כף/חשבון
Bon appétit!	bete'avon!	!בתאבון

Basics

Bread	lechem	לחם
Butter	chem'a	חמאה
Cheese	gvina	גבינה
Oil	shemen	שמן
Pepper	pilpel	פלפל
Salt	melach	מלח
Sugar	sucar	סוכר

Fruit

Apples	tapuchim	תפוחים
Bananas	bananot	בננות
Grapes	anavim	ענבים
Mangoes	mango	מנגו
Oranges	tapuzim	תפוזים
Pears	agassim	אגסים

Vegetables

Broccoli	broccoli	ברוקולי
Carrots	gzarim	גזרים
Garlic	shum	שום
Onions	btzalim	בצלים
Peppers	pilpelim	פלפלים
Potatoes	tapuchei adama	תפוחי אדמה

Fish

Mackerel	makrel	מקרל
Salmon	salmon	סלמון
Shellfish	peyrot yam	פירות ים
Tuna	tuna	טונה

Meat

Beef	baker	בקר
Chicken	off	עוף
Goat	ez	עז
Lamb	kevess	חזיר
Pork	chazir	כבש
Turkey	tarnegol hodu	תרנגול הודו

DRINKS

Beer	*bira*	בירה
Coffee	*kafeh*	קפה
Fruit juice	*mitz peyrot*	מיץ פירות
Milk	*chalav*	חלב
Tea	*teh*	תה
Water	*maim*	מים
Wine	*yain*	יין

SHOPPING

I'd like to buy...	*ani rotzeh (m)/rotzah (f) liknot...*	אני רוצה לקנות
How much is it?	*kama ze ole?*	כמה זה עולה?
I don't like it	*ani lo ohev (m)/ohevet (f) et ze*	אני לא אוהב/אוהבת את זה
I'm just looking	*ani rak mistakel (m)/mistakelet (f?)*	אני רק מסתכל/מסתכלת
It's too expensive	*ze yakar midai*	זה יקר מדי
I'll take it	*ani ekach et ze*	אני אקח את זה
Please may I have...	*bevakasha efshar...*	בבקשה אפשר...
Do you accept...?	*ata mekabel...?*	אתה מקבל...?
Credit cards	*cartis ashrai*	כרטיס אשראי
Travellers' cheques	*hamcha'at noss'im*	המחאת נוסעים
More	*yotair*	יותר
Less	*pachot*	פחות
Smaller	*katan yotair*	קטן יותר
Bigger	*gadol yotair*	גדול יותר

COMMUNICATIONS

I'm looking for...	*ani mechapess (m)/mechapesset (f) et ha...*	אני מחפש/מחפשת את ה...
Bank	*bank*	בנק
Post office	*sniff hadoar*	סניף_הדואר
Church	*knessiah*	כנסיה
Synagogue	*bet haknesset*	בית הכנסת
Mosque	*misgad*	מיסגד
...embassy	*...shagrirut*	...שגרירות
Currency exchange	*chalfan ksafim*	חלפן כספים
Internet café	*internet kafeh*	אינטרנט קפה
Tourist information office	*merkaz meidah tayarut*	מרכז מידע תיירותי

EMERGENCIES

Help!	*hatzilu!*	הצילו!
Call a doctor!	*tikre'u le rofeh!*	תקראו לרופא!
There's been an accident	*haita te'una*	היתה תאונה
I'm lost	*halachti le'ibud*	הלכתי לאיבוד
Go away!	*lech (m)/lechi (f) meepo!*	לך/לכי מפה!
Police	*mishtarah*	משטרה
Fire	*esh*	אש
Ambulance	*ambulance*	אמבולנס
Thief	*ganav*	גנב
Hospital	*beit cholim*	בית חולים
I am ill	*ani choleh (m)/cholah (f)*	אני חולה

GESTURES

Patience/please wait	joining all fingers and thumb together at the tips
Scepticism	putting one index finger to just under the eye
Hitchhiking	pointing at the ground with an index finger

HEALTH

Diarrhoea	shilshul	שלשול
Nausea	bchilah	בחילה
Doctor	rofeh	רופא
Prescription	nirsham	מרשם
Pharmacy	beit merkachat	בית מרקחת
Paracetamol	paracetamol	פאראסטמול
Antibiotics	antibiotika	אנטיביוטיקה
Antiseptic	chomer mechateh	חומר מחטא
Condom	condom	קונדום
Tampons	tamponim	טמפונים
Contraceptive	glulot neged herayon	גלולות נגד הריון
Sunblock	crem shizuf	קרם שיזוף
I am...	ani...	אני...
...asthmatic	...astmati	...אסטמתי
...epileptic	...epilepti	...אפילפטי
...diabetic	...choleh sokeret	חולה סוכרת
I'm allergic to...	ani elergi le...	...אני אלרגי ל
...penicillin	...penetzilin	פניצילין
...nuts	...egozim	...אגוזים
...bees	...dvorim	...דבורים

TRAVEL WITH CHILDREN

Is there a...?	ha'im yesh...?	?האם יש
...baby changing room	...pinat hachtalah	פינת החתלה
...a children's menu	...tafrit le yeladim	תפריט לילדים
Do you have...?	yesh lachem...?	? יש לכם
...infant milk formula	...tachlif chalav letinokot	'...תחליף חלב לתינוקות
Nappies	chitulim	חיתולים
Potty	sir layla	סיר לילה
Babysitter	shmartaf	שמרטף
Highchair	kisseh yeladim	כסא ילדים

OTHER

Mine/ours/yours	sheli/shelanu/shelcha	שלי/שלנו/שלך
And/some/but	ve/kama/aval	ו/כמה/אבל
This/that	ze	זה
Expensive/cheap	yakar/zol	יקר/זול
Beautiful/ugly	yaffeh/mecho'ar	יפה/מכוער
Old/new	yashan/chadash	ישן/חדש
Good/bad	tov/ra	טוב/רע
Early/late	mukdam/me'uchar	מוקדם/מאוחר
Hot/cold	cham/kar	חם/קר
Difficult/easy	kasheh/kal	קשה/קל
Boring/interesting	mesha'amem/me'anien	משעמם/מעניין

Appendix 2

FURTHER INFORMATION

BOOKS
Historical and religious

A History of Modern Israel by Colin Shindler. 2008. Cambridge University Press. ISBN 978 0 52 161538 9.

Everyman's Talmud by Abraham Cohen. 1995. Schocken Books. ISBN 978 0 80 521032 3.

History of Ancient Israel and Judah by J Maxwell Miller. 2006. SCM Press. ISBN 978 0 33 404117 7.

How to Read the Qu'ran by M Siddiqui. 2008. WW Norton & Co. ISBN 978 0 39 333080 9.

Introducing the Old Testament by John W Drane. 2000. Lion Hudson plc. ISBN 978 0 74 595016 7.

Israel: A History by Sir Martin Gilbert. 2008. Black Swan. ISBN 978 0 55 277428 4.

Israel: The Historical Atlas by The New York Times. 1997. John Wiley & Sons. ISBN 978 0 02 861987 3.

Kabbalah for Dummies by Arthur Kurzweil. 2006. John Wiley & Sons. ISBN 978 0 47 191590 4.

Lionhearts: Heroes of Israel by Michael Bar-Zohar. 2000. Little, Brown & Co. ISBN 978 0 44 652358 5.

Ploughshares into Swords: From Zionism to Israel by Arno Mayer. 2008. Verso Books. ISBN 978 1 84 467235 6.

Schindler's List by Thomas Keneally. 1994. Hodder and Stoughton. ISBN 978 0 34 060651 3.

The Politics of Sacred Space: The Old City of Jerusalem in the Middle East Conflict by Michael Dumper. 2001. Lynne Rienner Publishers Inc. ISBN 978 1 58 826016 1.

The Quest for the Historical Israel: Debating Archaeology and the History of Early Israel by Israel Finkelstein, Amihai Mazar and Brian Schmidt. 2007. Society of Biblical Literature. ISBN 978 1 58 983277 0.

The Torah: The Five Books of Moses by Sarna. 1992. Jewish Publication Society. ISBN 978 0 82 760015 7.

Fiction

Light Fell by Evan Fallenberg. 2008. SOHO Press. ISBN 978 1 56 947467 2.

My Michael by Amos Oz. 1992. Vintage. ISBN 978 0 09 974730 7.

A Tale of Love and Darkness by Amos Oz. 2005. Vintage. ISBN 978 0 09 945003 0.

In Search of Fatima: a Palestinian Story by Ghada Kharmi. 2009. Verso. ISBN 978 1 84 467368 1.

To the End of the Land by David Grossman. 2010. Jonathan Cape. ISBN 978 0 22 408999 9.

Guidebooks and general reference

A Photographic Guide to Birds of Israel and the Middle East by Richard Porter and David Cottridge. 2000. New Holland Publishers Ltd. ISBN 978 1 85 974508 3.

Israel: A Spiritual Travel Guide, 2nd edn: A Companion for the Modern Jewish Pilgrim by Rabbi Lawrence Hoffman. 2005. Jewish Lights. ISBN 978 1 58 023261 6.

Oxford English–Hebrew Hebrew–English Dictionary by Ya'acov Levy. 1999. Kernermann Publishing. ISBN 978 9 65 307027 1.

The Millennium Guide for Pilgrims to the Holy Land by Cardinal Edward Cassidy and James H. Charlesworth. 2000. D & F Scott Publishing Inc. ISBN 978 0 94 103793 8.

WEBSITES

www.jewishencyclopedia.com
www.parks.org.il Israel Nature and National Parks Authority.
www.eyeonisrael.com Interactive map of the country.
www.goisrael.com Israel Ministry of Tourism.
www.kabbalah.com Official website of the Kabbalah Centre.
www.kashrut.com Kosher and Jewish prayer time information service.
www.qibla.org Muslim prayer times.
www.jerusalem.muni.il Jerusalem Municipal Tourism department.

WIN A FREE BRADT GUIDE

READER QUESTIONNAIRE

**Send in your completed questionnaire and enter our monthly draw
for the chance to win a Bradt guide of your choice.**

To take up our special reader offer of 40% off, please visit our website at
www.bradtguides.com/freeguide or answer the questions below and return to us
with the order form overleaf.

(Forms may be posted or faxed to us.)

Have you used any other Bradt guides? If so, which titles? . . . .
. . . .

What other publishers' travel guides do you use regularly? . . . .
. . . .

Where did you buy this guidebook? . . . .

What was the main purpose of your trip to Nigeria (or for what other reason did
you read our guide)? eg: holiday/business/charity . . . .
. . . .

How long did you travel for? (circle one)

weekend/long weekend   1–2 weeks   3–4 weeks   4 weeks plus

Which countries did you visit in connection with this trip? . . . .
. . . .

Did you travel with a tour operator?' If so, which one? . . . .
. . . .

What other destinations would you like to see covered by a Bradt guide?
. . . .

If you could make one improvement to this guide, what would it be?
. . . .

Age (circle relevant category) 16–25   26–45   46–60   60+

Male/Female (delete as appropriate)

Home country . . . .

Please send us any comments about this guide (or others on our list).
. . . .
. . . .
. . . .

Bradt Travel Guides
IDC House, The Vale, Chalfont St Peter, Bucks SL9 9RZ, UK
✆ +44 (0)1753 893444 **f** +44 (0)1753 892333
e info@bradtguides.com
www.bradtguides.com

TAKE 40% OFF YOUR NEXT BRADT GUIDE!

Order Form

To take advantage of this special offer visit www.bradtguides.com/freeguide and enter our monthly giveaway, or fill in the order form below, complete the questionnaire overleaf and send it to Bradt Travel Guides by post or fax.

Please send me one copy of the following guide at 40% off the UK retail price

No	Title	Retail price	40% price
1	....	....	....

Please send the following additional guides at full UK retail price

No	Title	Retail price	Total
...	....	....	....
...	....	....	....
...	....	....	....

Sub total ....

Post & packing ....

(Free shipping UK, £1 per book Europe, £3 per book rest of world)

Total ....

Name ....

Address ....

Tel .... Email ....

☐ I enclose a cheque for £........ made payable to Bradt Travel Guides Ltd

☐ I would like to pay by credit card. Number: ....

Expiry date: .../....... 3-digit security code (on reverse of card) .....

Issue no (debit cards only) .....

☐ Please sign me up to Bradt's monthly enewsletter, Bradtpackers' News.

☐ I would be happy for you to use my name and comments in Bradt marketing material.

Send your order on this form, with the completed questionnaire, to:

Bradt Travel Guides
IDC House, The Vale, Chalfont St Peter, Bucks SL9 9RZ, UK
☏ +44 (0)1753 893444   f +44 (0)1753 892333
e info@bradtguides.com   www.bradtguides.com

Bradt Travel Guides

www.bradtguides.com

Africa

Access Africa: Safaris for People with Limited Mobility	£16.99
Africa Overland	£16.99
Algeria	£15.99
Angola	£17.99
Botswana	£16.99
Burkina Faso	£17.99
Cameroon	£15.99
Cape Verde	£15.99
Congo	£15.99
Eritrea	£15.99
Ethiopia	£16.99
Ghana	£15.99
Kenya Highlights	£15.99
Madagascar	£16.99
Malawi	£15.99
Mali	£14.99
Mauritius, Rodrigues & Réunion	£15.99
Mozambique	£15.99
Namibia	£15.99
Niger	£14.99
Nigeria	£17.99
North Africa: Roman Coast	£15.99
Rwanda	£15.99
São Tomé & Príncipe	£14.99
Seychelles	£14.99
Sierra Leone	£16.99
Sudan	£15.99
Tanzania, Northern	£14.99
Tanzania	£17.99
Uganda	£16.99
Zambia	£17.99
Zanzibar	£14.99
Zimbabwe	£15.99

The Americas and the Caribbean

Alaska	£15.99
Amazon Highlights	£15.99
Amazon, The	£14.99
Argentina	£16.99
Bahia	£14.99
Cayman Islands	£14.99
Colombia	£16.99
Dominica	£15.99
Grenada, Carriacou & Petite Martinique	£14.99
Guyana	£15.99
Nova Scotia	£14.99
Panama	£14.99
Paraguay	£15.99
Turks & Caicos Islands	£14.99
Uruguay	£15.99
USA by Rail	£14.99
Venezuela	£16.99
Yukon	£14.99

British Isles

Britain from the Rails	£14.99
Eccentric Britain	£15.99
Eccentric London	£13.99
Slow: Cotswolds	£14.99
Slow: Devon & Exmoor	£14.99
Slow: Norfolk & Suffolk	£14.99
Slow: North Yorkshire	£14.99
Slow: Sussex & South Downs National Park	£14.99

Europe

Abruzzo	£14.99
Albania	£15.99
Azores	£14.99
Baltic Cities	£14.99
Belarus	£15.99
Bosnia & Herzegovina	£14.99
Bratislava	£9.99
Budapest	£9.99
Cork	£6.99
Croatia	£13.99
Cross-Channel France: Nord-Pas de Calais	£13.99
Cyprus see North Cyprus	
Dresden	£7.99
Estonia	£14.99
Faroe Islands	£15.99
Georgia	£15.99
Greece: The Peloponnese	£14.99
Helsinki	£7.99
Hungary	£15.99
Iceland	£15.99
Kosovo	£15.99
Lapland	£13.99
Latvia	£13.99
Lille	£9.99
Lithuania	£14.99
Luxembourg	£13.99
Macedonia	£15.99
Malta & Gozo	£12.99
Montenegro	£14.99
North Cyprus	£12.99
Riga	£6.99
Serbia	£15.99
Slovakia	£14.99
Slovenia	£13.99
Spitsbergen	£16.99
Switzerland Without a Car	£14.99
Transylvania	£14.99
Ukraine	£15.99
Zagreb	£6.99

Middle East, Asia and Australasia

Armenia	£15.99
Bangladesh	£15.99
Borneo	£17.99
Eastern Turkey	£16.99
Georgia	£15.99
Iran	£15.99
Iraq: Then & Now	£15.99
Israel	£15.99
Kazakhstan	£15.99
Kyrgyzstan	£16.99
Lake Baikal	£15.99
Maldives	£15.99
Mongolia	£16.99
North Korea	£14.99
Oman	£15.99
Shangri-La: A Travel Guide to the Himalayan Dream	£14.99
Sri Lanka	£15.99
Syria	£15.99
Taiwan	£16.99
Tibet	£13.99
Yemen	£14.99

Wildlife

Antarctica: Guide to the Wildlife	£15.99
Arctic: Guide to Coastal Wildlife	£15.99
Australian Wildlife	£14.99
Central & Eastern European Wildlife	£15.99
Chinese Wildlife	£16.99
East African Wildlife	£19.99
Galápagos Wildlife	£16.99
Madagascar Wildlife	£16.99
New Zealand Wildlife	£14.99
North Atlantic Wildlife	£16.99
Pantanal Wildlife	£16.99
Peruvian Wildlife	£15.99
Southern African Wildlife	£19.99
Sri Lankan Wildlife	£15.99

Pictorials and other guides

100 Alien Invaders	£16.99
100 Animals to See Before They Die	£16.99
100 Bizarre Animals	£16.99
Eccentric Australia	£12.99
Northern Lights	£6.99
Tips on Tipping	£6.99
Wildlife and Conservation Volunteering: The Complete Guide	£13.99

NOTES

Index